Education and Earnings in Europe

Education and Earnings in Europe

A Cross Country Analysis of the Returns to Education

Edited by

Colm Harmon
University College Dublin and CEPR

Ian Walker
University of Warwick and Institute for Fiscal Studies

Niels Westergaard-Nielsen
Centre for Labour Market and Social Studies, University of Aarhus

Edward Elgar
Cheltenham, UK • Northampton, MA, USA

Published by
Edward Elgar Publishing Limited
Glensanda House
Montpellier Parade
Cheltenham
Glos GL50 1UA
UK

Edward Elgar Publishing, Inc.
136 West Street
Suite 202
Northampton
Massachusetts 01060
USA

A catalogue record for this book
is available from the British Library

Library of Congress Cataloguing in Publication Data
Education and earnings in Europe : a cross country analysis of the returns to education / edited by Colm Harmon, Ian Walker and Niels Westergaard-Nielsen.
    p. cm.
    Presents findings of a research project entitled Public Funding and Private Returns to Education.
    Includes bibliographical references and index.
    1. Education—Economic aspects—Europe—Cross-cultural studies. 2. Human capital—Europe—Cross-cultural studies. I. Harmon, Colm. II. Walker, Ian, 1954. III. Westergård-Nielsen, Niels C. IV. Public Funding and Private Returns to Education (Project)

LC67.E85 E39 2001
338.4'337'094—dc21   2001023727

ISBN 1 84064 530 X

Printed and bound in Great Britain by Bookcraft (Bath) Ltd.

Contents

v

List of Contributors

Rita Asplund (Research Institute of the Finnish Economy)
Mahmood Arai (Stockholm University)
Fernando Barceinas-Paredes (Universidad Metropolitana de México)
Erling Barth (Institute for Social Research, Norway)
Giorgio Brunello (University of Padua)
Arnaud Chevalier (London School of Economics)
Ioannis Cholezas (Athens University of Economics and Business)
Jens Jakob Christensen (CLS, University of Aarhus)
Simona Comi (Fondazione Eni Enrico Mattei, Milan)
Kevin Denny (University College Dublin & Institute for Fiscal Studies)
Josef Fersterer (University of Linz)   .
Marianne Guille (ERMES, Université Panthéon-Assas, Paris)
Colm Harmon (University College Dublin)
Joop Hartog (University of Amsterdam)
Christian Kjellström (Institute of Economic Research, Sweden)
Charlotte Lauer (ZEW, University of Mannheim)
Claudio Lucifora (Fondazione Eni Enrico Mattei, Milan)
Pedro Silva Martins (Universidade Nova de Lisboa, Lisbon)
Joop Odink (University of Amsterdam)
Josep Oliver-Alonso (Universitat Autónoma de Barcelona)
Pedro Telhado Pereira (Universidade Nova de Lisboa, Lisbon)
Jose Luis Raymond-Bara (Universitat Autónoma de Barcelona)
Marianne Røed (Institute for Social Research, Norway)
Jose Luis Roig-Sabaté (Universitat Autónoma de Barcelona)
Ali Skalli (ERMES, Université Panthéon-Assas, Paris)
Jeroen Smits (University of Amsterdam)
Viktor Steiner (ZEW, University of Mannheim)
Panos Tsakloglou (Athens University of Economics and Business)
Ian Walker (University of Warwick & Institute for Fiscal Studies)
Bernhard A. Weber (State Secretariat for Economic Affairs, Berne)
Niels Westergaard-Nielsen (CLS, University of Aarhus)
Rudolf Winter-Ebmer (University of Linz)
Aniela Wirz (University of Zurich)
Stefan Wolter (Swiss Coordination Centre for Research in Education, Aarau)

Acknowledgements

This book develops as a result of two years of research initiated in late 1998 funded by the European Commission under the Targeted Socio-Economic Research programme (contact number SOE2-CT98-2044). The project, Public Funding and Private Returns to Education or 'PURE', had an overarching objective to study the impact of different systems of public financial support for school attendance and of differences in educational differentiation and school admission rules (free or selective entry) on observed outcomes in the labour market, in particular, in terms of the levels and dispersion of private returns to education and education-related inequality in earnings. The project involved 15 European countries: Austria, Denmark, Finland, France, Germany, Greece, Ireland, Italy, Netherlands, Norway, Portugal, Spain, Sweden, Switzerland and the UK. We gratefully acknowledge the support of the European Commission in facilitating the cross-country network which allowed this research to develop and in particular of the scientific officers in DGXII who provided considerable guidance to the project managers.

We would also like to acknowledge the role of the scientists in charge of the PURE programme of research – Pedro Telhado Pereira of Universidade Nova de Lisboa, and in particular Rita Asplund of ETLA (the Research Institute of the Finnish Economy) who was the overall coordinator of PURE. This volume is a tribute to their efforts and dedication.

1. Introduction

Colm Harmon, Ian Walker and Niels Westergaard-Nielsen

INTRODUCTION

This volume is concerned with the returns to education, in particular on education as a private investment decision in "human capital", and explores the 'internal' rate of return to that private investment. While the literature is replete with studies that estimate this rate of return using regression methods, where the estimated return is obtained as the coefficient on year of education in a log wage equation containing controls for work experience and other individual characteristics, the issue is surrounded with difficulties.

In the following chapters we present the findings of a major EU-funded initiative under the 5th Framework Programme. Between 1998 and 2000 a 15 country network of research teams took part in a research project entitled Public Funding and Private Returns to Education (known as PURE). The main objective was to estimate private returns to education evaluating the relationship between wages and education across Europe giving us the opportunity to calculate and compare returns across the PURE member countries.

The research agenda encompassed a number of areas. A prime focus was the analysis and comparison of wage and human capital structures and private returns to education between countries and within countries over time in order to uncover distinct trends as well as similarities and dissimilarities across countries. This included analysis of the impact of country-specific trends in educational returns and of changes over time in underlying market forces (supply-side and demand-side factors), and analysis of carefully differentiated measures of private returns by type and level of education in order to highlight and compare national systems of education. The project also examined the structure and evolution of the national systems of education, admission rules and systems of financial support for school attendance. Finally the effect of differing systems of public funding and admission rules on private returns to education and on earnings inequality was considered.

In the chapters that follow our partners from the PURE project present estimates of the private return to schooling for their respective country. The chapters will explain in detail the educational system that generates the schooling, the datasets used in the analysis and straightforward estimates of the returns. Some countries, due to data availability for example, are able to extend the analysis to consider some of the possible difficulties in the literature.

In this opening chapter we consider the issues involved in estimating returns to schooling to establish the context for the subsequent country-specific chapters. We explore conventional estimates from a variety of datasets and pay particular attention to a number of the most important difficulties. For example, it is unclear that one can give a productivity interpretation to the coefficient if education is a signal of pre-existing ability. Indeed, the coefficient on years of education may not reflect the effect of education on productivity if it is correlated with unobserved characteristics that are also correlated with wages. In this case the education coefficient would reflect both the effect of education on productivity and the effect of the unobserved variable that is correlated with education. For example, "ability" to progress in education may be unobservable and may be correlated with the ability to make money in the labour market. Similarly, a high private "discount rate" would imply that the individual's privately optimal level of education would be low and, yet, such an unobservable characteristic conceivably may itself be positively correlated with high wages.

The signalling role of education may manifest itself in an effect of credentials on wages: there may be a pay premium associated with years of education that result in credentials being earned. This ought to manifest itself in a nonlinear relationship between (log) wages and years of education, and in there being a distribution of leaving education that is skewed away from years without credentials towards those years with credentials.

There may be other factors that affect the policy and economic interpretation of the statistical estimates: there may be "over"education where, because of labour market rigidities of some form, relative wages for different types of workers do not clear the markets for those types. For example, if the wage for highly educated workers is too high, then this type of worker may take a job that requires only a lower level of skill and commands a lower wage. This overeducation would manifest itself as a lower estimate of the average return to education and ought to result, in the long run, in a decline in education levels. That is, if there is some factor that prevents relative wages from adjusting then quantities will adjust instead. A related issue is the extent to which there is heterogeneity in the returns to education: returns may differ across individuals because they differ in the efficiency with which they can exploit education to raise their productivity. There may be individual-specific skills, for example social or analytical skills, which are complementary to formal education so that individuals with a large endowment of such skills reap a higher return to their investment in education than those with a small endowment. Thus, for example, some college graduates may not be well endowed with these complementary skills and may appear to be overeducated when, in fact, they are simply less productive than other graduates in graduate jobs.

Finally, we consider the "social" return to education, by which we mean the return to society over and above the private returns to individuals. Part of the private gross returns is given over to the government through taxation (and through reduced welfare entitlements). In addition to this tax wedge, the private return is indicative of whether the appropriate level of education is being provided, while the social return is suggestive of how that level should be funded. If there are significant social returns over and above the private returns there is then a case for providing public subsidies to align private incentives with social optimality. This literature is less well developed than the research on private returns but features some of the same difficulties – in particular, measurement error in the education variable and simultaneity between (aggregate) education and GNP (aggregate income) – that cloud the interpretation of the estimated education coefficient.

THEORETICAL FRAMEWORK

The analysis of the demand for education has been driven by the concept of human capital approach and has been pioneered by Gary Becker, Jacob Mincer and Theodore Schultz. In human capital theory education is an investment of current resources (the opportunity cost of the time involved as well as any direct costs) in exchange for future returns.

The benchmark model for the development of empirical estimation of the returns to education is the key relationship derived by Mincer (1974). The typical human capital theory (Becker, 1964) assumes that education, s, is chosen to maximise the expected present value of the stream of future incomes, up to retirement at date T, net of the costs of education, c_s. So, at the optimum s, the PV of the sth year of schooling just equals the costs of the sth year of education, so equilibrium is characterised by

$$\sum_{t=1}^{T-s} \frac{w_s - w_{s-1}}{(1+r_s)^t} = w_{s-1} + c_s$$

where r_s is called the internal rate of return (we are assuming that s is infinitely divisible, for simplicity, so "year" should not be interpreted literally). Optimal investment decision making would imply that one would invest in the sth year of schooling if $r_s > i$, the market rate of interest. If T is large then the right-hand side of the equilibrium expression can be approximated so that the equilibrium condition becomes

$$\frac{w_s - w_{s-1}}{r_s} = w_{s-1} + c_s .$$

Then, if c_s is sufficiently small, we can rearrange this expression to give

$$r_s \approx \frac{w_s - w_{s-1}}{w_s} \approx \log w_s - \log w_{s-1}$$

(where $\approx$ means approximately equal to). This says that the return to the sth year of schooling is approximately the difference in log wages between leaving at s and at s - 1. Thus, one could estimate the returns to s by seeing how *log* wages varies with s.

   In practice a number of further assumptions are typically made to give a specification that can be estimated simply. Mincer (1974) assumed that r_S is a constant - so

$$r = \Delta Y_t / h_t Y_t ,$$

where Y_t is potential earnings and h_t is the proportion of period t spent acquiring human capital. During full-time education $h_t = 1$ so

$$Y_s = Y_0 e^{rs} .$$

For post-school years, Mincer assumes that h_t declines linearly with experience,

$$h_t = h_0 - (h_0/T) t .$$

So, for x years of post-school work experience, earnings can be written as

$$Y_x = Y_s \exp\left(r \int_0^x h_t dt \right) .$$

Note that the rules of integration imply that

$$\int_0^x h_t dt = h_0 x - \frac{1}{2}\frac{h_0}{T} x^2 ,$$

and assuming that the Y_0 can be captured as a linear function of characteristics **X** we also have

$$Y_s = Y_0 e^{rs} = \mathbf{X}\beta e^{rs}.$$

Thus, we can write the expression for income after x years of experience and s years of schooling as

$$Y_x = Y_0 e^{rs} \exp r\left(h_0 x - \frac{h_0}{2T}x^2\right).$$

Thus, taking logs,

$$\log Y_x = \log Y_0 + rs + rh_0 x - \left(\frac{rh_0}{2T}\right)x^2$$

and, since actual earnings is

$$w_x = (1 - h_x)Y_x,$$

we finally arrive at the conventional Mincer specification:

$$\log w_x^{\cdot} = \mathbf{X}\beta + rs + rh_0 x - (rh_0/2T)x^2 + \log(1 - h_x).$$

Thus, the empirical approximation of the human capital theoretical framework is the familiar functional form of the earnings equation

$$\log w_i = \mathbf{X}_i\beta + rs_i + \delta x_i + \gamma x_i^2 + u_i,$$

where y_i is an earnings measure for an individual i such as earnings per hour/week, s_i represents a measure of their schooling, x_i is an experience measure (typically age minus age left schooling), $\mathbf{X}_i$ is a set of other variables assumed to affect earnings, and u_i is a disturbance term representing other forces which may not be explicitly measured, assumed independent of $\mathbf{X}_i$ and s_i. Note that experience is included as a quadratic term to capture the concavity of the earnings profile. In this context r can be considered the private return to schooling.

Clearly in this empirical derivation the schooling measure is treated as exogenous although education is the endogenous choice variable in the underlying human capital theory. Moreover, in the Mincer specification the disturbance term captures unobservable individual effects. However these individual factors may also influence the schooling decision, and induce a correlation between schooling and the error term in the earnings function. A common example is unobserved ability. This problem has been the preoccupation of the literature since the earliest contributions. If schooling is endogenous then estimation by least squares will yield biased estimates of the return to schooling. There have been a number of approaches to deal with this problem.

Firstly, measures of ability have been incorporated to proxy for unobserved effects. The inclusion of direct measures of ability should reduce the estimated education coefficient if it acts as a proxy for ability, so that the coefficient on education then captures the effect of education alone since ability is controlled for. Secondly the exploitation of within-twins or within-siblings differences is based on the assumption that unobserved effects are additive and common across twins so that they can be differenced out by regressing the wage difference between twins against the education difference. This approach is a modification of a more general fixed effect framework using individual panel data, where the unobserved individual effect is considered time-invariant. Finally the instrumental variable approach deals directly with the schooling/earnings relationship in a two-equation system. We return to these in detail later in this chapter.

Optimal Schooling Choice

It is useful at this point to consider theoretically the implications of endogenous schooling. One approach would be to consider a model similar to that presented by Willis (1986) which illustrates the concept of schooling as an optimizing investment decision based on future earnings, a decision based on the (discounted) difference in earnings from undertaking and not undertaking education and the total cost of education including foregone earnings. Investment in education continues until the difference between the marginal cost and marginal return to education is zero.

A number of implications stem from considering schooling as an investment decision. Firstly, the internal rate of return (IRR, or r in this review) is the discount rate that ensures that the present value of benefits equals the present value of costs. More specifically if the IRR is greater than market rate of interest more education is a worthwhile investment for the individual. In making an investment decision an individual who places more (less) value on current income than future income streams will have a higher (lower) value for the discount rates so individuals with high discount rates (high r_i) are therefore *less* likely to undertake education. Secondly, direct education costs (c_s) lower the net benefits of schooling. Finally, if the probability of being in employment is higher if schooling is undertaken a rising level of unemployment benefit will erode the reward from undertaking education. However, should the earnings gap between educated and non-educated individuals widen or if the income received while in schooling should rise (say, through a tuition subsidy or maintenance grant) the net effect on schooling should be positive.

A useful extension to the theory is to consider the role of the individual's ability on the schooling decision, whilst preserving the basic findings of the model of schooling as an investment. Griliches (1977) introduces ability (A) explicitly into the derivation of the log-linear earnings function. In this basic model the IRR of schooling is partly determined by foregone income (less any subsidy such as parental contributions) and any educational costs. Introducing ability differences has two effects on this basic calculus. The more able individuals may be able to 'convert' schooling into human capital more efficiently than the less able and this raises the IRR for the more able. One might think of this as inherent ability and education being complementary factors in producing human capital so that, for a given increment to schooling, a larger endowment of ability generates more human capital. On the other hand, the more able may have higher opportunity costs since they may have been able to earn more and this reduces the IRR.

The empirical implications of this extension to the basic theory are most clearly outlined in Card (2000) which embodies the usual idea that the optimal schooling level equates the marginal rate of return to additional schooling with the marginal cost of this additional schooling. Card (2000) allows the optimal schooling to vary across individuals for a further reason. Not only can different returns to schooling arise from variation in ability so that those of higher ability 'gain' more from additional schooling, but individuals may also have different marginal rates of substitution between current and future earnings. That is, there may be some variation in the discount rate. This variation in discount rates may come, for example, from variation in access to funds or taste for schooling.

If ability levels are similar between individuals the effects are relatively unambiguous - lower discount rate individuals choose more schooling. However, one might expect a negative correlation between these two elements: high-ability parents, who would typically be wealthier, will tend to be able to offer more to their children in terms of resources for education. Moreover high-education parents will have stronger tastes for schooling (or lower discount rates) and their children may "inherit" some of this. Moreover if ability itself is partly inherited then children with higher ability may be more likely than average to have lower discount rates. The reverse is true for children of lower-ability parents. Empirically this modification allows for an expression for the potential bias in the least squares estimate of the return to schooling to be derived. This bias will be determined by the variance in ability relative to the variance in discount rates as well as the covariance between them. This "endogeneity" bias arises because people with higher marginal returns to education choose higher levels of schooling. If there is no discount rate variance then the endogeneity will arise solely from the correlation between ability and education and since this is likely to be positive the bias in ordinary least squares (OLS) estimates will be upwards (if ability increases wages later in life more than it increases wages early in life). If there is no ability variance, then the endogeneity arises solely from the (negative) correlation between discount rates and OLS will be biased downwards if discount rates and wages are positively correlated (for example, if ambitious people earn higher wages and are more impatient).

Thus, the direction of bias in OLS estimates of the returns to education is unclear and is, ultimately, an empirical question.

STYLISED FACTS

The availability of microdata and ease of estimation resulted in many studies which essentially estimate the simple Mincer specification. In the original study, Mincer (1974) used 1960 US census data and an experience measure known as potential experience (i.e. current age *minus* age you left full time schooling). The returns to schooling were found to be 10% with returns to experience of around 8%. Layard and Psacharopoulos (1979) used the British General Household Survey (GHS) 1972 data and found returns to schooling of a similar level, around 10%. The Mincerian specification has also been used to address questions such as discrimination, effectiveness of training programmes, school quality, return to language skills, and even the return to "beauty" (see Hammermesh and Biddle (1994, 1998). See Willis (1986) and Psacharopolous (1994) for many examples of this simple specification. In a few studies it has been applied to panel data but this strand of research still suggests that most of the cross-section variance in earnings across individuals is persistent.

Within the PURE project it was possible to evaluate the relationship between wages and education across Europe. In a cross-country study like this, it is preferable that data be more or less comparable across countries, that is wages, experience and years of schooling should be calculated in a similar fashion. Since each country use their own national surveys, this condition is hard to maintain to some extent. However for the purpose of this review we formulated a common specification across our research partners and collected estimates of the return to schooling from each. All PURE partners have estimated this return to education using the log of the hourly gross wage where available (with the exception of Austria, Greece, Italy, Netherlands and Spain who use net wages). Figure 1.1 is a summary of the returns broken down by gender. We find that for some countries like the UK, Ireland, Germany, Greece and Italy there is a substantial variation in returns between gender. Returns to women are significantly higher than returns to men. Scandinavia (Norway, Sweden and Denmark) is characterized by relatively low returns. We see that the lowest returns in Europe are in fact found in Sweden, Norway and Denmark.

Most partners had access to longitudinal data (or at least a combination of cross-sections) for human capital variables and earnings which gives us the opportunity to identify trends in returns in the European countries. Table 1.1 contains such information. There does not seem to be a clear pattern in the trends. In total there seems to be 15 cases of no trend, 10 cases of increasing returns, and 5 cases of decreasing returns. Countries characterized by decreasing returns for both males and females are Austria and Sweden. Countries characterized by increasing returns are Denmark, Portugal and Italy. The remaining PURE countries are either characterized by no trend or by different male-female trends.

Figure 1.1 Returns to schooling: men and women (year closest to 1995)

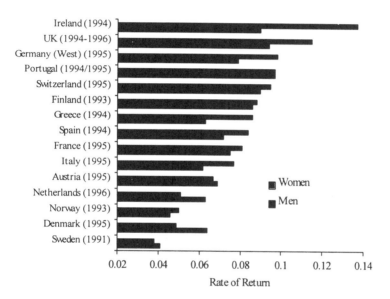

SPECIFICATION AND FUNCTIONAL FORM

Mincer's specification can be thought of as an approximation to a more general function of schooling (S) and experience (x) of the form

$$\log w = F(S,x) + e ,$$

where e is a random term that captures other (unobservable) determinants of wages. Many variants of the form of $F(.)$ have been tried. Murphy and Welch (1990), for example, concluded that

Education and Earnings in Europe

$$\log w = \mathbf{X}\beta + rS + g(x) + e$$

where $\mathbf{X}$ are individual observable characteristics that affects wages and $g(.)$ was a third or fourth order polynomial of the experience measure, provided the best approximation for the model. However, there are no examples in the empirical literature that suggest that the way in which x enters the model has any substantial impact on the estimated schooling coefficient.

Table 1.1   Trends in returns: men and women

| | Relative size of returns in 1980s | | Trend | Trend |
	Men	Women	Men	Women
Austria	+	+	down	Down
Denmark	÷	÷	up	Up
Germany	+	+	-	-
Netherlands	÷	÷	up	down
Portugal	+	+	up	up
Sweden	÷	÷	down	down
France	0	0	-	-
UK	÷	+	up	-
Ireland	+	+	- (up)	-
Italy	÷	÷	up	up
Norway	÷	÷	-	-
Finland	+	+	-	up
Spain	÷	+	-	up
Switzerland	+	+	-	-
Greece	÷	0	-	-

Notes
+ indicates relatively high returns, ÷ indicates relatively low returns, 0 indicates neither high nor low returns (returns close to average) and – indicates no obvious trend.

However, experience is seldom well measured in typical datasets and is often proxied by age minus the age left education, or even just by age alone. Note that to compare the specification that uses age with one that uses recorded or potential experience one needs to adjust for the difference in what is being held constant: the effect of S on log wages, holding age constant, is simply r while the experience-control specification implies that the estimate of education on wages that hold age constant needs to be reduced by the effects of S on experience – that is, one needs to subtract the effect of a year of experience. For example if the wage equation is

$$\log w_i = \mathbf{X}_i\beta + rS_i + \delta x_i + \gamma x_i^2 + u_i$$

then the adjustment is to subtract

$$\delta - 2\gamma(A-S).$$

Since the average value of $A-S$ is around 25, and (for men) δ is about 0.05 and γ is about -0.001 the adjustment is of the order of -0.25 or about 2.5%.

Table 1.2   Returns to education in Europe (year closest to 1995)

Definition of experience control	Men Pot.	Men Act.	Age	Women Pot.	Women Act.	Age
Austria	0.069	-	0.059	0.067	-	0.058
Denmark	0.064	0.061	0.056	0.049	0.043	0.044
W.Germany	0.079	0.077	0.067	0.098	0.095	0.087
Netherlands	0.063	0.057	0.045	0.051	0.042	0.037
Portugal	0.097	0.100	0.079	0.097	0.104	0.077
Sweden	0.041	0.041	0.033	0.038	0.037	0.033
France	0.075	-	0.057	0.081	-	0.065
UK	0.094	0.096	0.079	0.115	0.122	0.108
Ireland	0.090	0.088	0.065	0.137	0.129	0.113
Italy	0.062	0.058	0.046	0.077	0.070	0.061
Norway	0.046	0.045	0.037	0.050	0.047	0.044
Finland	0.086	0.085	0.072	0.088	0.087	0.082
Spain	0.072	0.069	0.055	0.084	0.079	0.063
Switzerland	0.090	0.089	0.076	0.095	0.089	0.086
Greece	0.063	-	0.040	0.086	-	0.064
Mean	*0.073*	*0.072*	*0.058*	*0.081*	*0.079*	*0.068*

Table 1.2 illustrates the effect of including different experience measures in schooling returns estimation based on data supplied by the PURE partners. In this table we report estimates based on OLS techniques controlling for different definitions of experience where experience is introduced as a quadratic term as suggested by the Mincer specification. Using a quadratic in age tends to produce the lowest returns, while using potential experience (age minus education leaving age) or actual experience (typically recorded in some datasets as the weighted sum of the number of years of part-time and full-time work since leaving full-time education) indicates a slightly higher return to education.

In Table 1.3 we estimate for men the return to schooling using the UK British Household Panel Survey (BHPS) including a range of different controls including union membership and plant size, part-time status, marital status and family size. As can be seen the result here is very robust to these different range of controls.

Table 1.3   Men in BHPS: sensitivity to changes in control variables

	None	Plant size and union	Part-time	Plant size union, and PT	All
Education	0.064 (0.002)	0.062 (0.002)	0.064 (0.002)	0.062 (0.002)	0.063 (0.002)
Medium plant	-	0.157 (0.012)	-	0.157 (0.012)	0.153 (0.012)
Large plant	-	0.241 (0.013)	-	0.242 (0.012)	0.243 (0.013)
Union member	-	0.079 (0.011)	-	0.079 (0.011)	0.080 (0.011)
No. of children	-	-	-	-	0.019 (0.005)
Married	-	-	-	-	0.144 (0.016)
Cohabitating	-	-	-	-	0.107 (0.020)
Divorced	-	-	-	-	0.058 (0.024)
Part time	-	-	−0.020 (0.041)	0.024 (0.039)	0.036 (0.040)

Notes: Figures in parentheses are robust standard errors. The models include age and age squared, year dummies, region dummies and regional unemployment rates.

Using Samples of Workers

A further point relates to the issue of using samples of working employees for the purposes of estimation of these returns. To what extent is the return to schooling biased by estimation based only on these workers? This has typically been thought not to be such an issue for men as for women since voluntary non-participation is thought to be much less common for men than women. There are two ways of illuminating the extent to which the estimated education return may be affected by this sample selection. One might compare OLS estimates with estimates of "median" regressions. Bias in OLS may arise if, for example, individuals with low wages tend to predominate among non-participants. Thus, using a selected sample of workers is to truncate the bottom of the wage distribution and hence raise the mean of the distribution over what it would otherwise be if no selection took place. Since OLS passes through the mean of the estimating sample it will be affected by the truncation in the data. However, the median of the data is unaffected by the truncation so there should be no bias in median regressions. Secondly, one could also use standard two-step methods (see Heckman *et al*, 1974) which attempt to control for the selection by modelling what determines it.

Table 1.4   BHPS: OLS, Heckman selection, and median regression

| | FRS Women | | |
	Education	Age	Age^2
OLS	0.109	0.026	−0.0003
	(0.002)	(0.003)	(0.000)
Heckman two-step	0.109	0.016	−0.0001
	(0.002)	(0.004)	(0.000)
Median regression	0.122	0.024	−0.0003
	(0.002)	(0.004)	(0.000)

Notes: Figures in parentheses are robust standard errors. The models includes year dummies, marital status, the number of children in three age ranges, region dummies, and regional unemployment rate. In the Heckman two-step case we use household unearned income as well as the variables from the wage equation in the participation equation.

Table 1.4 shows the parameter estimates for women using BHPS again. The results show slightly higher returns under the median regression method suggesting a small effect due to the selection into employment. While statistically significant the differences are small in absolute value. Since non-participation is more common among women than men we might imagine that the returns to women would be biased downwards relative to men and the size of this bias may depend on the relative participation rates. Figure 1.2 examines the relationship between the average participation rate for women in employment and the percentage difference between male and female returns to schooling for the countries in the PURE network. The figure shows that countries with the highest rates of female participation (typically the Nordic grouping) have the lowest differences in schooling returns while the countries with the lowest participation (including Ireland and the UK) have the largest. This suggests that there is some bias from using samples of participants alone and further research needs to be done to establish the size of this bias.

Variation in the Returns to Education across the Wage Distribution

It is possible that the returns to schooling may be different for individuals in the upper part of the wage distribution as compared to individuals in the lower portion of the wage distribution. One of the properties of OLS estimation is that the regression line contains or passes through the mean of the sample. An alternative methodology is available to OLS known as quantile regression (QR) which, based on the entire sample available, allows us to estimate the return to a particular level of education within different quantiles of the wage distribution. The idea with QR is to compare the returns at one part of the distribution, say the bottom quartile, with another part, say the top quartile. The comparison then allows us to infer the extent to which education exacerbates or reduces underlying inequality. Median regression, met earlier, is simply where the 50th percentile is the focus of attention.

Figure 1.2 Female/male differential in returns and female participation rates

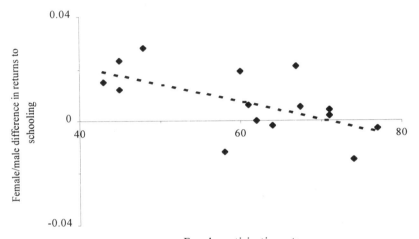

Female participation rate

Table 1.5 is based on the work of the PURE project and was compiled by Pedro Pereira and Pedro Silva-Martins. Comparisons are possible between two points in time across the range of countries, typically 15 - 20 years apart. The OLS results show that over the period the returns to schooling, on average, have broadly increased. There is a clear implication from the comparisons between the 90th and 10th percentile that the returns to schooling are higher for those at the top of the wage distribution compared to those at the bottom (although for some countries the profiles are flat across a range of the wage distribution). There is some suggestion that the returns have risen at the top of the distribution. One factor behind the distribution of wages is the distribution of inherent ability so that lower ability individuals predominate in the bottom half of the distribution. Thus education may have a bigger impact on the more able than the less able and this complementarity between ability and education is either getting stronger or not much weaker over time.

Table 1.5   Quantile regressions

	Year	1st Dec.	9th Dec.	OLS	Year	1st Dec.	9th Dec.	OLS
Austria	1981	9.2	12.6	10.5	1993	7.2	12.8	9.7
Denmark	1980	4.7	5.3	4.6	1995	6.3	7.1	6.6
Finland	1987	7.3	10.3	9.5	1993	6.8	10.1	8.9
France	1977	5.6	9.8	7.5	1993	5.9	9.3	7.6
Germany	1984	9.4	8.4		1995	8.5	7.5	
Greece	1974	6.5	5.4	5.8	1994	7.5	5.6	6.5
Italy	1980	3.9	4.6	4.3	1995	6.7	7.1	6.4
Ireland	1987	10.1	10.4	10.2	1994	7.8	10.4	8.9
Netherlands	1979	6.5	9.2	8.6	1996	5.3	8.3	7.0
Norway	1983	5.3	6.3	5.7	1995	5.5	7.5	6.0
Portugal	1982	8.7	12.4	11.0	1995	6.7	15.6	12.6
Spain	1990	6.4	8.3	7.2	1995	6.7	9.1	8.6
Sweden	1981	3.2	6.6	4.7	1991	2.4	6.2	4.1
Switzerland	1992	8.2	10.7	9.6	1998	6.3	10.2	9.0
UK	1980	2.5	7.4	6.7	1995	4.9	9.7	8.6

Summary: Meta Analysis

To summarize the various issues discussed above we use the methods common in meta-analysis to provide some structure to our survey of returns to schooling and to provide a framework to determine whether our inferences are sensitive to specification choices. A meta-analysis combines and integrates the results of several studies that share a common aspect so as to be 'combinable' in a statistical manner. The methodology is typical in the clinical trials in the medical literature. In its simplest form the computation of the average return across a number of studies is now achieved by weighting the contribution of an individual study to the average on the basis of the standard error of the estimate (see Ashenfelter et al., 1999, for further details).

In Figure 1.3 we present the findings of a simple meta-analysis based on the collected OLS estimated rates of return to schooling from the PURE project supplemented by a number of findings for the USA. Well over 1000 estimates were generated across the PURE project on three main types of estimated return to schooling- existing published work (labelled PURE1), existing unpublished work (PURE2), and new estimates produced for the PURE project (PURE3). Each column refers to a different sample of studies (for example only studies based on US-originated studies).

Education and Earnings in Europe

Figure 1.3 Meta- analysis

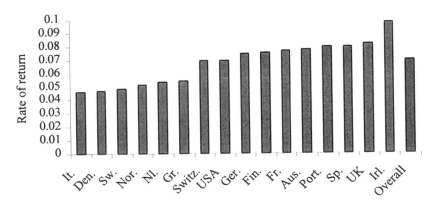

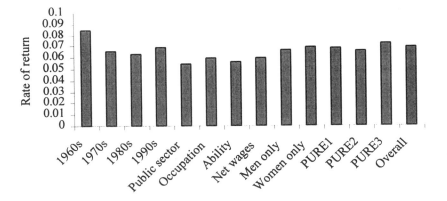

A number of points emerge from the figure. Despite the points raised earlier in this chapter there is a remarkable similarity in the estimated return to schooling for a number of possible cuts of the data with an average return of around 6.5% capturing to a large extent the returns for different countries and different model specifications. There are a number of notable exceptions. The Scandinavian countries generally have lower returns to schooling while at the other extreme the returns for the UK and Ireland are indeed higher than average. In addition estimated returns from studies of public sector workers, and from studies where net (of tax) wages are only available average about 5% (although we would expect the net returns to be lower than those from gross earnings by an amount approximately equal to the average tax rate). Estimates produced using samples from the 1960s also seem to have produced higher than average returns.

ENDOGENEITY OF SCHOOLING

Isolating the Effect of Exogenous Variation in Schooling

If you want to know how an individual's earnings are affected by an extra year of schooling you would ideally compare an individual's earnings with N years of schooling with the same individual's earnings after $N + 1$ years of schooling. The problem for researchers is only one of the two earnings levels of interest are observed and the other is unobserved (Harmon *et al.*, 2000). The problem is analogous to those encountered in other fields, such as medical science: either a patient receives a certain treatment or not so observing the effectiveness of a treatment is difficult as all we actually observe is the effect of treatment on those who are treated. In medical studies the usual solution to this problem is by providing treatment to patients on the basis of a random assignment scheme. In the context of education studies this is sometimes possible but is usually not feasible. However, there are still possibilities to tackle the problem that the treated are not the same as the untreated in unobservable ways and labour economists have made significant progress in this area in the past 10 years. The key idea is to look for real-world events (as opposed to real experiments), which can be arguably considered as events that assign individuals randomly to different treatments. Randomly here has as its more precise definition that there is no relation between the event and the outcome of interest. Such events have been dubbed "natural experiments" in the literature. The essence of this natural experiment approach is to provide a suitable instrument for schooling which is not correlated with earnings and in doing so provide the closest equivalent to a randomized trial in an experiment in a clinical study.

A very direct way of addressing the issue of the effect of an additional year of education on wages can be seen where we examine the wages of people who left school at 16 when the minimum school leaving age was raised to 16 compared to the wages of those who left school at 15 just before the minimum was raised to 16. The Family Resources Survey for the UK is large enough for us to select the relevant cohort groups to allow us do this and Table 1.6 shows the relevant wages.

The effect of the treatment of having to stay on at school gives the magnitude of interest for policy work – the effect of additional schooling for those who would not have normally chosen an extra year. This is 14.9% for men and 10.7% for women. The former figure is very close to that obtained in Harmon and Walker (1995) using more complex multivariate methods. In contrast the effect of an additional year of schooling that had been chosen earned a larger premium of 24.8% for men and 19.0% for women which reflects the fact that these are different people to those that left at 15 in terms of their other characteristics.

Table 1.6   Wages and minimum school leaving ages (£/hour)

	(1) Left at 15 pre-reform	(2) Left at 16 pre-reform	(3) Left at 16 post-reform	% difference between (3) and (1)	% difference between (2) and (1)
Men	7.66	9.56	8.90	14.9	24.8
Women	5.25	6.25	5.81	10.7	19.0

More formally the treatment group is chosen (albeit not randomly) independent of any characteristics that affect education. Thus, one should not, of course, group the data according to ability. The variable that defines the natural experiment can be thought of as a way of "cutting the data" so that the wages and education of one group can be compared with those of the other: that is, one can divide the between-group difference in wages by the difference in education to form an estimate of the returns to education. The important constraint is that the variable that defines the sample separation is not, itself, correlated with education. There may be differences in observable variables between the groups - so the treatment group may, for example, be taller than the control group – and since these differences may contribute to the differences in wages and/or education one might eliminate these by taking the differences over time within the groups and subtract the differences between the groups. Hence, the methodology is frequently termed the difference-in-differences method.

Table 1.7   Wald estimates of the return to schooling

Even GHS 78-96		Smoker (at 16)	Non-smoker (at 16)	Difference	Wald estimate
Men	Log wage	2.36	2.51	0.16	0.16/0.97 =
	Educ years	12.11	13.08	0.97	0.164
Women	Log wage	2.01	2.18	0.17	0.17/0.90 =
	Educ years	12.52	13.42	0.90	0.188

If the data can be grouped so that the differences between the levels of education in the two groups is random, then an estimate of returns to education (known here as a Wald estimate) can be found from dividing the differences in wages across the groups by the difference in the group average education. A potential example is to group observations according to their childhood smoking behaviour. This information is contained in the General Household Survey for the UK, for even years from 1978-96, and Table 1.7 shows that by examining these differences between groups the estimated return to schooling is around 16% for men and 18% for women.

A closely related way of controlling for the differences in observable characteristics is to control for them using multivariate methods. This is the essence of the instrumental variables approach. By constructing instruments for schooling that are uncorrelated with the earnings equation the instrumental variables (IV) approach will generate unbiased estimates of the return to schooling. Consider the following model

$$y_i = \mathbf{X_i}'\delta + \beta S_i + u_i$$

where

$$S_i = \mathbf{Z_i}'\alpha + v_i$$

where in addition to those variables described earlier $\mathbf{Z}$ is a vector of observed attributes. We assume

$$E(\mathbf{X_i}\, u_i) = E(\mathbf{Z_i}\, v_i) = 0.$$

We can, as before, interpret β as the return to schooling. Estimation by OLS will yield an unbiased estimate of the return only if schooling is exogenous, so that there is no correlation between the error terms. If this condition is not satisfied alternative estimation methods must be employed. The correlation might be non-zero because some important variables related to both schooling and earnings are omitted from the vector $\mathbf{X}$. Motivation, or other ability measures, besides IQ are examples. It is important to note that even a very extensive list of variables included in the vector $\mathbf{X}$ will never be exhaustive. An estimate of the return to schooling based on OLS will not give the causal effect of schooling on earnings as the schooling coefficient β captures some of the effects that would otherwise be attributed to the omitted ability variable. For instance, if the omitted variable is motivation, and if both schooling and earnings are positively correlated with motivation, the estimation ignores that more motivated persons are likely to earn more than less motivated persons even when they have similar amounts of schooling.

In order therefore to model the relationship between schooling and earnings we must use the schooling equation to compute the predicted or fitted value for schooling. We then replace schooling in earnings function with this predicted level. As predicted schooling is correlated with actual schooling this replacement variable will still capture the effect of education on wages. However there is no reason that predicted schooling will be correlated with the error term in the earnings function so the estimated return based on predicted schooling is unbiased. This is the two-stage-least-squares method that captures the essence of the IV method.

The difficulty for this procedure is one of "identification". In order to identify or isolate the effect of schooling on earnings we must focus our attention on providing variables in the vector $\mathbf{Z_i}$ that are not contained in $\mathbf{X_i}$. That is, there must exist a variable which is a determinant of schooling that can legitimately be omitted from the earnings equation. This variable is provided by the natural experiment. In essence this amounts to examining how wages differ between groups whose education is different for exogenous reasons. For example, some individuals may have faced a minimum school-leaving age that differed from that faced by others, or may have started school at an earlier age for random reasons (i.e. reasons that are uncorrelated with the wages eventually earned).

Results from IV Studies – International Evidence

In Figure 1.4 we present results of a meta-analysis of studies which treat schooling as endogenous based on the PURE dataset of results used in Chapter 2. Compared to an average from OLS of 6.5% we see much larger returns to schooling in IV studies (of about 9%) and from IV studies based on interventions in particular (of around 13% to 14%). IV studies based on family background sourced instruments have returns an average close to the OLS estimate.

Figure 1.4 Meta-analysis of models with endogenous schooling

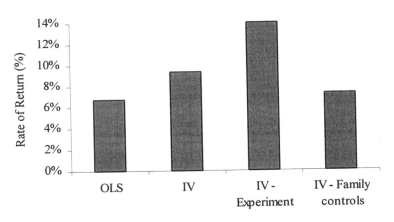

Table 1.8 outlines the key results in this literature for the non-UK studies. Angrist and Krueger (1991) use the presence of compulsory schooling law variation across US states and the quarter of the year in which a person was born as the basis of their instruments. The underlying idea here is that a person who has been born early in the year (the first quarter) reaches the minimum school leaving age after a smaller amount of schooling than persons born later in the year. The actual amount of schooling attained is directly related to the quarter in which they were born while at the same time there seems no reason to believe that quarter of birth has an own independent effect on earnings. Direct estimation by OLS gives an estimate of the return to schooling of 0.063 whereas the IV method gives an estimate of 0.081. The study of Angrist and Krueger has been criticized by Bound *et al.*, 1995. They argue that quarter of birth may have an impact on earnings other than only through the effect on schooling. Studies from other social sciences indicate that the timing of births over a year is related to social background. Parents with lower social backgrounds tend to get children spread evenly over the year, while parents from higher social classes get children during more concentrated in particular seasons.

In another study, Angrist and Krueger (1992) exploit the idea that because college enrolment led to draft exemptions potential draftees for the Vietnam campaign had this exogenous influence on their schooling decision. The instruments are based around numbers assigned on the basis of month and day of birth from which a 'draft lottery' was conducted. Again the IV results are higher than OLS but the difference is insignificant, perhaps reflecting later work which suggested the instrument was only marginally significant to the education decision (see Bound *et al.*,1995). Card (1995) uses an indicator for the distance to college as an instrument for schooling based on the observed higher education levels of men who were raised near a four-year college and finds returns of 13.2% compared to OLS estimates of closer to 7%. However, again, the estimates were rather imprecise so this finding lacked precision. Butcher and Case (1994), in one of the few examples based on a sample of women, again find IV exceeding OLS and in fact the estimated return more than doubles in this study.

A somewhat different approach is used in the paper by Duflo (1999) where estimation is based on the exposure of individuals to a massive investment programme in education in Indonesia in the early 1970s. Individuals were assigned to the treatment on the basis of their date of birth (pre-and post- reform) and the district they lived in (as investment was a function of local level needs assessment). Meghir and Palme (1999) pursue a similar strategy in their analysis of reforms in Sweden in the 1950s that were intended to extend the schooling level nationally. This was piloted in a number of school districts prior to its adoption nationally and it is from this pre-trial experiment that the variation in attainment comes. Both these papers rely on large-scale reforms or 'natural experiments' whose effect differed across individuals. A similar approach is used in Denny and Harmon (2000) in looking at a fundamental change in the educational system in 1960s Ireland which not only affected the entire population of school-going individuals but in a way which differed across socio-economic backgrounds.

Table 1.8   IV studies – Estimated Rate of Return to Schooling

Study	Sample	OLS	IV	Instruments
Angrist and Krueger (1991)	*US 1970/1980 Census: men born 1920-29, 1930-39, 1940-49*	6.3	8.1	Year/State/ Quarter of Birth
Angrist and Krueger (1992)	*US 1979-85 CPS: men born 1944-53 (potential Vietnam War draftees)*	5.9	6.6	Draft Lottery Number
Card (1995)	*US NLS: men aged 14-24 in 1966 sampled as employed in 1976*	7.3	13.2	Nearby college to place of residence
Butcher and Case (1994)	*US PSID 1985: white women aged 24+*	9.1	18.5	Presence of older sisters
Harmon and Walker (1995)	*UK FES 78-1986. males 16-64.*	6.1	15.2	School- leaving age changes
Dearden (1998)	*UK NCDS: women born in 1958*	8.3	9.3	Family variables
Harmon and Walker (1999)	*UK GHS 1985- 1992 : males 16-64.*	4.1	14.0	School leaving-age changes
Meghir and Palme (1999)	*Sweden – males*	2.8	3.6	Curriculum reforms
Duflo (1999)	*Indonesian – males*	7.7	9.8	School building project
Harmon and Walker (2000)	*UK NCDS: men*	5.1%	9.9%	Peer effects, education reforms
Denny and Harmon (2000)	*Irish ESRI 1987 Data – Males*	8.0	13.6	Abolition of fees for secondary schooling.

Notes: See Card (2000) for further details.

Dearden (1998) repeats the idea in Butcher and Case (1994) by using sibling presence as an instrument for schooling. This study employed National Child Development Study (NCDS) data from the UK and found increased estimates of the return to schooling compared to the the OLS equivalents. In a series of papers Harmon and Walker (1995, 1999, 2000) use changes in the compulsory school-leaving age laws in the 1950s and 1970s as instruments, as well as other educational reforms and peer effects. Across a number of datasets a robust finding emerges that compared to OLS estimates of the order of 5% or 6% per year of schooling the IV estimated returns could be significantly higher.

Why are the IV estimates higher than OLS?

As discussed above Card (1995, 2000) presents a model of endogenous schooling which shows that individuals invest in schooling until the marginal return to schooling is equal to their marginal discount rate. Therefore less educated workers have either lower returns to schooling (less able) or higher discount rates (less taste for education, poorer backgrounds). If an intervention used as an instrument in an IV estimation induces those from the low-education group to participate further the associated return will reflect the marginal returns for the low-education group, which may well exceed the return for the population as a whole.

In the Card (2000) model the return to education can vary across the population, and the marginal return to schooling is a decreasing function of schooling. When the instrument is formed on the basis of membership of a treatment group the IV estimate of the return to schooling is the difference in expected log earnings between the control group and the treatment group, divided by the difference in expected schooling for the two groups. This implies that if all individuals in the population have the same marginal return the IV estimate is a consistent estimate of the average marginal rate of return. However, if the return to schooling is allowed to vary across individuals the IV estimate is the rate of return for the subgroup most affected by the treatment/instrument. If only one subgroup is affected by the intervention the IV estimator will yield the marginal rate of return *for that subgroup*.

In this respect the IV estimator can exceed the conventional OLS estimator if the intervention affects a subgroup with relatively high marginal return to schooling. In the context of Card's model this is possible as low amounts of schooling can imply higher marginal returns to schooling if the relative variation in ability is small. If the intervention affects those with below-average schooling levels the IV estimate will be larger than the 'average' OLS result. This is suggested as a rationale for the results in, for example, Angrist and Krueger (1991, 1992) concerning changes in compulsory schooling laws, and is a specific example of the more general issue of estimating returns for the marginal groups hit by the treatment known as Local Average Treatment Effects or LATE.

As noted by Dearden (1995) if the instrument(s) is correlated with the true measure of education but uncorrelated with any measurement error in schooling, the IV approach can be used, and the presence of measurement error should not affect the estimated IV return to education which will be consistent. What will differ is the interpretation placed on the difference between OLS and IV results. As such the difference can now be attributed to a combined effect of measurement error and the endogeneity of schooling. The research by Ashenfelter and Krueger (1994) calculates the reliability ratio (the ratio of variance of the measurement error to total variance in S) in years of schooling measures in survey data at 90%, suggesting that approximately 10% of the total variance in schooling is due to measurement error, but still finds large and significant downward bias in the least squares estimates. On this evidence measurement error appears an unlikely candidate for explaining the IV/OLS difference.

Finally, the negative correlation may be a result of optimizing behaviour of individuals. Assuming another unmeasured factor which affects income but is unrelated to ability is the approach of Griliches (1977). For example if there is a component that affects the marginal costs of education but not the marginal benefits, such as foregone earnings, the optimizing framework will lead to a negative correlation between schooling and the earnings function residual.

Instrument Relevance and Instrument Validity

Bound *et al.* (1995) urge caution in the use of IV. In this context IV can be simply explained as the splitting of the variance in schooling into an endogenous and exogenous component, with the exogenous component used in estimation of the first stage equation. The essence of their argument is that the consistency of IV assumes the instruments are correlated with schooling but not associated with the earnings outcome. Moreover, if this is not the case, and there is only a tenuous relationship between the instrument and schooling, estimation by IV will lead to large inconsistencies. Thus, we find two main results. Firstly, a weak relationship between schooling and the instruments will raise IV inconsistency. Secondly, a strong relationship between the instruments and the error in the wage equation will also raise the inconsistency, with this effect magnified by the presence of a poor schooling/instrument relationship. As an example Bound *et al.* (1995) re-estimate the results from Angrist and Krueger (1991) and find that the hundreds of instruments used in that study are mostly uncorrelated with S which can result in IV being more biased that OLS.

A similar argument has been put forward for the case of invalid instruments. Again Bound and Jaeger (1996), based on a replication of the original paper, fnd that quarter of birth does seem to have an effect on wages invalidating the case of Angrist and Krueger (1991). Family background variables come into this category.

Non-random assignment to treatment and control groups can potentially arise in natural experiments. As suggested in Card (2000), in the study by Harmon and Walker (1995) people born before 1958 were considered as the control group and those post 1958 were the treatment group on the basis of the implementation of the change in school-leaving age. However older cohorts may be different in other ways – their education may have been affected by World War II for example (see Ichino and Winter-Ebmer, 2000).

Finally, publication bias is suggested by Ashenfelter *et al.* (1999). The average return to schooling in a meta analysis of schooling returns estimated by OLS is 6% compared to an average of over 9% from IV estimates. Ashenfelter *et al.* (1999) estimate the probability of being observed in a sample of estimated returns as a declining function of the *p*-value on your result. In other words more significant results have a higher chance of being observed. When this is corrected about two-thirds of the gap between the average OLS estimated return and the average IV estimated return is accounted for.

Fixed Effect Estimators

Table 1.9 illustrates some recent findings from the literature based on samples of siblings or twins. This approach exploits a belief that siblings are more alike than a randomly selected pair of individuals, given that they share common heredity, financial support, peer influences, geographic and sociological influences etc. This literature attempts to eliminate omitted ability bias by estimating the return to schooling from differences between siblings or twins in levels of schooling and earnings, based on a belief that these differences represent differences in innate ability or motivation, a truer picture of ability bias than simple test scores. This approach received much attention in the schooling-earnings literature in the late seventies and early eighties, possibly as a result of the availability of suitable panel data or specialist studies. If the omitted variable, say ability (A), is such that siblings have the same level of A, then any estimate of β from within family data, i.e., differences in salary between brothers, will eliminate this bias. The survey by Griliches (1979) concludes that the estimated return to schooling where ability bias is purged via differencing is lower than the estimated return from the whole sample.

The research of Blanchflower and Elias (1999) argues that twins may represent a quite distinct population grouping, making generalizations to the population as a whole difficult. Bound and Solon (1998) point out that the US twins data seems to have larger differences in S than randomly matched unrelated invididuals would have casting doubt on the data. However more fundamental criticisms of this approach have focused on the underlying assumptions. If ability has an individual component as well as a family component, which is not independent of the schooling variable, the within-family approach may not yield estimates which are any less biased. Also, although more desirable than the approach of ability 'proxies' outlined above the problem of poorly specified data may be particularly damaging to this more sophisticated approach, particularly if the measurement of schooling is prone to error both in the choice of measure and the reporting of the data, even in cross-sectional studies. If schooling is measured with error, this will account for a larger fraction of the differences between the twins than across the population as a whole. This would imply that the bias from measurement error in schooling is likely to increase by forming differences between twins.

Table 1.9   Twins/Siblings Research on Schooling Returns

		OLS	IV
Ashenfelter and Rouse (1999)	Princeton Twins Survey	7.8%	10%
Rouse (1997)	Princeton Twins Survey	7.5%	11%
Miller et al (1995)	Australian Twins Register	4.5%	7.4%
Isacsson (1999)	Swedish same sex twins	4%	5.4%
Ashenfelter and Zimmerman (1997)	NLS Young Men	4.9%	10%

Recent contributions to the twins literature have attempted to deal with the measurement error problem by instrumenting the education of twin A using the measure of the education of Twin A *as reported by Twin B*. Ashenfelter and Krueger (1994) collected data at an annual twins festival in 1991 and found against the conventional result of upward bias in OLS estimates. Moreover, correcting for measurement error in the self-reported schooling level generates a much larger estimate of the schooling return, in the order of 14%. The possible non-randomness of this dataset and the relatively small samples used led to criticisms. However, the findings of Ashenfelter and Zimmerman (1992) support this result. The recent paper by Miller *et al.* (1994), which uses a much larger sample of twins from a representative survey and employs the same technique as Ashenfelter and Krueger (1994), also finds strong evidence of downward bias in the least squares estimates.

Other panel data techniques have been employed to this problem. By treating the unobserved heterogeneity as fixed, individual panel data can be used to eliminate the fixed effect. It is assumed that the unobservables are time invariant, and hence observations on the same individual at different time periods yield the information necessary to isolate the effect of the unobservable. The applicability of panel data to estimates of schooling returns is limited. This is due to the nature of the panel that we only observe earnings information following completion of schooling. Taking first differences in earnings will eliminate not only the unobservable fixed effect but the schooling information also. Information is therefore required on individuals' earnings before and after schooling, and as such is only available for those who return to education later in their lives. While this appears unlikely, Angrist and Newey (1991) find some 19% of working male respondents in National Longitudinal Study of Youth (NLSY) reporting a higher level of schooling in later waves of the data, removing the fixed effect designation of schooling.

SOCIAL RETURNS TO EDUCATION

Externalities from Education

A clear message of the previous section is the presence of a significant private return to education (which just includes the costs and benefits that flow to the student) of which the OLS estimates can be considered at least a lower bound. As noted in Sianesi and Van Reenen (1999) and Dutta *et al.* (1999) persistently high returns to individuals undertaking higher education suggests that individuals may be underinvesting in education for some reason. However, given this high private return, it is not clear why taxpayers resources should be invested in encouraging educational participation unless there are benefits to society over and above the benefits to the individual. Greenaway and Haynes (2000) discuss the possibility that graduates raise the productivity of non-graduates such that aggregate productivity is higher. Moreover, there may be socially cohesive benefits from education participation rates being increased through government interventions. Dutta *et al.* (1999) calculate social rates by comparing the earnings profiles for male university graduates and non-graduates who have A levels and using a baseline assumption for the cost of producing a graduate of £4790 per annum plus earnings foregone while studying. Social rates of return for three groupings of degree subjects are then estimated. These rates of return for graduates range from zero (for broadly humanities and biological sciences) to over 11% (for medicine, science and computing, business studies and social studies). These are lower than their private rate of return estimates but are still relatively high and crucially exceed the rate of return expected by the UK Treasury for support of investment projects. Evidence in OECD (1998) cited in Greenaway and Haynes (2000) suggests that social rates of return in the OECD are around 10% and higher in countries where students make a contribution to costs (such as Australia, Canada and the USA). This analysis makes no allowance for wider benefits to the economy.

Human Capital and Growth – Macroeconomic Evidence

Aggregating a Mincer human capital earnings function to the economy level we get

$$\ln \overline{w}_{jt} = r_{jt} \overline{S}_{jt} + e_{jt}$$

where the overbar denotes country-specific means for schooling and incomes (although, for income, in practice, GDP per capita is used), for country j at time t. Differencing removes technological differences that are part of the error term terms to give

$$\Delta \ln \overline{w}_j = \Delta r_j \overline{S}_{jt} + r_{jt} \Delta \overline{S}_j + \Delta e_{jt}$$

so the S coefficient shows how returns have changed over time, while the ΔS coefficient gives the (social) rate of return in j at time t. Psacharopoulos (1994) found that the Mincerian return fell on average by 1.7% over 12 years while O'Neill (1995) found that the (social) return rose by 58% in developed countries and 64% in less developed countries (LDCs) between 1967 and 1985. The implication is that the externality has been growing over time.

The idea that growth rates should converge is in a feature of many macro-studies – those below their steady-state growth rate should catch up with those above, that is

$$\Delta W_j = \beta \left(W_{jt-1} - W_j^* \right) + u_j$$

where $W = $ log of w and W^* is the steady state level of GDP (per capita). Then the macro growth equation would become

$$\Delta W_j = \beta W_{jt-1} + r S_{j,j-1} + \ldots\ldots + e_j$$

where variables such as "rule-of-law" index, inflation and capital are sometimes included. In addition an interaction

$$W_{jt-1} S_{j,t-1}$$

may be included to capture the idea that the speed of convergence may be faster the higher is the level of education. Such growth equations are usually estimated from pooled cross-section data spanning five (or more) years.

Classic examples are Barro and Lee (1993) and Benhabib and Spiegel (1994). However, there are some differences between what is usually estimated in the growth modelling literature and micro-work in the Mincer tradition. Much of the macro-growth literature excludes ΔS, the change in schooling levels in the economy. The growth literature also typically includes controls to capture the steady state level of GDP. There are a number of empirical difficulties with this literature mainly related to the nature of the causal relationship between schooling and growth. The interpretation of the S coefficient in

$$\Delta W_j = \beta W_{jt-1} + r S_{j,t-1} + \ldots\ldots + e_j$$

could be interpreted as a return in terms of the 'steady state' growth of the economy - educated countries grow faster. However, more indirect effects are possible. Schooling may better enable the workforce to develop and adapt to new technologies which will also allow educated countries to grow faster. But paradoxically countries with low levels of average schooling might have better opportunities to grow by adopting technology developed abroad. The return to S may have risen or fallen which can jeopardize the interpretation in these growth models. However anticipated growth in an economy could cause an increase in the demand for education. Indeed Topel (2000) has argued that "little can be learned" from macro-growth equations because either a positive or a negative coefficient on human capital is "consistent with the idea that human capital is a boon to growth and development".

Human Capital and Growth – Microeconomic Evidence

Krueger and Lindahl (1999) strongly criticize many of the macro contributions in this area and point to the micro-foundations of the analysis and the strong assumptions underpinning the findings. For example many of the more general results linking education and growth might stem from imposing constant coefficient and linearity restrictions on the data. This point is reaffirmed in Trostel (2000) who shows how the limited microeconomic evidence on human capital production is not helpful as it imposes important restrictions on the estimates of the returns to scale to the inputs. Although constant returns may be an appropriate assumption for some educational services (i.e., teaching) this does not imply constant returns to scale in producing human capital which is embodied in individuals. In Trostel's model the returns to scale is inferred from the rate of return to education. Data from the International Social Survey Programme is used to estimate (private) rates of return to education and rejects a constant marginal rate of return to education which is shown to equate to a rejection of constant returns to scale in producing human capital. The marginal rate of return to schooling is shown to be significantly increasing at low levels of education indicating significant increasing returns, and the marginal rate of return decreases significantly at high levels of education (thus indicating significant decreasing returns).

Krueger and Lindahl (1999) also stress how causality can be confused – it is not clear that cross-country differences in education are a cause of income, or a result of income or income growth. Therefore, while considerable effort has been placed in the exogeneity or endogeneity of schooling in private returns estimation based on microeconomic data, little or no effort has been made in the possible endogeneity of education in cross-country macro-specifications. Similarly human capital enhancement projects can result in other investments to enhance growth introducing a second source of omitted variable bias in cross-country study. The call in the Krueger and Lindahl research is for an experimental approach to be adopted in the social returns literature to repeat in essence what we extensively discussed earlier in the report for the estimation of private returns. In view of the difficulty in finding a 'one size fits all' experiment the conjecture in this research is that establishing the social returns and quantifying the likely externalities from education is likely to be more successful from within region study rather than between country study.

A literature is beginning in this vein but unfortunately the evidence is already conflicting. Moretti (1998) examines US census information for otherwise similar workers within cities with higher and lower education levels. He differences out the potential draw of the city for particular workers as well as the endogeneity of the growth in education across cities. What is found is that a 1% increase in the share of college-educated workers raises the earnings of school dropouts by 2.2%, of high school graduates by 1.3% and college graduates by 1.1%. All gains are net of costs. In this paper Moretti instruments for average schooling - individual schooling is however left as exogenous. Acemoglu and Angrist (1999) consider implications of, like Moretti (1998), treating average schooling as endogenous. However, they also allow for the endogeneity of individual schooling on the basis that instrumenting average schooling if the OLS and IV estimates of the private return to schooling differ can raise more considerable specification problems. They use compulsory schooling laws in the USA to instrument individual schooling while basing their treatment of average schooling by exploiting differences in child labour laws across the US states. Compared to least square estimates of the private return to education of around 6% estimates based on IV range from 7% to just over 9%. However the social returns estimated in this paper are smaller at around 2% per year of average schooling. Acemoglu and Angrist conclude that their study offers little evidence for sizeable social returns to education, at least over the range of variation in average state-wide education induced by changing the compulsory schooling laws.

Other Externalities from Education

Blundell *et al.* (1999) consider the evidence on the returns to the employer of education and training.   The difficulty is well known here – data is hard to obtain which measures elements such as productivity, competitiveness and profitability, and this is confounded by the need to consider the role the employer may take in funding the investment in human capital particularly in the case of training.

Other more indirect benefits from education may be possible.   Freeman (2000) suggests that there is little *direct* evidence linking education to reductions in crime and the perceived linkage relates to the effect that education has on factors such as unemployment and inequality. For example upward trends in inequality are associated with higher levels of both property and violent crime (Kelly, 2000).   Winter-Ebmer and Raphael (1999) find positive effects of unemployment on crime which are not just statistically significant but large in size.   Leigh (1998) in a review of work published in this areas concludes that increased education is positively and strongly correlated with absence of violent crime, measures of health, family stability and environmental benefits.

Lochner (1999) develops and estimates a model of the decisions to work, to educate yourself, and to commit crime and allows for the possibility of all of these choices being endogenous.   The model suggests that education is correlated with crimes *that require less skill*.   Part of the model allows for simulation of the effects of education subsidies on external outcomes and predicts that education subsidies reduce crime.   In so far as possible, empirical implications were explored using various large scale US micro-datasets.   Ability and high school graduation significantly reduce the participation of young men in crime and the probability of incarceration. Evidence from the census data supports a general finding that states with higher rates of high school participation and tougher penalties have the lowest index for property crime.

CONCLUSIONS

Despite a well-developed theoretical foundation estimation of the return to a year of schooling has been the focus of considerable debate in the economics literature. A dominant feature of the simple human capital earnings function, that schooling is exogenous, has in particular been the focus of recent research efforts. With respect to the returns for an individual from schooling a number of conclusions can be drawn.

Simple analysis of average earnings for different levels of education can mask a number of issues. The omission of additional controls assumes that variables that affect wages are uncorrelated with schooling – which seem implausible. For example older people are likely to have lower levels of education but higher levels of work experience giving very different 'returns' for a given level of schooling. Multivariate regression analysis based on OLS suggests a return to a year of schooling of between 3% and 9% depending on the country of analysis when a relatively parsimonious specification is used based on controlling for schooling and experience (measured with age and its square to capture the potential for diminishing returns to experience).

The returns to schooling are relatively stable to changes in this simple OLS specification (such as including controls for marital status/family size/union membership) but some differences are worth noting. Using different measures of experience (based on actual reported experience and so-called 'potential' experience or the difference between current age and the age left school) will tend to raise the return to schooling by approximately 1%. Including occupational controls will tend to have the opposite effect, lowering the return by around 1%. Basing the estimation on samples of employed persons may also bias the returns to schooling downwards slightly, at least for samples of women.

The basic specification assumes that earnings are linear in education, or that each year of education adds the *same* amount to earnings irrespective of the particular year. This may seem implausible but it has been difficult to find examples in the literature that conclusively prove that linearity is not a valid assumption. There is limited evidence that some years of schooling carry 'sheepskin' effect – leaving school the year immediately following a credential awarding year for example may generate a lower return for that year generating a dip in the education/earning profile.

Returns to education may also differ across the wage distribution. Evidence based on quantile regression methods suggest that the returns are higher for those in the top decile of the income distribution compared to those in the bottom decile. Moreover this inequality may have increased in recent years. One explanation for this phenomenon is a complementarity between ability and education – if higher ability persons earn more this might explain the higher returns in the upper deciles of the wage distribution.

Given the increase in the supply of educated workers in most OECD countries there is a concern that the skills workers bring to their job will exceed the skills required for the job. This will manifest itself in a lower return to schooling for the years of schooling in excess of those required for the employer. One of the main problems with this literature is the often poor definition of overeducation in available datasets, typically based on subjective measures given by the individual respondent. Where a more encompassing definition is used based on job satisfaction the apparent negative effect of overeducation is eliminated when ability controls are included and moreover when overeducation appears genuine the penalty may be much larger than was first thought.

Ideally the way we would wish to measure the return to schooling would be to compare the earnings of an individual with two different levels of schooling, but only one level of education is observed for a particular individual. The literature has recently attempted to deal with this problem by finding 'experiments' in the economy that randomly assign groups of individuals to different levels of schooling. We can, for example, examine the wages of people who left school at 16 when the minimum school-leaving age was raised to 16 compared to those who left school at 15 before the change in the minimum age legislation. This gives us a measure of the return to schooling for those that would not have chosen an extra year of schooling. The return to schooling from studies that use this methodology seem to be larger than those obtained using OLS. Alternatively a more sophisticated modelling procedure based on IV can be used to deal with this problem.

The effect of this change in procedure can be considerable. Average returns to schooling from OLS are around 6% internationally and over 9% from these alternative methods. A concern about this methodology is that the higher returns found may reflect the return for the particular subgroup affected by the policy intervention. Thus, for example, changes in compulsory schooling laws may affect those individuals who place the least *value* on education – and as such estimates of the return to schooling based on these changes may be estimating the returns for that group. An alternative explanation is that the intervention actually has a weak effect on schooling which for econometric reasons can introduce or exaggerate bias in the estimated returns. In short, care should be taken in the interpretation of IV estimated returns to schooling as an indicator of the return to all individuals without careful knowledge of the effect of the interventions used in estimation of the return.

The evidence on private returns to the individual is compelling and despite some of the subtleties involved in estimation there is still an unambiguous positive effect on the earnings of an individual from participation in education. Given this high return unless there are benefits to society (social returns) over and above the private returns there is little argument for the taxpayer to subsidize individual study. There is a limited amount of evidence that suggests social returns to education may be positive. Direct macroeconomic evidence that links growth to education in confounded by the unclear nature of the causal relationship between average schooling levels and measures such as GNP growth. The microeconomic studies that are available confirm this and show how many important findings linking education to growth are based on restrictive functional form assumptions.   What is possibly needed in order to solve the issue of the wider impact of education on society is a parallel to the experiments approach adoped in the estimation of private returns which does suggest that within-country rather than between-country analysis may be the route to quantifying the externality from education.

REFERENCES

Acemoglu, Daron and Joshua Angrist (1999), "How Large are the Social Returns to Education? Evidence from Compulsory Schooling Laws", NBER Working Paper no. 7444.

Angrist, Joshua and Alan B. Krueger (1991), "Does Compulsory School Attendance Affect Schooling and Earnings", *Quarterly Journal of Economics,* 106, 979-1014.

Angrist, Joshua and Alan B. Krueger (1992), "Estimating the Payoff to Schooling Using the Vietnam-Era Draft Lottery", NBER Working Paper no. 4067.

Angrist, Joshua and Whitney Newey (1991), "Over-Identification Tests in Earnings Functions with Fixed Effects", *Journal of Business and Economic Statistics*; 9(3), 317-23.

Ashenfelter, Orley and Alan Krueger (1994), "Estimates of the Economic Return to Schooling for a New Sample of Twins", *American Economic Review*, (84), 1157-73.

Ashenfelter, Orley and Cecelia Rouse (1998), "Income, Schooling, and Ability: Evidence from a New Sample of Identical Twins", *Quarterly Journal of Economics*, 113, 253-284.

Ashenfelter, Orley and David Zimmerman (1997), "Estimates of the Return to Schooling from Sibling Data: Fathers, Sons and Brothers." *Review of Economics and Statistics,* 79, 1-9.

Ashenfelter, O., Harmon, C. and Osterbeek, H. (1999), "Empirical Estimation   of the School/Earnings Relationship-A Review.", *Labour Economics*, 6(4), 453-70.

Becker, Gary (1964), *Human Capital: A Theoretical and Empirical Analysis, with Special Reference to Education.* Columbia University Press, New York.

Benhabib, Jess and Mark Spiegel (1994), "The Role of Human Capital in Economic Development: Evidence from Aggregate Cross Country Data.", *Journal of Monetary Economics*, 34(2), 143-73.

Blanchflower, David and Peter Elias (1999), "Ability, Schooling and Earning – Are Twins Different", mimeo, Dartmouth College.

Blundell, R.W., L.Dearden, A.Goodman, A. and H.Reed (1999) "Higher Education, Employment and Earnings in Britain", Institute for Fiscal Studies.

Bound, John, David Jaeger and Regina M. Baker (1995), "Problems with Instrumental Variables Estimation when the Correlation between the Instruments and the Endogenous Explanatory Variables is Weak", *Journal of the American Statistical Association*, 90, 443-50.

Bound, John and David Jaeger (1996), "On the Validity of Season of Birth as an Instrument in Wage Equations: A Comment on Angrist and Krueger's 'Does Compulsory School Attendance Affect Schooling and Earnings?' NBER Working Paper no.5835.

Bound, John and Gary Solon (1998), "Double Trouble: On the Value of Twins-Based Estimation of the Return to Schooling", NBER working paper no.6721.

Butcher, Kristin and Anne Case (1994), "The Effect of Sibling Composition on Women's Education and Earnings", *Quarterly Journal of Economics*, 109, 531-563.

Card David (1995), "Earnings, Schooling, and Ability Revisited", in Solomon Polacheck (ed), *Research in Labor Economics*, Vol.14, JAI Press, Greenwich Connecticut..

Card, David (2000), "Education and Earnings", in Orley Ashenfelter and David Card (eds), *Handbook of Labor Economics*, North Holland, Amsterdam and New York.

Card, David and Alan Krueger (1996), "School Resources and Student Outcomes: An Overview of the Literature and New Evidence from North and South Carolina", *Journal of Economic Perspectives*, 10(4), 31-50.

Dearden, Lorraine (1995), "Education, Training and Earnings" Ph.D. thesis, University College London.

Dearden, Lorraine (1998), "Ability, Families, Education and Earnings in Britain", Institute for Fiscal Studies Working Paper no.W98/14.

Denny, Kevin and Colm Harmon, (2000), "Educational Policy Reform and the Return to Schooling from Instrumental Variables", IFS Working Paper no. W00/06.

Duflo, Esther (1999), "Schooling and Labor Market Consequences of School Construction in Indonesia: Evidence from an Unusual Policy Experiment", mimeo, MIT.

Dutta, J., J.Sefton and M.Weale (1999), "Education and Public Policy", *Fiscal Studies*, 20, 351-86.

Freeman, Richard (2000), "The Economics of Crime", in Orley Ashenfelter and David Card (eds), *Handbook of Labor Economics*, North Holland, Amsterdam and New York.

Griliches, Zvi (1977), "Estimating the Returns to Schooling: Some Econometric Problems", *Econometrica*, 45(1), 1-22.

Griliches, Zvi (1979), "Sibling Models and Data in Economics: Beginnings of a Survey", *Journal of Political Economy*, 87, S37-S64.

Greenaway, David and Michelle Haynes (2000), "Funding Universities to Meet National and International Challenges." mimeo, University of Nottingham.

Harmon, Colm, Hessel Oosterbeek and Ian Walker (2001), "The Returns to Education: A Review of Evidence, Issues and Deficiencies in the Literature", mimeo, University of Warwick.

Harmon, Colm and Ian Walker (1995), "Estimates of the Economic Return to Schooling for the United Kingdom", *American Economic Review*, 85, 1278-1286.

Harmon, Colm and Ian Walker (1999), "The Marginal and Average Return to Schooling in the UK", *European Economic Review*, 43(4-6), 879-87.

Harmon, Colm and Ian Walker (2000), "Returns to the Quantity and Quality of Education: Evidence for Men in England and Wales." *Economica*, 67, 19-35.

Heckman James and Soloman Polachek (1974), "Empirical Evidence on the Functional Form of the Earnings-Schooling Relationship", *Journal of the American Statistical Association*, 69, 350-354.

Isacsson, Gunnar (1999), "Estimates of the Return to Schooling in Sweden From a Large Sample Of Twins", *Labour Economics*, 6(4), 471-489.

Kelly, M. (2000), "Inequality and Crime." *Review of Economics and Statistics*, November.

Krueger, Alan and Mickael Lindahl (1999), "Education for Growth in Sweden and the World", NBER Working Paper no. 7190.

Layard, Richard and George Psacharopoulos (1979), "Human Capital and Earnings: British Evidence and a Critique", *The Review of Economic Studies*, Vol. 46, No. 3.

Leigh, John (1998), "The Social Benefits of Education: A Review Article", *Economics of Education Review:*,17(3), 363-68.

Lochner, Lance (1999), "Education, Work and Crime: Theory and Evidence", Rochester Center For Economic Research Working Paper no. 465.

Meghir, Costas and Martin Palme (1999), "Assessing the Effect of Schooling on Earnings using a social experiment", IFS Working Paper no. W99/10.

Miller Paul, Charles Mulvey and Nick Martin (1995), "What do Twins Studies Reveal about the Economic Return to Education? A Comparison of Australian and US Findings", *American Economic Review*, 85, 586-99.

Mincer, Jacob (1974), *Schooling, Experience and Earnings*, Columbia University Press, New York.

Moretti, Enrico (1998), "Social Returns to Education and Human Capital Externalities; Evidence from Cities", Centre for Labour Research Working Paper no. 9, University of California, Berkeley.

Murphy Kevin and Finis Welch (1990), "Empirical Age-Earnings Profiles", *Journal of Labor Economics*, 8, 202-229.

O'Neill, Donal (1995), "Education and Income Growth: Implications for cross-country inequality", *Journal of Political Economy,* 103, 6, 1289-1301

Psacharopoulos, George (1994), "Returns to Investment in Education: A Global Update", *World Development*, 22, 1325-1343.

Rouse, Cecilia E. (1997), "Further Estimates of the Economic Return to Schooling from a New Sample of Twins", Unpublished Discussion Paper, Princeton University Industrial Section.

Sianesi, Barbara and John Van Reenen (1999), "The Returns to Education – A Review of the Macroeconomic Literature.", mimeo, University College London.

Topel, Robert H (2000), "Labor Markets and Economic Growth", in Orley Ashenfelter and David Card (eds) *Handbook of Labor Economics*, North Holland, Amsterdam and New York.

Trostel, P. (2000), "Micro Evidence on Education as an Engine of Growth.", mimeo, University of Warwick.

Willis, Robert (1986), "Wage Determinants: A Survey and Reinterpretation of Human Capital Earnings Functions", in Orley Ashenfelter and Richard Layard (eds) *Handbook of Labor Economics*, North Holland, Amsterdam and New York.

Winter-Ebmer, Rudolf and S. Raphael (1999), "Identifying the Effect of Unemployment on Crime", mimeo, University of Linz.

2.   Austria

Josef Fersterer
and
Rudolf Winter-Ebmer

INTRODUCTION

This study is an attempt for Austria to establish a systematic presentation of the development of returns to education in the last two decades.[1] Comprehensive studies in the past have been hampered by the lack of comparable data over time. We start with simple human capital earnings functions of the Mincer type. Especially for women, sample selectivity issues warrant a closer look at the base specification to check for selectivity bias. We then expand the analysis to check for robustness of the results by including other control variables often used in earnings regressions. We also consider other issues, such as different returns for specific subgroups of the population. In doing this, personnel policies in the public sector can be analysed; also, the difference between returns to education for employees and self-employed allows us to consider the signalling issue, that is higher education might not be productive as such but might serve only as a signal to the potential employer. The basic specification condenses educational attainment simply to the number of years of schooling the individual has attended but returns to education may be very different for secondary or tertiary education, between different types of schools and so on. A specific consideration of school types allows also the investigation of issues of linearity of returns to education, as well as the calculation of marginal returns for further years. Due to a lack of suitable instruments, which are also available over time, the question of endogeneity of schooling decisions is not dealt with.[2]

THE EDUCATIONAL SYSTEM IN AUSTRIA

The schooling system in Austria is split up in primary, secondary and tertiary levels. Nowadays compulsory schooling takes nine years from age 6 to age

15. In the School Organization Act of 1962, which aimed to increase educational participation, the minimum school leaving age was raised by one year.

Primary education usually starts at age 6 and comprises four grades. Lower secondary education (four years) takes place either in general secondary or in academic secondary schools. After completing lower secondary education, students may continue education in an upper secondary school or take up an apprenticeship. If you opt for apprenticeship training you have to attend first a fifth year of lower secondary education (polytechnic course), which also offers vocational orientation. The apprenticeship is organized as a dual system: besides their practical training in an enterprise, trainees are subject to compulsory vocational schooling (8 to 12 weeks per year). Traineeships last between two and four years.

Upper secondary education takes place in the upper cycle of the academic secondary schools or in upper vocational schools. Whereas pre-academic general education is provided in the former ones, general education is combined with advanced vocational education in the latter, qualifying students for professional activity in technical and business areas. At the end of the courses, students take a matriculation examination (Matura), which gives them the right to enter tertiary education. Besides these upper secondary schools there exist intermediate vocational schools. These two to four year courses offer technical and business knowledge equivalent to the dual system of school and apprenticeship. Passing intermediate vocational schools do not allow entry into tertiary education without further examinations.

Admission to intermediate vocational and upper secondary schools presupposes successful completion of grade 8 of compulsory schooling, either lower secondary or academic secondary school. Depending on the school type, admission is also made conditional upon the assessment of the student's performance in certain subjects and an entrance exam.

Public universities traditionally provide tertiary education, which requires Matura for admission. The master's course (the first degree) legally takes four to five years (minimum duration), depending on the discipline studied. But actually, students need between six (business economics) and eight and a half years (psychology) to finish their master's course. Moreover, only about 60% of male and about 40% of female students graduate. The doctoral course, which may follow a master's course, is of two years' minimum duration.

Besides universities, there is a short non-university sector, which comprises teacher-training academies, academies for social workers, medico-technical schools and military academies. Graduates of these two to three year courses receive non-academic diplomas. Since 1993, polytechnic colleges (non-university post-secondary institutions for professions other than teachers and social workers) have been established which offer four-year courses in predominantly technical areas. These institutions are strongly orientated towards practical training, while universities are devoted to basic research and more general training of students. Applicants to technical colleges have to pass an entrance exam. Quantitatively, the non-university post-secondary sector still plays a marginal role. In 1995, about 90% of all post-secondary students were enrolled at university, 8% at teachers academies, 1.5% at medico-technical schools and social academies and 0.5% at technical colleges. Technical colleges are designed to attract students from university, so that the last figure is expected to rise in the years to come.

METHODOLOGY AND DATA

Ordinary least squares methods are applied to standard Mincerian earnings functions. The dependent variable is net hourly wages in logarithmic terms. Schooling is defined as years of schooling. Controls for experience are also included and the error term is assumed to be independent and identically normally distributed with fixed variance σ^2. All regressions were run for men and women separately and are performed for the period $t = 1981-1997$ every second year. This parsimonious specification has the advantage of easy comparability with other studies. It measures returns to education in a comprehensive way: all indirect influences of education on wages (such as better occupations and sectors) are attributed to education directly. We get, therefore, a reduced form coefficient for schooling. It should be clear, that all other variables typically used in wage regressions are potentially endogenous and influenced by education itself.

We use the Austrian Mikrozensus, the only available data source for Austria for such a time period. These datasets are representative 1% household surveys, and include detailed information about human capital variables. Net monthly earnings are reported in odd years only, so the cross-section regressions are run every second year. Children allowances, which originally had been included in the earnings data until 1993, were eliminated throughout. Net hourly wages can then be constructed by apportioning monthly earnings into the weekly equivalents and dividing through by weekly hours worked. The Mikrozensus contains information about the highest level of schooling achieved. Years of schooling can easily be identified up to the secondary level.[3] Completing the tertiary level is assumed to take 17 years, so students are on average four to five years at university. For the framework with years of schooling one additional year of schooling has been added for people holding an apprenticeship degree (Lehrabschluß). There is no information about actual work experience or years of work interruption. Therefore we used potential experience defined as (age – years of schooling – 6) in the regressions. All employees[4] (white-collar, blue-collar and civil servants) aged between 15 and 65 years are included in the sample. Apprentices have been eliminated from the analysed population.

Income taxes in Austria are highly progressive. It follows that net hourly wages of full-time workers are lower compared to net hourly wages of part-time workers. Therefore, we opted for the following procedure. In a first step we eliminated all employees working less than 15 hours per week. Since only approximately 1% of the remaining male workers operate fewer than 35 hours per week, we concentrated only on those workers who work full time. For women, we added a part-time dummy for those who work between 15 and 34 hours a week, since between one-fifth and one-quarter of all female employees follow a part-time schedule. To avoid bias from incorrect income data (outliers) we omit all employees whose net monthly wages are below the minimum contribution level (Mindestbeitragsgrenze) of the Social Security System.[5]

The Austrian Mikrozensus reports the highest level of schooling achieved; however, graduates from teachers' academies were often coded incorrectly as secondary instead of tertiary educated persons. This mistake has been corrected in the Central Statistical Office by consistency checks since 1987, seemingly leading to a sharp increase of graduates from university. Therefore, before 1987 the relatively low reported years of schooling for teachers implied an upward bias in the estimated rates of return. The bias is especially strong for females, because proportionately more girls attend teachers' colleges than boys. To our knowledge, this is the first study to acknowledge this issue. Several earlier studies excluded civil servants from the sample, which avoids this consistency problem (see Fersterer and Winter-Ebmer, 1999 for more details). There is no simple procedure to overcome this consistency problem. In particular, recoding the observations is impossible. In order to get comparable results over the entire period, we decided therefore to exclude teachers from our sample (about 200 males and 400 females in each year). This procedure also overcomes the problem that information about hours worked by teachers should be viewed with caution.

RESULTS

Returns to Education

Generally, we find a slightly downward trend in the evolution of returns to schooling. Average returns to one additional year of education fell from 10.3% (11.6%) in 1981 to 7.4% (8.0%) for men (women) in 1997 (see Tables 2.1 and 2.2.) At the beginning of the period, average returns to schooling are slightly higher (about 1%) for females than for males. But this difference disappears gradually. The estimates for males are somewhat higher compared to the figures presented by Hofer and Pichelmann (1997),[6] but the trend is the same.

Table 2.1 Estimates of basic equation 1981–1997, males (without teachers)

	Years of schooling	Constant	R² adj.	Sample size
1981	0.103	2.656	0.224	9983
	(0.002)	(0.025)		
1983	0.098	2.744	0.244	8541
	(0.002)	(0.026)		
1985	0.096	2.812	0.264	8094
	(0.002	(0.026)		
1987	0.093	2.967	0.248	8509
	(0.002)	(0.024)		
1989	0.097	3.034	0.228	7879
	(0.002)	(0.027)		
1991	0.088	3.261	0.230	7311
	(0.002)	(0.026)		
1993	0.094	3.277	0.241	7171
	(0.002)	(0.028)		
1995	0.080	3.440	0.283	7215
	(0.002)	(0.023)		
1997	0.074	3.551	0.275	5385
	(0.002)	(0.026)		

Notes: Standard errors in parenthesis.

Although a very parsimonious specification is used, about 25% of the variance in log net hourly wages is explained by the human capital earnings function. Women following a part-time job earn significantly higher net hourly wages compared to their full-time employed counterparts. The extent of the difference fell considerably within the period: from about 10% at the beginning to only 3% at the end of the period.

Returns to Experience

Earnings-experience profiles illustrate the extent to which employers honour additional years of work experience. In human capital theory, returns to experience arise due to general on-the-job training. Therefore earnings-experience profiles are expected to show a concave pattern, indicating rising marginal costs and/or falling marginal returns to training over the live cycle. In Figure 2.1 our estimated profiles show the expected concave pattern for both genders. However, the profiles behave very differently over time. For males, returns to experience are relatively stable within the period examined. On the contrary, in 1997 for women the profile became extremely flat compared to that in 1981. Note that we use potential instead of actual experience in the regressions. This will bias the estimated earnings-experience profile downwards, especially for women, since potential experience will overstate actual experience grossly if there are significant work interruptions.

Table 2.2 Estimates of basic equation 1981–1997, females

	Years of schooling	Part-time (0,1)	Constant	R^2 adj.	Sample size
1981	0.116 (0.003)	0.080 (0.012)	2.268 (0.036)	0.240	5284
1983	0.113 (0.003)	0.113 (0.013)	2.409 (0.036)	0.272	4629
1985	0.110 (0.003)	0.097 (0.012)	2.478 (0.034)	0.288	4638
1987	0.095 (0.003)	0.082 (0.011)	2.767 (0.033)	0.233	4950
1989	0.104 (0.003)	0.054 (0.012)	2.772 (0.037)	0.221	4546
1991	0.098 (0.003)	0.014 (0.011)	2.963 (0.034)	0.223	4703
1993	0.089 (0.003)	0.050 (0.012)	3.139 (0.036)	0.200	4461
1995	0.079 (0.002)	0.032 (0.009)	3.358 (0.030)	0.220	4700
1997	0.080 (0.003)	0.026 (0.010)	3.409 (0.034)	0.232	3492

Notes: Standard errors in parenthesis.

Figure 2.1 Earnings-experience profiles (selected years)

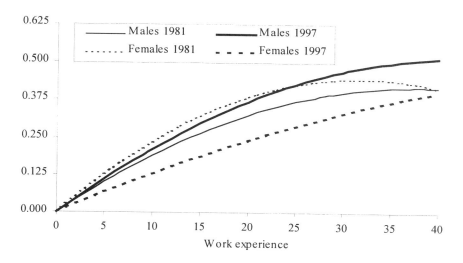

EXTENSIONS

In this section we extend the basic specification in order to check for robustness of the results. The first issue concerns the problem of inferring returns to education from a sample of working people only (sample selectivity problem). Standard economic theory would suggest that those who do supply zero hours of labour would do so because they have lower market wages and possibly also lower expected returns to their education. Heckman's sample selectivity approach will be used to deal with this issue.

Later we will add further explanatory variables to the simple Mincer equation. Results for various subgroups are presented as well as more detailed results for different types of schools. For the most part of the extensions we use only the 1995 cross-section of the Austrian Mikrozensus.

Sample Selectivity Correction for Women

Table 2.3 Selectivity correction for women (1995)

| | Selectivity correction | | Median |
	No	Yes	Regression
Years of schooling	0.068	0.066	0.071
	(0.002)	(0.002)	(0.002)
Experience (potential)	0.016	0.017	0.017
	(0.001)	(0.001)	(0.002)
Experience squared [a]	-0.017	-0.015	-0.020
	(0.003)	(0.003)	(0.004)
Part-time [b]	0.027	0.047	0.013
	(0.009)	(0.009)	(0.010)
λ	-	-0.085	-
		(0.013)	
Constant	3.480	3.530	3.436
	(0.023)	(0.024)	(0.027)
Adjusted R^2	0.255	-	-
Sample size	5058	10442/5058	5058

Notes: Standard errors in parenthesis. [a] Parameter multiplied by the factor 100. [b] Parameter transformed by $\exp(\beta)-1$.

Estimates of human capital functions for women may potentially be biased, because the sample used in the estimation may not be randomly drawn. We therefore included a Heckman correction term to control for such a bias. Variables concerning personal characteristics (years of schooling, age, age squared, nationality) as well as family background (marital status, number of children at different ages) are used to identify participation in the labour force.

Estimates of the human capital function with and without a Heckman correction term are presented in Table 2.3. Although the Heckman correction term is highly significant, the only parameter in the earnings function that changes significantly is the part-time dummy. A more informal way of controlling for selection bias is to use median regression (Buchinsky, 1994), which is especially robust with respect to outliers.[7] The results in Table 2.3, column 3, concur with the estimates above: the returns to education are in a very narrow band, between 6.6% and 7.1% earnings gain per year of education. The same applies to returns to experience. The coefficient for part-time work is cut in half in the median regression, which might be due to the discounting of outliers.

Table 2.4 Inclusion of additional control variables (men, 1995)

	None	Family	Family, nationality	County, city size	County, city size, industry	All
Years of schooling	0.071 (0.002)	0.069 (0.002)	0.066 (0.021)	0.070 (0.002)	0.073 (0.002)	0.069 (0.002)
Experience	0.029 (0.001)	0.024 (0.001)	0.023 (0.001)	0.029 (0.001)	0.029 (0.001)	0.024 (0.001)
Experience squared [a]	-0.039 (0.002)	-0.032 (0.003)	-0.031 (0.003)	-0.039 (0.002)	-0.039 (0.002)	-0.031 (0.002)
Married (0,1)[b]	-	0.069 (0.009)	0.081 (0.009)	-	-	0.081 (0.008)
Children<4 years	-	0.000 [c] (0.007)	0.004 [c] (0.007)	-	-	0.003 [c] (0.007)
Nationality (0,1)[b]	-	-	-0.153 (0.011)	-	-	-0.171 (0.011)
Constant	3.537 (0.021)	3.568 (0.021)	3.607 (0.021)	3.570 (0.024)	3.453 (0.177)	3.690 (0.174)
Counties (9)[d]	-	-	-	7.20	7.24	10.31
City size (4)[d]	-	-	-	3.99	3.23	7-79
Industries (57)[d]	-	-	-	-	11.65	11.23
R^2 adj.	0.302	0.309	0.327	0.309	0.364	0.391
Sample Size	7022	7022	7022	7022	7022	7022

Notes: Standard errors in parenthesis. [a] Parameter multiplied by the factor 100. [b] Parameter transformed by $\exp(\beta)-1$. [c] Not significant. [d] F-value presented.

Additional Control Variables

Table 2.4 compares the return to education obtained from the inclusion of various additional control variables. The Mincerian specification for men now controls for family background (marital status, number of children below age 4), nationality (native / foreigner) as well as nine counties, four city size, and 57 industry dummies. This check indicates that the standard earnings functions are rather robust, since none of the additional included variables change the estimates of returns to schooling, experience or experience squared significantly. The table reveals other well known results: foreign citizens – who are predominantly from former Yugoslavia – earn about 15% less compared to their native counterparts. There also exists a sizeable marriage premium for men: married males earn significantly more (6.9%) than singles.

Returns to Human Capital for Different Subgroups of Workers

Returns to schooling can be expected to differ substantially across different subgroups of workers, between employees and self-employed persons and between private and public employees. Several issues can be discussed under this heading: (1) educational attainment as a signalling device, (2) the difference of pay determination in the market versus administrative wage setting, and (3) returns to education and career paths for white- and blue-collar jobs. The returns to human capital for various sub-populations are reported in Tables 2.5a and 2.5b. There is a survey non-response problem for self-employed (only 10% of the self-employed persons report their income, see Table 2.6), hence we pool observations from three subsequent years (1991, 1993 and 1995) to increase our sample size and include annual dummies to control for changes over time affecting all persons equally.

Table 2.5a Returns to human capital for various subgroups (men)

	Years of schooling	Experience (potential)	Experience squared [a]	Constant	R^2 adj.	Sample Size
All	0.077 (0.001)	0.023 (0.001)	-0.027 (0.002)	3.430 (0.014)	0.301	21357
Self employed	0.102 (0.012)	0.043 (0.011)	-0.062 (0.022)	2.780 (0.206)	0.372	155
All employees	0.077 (0.001)	0.023 (0.001)	-0.026 (0.002)	3.519 (0.014)	0.301	21202
Civil Servants	0.067 (0.001)	0.018 (0.001)	-0.011 (0.003)	3.585 (0.022)	0.417	5055
All private employees	0.097 (0.002)	0.026 (0.001)	-0.033 (0.002)	3.310 (0.019)	0.292	16147
White collar employees	0.080 (0.002)	0.040 (0.002)	-0.051 (0.004)	3.241	0.367	4964
Skilled manual employees	0.043 (0.006)	0.022 (0.001)	-0.031 (0.003)	3.896	0.188	6504
Unskilled manual empl.	0.038 (0.005)	0.012 (0.001)	-0.016 (0.003)	3.877 (0.053)	0.100	4679

Notes: Standard errors in parenthesis; observations pooled over the years 1991, 1993 and 1995; annual dummies included in all regressions. [a] Parameter multiplied by the factor 100.

Table 2.5b Returns to human capital for various subgroups (women)

	Years of schooling	Experience (potential)	Experience squared a)	Part-time (0,1)b)	Constant	R² adj.	Sample Size
All Females	0.072 (0.001)	0.019 (0.001)	-0.021 (0.002)	0.032 (0.006)	3.240 (0.015)	0.29	14879
Self employed	0.073 (0.017)	0.016 c) (0.012)	-0.022 c) (0.022)	0.395 (0.114)	3.146 (0.296)	0.25	97
All employees	0.072 (0.001)	0.018 (0.001)	-0.021 (0.002)	0.030 (0.006)	3.238 (0.015)	0.29	14782
Civil Servants	0.046 (0.002)	0.019 (0.002)	-0.022 (0.004)	0.047 (0.012)	3.685 (0.027)	0.28	3365
All private employees	0.089 (0.002)	0.018 (0.001)	-0.019 (0.002)	0.029 (0.006)	3.144 (0.022)	0.26	11417
White collar employees	0.076 (0.002)	0.024 (0.001)	-0.026 (0.003)	-0.002 c) (0.008)	3.356 (0.028)	0.29	6663
Skilled manual empl.	0.039 (0.013)	0.011 (0.003)	-0.010 c) (0.008)	0.034 c) (0.025)	3.358 (0.136)	0.14	889
Unskilled manual empl.	0.009 (0.005)	0.006 (0.001)	-0.007 (0.003)	0.072 (0.009)	3.931 (0.048)	0.15	3865

Notes: Standard errors in parenthesis. Observations pooled over the years 1991, 1993 and 1995. Annual dummies included in all regressions. a) Parameter multiplied by the factor 100. b) Parameter transformed by $\exp(\beta)-1$. c) Not significant.

The signalling hypothesis (Spence, 1973) can explain higher wages for more highly educated workers even in the absence of productivity-enhancing effects of schooling. Education could simply sort inherently productive workers from the rest. Students with higher productivity find it easier to obtain more schooling and, therefore, employers choose more educated students and pay them higher wages. One simple way to test for signalling is to compare returns to education for employed and self-employed workers. For self-employed there is no need to signal one's competence by presenting a schooling degree; higher wages should only be due to higher productivity as such.

In Table 2.6 returns to education are compared for self-employed and all employees. Owing to strict pay scales in the public sector, the proper comparison group is all private sector employees. For males, we find practically no difference in the returns to education for self-employed and private-sector employees. In the case of females, private sector employees get returns per year of schooling 1.6% higher than the self-employed; a difference which can be attributed to signalling effects.[8]

Wage determination in the private and public sector is markedly different. Both men and women get lower returns to education in the public sector: men (women) in the public sector get only 70% (52%) of possible returns in the private sector. Together with higher entry wages, this phenomenon speaks for a compressed administrative wage scale for public servants.

Table 2.6   Income variable survey non-response (%)

	Women		Men	
	Not reported	Reported	Not reported	Reported
Self employed	90.5	9.5	89.5	10.5
Civil servants	36.5	63.5	43.0	57.0
White collar workers	32.7	67.3	32.3	67.7
Skilled blue collar	33.9	66.1	32.4	67.6
Unskilled blue collar	28.1	71.9	30.3	69.7

Table 2.7   Returns to human capital for natives and foreigners (1995)

	All	Natives	Foreigners
Men			
Years of schooling	0.071 (0.002)	0.070 (0.002)	0.039 (0.006)
Experience (potential)	0.029 (0.001)	0.030 (0.001)	0.014 (0.004)
Experience squared [a]	-0.041 (0.003)	-0.019 (0.008)	-0.039 (0.002)
Constant	3.537 (0.021)	3.534 (0021)	3.910 (0.072)
R^2 adj.	0.302	0.256	0.106
Sample size	7022	6522	500
Women			
Years of schooling	0.068 (0.002)	0.067 (0.002)	0.040 (0.007)
Experience (potential)	0.017 (0.001)	0.018 (0.002	0.000 (0.005)
Experience squared [a]	-0.018 (0.003)	-0.021 (0.003)	0.010 (0.013)
Part-time $(0,1)$[b]	0.025 (0.009)	0.018 (0.009)	0.040 (0.037)
Constant	3.477 (0.023)	3.479 (0.024)	3.804 (0.091)
Adjusted R^2	0.259	0.264	0.092
Sample size	5056	4747	309

Notes: Standard errors in parentheses. [a] Parameter multiplied by the factor 100. [b] Parameter transformed by $\exp(\beta)-1$.

It must be noted, however, that sector selection cannot be taken as randomly assigned. Education, on the one hand, is influencing sector choice, together with risk-aversion, motivation and different occupational amenities in private and public sector jobs. Therefore, the results should be interpreted cautiously. Returns to education in the public sector are particularly low for females. Given relatively strict career schemes – relying on education and tenure, our use of potential experience instead of actual experience will in the public sector not only bias returns to experience downwards, but also those for education.[9] Moreover, as most jobs in the public sector are white-collar jobs, returns for public sector workers could be compared with those for white-collar workers only, which gives us somewhat lower differentials.[10] As expected, returns to education are twice as high for white-collar as compared to blue-collar workers (approximately 8% versus 4%). Returns are particularly low for unskilled female blue-collars, which might be due to the low variation in educational attainment in this group. Moreover, more highly educated workers would certainly be overeducated for these jobs (Sicherman, 1991).

Earnings-experience profiles differ substantially by gender as well as across various occupational categories. The profiles for men are rather steep compared to those for women, giving rise to much higher earnings later in the career. We believe that this is related to the influence of potential experience, as discussed above. Whereas the curvature of earnings-experience profiles of males is steepest for self-employed and white-collar workers, the curvature of the profiles for women is rather similar across various occupational categories.

Returns to education for foreigners are much lower than those for natives; they are approximately at a level of 55% for males and 60% for females (see Table 2.7). Similar reasoning applies to returns to work experience. Without a proper consideration of issues of adaptation to the Austrian labour market, especially concerning the length of stay in Austria and the transferability of schooling degrees from abroad or the language problem, the presentation of these differentials must be seen as preliminary.

Returns to Different Types of Schools

So far we have used years of schooling as our measure of educational attainment. In this section we look at returns to specific school types. The linearity assumption implicit in the Mincerian years-of-schooling specification can now be tested. This is particularly interesting given the recent discussion about heterogeneous returns for specific groups.[11] We can also test the credentialism argument that it is not years actually spent in education that is the most important, but the degree gained.[12] Moreover, for choice of schooling type, returns to different types of schooling (at the same level, say secondary) are important in itself.

Returns to the different types of secondary and tertiary education are given in Table 2.8. School types are ranked by increasing number of (required) years of schooling. Returns to degrees achieved are rising unequivocally with required years of education. The differences between two adjacent school types are generally significant. The only exceptions are the difference between females with secondary academic schools and females with vocational colleges completed,[13] as well as the difference between males having finished vocational colleges and short non-university education, respectively.

In general, differences by gender at various educational levels are not significant. The gap of about 12 percentage points between male and female short non-university graduates is at the 10% level statistically significant. For a proper interpretation of these differences, the proportion of students in the different school types among "short non-university" i.e. teacher's colleges, military academy, etc. must be taken into account. On the other hand, male university graduates earn a wage premium of 10 to 11 percentage points over their female colleagues.[14]

The estimates of the returns to different types of schooling suggest that it may be worth while to calculate average returns for a year spent in school for different types of school. This can be taken as a measure of school productivity. There are several difficulties with this estimation. First, to calculate average returns by year, it must be assumed how long a student has attended a specific school. Here we use statutory years for all types of secondary education. For university students we propose two approaches; one where we assume five years of study (close to statutory years, which are different by study type) and seven years (close to the actual number of years students spend at universities).

A second difficulty is that for students in tertiary education the marginal gain from tertiary education has to be calculated. Therefore, we deduct from the respective coefficients for tertiary education in Table 2.8 the average return to secondary academic schools (0.409 for women, 0.418 for men). Secondary academic schools are the typical entrance gate to universities in Austria.

Marginal returns to a further year of education are strongly declining, both for males and for females. A year of vocational school offers the highest returns. Interestingly, years of vocational colleges do not offer higher returns than those spent in secondary academic schools. This is contrary to widespread expectations that vocational colleges (business or especially technical ones) offer a more practical education as compared to the secondary academic schools, which are primarily seen as a preparatory school for university entrants. This issue warrants further investigation, especially because of the selective character of the sample: we measure the returns to secondary schooling only for those who refrain from tertiary education. Returns to tertiary education are particularly low, especially if we calculate the returns by using actual years spent in the university: around 3% per year.

Table 2.8 Returns to different types of schools (1995)

	Women	Men
Compulsory schooling (base)		
Apprenticeship [a]	0.127	0.149
	(0.010)	(0.009)
Secondary		
Vocational schools [a]	0.317	0.289
	(0.013)	(0.015)
Secondary academic schools [a]	0.409	0.418
	(0.020)	(0.020)
Vocational colleges [a]	0.494	0.510
	(0.017)	(0.016)
Tertiary		
Short non-university [a]	0.610	0.491
	(0.024)	(0.032)
University [a]	0.696	0.804
	(0.027)	(0.021)
Experience (potential)	0.019	0.030
	(0.001)	(0.001)
Experience squared [b]	-0.026	-0.046
	(0.003)	(0.002)
Part-time (0,1) [a]	0.034	-
	(0.008)	
Constant	4.007	4.097
	(0.014)	(0.013)
R^2 adj.	0.291	0.309
Sample Size	5186	7475

Notes: Standard errors in parentheses; *Vocational schools (berufsbildende mittlere Schulen):* vocational, technical, artistic schools, business schools, schools for social professions (nurses etc.), agricultural schools which last 2-4 years; *Vocational colleges (berufsbildende höhere Schulen):* like vocational schools but they last 5 years and give access to further short non-university and university education; *Secondary academic schools (allgemeinbildende höhere Schulen):* 4 years of higher general education giving access to further short non-university and university; *Short non-university (hochschulverwandte Lehranstalten):* academies for social professions, colleges for higher medical-technical services, military academies, teachers' colleges (3 year courses). [a] Parameter transformed by $\exp(\beta)$-1. [b] Parameter multiplied by the factor 100.

CONCLUSION

We calculate returns to education for Austria using a unified data framework for the period 1981 to 1997. We find falling returns both for males and females. Returns per year of schooling were more than 10% at the beginning of the 1980s and decreased to 8% at the end of the 1980s. This drop may be related to the expansion of higher education in Austria, which started in the mid-seventies. These results are robust once we control for specific problems in the data, when we use robust estimation techniques or when we add more variables to the simple Mincer framework. Returns are higher in the private sector as compared to the public sector. Given the higher starting wages in the public sector this could simply be a consequence of wage compression in the highly unionized public sector. Finally, returns to further education are falling; the more schooling you acquire the lower is the return by year. Returns for years spent in secondary schooling are more than 10%, whereas those spent in university yield less than 4% per year.

NOTES

1. See Fersterer and Winter-Ebmer (1999) for a survey on previous work on returns to education in Austria and Christl (1984) for a first study on returns to education for Austria.
2. Ichino and Winter-Ebmer (1998) present instrumental variables estimates for a very specific situation, which are considerably higher than ordinary least squares estimates. Due to this local average treatment effect (LATE) situation, these results are not easily generalized.
3. Only statutory years were coded; for individuals who had to repeat a year of secondary school, the actual number of years spent in school is underestimated.
4. Results for self-employed persons are shown below.
5. The minimum contribution level is routinely adapted to the inflation rate; it was $320 in 1991. Approximately 120 to 150 observations (males and females) have been eliminated each year due to this condition.
6. Hofer and Pichelmann (1997) use the same dataset and estimate earnings functions from 1981 to 1995 for males, again every second year. Besides the standard human capital variables, they additionally include a dummy for white-collar workers, interaction terms between white-collar and experience and its quadratic, a vector of eight industry dummies and a foreigner dummy in their regression. Moreover, they excluded civil servants from the analysed population.
7. Median regression was also performed using the whole sample including the workers with earnings below the social security's minimum contribution level. The results are very robust.
8. As Zweimüller (1992) points out, sample selection bias due to survey non-response might be a serious problem, which in our case, given the very high non-response rate for self-employed, could affect the returns for self-employed severely.
9. Winter-Ebmer and Zweimüller (1994) use actual experience for 1983 and find a much lower difference in returns to education for females in private versus public sector jobs.
10. See Boss *et al* (1997) for an extensive study on lifetime earnings profiles of private and public-sector workers.
11. See Card (1999) for a model, Ichino and Winter-Ebmer (1999) for an application to Germany.
12. Here, both the information about the actual number of years spent in school and the highest degree attained is necessary, which is not available so far. Especially in Austria, many students have to repeat years in secondary school. Likewise, average time for a tertiary degree is much higher than the minimum number of years required.
13. The difference is significant at 10%.
14. See Lassnigg *et al* (1998) on earnings of university graduates.

REFERENCES

Altrichter Herbert and Peter Posch (1995), 'Austria', in N.T. Postlethwaite, *International Encyclopedia of National Systems of Education*, 2nd Edition, Pergamon, Cambridge, 48-57.

Buchinsky, Moshe (1994), 'Changes in the U.S. Wage Structure 1963–1987: An Application of Quantile Regression', *Econometrica*, 62(2), 405–58.

Boss, Michael, Hofer, Helmut, Mitter, Peter and Josef Zweimüller (1997), 'Lebenseinkommen im Privaten und Öffentlichen Sektor', mimeo, Institute for Advanced Studies, Vienna.

Card, David (1999), 'The Causal Effect of Education on Earnings', in Orley Ashenfelter and David Card (eds), *Handbook of Labor Economics*, vol. 3, North-Holland, Amsterdam, 1801–63.

Christl, J. (1984). 'The Explanatory Power of the Human Capital Earnings Function'. *Empirica* 11(1), 47–57.

Fersterer, Josef and Rudolf Winter-Ebmer (1999): 'Human Capital and Earnings in Austria', mimeo, University of Linz, Austria.

Hofer, Helmut and Karl Pichelmann (1997): 'A note on earning inequality in Austria', mimeo, Institute for Advanced Studies, Vienna.

Ichino, Andrea and Rudolf Winter-Ebmer (1998): 'The Long-run Educational Cost of World War II: An Example of Local Average Treatment Effect Estimation', WP 9802, University of Linz.

Ichino, Andrea and Rudolf Winter-Ebmer (1999): 'Lower and Upper Bounds of Returns to Schooling: An Exercise in IV Estimation with Different Instruments', *European Economic Review*, 43(4-6), 889–901.

Lassnigg, Lorenz, London, Susanne, Schramm, Brigitte and Peter Steiner (1998): 'Zur Beschäftigung von Hochschulabsolventen', mimeo, Institute for Advanced Studies, Vienna.

Sicherman, Nachum (1991): '"Overeducation" in the Labor Market', *Journal of Labor Economics* 9(2), 101–22.

Spence, Michael (1973): 'Job Market Signalling', *Quarterly Journal of Economics*, 87(3), 355–374.

Winter-Ebmer, Rudolf and Josef Zweimüller (1994): 'Gender Wage Differentials in Private and Public Sector Jobs', *Journal of Population Economics* 7(3), 271–285.

Zweimüller, Josef (1992): 'Survey non-response and biases in wage regressions', *Economics Letters* 39(1), 105–109.

3. Denmark

Jens Jakob Christensen
and
Niels Westergaard-Nielsen

INTRODUCTION

The objective of this chapter is to present empirical evidence on returns to human capital variables in Denmark. The data sources used in the analysis are the Longitudinal Labour Market Register (LLMR) and the Integrated Database for Labour Market Research (IDA), and we focus on the period 1981-1995. We investigate gender-specific returns to both education and labour market experience, examine the time trends in the data, and test the robustness of our estimates under different specifications of the model. We follow up on previous studies of returns to human capital carried out in Denmark, in particular Asplund *et al.* (1996a), which is a cross-country comparison of the Nordic countries.[1] Inspiration is also provided by Asplund et al. (1996b) and Bingley and Westergaard-Nielsen (1997). The study by Asplund *et al.* (1996b) is also part of above-mentioned cross-country comparison of the Nordic countries, whereas the last three only focus on the Danish labour market. The unit of observation for all studies is the individual, and the theoretical approaches are, in a broad sense, all based on various and augmented specifications of the standard human capital earnings function as proposed by Mincer (1974). However, the objectives differ to some extent. Where Asplund *et al.* (1996a) focus on the wage distribution across individuals in general, the target of Asplund *et al.* (1996b) is the wage differentials due to gender alone. Bingley and Westergaard-Nielsen (1997) estimate the size of demand-induced firm wage determinants, while accounting for individual worker supply wage determinants.

DATA AND VARIABLES

The dependent variable used is the natural logarithm of gross hourly wages. Schooling is defined as years of schooling beyond basic school (nine years), and we consider the impact of both potential and actual experience.[2] Table

3.1 shows the descriptive statistics for the variables used in the analysis. Actual experience is the number of years of labour market experience (provided by contributions to the supplementary pension system, ATP), and potential experience is age minus years of schooling minus school starting age. The gross hourly wage is calculated using information on annual wage income and number of hours worked in a year (also provided by ATP).

Table 3.1 Descriptive statistics (1981-1995)

Variable	Observations	Mean	Std. dev.	Min	Max
Age	130283	37.53	11.90	16	64
Woman	130283	0.48	0.50	0	1
Public	130283	0.36	0.48	0	1
Province	130283	0.64	0.48	0	1
Schooling	130283	2.86	2.44	0	9
Actual experience	129306	13.48	9.81	0	54.79
Potential experience	130092	18.85	12.11	0	48
Wage	119111	112.72	54.13	31.39	856.20
ln (wage)	119111	4.64	0.40	3.44	6.75
Ninth level (0)	130283	0.227	0.419	0	1
Tenth level (1)	130283	0.141	0.348	0	1
Vocational (3)	130283	0.327	0.469	0	1
High school (4)	130283	0.061	0.240	0	1
Short non univ. (5)	130283	0.118	0.323	0	1
Bachelor (7)	130283	0.080	0.272	0	1
Graduate (9)	130283	0.045	0.207	0	1

Notes: Numbers in parentheses are the number of years beyond basic school typically required to obtain the associated educational level.

SIMPLE ESTIMATION OF THE EARNINGS FUNCTION

While ordinary least squares (OLS) may be biased due to the fact that the level of education is not truly exogenous, the obvious advantage of OLS is that it is easy to apply. In addition, Dearden (1999) has shown that conventional OLS (which typically controls for age, gender, ethnicity, and region of residence, and ignores the endogeneity of schooling) is a rather good approximation. Thus, the effect of omitted ability and family background biases are generally offset by the effect of measurement error bias and composition (self-selection) bias.

However, we have no evidence that this finding is valid in general or if it only applies to the UK data. Nevertheless, national surveys containing no information on ability or parental background have been given a lease of new life in the context of estimating returns to education.

Returns to Schooling

Table 3.2 and Figure 3.1 show the simple OLS estimates of the human capital earnings function (HCEF). It appears that the model explains approximately 20 to 30% of the male wage variation and approximately 10 to 20% of the female variation. Regardless of gender, it also appears that the 'goodness-of-fit' strongly depends on the year in question. In other words the results suggest that the HCEF is more applicable in terms of men.

For some reason and regardless of gender, wages are relatively poorly explained by the model in the years 1982, 1983 and 1984. As regards estimated (average marginal) returns to years of schooling, the following conclusions can be drawn: (1) Male returns are approximately 5%, and female returns are approximately 3%. (2) The gender gap in returns to education has remained fairly constant throughout the years examined. (3) The trend in returns in the period examined is that of increasing returns for both men and women.

Figure 3.1 Trend in estimated returns to schooling (1981-1995)

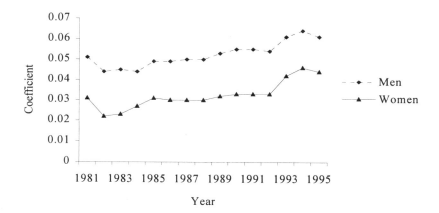

Table 3.2 OLS estimates of returns to education, 1981 to 1995

| | Men | | Women | |
	Return	Adj. R^2	Return	Adj. R^2
1981	0.051 (0.002)	0.246	0.031 (0.002)	0.071
1982	0.044 (0.002)	0.170	0.022 (0.002)	0.034
1983	0.045 (0.002)	0.186	0.023 (0.002)	0.035
1984	0.044 (0.002)	0.182	0.027 (0.002)	0.041
1985	0.049 (0.002)	0.231	0.031 (0.002)	0.084
1986	0.049 (0.002)	0.257	0.030 (0.002)	0.084
1987	0.050 (0.002)	0.269	0.030 (0.002)	0.087
1988	0.050 (0.002)	0.255	0.030 (0.002)	0.091
1989	0.053 (0.002)	0.260	0.032 (0.002)	0.103
1990	0.055 (0.002)	0.261	0.033 (0.002)	0.110
1991	0.055 (0.002)	0.251	0.033 (0.002)	0.099
1992	0.054 (0.002)	0.243	0.033 (0.002)	0.102
1993	0.061 (0.002)	0.294	0.042 (0.002)	0.180
1994	0.064 (0.002)	0.286	0.046 (0.002)	0.207
1995	0.061 (0.002)	0.294	0.044 (0.002)	0.191
Pooled	0.052 (0.000)	0.244	0.033 (0.000)	0.098

Notes: Standard errors in parentheses. All numbers significant at the 1% level. Number of observations is 3000 – 5000, depending on year and gender.

Returns to Experience

According to the HCEF above, wages are thought to be parabolicly related to years of experience, that is the wage-experience profile is bell-shaped. Consequently, average marginal returns depend on years of experience. Average marginal returns to experience can either be calculated or be recorded directly as the slope of the wage-experience curve.

Figure 3.2 summarizes the estimated wage effects of experience for each gender separately. The male profile is clearly bell-shaped, however, the female profile is closer to being linear in that the squared term has only a small impact on wages (in fact no significant impact). Maximum male wage growth due to experience is (on average) obtained at around 31 years of experience, corresponding to a wage growth of approximately 48% since labour market entry. Female maximum is obtained at 45 years of experience corresponding to a total wage growth of approximately 22%. The nature of the functional form implies that the maximum *marginal returns* are obviously obtained at the moment of entry into the labour market, when experience equals zero. In order to evaluate the trend in marginal returns to experience throughout the years 1981-1995, we have calculated average marginal returns for a person with 10 years of experience (Figure 3.3).

Denmark

Figure 3.2 Estimated wage effect of experience (1995)

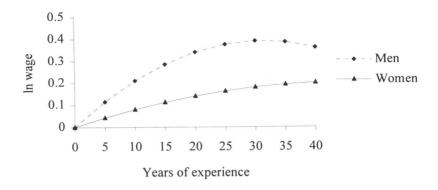

Figure 3.3 Trend in marginal returns to experience for an individual with 10 years of experience (1981-1995)

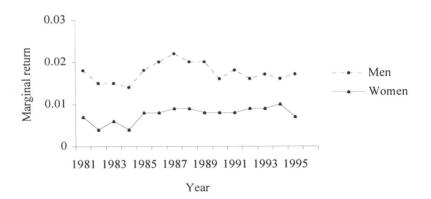

Allowing for Non-Linearities (Levels of Education)

Implicit in the HCEF proposed by Mincer is the assumption that the correct measure of education is number of years of completed education, and that each additional year of schooling has the same effect on earnings (linear function).

However, it is often argued that credentials matter more than years of schooling. This "sheepskin effect" posits the existence of a wage premium for fulfilling the final year of elementary school, high school, or college (see Card, 1999). In order to investigate whether the Danish data are characterized by linearity or non-linearity between years of schooling and wages, the schooling variable in the regression equation is replaced by a variable for each educational level (k in total) minus 1. The omitted level, which can be chosen arbitrarily, is represented by the general intercept term of the regression equation (equivalent to including levels for all educational levels and then run the regression with the general intercept suppressed).

Figure 3.4 Returns to levels of education, men (1995)

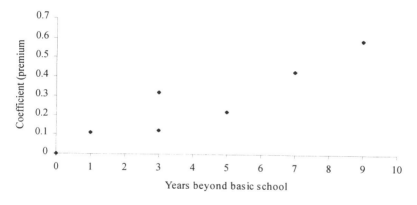

Figures 3.4 and 3.5 contain the results of an estimation of the model above. It appears that returns to schooling do in fact not form a straight line when relating wage premiums to years of schooling typically associated with each level, i.e. each additional year of schooling does not have the same proportional effect on wages. Obviously, the linearity assumption is mainly violated by the fact that people with a high school diploma as the highest attained level of formal education seem to be very generously rewarded – especially in terms of men. The reason is probably that the high school diploma and, previously, the 10th grade give access to a number of private educations that are not recorded in the official statistics. One example is bankers (we have corrected for a number of these omissions, but have not been able to identify all).

Another deviation from the linear returns to education is found for the apprentice training compared to 10 years of schooling. The increment in income between the two is very small – regardless of gender. Furthermore, going from bachelor to graduate grade is associated with a relatively big increase in female wages (creating some convexity). Despite these observations of a hammock-like shape, we conclude that the linearity assumptions is, as an approximation, reasonable, but not perfect.

Figure 3.5 Returns to levels of education, women (1995)

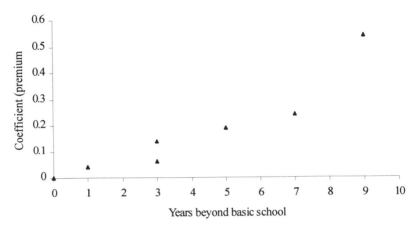

Years beyond basic school

Private versus Public Sector

If the public and private sector wage functions differ significantly (which may very well be the case), one should consider not pooling the two sectors into one single restricted estimation. In order to formally test whether public and private sector differ in terms of returns to schooling and experience, we have estimated a model where all variables in the HCEF are interacted with a private sector dummy (Table 3.3).[3]

If there was no significant difference between the two sectors in terms of returns to schooling and experience, the coefficients (2), (4), (6), and (8) should all be equal to zero. As regards the constant term (2) and returns to schooling (4) this appears to be true - we are not able to reject the hypothesis of no difference. However, returns to experience differ significantly between the two sectors.

Table 3.3 Private and public sector returns (1995)

		Men	Women
(1)	β_0	4.49 (153)	4.51 (217)
(2)	$\beta_1 - \beta_0$	-0.014 (-0.42)	-0.023 (-0.8)
(3)	β_2	0.063 (20.1)	0.045 (20.4)
(4)	$\beta_3 - \beta_2$	0.004 (1.1)	0.005 (1.3)
(5)	β_4	0.017 (5.4)	0.005 (2.1)
(6)	$\beta_5 - \beta_4$	0.011 (3.2)	0.008 (2.2)
(7)	β_6	-0.00017 (-2.4)	0.00008 (1.1)
(8)	$\beta_7 - \beta_6$	-0.00023 (-2.7)	-0.00016 (-1.5)
N		4137	3787
Adj. R^2		0.31	0.20

Notes: t-values in parentheses. (1) public sector intercept, (2) private minus public sector intercepts, (3) public sector return to schooling, (4) private minus public sector returns to schooling, (5) public sector return to experience, (6) private minus public sector returns to experience, (7) coeff. of public sector experience squared, and (8) private minus public sector experience squared coefficients.

Addition of Control Variables to HCEF

Table 3.4 Estimated returns with controls for sector and province (1995)

	Men		Women	
	Coef.	St. Error	Coef.	St. Error
Intercept	4.56	0.016	4.58	0.015
Schooling (S)	0.063	0.002	0.045	0.002
Experience (E)	0.026	0.002	0.011	0.002
Exp^2 x 100	-0.038	0.000	-0.005	0.005
Province	-0.076	0.010	-0.082	0.009
Public	-0.104	0.010	-0.053	0.009
Observations	4137		3787	
Adjusted R-Sq	0.32		0.22	

In the analyses above, we have - among other things - implicitly assumed that there are no differences in returns between private and public sector employees and that there are no regional differences either. This omission of potentially relevant and important control variables may thus give a wrong picture of the true returns (or, at least, provide estimates that are too general).

Consequently, and if returns are thought to differ between different sub-groups, one should include relevant control variables. Table 3.4 contains the results of an estimation of HCEF including controls for region and sector.[4]

Compared to the estimates of Table 3.2, we find that the addition of the two control variables has no major impact on marginal returns (except for a slight increase in male returns to schooling). Furthermore, it emerges that public sector employees (on average) earn approximately 5% (women) and 10% (men) less than private sector employees, and that living in the province is associated with an average wage discount of approximately 7-8%, depending on gender.

Actual versus Potential Experience

Researchers rarely have access to information on actual labour market experience, which is why potential experience is typically used instead, and has gradually become the preferred experience concept.[5] In order to analyse the sensitivity on returns of switching from actual to potential experience, we have estimated HCEF using both concepts (compare Table 3.4 with Table 3.5).

Table 3.5 HCEF using potential experience (1995)

	Men		Women	
	Coef.	St. Error	Coef.	St. Error
Intercept	4.51	0.016	4.50	0.015
Schooling (S)	0.067	0.002	0.051	0.002
Experience (E)	0.028	0.002	0.016	0.001
Exp^2	-0.040	0.003	-0.023	0.003
Province	-0.113	0.010	-0.060	0.009
Public	-0.078	0.010	-0.090	0.009
Observations	4324		3929	
Adjusted R-Sq	0.33		0.23	

Notes: Standard error in parentheses

Apparently using potential experience when estimating the HCEF is associated with upward biased returns. Thus, both returns to experience and returns to schooling increase substantially when switching from actual to potential experience – regardless of gender. We also find that the model fit is better when using potential experience given the adjusted R^2 is higher.

SELECTIVITY BIAS

According to the conventional wisdom especially women have a choice whether to work, and thus, whether we observe their wages in our data.[6] This decision is not made randomly, but is typically linked to certain characteristics. Thus, women who would be facing low wages in the labour market (due to lack of skills, age, children and so on) may be unlikely to work.

Table 3.6 Estimated female returns, with and without selectivity correction (1995)

	No correction		Heckman´s 2-step correction	
	Coef.	St. Error	Coef.	St. Error
Schooling	0.044	0.002	0.045	0.004
Experience	0.009	0.002	0.010	0.003
Experience^2 x 100	-0.003	0.006	-0.0014	0.008
Lambda (λ)	-	-	0.022	0.111
N (inc. missing)	-	-	4180	-
N (excl. missing)	3787	-	3787	-
R^2 (adjusted)	0.19	-	-	-

Notes: Standard errors in brackets. The following variables have been used in the probit (selection) equation: *Dummy for partner, dummy for children aged 0-7, Schooling, Experience,* and *Experience squared.* All variables in the selection equation significant at the 1% level.

Consequently, the sample of observed wages is biased upward. In order to correct for this potential selectivity bias, we have estimated the female (1995) wage equation in combination with a (probit) selection function using Heckman's (1979) two-step procedure. According to Table 3.6, we find neither evidence nor a minor indication of the presence of selectivity bias, Lambda (λ) is not significantly different from zero. The estimated coefficients of the Heckman two-step selection model are however very sensitive to the model specification.

The selection equation (probit function) has to be properly specified. In order to eliminate the possibility of reaching a conclusion regarding selectivity bias based on a misspecification of the model, we have experimented with several specifications. Though the size of lambda varies quite a lot with the specific choice of variables included in the probit function, all specifications lead to the conclusion that no serious selectivity bias is present in the data. Since most women work in Denmark this result is expected.

SIGNALLING VERSUS HUMAN CAPITAL

Education may also have a value from signalling innate productivity. This value may be close to zero for self-employed in that the returns to education for self-employed are to a higher extent due to the impact on productivity (see Weiss,1995). One may therefore identify the signalling value of education as the difference in returns between wage earners and self-employed. This signalling may be rather substantial with in excess of 60% of returns to education due to the signalling value. Whether this conclusion is to be trusted depends on the implicit assumption that self-employment is randomly assigned. In other words self-employment may very well be endogenous, and if this endogeneity is controlled for, the numbers might change significantly. At this moment we do not have access to variables to instrument self-employment (parental characteristics for instance). Another crucial assumption is that self-employed declare as much of their income as employed. With a 25% VAT rate this assumption seems rather heroic.

ENDOGENOUS SCHOOLING

OLS estimates of returns to schooling may be biased if the schooling variable is not exogenous. Thus, if there is reason to believe that years of schooling is in fact endogenous in that the determinants of schooling are correlated with the determinants of income, other estimation techniques should be employed to measure the true returns. We have tried to control for the endogeneity of schooling by instrumenting education with sibling's education (males instrumented with older brother and females instrumented with older sister). Since the estimation is carried out using the CLS-IDA database, we had access to *all* persons with an older brother/sister.[7] Estimated returns using both OLS and instrumental variables (IV), contrary to most IV studies conducted so far, do not find that returns increase dramatically once the endogeneity is controlled for. Based on this analysis, the conclusion is that the bias arising from the fact that schooling is not exogenous is present and significant, but not as large as found elsewhere.

ABILITY AND FAMILY BACKGROUND

As mentioned above, education is not randomly assigned, but depends on individual-specific factors such as "ability" and family background characteristics. As regards the ability issue the problem is that we basically do not know whether people with high wages earn more *because* of the higher education, or if people with a higher ability have chosen to acquire more education. In other words, OLS does not separate the effect on wages of unobserved ability, but ascribes it all to education. If in fact people with a high earnings capacity choose to acquire more education, OLS will thus overstate the true causal effect of education on wages.

In order to identify the causal effect of schooling, researchers have often stated that account also has to be taken for family background information. The interest in family background issues is due to the fact that the empirical correlation between parents' education and the child's education is high. Technically the solution to the problem is adding control variables for ability (IQ test scores, for instance) and family background (parents' education, for instance), which will catch (hopefully most of) the effects on earnings of unobserved individual attributes. Alternatively one might use the information on ability bias provided in the various twin studies. However, unless the family background control variables catch all the unobserved ability components (which is only a realistic assumption when dealing with identical twins), returns to education may still be biased.

Estimated returns based on both OLS and IV but with two control variables added to the earnings equation, i.e. mother's and father's education (years), suggest that nothing really happens to the returns to schooling when the parent's education is controlled for. In the case of IV estimation on a sample of males the return to schooling increases from 0.055 to 0.063 possibly suggesting an omitted variable bias in the male IV returns.

CONCLUSION

The ability of HCEF as proposed by Mincer to explain wages depends very much on the year examined and - especially - gender. Nevertheless, we find that the model explains approximately 20% to 30% of male wages, and approximately 10% to 20% of female wages – a finding that is in tune with various international findings based on OLS. However, the assumption that years of schooling is randomly assigned may be so far from the truth, that we – when using conventional OLS – do not identify the true causal relationship between schooling and wages. Bearing this weakness of OLS in mind, we hereby sum up the major findings of the study.

Estimated (average marginal) returns to schooling and experience are rather different between men and women in Denmark. Based on the most recent observations, estimated male returns to schooling are approximately 5%, which is 2 percentage points more than the equivalent female estimates. The gap in returns to schooling has, roughly speaking, been constant in the period examined; a period which has been characterized by increasing returns, that is an upward trend. Men and women do also differ in terms of the experience-wage profile. The profile for men is significantly bell-shaped, whereas the female ditto is close to linear. As regards marginal returns to years of experience (evaluated for an individual with 10 years of labour market experience), the male returns are approximately twice the female returns; a gap that - after some years of contraction - has expanded in 1995.

Replacing the linear schooling term in the HCEF by dummies for each educational level, we allow for nonlinearities in education, and it appears that returns to schooling is in fact not strictly linear. Especially in terms of women, wages and years of schooling seem to be related in a convex manner. The gender differences also appear to be large for all other educations than the MA level.

We find that public sector returns to years of schooling are lower than the private sector returns – regardless of gender – and that the average discount of being employed in the public sector is approximately 5% to 10%. In addition, female returns to years of schooling in the province are substantially smaller than in the area of Greater Copenhagen. The average discount of living in the province is approximately 7%. We also find that using potential experience at the expense of actual experience is associated with partly a rise in the goodness-of-fit of HCEF and partly upward biased returns.

Based on the Heckman correction procedure, we have not managed to identify any presence of selectivity bias (endogenous female labour supply) in the Danish labour market. This is probably due to the high female participation rates). Furthermore, and in order to test whether returns to education reflect more than just the impact of education on productivity (returns may partly be due to signalling innate productivity due to education), we have compared returns for wage earners with returns for self-employed. We find that the signalling value is quite substantial, but since we have not been able to control for the likely endogeneity of being self-employed, this outcome may be more or less biased.

Finally, we have been able to control for the endogeneity of schooling by instrumenting with siebling's education (IV). In short, we find that once the endogeneity is controlled for, returns increase by approximately 20%. This increase is significant, but far from the 100% increase that is found in other IV studies. Controlling for parent's education in the earnings equation generally does not change returns to schooling significantly.

NOTES

1. The Nordic Labour Market in the 1990's, edited by E. Wadensjö (1996).
2. We use LLMR (*Longitudinal Labour Market Register*), which is a random 0,5% sample of the adult population (the age span is 13-78, depending on the year of observation) covering the years 1976-1995. All information in LLMR is drawn from administrative registers and is merged by Statistics Denmark
3. Estimating the full interaction-model is equivalent to fitting separate regressions to the sectors. However, the dummy specification provides a simple means of testing for

homogeneity of intercepts and slopes between sectors. In $w = \beta0+(\beta1-\beta0)*D2+\beta2*S+(\beta3-\beta2)*D2*S+\beta4*EXP+(\beta5-\beta4)*D2* EXP+\beta6*EXP2+(\beta7-\beta6)D2*EXP2 + u$, where D2 is a dummy taking the value 1 when employed in the private sector.

4. In the literature, dummy variables are typically added to control for region, sector and race. However, LLMR does not contain information on race, which is why we only focus on sector and region.
5. Potential experience is defined as the individuals age minus number of years of formal schooling minus school starting age (Age - S - 7).
6. Throughout the literature, it is assumed that selectivity bias is not a substantial problem in terms of men, see Dearden (1999).
7. IDA is created by Statistics Denmark and contains information on labour market conditions for the total population of individuals (5,2 mio) and establishments (around 230,000) in Denmark over the years 1980-1991. The information originates in various administrative registers and is merged by Statistics Denmark.

REFERENCES

Asplund, R., Barth, E., Le Grand, C., Mastekaasa, A. and Westergaard-Nielsen, N. (1996a), in E. Wadensjö (ed.), *The Nordic Labour Market in the 1990s*, North-Holland, Amsterdam.

Asplund, R., Barth, E., Smith, N. and Wadensjö, E. (1996b), in E. Wadensjö (ed.), *The Nordic Labour Market in the 1990s*, North-Holland, Amsterdam.

Bingley, P. and Westergaard-Nielsen, N. (1997), 'Worker and establishment wages: estimates from a multilevel model', mimeo, Centre for Labour Market and Social Research.

Card, David (1999), 'The Causal Effect of Education on Earnings', in Orley Ashenfelter and David Card (eds), *Handbook of Labor Economics*, vol. 3, North-Holland, Amsterdam, 1801–63.

Dearden, L. (1999), "Qualifications and Earnings in Britain: How Reliable are Typical OLS Estimates of the Returns to Education? " mimeo, IFS.

Mincer, Jacob (1974). *Schooling, Experience, and Earnings.* National Bureau of Economic Research, New York.

Wadensjö, E. (1996). *The Nordic Labour Market in the 1990's*, North-Holland, Amsterdam.

Weiss, A. (1995), "Human Capital vs. Screening Explanations of Wages", *Journal of Economic Perspecitves*, Vol. 9(4), 133-54.

4.   Finland

Rita Asplund

INTRODUCTION

This study explores the evolution of private returns to education in Finland. The results to be presented are obtained from estimating simple Mincerian earnings equations using cross-sections of the Finnish Labour Force Survey (LFS) compiled by Statistics Finland. Attempts are also made to examine the sensitivity of educational returns to the specification of the earnings equation as well as to the adopted estimation technique.

The primary reason for basing the analysis of the interplay between interpersonal differences in wages and educational attainment levels on the LFS is that this is the only individual-level data set for Finland that allows the calculation of average hourly wages.[1] Moreover, the LFS has recently been supplemented with income data for two more years – 1984 and 1995 – in addition to the four years having been made available so far, that is, 1987, 1989, 1991 and 1993. Needless to say, the time period is nevertheless still too short to uncover longer-run trends over time.[2]

The subsequent analysis is undertaken separately for men and women in paid employment, thus excluding all self-employed. The investigated category of male workers is restricted to those .in full-time employment, whereas the category of female workers comprises all women, that is, also those employed on a part-time basis. As such, this difference in the definition of the male and female samples has a negligible impact on the estimated returns to education for Finland; the share of part-timers in the Finnish labour force was still minor in 1995. In international perspective, on the other hand, the chosen definition of the male and female samples clearly improves the comparability of estimation results across countries, since the share of part-timers among women varies considerably across countries while the corresponding share among men is still small in most European countries.[3]

The next section presents briefly the data used and the specification of the basic earnings model to be estimated. Section three reports and discusses the estimated average returns to human capital with the emphasis on returns to years of schooling. Section four shifts the focus from the number of completed years of schooling to the acquired educational level. Section five compares gross and net (before and after tax) returns to education. Section six explores the possibility of a sample selection bias affecting the estimation results for female workers. Concluding remarks are given in Section seven.

DATA AND MODEL SPECIFICATION

The LFS is a representative sample of the whole Finnish population. The sample has traditionally contained some 9,000 individuals aged 15–64 as stratified according to age, sex and region. Apart from these individual characteristics, also the information on education and income is register based. The rest of the information is self-reported through questionnaires and interviews undertaken by Statistics Finland.

The basic earnings equation to be estimated is identical to the simple Mincer earnings model, with the natural log of individual earnings regressed on the individuals' completed years of schooling and their potential work experience (and its square). The earnings concept refers to the individual's average gross hourly wage as calculated from tax record information on taxable annual earnings and self-reported numbers of months and normal hours worked. The annual earnings comprise all kinds of compensation, such as overtime and vacation pay. Separate information is provided on the taxable pecuniary value of fringe benefits, but the addition of fringe benefits to annual earnings exerts no significant influence on the estimation results.[4] The gross hourly wage appearing in the estimations reported in subsequent sections is exclusive of fringe benefits.

The education acquired by each individual is, according to the Register of Degrees and Examinations, compiled by Statistics Finland and based on information collected annually from educational institutions. The register gives the single highest education completed by the individual. If the individual has completed two or more degrees at the same level, only the most recent one is recorded with no indication of previous same-level degrees. Another shortcoming is that the register is restricted to completed degrees. Thus, a university student is assigned an upper secondary degree (mostly the matriculation examination from a Gymnasium) until (s)he has completed a university degree, which is estimated to take on average three and a half years at the lower candidate (BA) level and five and a half years years at the higher candidate (MA) level. Considerable variation in finishing times occurs, however, depending on the student's educational field as well as degree of activity in working life while studying.

A distinction is made between a total of seven educational levels. The starting level is a nine–year basic education, which is compulsory for all children aged 7–16. The next level covers upper secondary education, which divides into general and vocational education. The general education is provided in Gymnasium and leads to a matriculation examination (= 12 years of schooling). The vocational education is provided by vocational schools and may last for less than three years (= lower level, 10–11 years) or about three years (= upper level, some 12 years). Higher (or tertiary) education comprises both vocational colleges and universities. Vocational colleges provide short non-university vocational education (= 13–14 years). Lower candidate (BA–level) degrees (= some 15 years), higher candidate (MA–level) degrees (= some 16 years) as well as post–graduate degrees (licentiate and doctoral degrees = 18 years or more) are taken at universities. This information on educational levels may be transformed into years of schooling by using the number of years given in parentheses, which correspond to the stereotype key constructed by Statistics Finland for turning degrees into years. The actual years used by the individual for completing the degree are not known.

Work experience is defined as the potential number of years an individual has spent in working life; that is, each sample individual's work experience is calculated as age minus completed years of schooling minus age of school start (seven years in Finland). For men an extra year has been subtracted since military service is compulsory for all Finnish men. Underlying this definition of experience is the assumption that all schooling is performed on a full-time basis and that the individual enters the labour market immediately after having completed his/her schooling and stays employed until retirement. This measure of work experience may, as a consequence, either underestimate or overestimate the individual's actual work experience. The rather common habit especially among more 'mature' university students of combining studies and work will underestimate the true experience the individual has gained in working life, while breaks in the working career due to unemployment spells or family responsibilities will overestimate the work experience acquired by the individual. The seriousness of this bias and its impact on the estimation results are explored in some detail in the next section. Separate wage equations are specified for male and female workers. As noted in the outset, the analysis focuses on all female workers but only on full-timers among male workers. The female wage equation is therefore supplemented with a dummy capturing the wage effect of being employed on a part-time instead of a full-time basis. The LFS indicates explicitly whether the worker is in part-time or full-time employment.[5]

RETURNS TO YEARS OF SCHOOLING

This section presents returns to years of schooling obtained from estimating conventional Mincer wage equations separately for men and women using the six cross-section LFS years available. Furthermore, the sensitivity of the estimated rates of return to an extra year in schooling is explored by adding additional wage-relevant background variables to the equations, by replacing potential experience with actual experience and by estimating separate wage equations for private-sector and public-sector workers. These sensitivity tests are restricted to the year 1993.[6]

Basic results

Tables 4.1A and 4.1B give the coefficients of the schooling and experience variables obtained from estimating the basic wage model. Comparing the estimates for 1984 and 1995 points to a weakly increasing trend in educational returns for women but a weakly declining trend for men. For most of the investigated time period, however, the average return of male workers to an additional year in schooling has remained roughly unchanged (according to a simple *t*-test), amounting to some 9.4 per cent.[7] Among female workers, on the other hand, the average return to an extra year in school was significantly lower in the boom years of the 1980s, but rose to approximately the same level as for male workers in the deep recession years of the early 1990s.[8]

This diverging trend in the average return to schooling between genders might be due to a more profound re-structuring of the female than of the male labour market. The explosion in unemployment rates from 1991 onwards first affected men more strongly, but spread gradually to female-dominated industries and sectors causing the unemployment rate of women to rise faster than that of men. As a consequence, in the mid-90s female unemployment was more severe than male unemployment. When further noting that the risk of becoming unemployed has been strongly biased towards low-skilled, low-paid people,[9] the rise in the return to education among women seems to be primarily the outcome of relatively more low-skilled, low-paid female workers having become unemployed during the recession years. This hypothesis receives support from the stronger rise in both hourly wages and average education between 1991 and 1993 among employed women compared with employed men, but surely deserves more in-depth investigation.

The return to work experience improved markedly among male workers in the early 1990s. Simultaneously the curvature of their experience-wage profile steepened substantially. In contrast, the work experience accumulated by female workers has persistently been only moderately reflected in their wages. In 1993, the initial experience-induced wage effect of female workers amounted to less than one-fourth of that of their male colleagues, and their experience-wage profile was on average flat compared to an increasingly steeper male wage profile. The sudden trend break in 1995 is obviously explained by the previously mentioned re-structuring of the LFS.

Table 4.1A Basic estimation results: men in full-time employment, gross hourly wage

	1984	1987	1989	1991	1993	1995
Years of schooling	0.095	0.090	0.090	0.092	0.086	0.089
	(0.003)	(0.004)	(0.004)	(0.004)	(0.004)	(0.005)
Experience (potential)	0.029	0.028	0.025	0.032	0.038	0.037
	(0.002)	(0.002)	(0.002)	(0.003)	(0.004)	(0.004)
Experience squared [a]	-0.046	-0.045	-0.035	-0.051	-0.059	-0.057
	(0.005)	(0.006)	(0.006)	(0.006)	(0.008)	(0.010)
R^2 adjusted	0.342	0.302	0.290	0.338	0.349	0.309
Number of observations	2274	1876	2089	1975	1175	1016

Table 4.1B Basic estimation results: all women (incl. of part-time dummy), gross hourly wage

	1984	1987	1989	1991	1993	1995
Years of schooling	0.079	0.078	0.082	0.091	0.088	0.095
	(0.004)	(0.004)	(0.004)	(0.004)	(0.005)	(0.005)
Experience (potential)	0.014	0.014	0.009	0.017	0.008	0.026
	(0.002)	(0.003)	(0.002)	(0.002)	(0.004)	(0.004)
Experience squared [a]	-0.018	-0.021	-0.008[b]	-0.023	-0.004[b]	-0.036
	(0.005)	(0.006)	(0.005)	(0.005)	(0.008)	(0.008)
R^2 adjusted	0.221	0.201	0.207	0.292	0.258	0.293
Number of observations	2275	1966	2118	2113	1336	1164

Notes:
Standard errors are in parentheses below the estimates. [a] Parameter multiplied by the factor 100. [b] The estimate is insignificant at the 5% level.

Addition of other explanatory variables

The variation in wages across individuals reflects only partially individual differences in human capital endowments. As can be seen from Tables 4.1A and 4.1B, schooling and work experience can, at most, explain about one-third of the observed dispersion in individual gross hourly wages. Moreover, the estimated returns to education might capture at least part of the wage effect of some crucial personal or job-related background characteristic omitted in the simple human capital model. The sensitivity of the years-of-schooling estimate to the inclusion of a selected number of other wage-relevant variables is evident from Table 4.2.

Adding a tenure variable (and its square) to capture the influence on wages of individual differences in the length of the current employment relationship, leaves the estimated rate of return to years of schooling unchanged for both genders. The inclusion of a set of variables reflecting differences in family responsibilities and residential location[10] causes a slight drop in the schooling estimate for both men and women, but for both groups the decline in the estimate is insignificant according to a simple t-test. Extending the wage equation with variables related to the individual's job has no significant effect on the schooling estimate, either. The same holds for industry affiliation.

Table 4.2 Sensitivity of the schooling-year-return estimate to the addition of other explanatory variables, 1993

	Men:		Women:	
	Years of schooling	R^2 adj.	Years of schooling	R^2 adj.
Basic wage model	0.085 (0.004)	0.356	0.088 (0.005)	0.256
Addition of:				
Tenure, tenure squared	0.085 (0.004)	0.372	0.087 (0.005)	0.270
Family variables [a]	0.078 (0.004)	0.394	0.085 (0.005)	0.267
Job-related variables [b]	0.086 (0.004)	0.367	0.090 (0.005)	0.259
2-digit industry dummies	0.090 (0.005)	0.410	0.084 (0.005)	0.284
12 socio-economic dummies	0.049 (0.006)	0.441	0.056 (0.006)	0.304

Notes:
Standard errors are in parentheses below the estimates. The number of observations amounts to 1119 for men (full-timers) and 1305 for women (all, including part-timers). [a] Dummy for married, children aged 0-7, children aged 8-17, living in the capital (Helsinki) area. [b] Dummy for temporary job contract, other than regular day-time work, other than normal pay scheme, unemployment during past 12 months, unionized.

In line with empirical evidence for other countries, the addition of variables stating the individuals' position in the socio-economic hierarchy causes a substantial decline in the estimated return to an additional year in schooling. This outcome is hardly surprising, though, since the socio-economic classification relies heavily on the individuals' acquired education. Moreover, the decline is of much the same magnitude (some 40 per cent) among male and female workers, thus retaining the aforementioned equality in educational returns across genders obtained for 1993.

Potential versus actual work experience

As discussed earlier, the individual's potential years in working life may, for several reasons, deviate from his/her actual – i.e. self-reported – years spent working. The LFS allows a comparison of the two experience measures since the survey includes a question concerning each individual's actual number of working years.[11] As is to be expected, the two measures differ only slightly for male workers. In the 1993 LFS they are, in effect, almost identical (about 19.5 years on average). Among female workers, on the other hand, there is on average a three – year gap between the two measures; in 1993 the average length of potential experience amounted to some 21.6 years compared to 18.6 years for the average length of actual experience. Replacing potential experience with actual experience in the basic wage model could, as a consequence, be expected to produce a larger change in the impact of accumulated work experience on female than on male wages.

Table 4.3 Potential versus actual experience, 1993

	Men Model 1	Model 2	Women Model 1	Model 2
Years of schooling	0.086 (0.004)	0.085 (0.004)	0.088 (0.005)	0.087 (0.004)
Experience, potential	0.038 (0.004)		0.008 (0.004)	
Experience squared, potential [a]	-0.059 (0.008)		-0.004 [b] (0.008)	
Experience, actual		0.037 (0.004)		0.012 (0.004)
Experience squared, actual [a]		-0.056 (0.008)		-0.009 [b] (0.008)
R^2 adj.	0.349	0.342	0.258	0.270
Number of observations	1175	1175	1336	1336

Notes:
Standard errors are in parentheses below the estimates. The male sample contains full-timers only while the female sample includes all employed women. [a] Parameter multiplied by the factor 100. [b] The estimate is insignificant at the 5% level.

Table 4.3 shows that the experience estimates do change – more so for women than for men, but this change is insignificant throughout.[12] The marginal change in the female estimates of work experience is obviously

explained by the overall minor effect of work experience on female wages.
Also the schooling estimates remain unaffected.

Is there a sectoral gap in returns?

The estimation results obtained from estimating the basic wage equation
separately by gender and sector point to notable similarities as well as
dissimilarities in the rewarding of human capital endowments (Table 4.4).
Among male workers the average return to an additional year of schooling is
significantly higher in the private sector while the opposite pattern is
discernible among female workers.

Indeed, the estimated rate of return is of approximately the same
magnitude (over 9 per cent) for men in private-sector employment as for
women in public-sector employment. Public-sector men, on the other hand,
are faced with an average return to schooling that is close to that of private-
sector women (about 8 per cent).

Table 4.4 Private versus public sector, 1993

	Men		Women	
	Private sector	Public sector	Private sector	Public sector
Years of schooling	0.092 (0.007)	0.080 (0.006)	0.077 (0.008)	0.095 (0.006)
Experience (potential)	0.037 (0.004)	0.042 (0.006)	0.005 [b] (0.006)	0.011 (0.005)
Experience squared [a]	-0.053 (0.011)	-0.072 (0.013)	0.002 [b] (0.011)	-0.010 [b] (0.010)
R^2 adj.	0.322	0.455	0.131	0.361
Number of observations	832	343	677	659

Notes:
Standard errors are in parentheses below the estimates. The male sample contains full-timers
only while the female sample includes all employed women. [a] Parameter multiplied by the
factor 100. [b] The estimate is insignificant at the 5% level.

In contrast to the schooling results, a distinction between sectors does not
change the overall pattern of experience-induced wage effects. The
accumulation of (potential) work experience is strongly reflected in male
wages irrespective of sector. Female wages are, at most, only weakly affected
by increasing work experience and the experience-wage profile is practically
flat in both sectors.

RETURNS TO EDUCATIONAL DEGREES

Giving the schooling variable the form of a continuous measure contains the implicit assumption of there being a strict linear relation between wages and the completed number of years of schooling. Put differently, each additional year in school is assumed to increase wages to the same extent, irrespective of the level at which the schooling is undertaken.

Table 4.5 Returns to educational degrees, 1993

	Men		Women	
	Dummy estimates	Year-based estimate (and corresponding %)	Dummy estimates	Year-based estimate (and corresponding %)
Lower secondary (10–11 years)	0.051 (0.022)	+1 = 0.051 +2 = 0.025	0.053 (0.022)	+1 = 0.053 +2 = 0.026
Upper secondary (12 years)	0.230 (0.028)	+3 = 0.071	0.154	+3 = 0.049
Short non-univ. (13–14 years)	0.344 (0.045)	+4 = 0.077 +5 = 0.061	0.385 (0.036)	+4 = 0.085 +5 = 0.067
BA-level (15 years)	0.409 (0.062)	+6 = 0.059	0.475 (0.049)	+6 = 0.067
MA-level or more (16 years +)	0.640 (0.036)	+7 = 0.073 +8 = 0.064 +9 = 0.056	0.632 (0.039)	+7 = 0.072 +8 = 0.063 +9 = 0.056
Experience (potential)	0.039 (0.037)		0.011 (0.038)	
Experience squared [a]	-0.065 (0.008)		-0.011 [b] (0.008)	
R^2 adj.	0.368		0.274	
N	1175		1336	

Notes: Standard errors are in parentheses below the estimates. The male sample contains full-timers only while the female sample includes all employed women. [a] Parameter multiplied by the factor 100. [b] The estimate is insignificant at the 5% level.

Replacing the years–of–schooling variable with educational level dummies allows for a simple test of whether this is a reasonable assumption. Estimation results for 1993 are reported in Table 4.5, with those having completed, at most, a basic education standing as the reference group. As is to be expected, the hourly wages increase with education. Moreover, the pattern is almost identical for men and women with upper secondary education being the only level at which female workers are significantly less rewarded for their education[13].

Another way of comparing the size of the rate of return at different educational levels is to account for the number of years usually required for completing a degree at each particular level. This is done in columns two and four of Table 4.5. The numbers reported are calculated from the coefficients in columns one and three, with the corresponding anti-log percentages given in parentheses. The outcome varies considerably depending on the number of years assigned to each educational level. Nevertheless, there seems to be no clear tendency of annual average returns to education to decline at the higher educational levels, not even when the MA-level university degree is assumed to require six years to complete.

Furthermore, also the returns to different educational levels are only marginally affected when supplementing the wage equation with the same set of personal and job-related background characteristics as in the years-of-schooling based estimations above. Again the only information that causes a significant decline in the estimated returns to education is the individuals' socio-economic status.

In a previous section men employed in the public sector were found to have a lower average return to years of schooling as compared to their colleagues in the private sector. When repeating this comparison on an educational-level basis, the wage premium of private-sector men shows up at all educational levels except for lower secondary education (a few years in vocational school). The favourable situation of women in public-sector employment, on the other hand, seems to be explained primarily by the much better rewarding of a lower secondary education in the public sector than in the private sector. These gaps in educational returns no doubt reflect the conspicuous differences between the two sectors when it comes to occupational and industrial structures as well as pay and tenure systems.[14]

GROSS VERSUS NET RETURNS TO EDUCATION

The analysis has so far focused on the effects of education on individual *gross* (before-tax) hourly wages. Especially in countries with strongly progressive income tax systems, wage and salary earners may, however, be more concerned about their return to educational investments measured by means of *net* (after-tax) rather than gross hourly wages.

The tax register data added to the LFS include information not only on the individuals' annual taxable earnings but also on the total amount of income taxes *actually paid* to the state, to the local authority (the municipality) and to the state church. This means that the available information refers to the individuals' income tax burden after adjustment for both personal and family-related tax allowances and deductions. The individuals' after-tax earnings can thus be obtained by subtracting the sum of paid income taxes from the annual taxable earnings.

However, this way of calculating net earnings is straightforward only if taxes have been paid merely out of income earned at the main job. This is because the available information on paid income taxes refers to all taxable earnings of the individual. Thus income taxes paid on earnings from, for instance, a second job are also included. This turned out to be a minor problem in the 1993 LFS, though. According to the tax register data a large majority of the sample workers has taxable earnings reported from one (the main) job only, and in the case of other taxable earnings, these are for the most part minor compared with the taxable earnings from the main job. In view of this it is hardly surprising that experiments to reduce the paid income taxes in proportion to eventual other than main-job taxable earnings, changed the estimation results only marginally.

Table 4.6 Gross versus net hourly wage, 1993

	Men:		Women:	
	Gross hourly wage	Net hourly wage	Gross hourly wage	Net hourly wage
Years of schooling	0.085 (0.004)	0.072 (0.004)	0.089 (0.005)	0.074 (0.004)
R^2 adj.	0.357	0.303	0.266	0.217
Lower secondary (10–11 years)	0.057 (0.022)	0.021 [a] (0.022)	0.056 (0.022)	0.033 [a] (0.022)
Upper secondary (12 years)	0.241 (0.027)	0.221 (0.026)	0.166 (0.026)	0.145 (0.026)
Short non-univ. (13–14 years)	0.341 (0.045)	0.312 (0.044)	0.375 (0.035)	0.311 (0.033)
BA-level (15 years)	0.407 (0.062)	0.281 (0.066)	0.496 (0.046)	0.413 (0.047)
MA-level or more (16 years +)	0.637 (0.036)	0.535 (0.033)	0.631 (0.039)	0.516 (0.037)
R^2 adj.	0.376	0.332	0.281	0.230
N	1158	1158	1316	1316

Notes: Standard errors are in parentheses below the estimates. The male sample contains full-timers only while the female sample includes all employed women. [a] The estimate is insignificant at the 5% level.

The average rate of return to an additional year of schooling drops for both men and women from about 9 per cent to some 7.5 per cent when turning from gross to net hourly wages (Table 4.6). The returns to secondary education levels remain roughly unchanged while, as is also to be expected, the wage premium of higher education degrees is significantly lower when accounting for the progressivity of income taxes.[15]

TESTING FOR PRESENCE OF SAMPLE SELECTION BIAS

Women tend to have a more interrupted working career than men. Observing those employed at a specific point in time may accordingly cause a greater problem of sample selection among women than among men. To test for the potential presence of a sample selection bias in the estimation results for women, the basic wage equation for female workers is re-estimated together with a probit equation thought to capture women's choice between employment and non-employment. The selection process is assumed to be affected by the women's education, age, marital status, children and regional residence. The chosen explanatory variables predict the (non)employment status correctly for over 73 per cent of the sample women.

Two methods of estimation are adopted: Heckman's two-stage least squares technique and full information maximum likelihood estimation (FIML) where the Heckman estimates as used as values of departure. As is evident from Table 4.7, the results point to a non-negligible sample selection bias affecting the estimation results for female workers. This bias does not seem to influence the estimated returns to education to any significant extent, however. The estimates of potential work experience, in contrast, increase remarkably and approach, in the FIML-estimations, those of male workers.

Ignoring the potential presence of a sample selection bias thus turns out to leave the variable of main interest in this context – the return to education – unaffected. Nevertheless it may be justified to make two comments on the use or non-use of a sample selectivity approach. First, the Heckman correction for sample selection has, in recent years, been subject to rather serious critique due to the usually high correlation between the exogenous variables in the selection equation and the wage equation making even the FIML estimator very unrobust. In fact, such collinearity problems show up in the LFS data.[16] Second, the sample selection bias problem tends to disappear when more explanatory variables are added to the wage equation.[17]

Education and Earnings in Europe

Table 4.7 Sample selection correction for women, 1993

	OLS	Heckman 2-stage	ML-estimates
Years of schooling	0.088	0.095	0.096
	(0.005)	(0.005)	(0.004)
Experience	0.008	0.028	0.031
(potential)	(0.004)	(0.006)	(0.004)
Experience	-0.004 [b]	-0.048	-0.053
squared [a]	(0.008)	(0.014)	(0.009)
Lambda		0.219	
		(0.060)	
Rho(1,2)			0.671
			(0.054)
R^2 adj.	0.258	0.265	
Log-Likelihood			-1677.05
Lower secondary	0.053	0.092	0.073
(10–11 years)	(0.022)	(0.027)	(0.026)
Upper secondary	0.154	0.201	0.179
(12 years)	(0.026)	(0.030)	(0.027)
Short non-univ.	0.385	0.431	0.410
(13–14 years)	(0.036)	(0.038)	(0.036)
BA-level	0.475	0.524	0.501
(15 years)	(0.049)	(0.047)	(0.042)
MA-level or more	0.632	0.706	0.681
(16 years +)	(0.039)	(0.043)	(0.038)
Lambda		0.253	
		(0.068)	
Rho(1,2)			0.612
			(0.067)
R^2 adj.	0.274	0.281	
Log-Likelihood			-1663.65
N	1336	1336	1336
Total N			2536

Notes: Standard errors are in parentheses below the estimates. [a] Parameter multiplied by the factor 100. [b] The estimate is insignificant at the 5% level.

CONCLUSION

The average return to an additional year of schooling has remained roughly unchanged among male workers over the 12-year period investigated. Among female workers, it was significantly lower in the 1980s, but increased in the early 1990s to approximately the same level as for men. In 1993, men and women fared equally well also when comparing average returns to different levels of education. These level-of-education returns further suggest that the marginal return to additional years invested in higher education is rather constant than declining. This outcome is not affected when trying to correct the female estimation results for the potential presence of a sample selectivity bias.

The addition of a broad set of personal and job-related background characteristics to the gender-specific wage equations has a minor influence on the estimated returns to education. The only exception is the individuals' socio-economic status, which overtakes a considerable part of the wage impact estimated to arise from investments in education. The results further indicate that this 'trade-off', between the individuals' position in the socio-economic hierarchy and education, increases with the length of schooling.

A comparison between the private and the public sector, finally, suggests that men are on average better rewarded for their education when employed in the private sector, while the opposite holds among women. Sector-specific returns to educational levels reveal that men in public-sector employment fare slightly worse at principally all levels. The more advantageous position of women in public-sector employment, on the other hand, seems to arise primarily from notably better rewarding of lower secondary educations than in the private sector. The results also indicate that male workers have faced a marked improvement in the rewarding of experience accumulated in working life. The experience of female workers, on the other hand, has persistently been only weakly rewarded in the Finnish labour market. Moreover, this finding obviously explains why, in contrast to what would be expected, also the female estimates remain roughly unchanged when replacing the sample workers' potential work experience with their actual work experience.

Unfortunately, the LFS offers no possibilities to investigate other crucial aspects of private returns to education, such as the impact of innate ability and family background. The LFS data set also proved to be too thin to allow for robust tests of the human capital theory against the screening hypothesis. However, these shortcomings do not concern the LFS data only. The same drawbacks characterise also other individual–level data sets readily available. This is the simple explanation for the so far rather limited perspective on private returns to education in Finland.

NOTES

1. Accordingly the LFS is also the only dataset that allows a comparison of rates-of-return estimates when using annual earnings instead of hourly wages. For all years investigated, the estimated returns are significantly higher with annual earnings being the dependent variable. For example, for both male and female workers the hourly wage based return to an additional year in schooling amounted in 1993 to 9 per cent as compared to an annual earnings based return of 11 per cent.
2. Previous studies for Finland based on Population Census data for the period 1970–90 and individual annual earnings indicate that the return to education declined considerably in the 1970s but remained largely unchanged in the 1980s. For a review of Finnish evidence, see Asplund (1999).
3. See e.g. Asplund and Persson (2000).

4. Evidence for Finland on the effect of fringe benefits is provided in e.g. Asplund (1993) and Granqvist (1998).
5. For detailed information on the LFS and the variables used in the current analysis, see e.g. Asplund (1993).
6. The reason for undertaking the sensitivity tests for the year 1993 and not for the most recent year available, 1995, is that the information content of the 1995 LFS differs in some crucial dimensions from that of previous surveys. Most importantly, the 1995 LFS does not allow hourly wages to be calculated in an equally detailed way as previous surveys do. Furthermore, some of the key variables used for the sensitivity tests are simply missing from the 1995 LFS.
7. $(e^{0.09} - 1) * 100 \approx 9.4$
8. The difference in the years-of-schooling coefficients estimated for men and women was statistically insignificant for 1991, 1993 and 1995.
9. See e.g. Asplund and Lilja (2000).
10. Moreover, interacting regional variables with the years-of-schooling variable revealed no significant variation in average returns to education across regions.
11. Unfortunately this information has no longer been collected in the 1995 LFS.
12. Experiments with specifications including both age and actual experience (both given the exponential shape) produced statistically insignificant coefficients for the age variables for both men and women, for which reason these estimation results are not displayed.
13. The use of actual instead of potential work experience leaves the educational dummy coefficients roughly unchanged. The work experience estimates, in turn, are almost identical to those reported in Table 4.3 above. The estimation results obtained when using actual work experience are therefore not shown.
14. More detailed results can be found in e.g. Asplund (1998a).
15. More detailed results are reported in Asplund (2000).
16. See further Asplund (1998b).
17. This is certainly the case for Finland (see Asplund, 1993).

REFERENCES

Asplund, R. (1993), *Essays on Human Capital and Earnings in Finland*, Helsinki: The Research Institute of the Finnish Economy ETLA, Series A 18.

Asplund, R. (1998a), 'Private- vs. Public-Sector Returns to Human Capital in Finland', *Journal of Human Resource Accounting* **3** (1), 11–44.

Asplund, R. (1998b), *Are Computer Skills Rewarded in the Labour Market? – Evidence for Finland*, Bergen: SNF Yearbook 1998.

Asplund, R. (1999), 'Earnings and Human Capital: Evidence for Finland', in Asplund, R. and P.T. Pereira (eds), *Returns to Human Capital in Europe. A Literature Review*, Helsinki: The Research Institute of the Finnish Economy ETLA, Series B 156.

Asplund, R. (2000*), Gross and Net Returns to Education in Finland*, Helsinki: The Research Institute of the Finnish Economy ETLA. (forthcoming)

Asplund, R. and R. Lilja (2000), 'Has the Finnish Labour Market Bumped the Least Educated?', in Borghans, L. and A. de Grip (eds), *The Overeducated Worker? The Economics of Skill Utilization*, Cheltenham: Edward Elgar Publishing Ltd.

Asplund, R. and I. Persson (2000), 'Low Pay – A Special Affliction of Women', in Gregory, M., W. Salverda and S. Bazen (eds), *Labour Market Inequalities: Problems and Policies in International Perspective*, Oxford: Oxford University Press. (forthcoming).

Granqvist, L. (1998), *A study of fringe benefits. Analysis based on Finnish micro data.* Stockholm: Swedish Institute for Social Research – Dissertation Series 33.

5. France

Marianne Guille
and
Ali Skalli

INTRODUCTION

In this chapter, we present a series of estimates of the returns to education using French labour market data. We distinguish between the public and the private sectors, men and women and between part-time and full-time female employees. We also analyse changes in the returns to education between the early 1970s and the end of the 1990s.

We have three main goals. First, we analyse the stability of the estimated returns to education and evaluate their sensitivity to different specifications of key variables, in particular earnings and measures of educational attainment. In the process, we update results of previous studies of the returns to education in France.[1] Second, we investigate two important sources of bias by providing new evidence for the endogeneity of schooling and by taking account of women's participation in the labour market. Third, we propose tests of predictions of the screening hypothesis.

The structure of the chapter is as follows. We briefly introduce the French educational system and our data. Our main results are then presented in the following sections: the evolution over time of the returns to education, the sensitivity of estimates to two possible sources of bias: endogeneity and selectivity and the issue of signaling. The last section concludes the chapter.

THE FRENCH EDUCATIONAL SYSTEM

In France, schooling is compulsory for children aged between 6 and 16. Hence, they all attend primary and lower secondary schools. In addition, enrolment rates as well as schooling expectancy have soared since the mid 1980s.[2] As a consequence, more than three-quarters of the children reach the upper secondary level, which is composed of three main branches: general, technological and vocational education.

The first two include three years in traditional *lycées* (high schools) where successful students are then given the general or technological *Baccalauréat*. Vocational upper secondary education, on the other hand, offers different qualifications, which require two or three years of schooling in apprenticeship training centres or vocational high schools where various specializations are proposed.

In 1996, 85% of the pupils in the age cohort eligible to pass these upper secondary degrees have been successful. 70 per cent of the graduates have been given the *Baccalauréat*.[3] These figures are the result of a spectacular rise in the number of *bacheliers*, since only 35% of a generation passed the *baccalauréat* fifteen years ago. As a consequence, 60% of a generation reach tertiary education nowadays. Such a transition from *élite* to mass higher education has then led to a considerable diversification of the French higher education system.

A distinguishing feature of the French higher education system was the coexistence of an open and a closed sector. The former comprises universities where vocational and selective programmes have been progressively introduced in addition to the traditional long streams of general content. The latter comprises the old and prestigious *Grandes Ecoles,* but also more recent schools offering short vocational courses.

While the *Baccalauréat* is sufficient to enter universities, the best *bacheliers* are selected for two further years in preparatory classes before application to enter a *Grande Ecole*. Students are then selected among those applicants who have had the highest scores in national competitive exams (*Concours d'Entrée*). Note, however, that only access to *Grandes Ecoles* is selective since students meet no further selection process during their schooling career. This is not true in universities where access to either doctoral programmes or vocational ones depends on the scores students have had during their previous years in higher education.

Apart from health training where there is selection through a competitive exam at the end of the first year, all the traditional long streams offered by universities (law, economics, science, humanities) have similar structures: successful students are given a first qualification (*DEUG*) after two years, a second one (*Licence*) a year later and, finally, the college degree (*Maîtrise*), a further year later. The only requirement to access any of these is graduation from the previous level.

However, the increasing importance of vocational programmes has led not only to an increase in the vocational content of these traditional long streams, but also to compel students sometimes to within-firm placements even when they are not involved in vocational programmes. Moreover, new vocational programmes were created within universities. Short ones last two to three years beyond the *Baccalauréat* (*DUT, DEUST*). Application to long ones necessitates a general degree: the first year of the *DEUG* for an *Institut Universitaire Professionnel* (three years of schooling), the *DEUG* for a *MST* (two years of schooling) and a *Maîtrise* for a *DESS* (one year of schooling). Though offered by universities, these vocational programmes are selective since they are open to limited numbers of students.

Grandes Ecoles are traditionally specialized in three major fields: administration, business and engineering. Schooling lasts between three and four years beyond preparatory classes. As well as these, there are specialized schools (arts, paramedical training...) and short programmes leading to vocational degrees (*BTS*), which require two or three years of schooling beyond the *Baccalauréat*. Though less selective than *Grandes Ecoles*, access to these short vocational streams requires success in an exam, a test or an interview.

This seemingly high segmentation of the French system of higher education is, however, only partial. Indeed, university graduates may choose to enter *Grandes Ecoles* though they still need to pass the admission process. Alternatively, there are admission rules defining the level at which a *Grande Ecole* student may enter a university. Students having attended short vocational programmes, however, have to pass a special exam to enter a university beyond the first degree (*DEUG*).

It is worth noting that any pattern remains virtually permissible, the only exception being that entry to a given level requires graduation from the preceding level. Therefore, the actual number of years of schooling of an individual holding a given qualification may be either lower or higher than the number of years which is typically required to attain that qualification. Not only do some individuals skip one or more primary school classes, but, at each step of their schooling career, they may also have to repeat a year if their scores are too low. They may also attend classes of a given level and drop out before graduation at that level. Note finally that not all patterns that end up at the same level of certification are equally efficient.[4]

DATA

The results we report in the following sections are drawn from two datasets conducted by INSEE, the French national statistics institute.

The household survey called *Formation et Qualifications Professionnelles* (FQP, Training and Professional Qualifications) presents very interesting characteristics. Not only is it the richer French dataset in terms of initial as well as post-school education and their professional outcomes, but the five FQP data sets that are available (1963, 1970, 1977, 1985, 1993) imply that the same information can be observed for as many points in time.

Because of the eight year cycle of FQP, we also use the household survey called *Emploi* (Emploi, Employment Survey) for the years 1993 to 1998. Both FQP and Emploi contain the actual number of years of schooling as well as individuals' highest qualifications, but only FQP gives detailed information on individuals' educational records and family background.

Both FQP and Emploi provide direct information on individuals' gross earnings (excluding social contributions). However, in FQP, only gross annual earnings are available, while in Emploi gross monthly earnings as well as the usual number of weekly work hours are provided. As a result, gross hourly earnings can be calculated from Emploi as monthly gross earnings divided by four times the usual number of weekly worked hours.

Therefore, no measure of net earnings is available to us and this is due to the French tax system where taxes are calculated on a household basis.[5]

TRENDS OVER TIME OF THE RETURNS TO EDUCATION

In estimating the returns to education, it is important to examine the extent to which the results are sensitive to the choice of specification. Hence, the first step of our analysis consisted in considering different measures of individuals' remuneration and/or human capital and in including a large set of potential wage determinants. The results, which we do not report in detail here, could be summarized as follows.

The effect of schooling on hourly wages is slightly lower than that on annual remuneration for men as well as for women. This indicates that schooling has an impact on wages as well as on the number of worked hours. Indeed, by increasing wage rates, schooling is very likely to influence positively individuals' labour supply and, by reducing the likelihood of unemployment, it reduces the number of unemployed hours.[6]

While the returns to actual experience are systematically lower than the returns to potential experience for men and for women, the effect of schooling on wages differs according to gender. For men (women), the returns to education are systematically lower (higher) in the specification including actual experience. The estimated returns to education using either actual or potential experience remain, however, very close, while the returns using age are systematically and significantly lower (see Card, 1999).[7]

The inclusion of additional variables (job tenure, marital status, number of children, region, industry and employer size) results in a decrease of the estimated rates of returns to education. However, this decrease is mainly noticeable for women since the estimates fall from 0.073 (in the most parsimonious Mincer-type equation) to 0.058. Compared to these figures, the returns to education for men seem to be less sensitive to specification augmenting as they fall by less than one percentage point (from 0.076 to 0.066).

We have also separated individuals according to gender and to whether they were employed in the private or in the public sector.[8] In a simple specification where individuals' wages are explained by their actual number

Education and Earnings in Europe

of years of schooling and their potential labour market experience (see endnote 7), several interesting features emerge from the results. Although the returns to education were higher for men in 1970, the gender differential seems to be significantly changing over time. Indeed, not only has it been decreasing prior to 1993, but it also turned out to be in favour of women during the 1990s, which is the case in most European countries. A possible explanation of this evolution is the change in women's demand for education. As female enrolment rates as well as their investment in education increase, women are less frequently assigned to those jobs or occupations not requiring high education levels and have a lower propensity to choose educational programmes of relatively low value in the labour market.[9] Furthermore, their higher investment in education results in an increase of the productive capabilities of the average women observed in the labour market.

Figure 5.1   OLS estimates 1970, 1977, 1985 and 1993

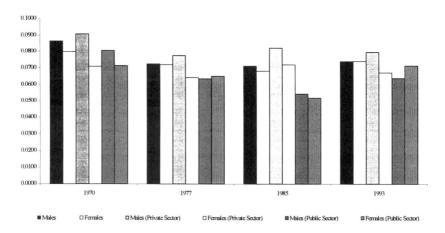

Source: Own calculations based on FQP data.

Secondly, while the estimated rates of return are systematically higher in the private sector than in the public sector for men, the difference is larger for men than for women prior to 1993 and negative for women after this date. This means that the observed evolution (in favour of women) of the gender differential in the returns is mainly taking place in the public sector. Note that qualifications are almost the main determinant of the hiring decision in the public sector: to become a civil servant, each applicant needs to hold the specific qualification required for the supplied job and to successfully pass a competitive exam. Obviously, such a hiring procedure is based on objective criteria and leaves little room for discrimination.

Thirdly, there is no clear trend in the returns to education. To see whether these returns are rather stable or changing over time, we have performed a pseudo-panel analysis based on two specifications suggested by Baudelot and Glaude (1989). The first one included the actual number of years of schooling, labour market experience and its square a cohort variable defined according to the year of entry into the labour market and an interaction variable of schooling and cohorts. In the second one, the cohort variable is replaced by an indicator of the sampling year. All variables are deviations from the corresponding characteristics of the average cohort. In FQP data, the reference men (women) cohort entered the labour market in 1957 (1962) and is endowed with 10.24 (11.20) years of schooling and 20.51 (15.85) years of potential experience. Similarly, in Emploi data, the reference men (women) cohort entered the labour market in 1974 (1975) and is endowed with 12.07 (12.51) years of schooling and 21.09 (20.68) years of potential experience.

For both men and women and in both data sets, the evidence suggests that, on average, the returns to education are declining over time. This may be due to business cycle as well as to cohort effects. Jarousse (1988) suggests that declining returns might be due to the low influx of *Bacheliers* into those programmes with the highest values and the persistence of enrolments in declining fields, offering the lowest returns but requiring a minimal level of effort. An alternative interpretation is suggested by Baudelot and Glaude (1989) who also highlight a declining trend in the returns to education for the period 1970–1985. They argue that the decreasing trend is mainly due to the increase of low wages, particularly the minimum wage (SMIC), which has led to less wage dispersion and thus has contributed to the depreciation of the returns to high level qualifications. Overeducation is also a possible explanation: if higher unemployment rates lead to lower matching quality of individuals to their jobs and if overeducated individuals earn less than if their job required exactly the qualifications they hold, then one would expect the returns to education to decrease with the level of unemployment.

CORRECTION FOR TWO POTENTIAL SOURCES OF BIAS

In this section, the two main questions we address are: (1) To what extent does the labour supply behaviour of women affect their returns to education? (2) Could the actual effect of education on earnings be accurately measured if education is thought of as any exogenous variable?

Selectivity Bias

Although the participation rate of women is increasing over time, it remains significantly lower than that of men. Indeed, the participation rate of 25-60 year old individuals has increased from 75% in 1975 to 82% in 1994. But, this increase is due to women's changing behaviour since males' participation rate has slightly decreased from 95% to 91% while that of women has largely increased from 55% to 72%. Moreover, differences in the participation rates between the lowest and the highest educational level have increased for men (from 93% to 98% in 1975, from 84% to 95% in 1994), not for women (46% to 75% in 1975, 56% to 85% in 1994).

Even among participants to the labour market, it is a stylized fact that men and women differ in the amount of labour they supply. According to the Emploi survey, 25% (20%) of women worked part-time in 1992 (1982) while only 3.5% (2.5%) of men did so. Moreover, not only are there differences among occupations, but it seems that education influences the distribution of female part-time workers: 16% (30%) of female white collar (service employees) worked part-time in 1992. Indeed, part-time work is more frequent among low-educated women, while the difference between men and women decreases along the hierarchy of educational levels.

This discussion suggests that the proportions of women not participating to the labour market or working only part-time are so high that selectivity might be a serious problem. Since the amount of labour supply is a matter of choice, the categories of women one observes (participants, full and part-time employees) are not randomly determined and observed earnings can no more be thought of as random samples of women potential earnings.

Table 5.1 The impact of selectivity bias

	OLS		Ordered Probit		Nakamura	
	Full–time	Part–time	Full–time	Part–time	Full–time	Part–time
Constant	1.9014	1.5196	1.8605	1.5137	1.8699	1.5114
	(0.0325)	(0.0717)	(0.0390)	(0.0786)	(0.0384)	(0.0765)
School	0.0554	0.0957	0.0560	0.0959	0.0558	0.0959
	(0.0007)	(0.0016)	(0.0008)	(0.0018)	(0.0007)	(0.0018)
Age	0.0548	0.0455	0.0561	0.0458	0.0559	0.0460
	(0.0016)	(0.0035)	(0.0017)	(0.0037)	(0.0017)	(0.0038)
Age^2/100	-0.0513	-0.0353	-0.0530	-0.0357	-0.0528	-0.0359
	(0.0020)	(0.0043)	(0.0022)	(0.0047)	(0.0022)	(0.0047)
Lambda			0.0141	0.0024	0.0143	0.0025
			(0.0074)	(0.0130)	(0.0093)	(0.0128)
Adjusted R^2	0.32	0.40	0.32	0.40	0.32	0.40
Fisher	2940.64	1374.61	2206.68	1030.80	2206.23	1030.43
N	19,155	6,182	19,155	6,182	19,155	6,181

Notes: Robust standard errors in parentheses.
Source : Own calculations based on the 1995 Emploi survey.

In order to simultaneously take into account part-time and non-participation selectivity biases, Ermisch and Wright (1993) suggest that the selection process be modeled as an ordered probit, the endogenous variable of which has three response levels (full-time work, part-time work and non participation). A slightly different approach is that suggested by Nakamura & Nakamura (1983) who estimate two separate probit equations for full-time work and for non-participation using the whole sample.[10]

Table 5.2 Reduced form probit equations

	Ordered probit		Work/not work		Full-time/part-time	
	Coef.	Std. dev.	Coef.	Std. dev.	Coef.	Std. dev.
Constant	-3.7025	0.0908	-3.4156	0.1055	-3.3980	0.1005
Schooling	0.0521	0.0021	0.0759	0.0026	0.0405	0.0023
Age	0.2226	0.0045	0.2269	0.0051	0.2107	0.0050
Age Sq.	-0.0030	0.0001	-0.0031	0.0001	-0.0029	0.0001
Married	-0.2962	0.0196	-0.3800	0.0238	-0.2582	0.0206
Divorced	0.2764	0.0307	0.3304	0.0391	0.2560	0.0321
Widowed	-0.7782	0.0406	-0.0942	0.0460	-0.0932	0.0449
Foreigner	-0.3400	0.0293	-0.2976	0.0321	-0.3808	0.0329
NBC18	-0.3579	0.0711	-0.3821	0.0081	-0.3407	0.0078
NBUNE	-0.3746	0.0197	-0.4074	0.0216	-0.3497	0.0219
First cut	0.5232	0.0612				
Second cut	1.1306	0.0078				
Log likelihood	-32733.6		-18727.2		-22330.4	
Full-time sample	19155				19155	
Part-time sample	6182					
Full + part time			25337			
Non Participation	15151		15151			
Non full-time					21333	
Total	40488		40488		40488	

Source : Own calculations based on the 1995 Emploi survey.

Table 5.2 reports the results from our replication of both approaches using the 1995 Emploi survey. In the work/not work equation, the endogenous variable takes value 1 if the woman works either full or part-time and 0 otherwise. In the full/part-time equation, the choice variable takes value 1 if the woman works full-time and 0 if either she works part-time or does not work at all. As can be seen from Table 5.2, the reduced-form choice equations include, in addition to the regressors in the earnings function (see

Table 5.1), marital status indicators, the number of children aged less than 18 (NBC18), citizenship and the number of unemployed in the household (NBUNE). All the variables we have included seem to have a significant impact on the decision to participate and on the decision to work full-time.

An examination of Table 5.1, which compares OLS estimates to those resulting from both correction methods, shows that both approaches lead to very similar results. There is a positive selection into the full-time work category, but no significant selection effect into the part-time work category. However, with both methods, correction for selectivity bias results in a very slight increase in the returns to schooling. For full-time (part-time) workers, the OLS estimated return is 5.54% (9.57%) while the corrected one is around 5.59% (9.59%).

Endogeneity Bias

As mentioned above, another potential source of bias is the assumption we have adopted so far that the number of years an individual spends at school is exogenous. In this subsection, we test the endogeneity hypothesis using the 1993 FQP survey. The instruments we use are the education level of the individual's father and mother as well as the number of his or her siblings. The accuracy of these instruments is validated by a severe testing procedure.

Table 5.3 OLS and IV estimates

| | OLS log wages | | IV log wages | |
	Men	Women	Men	Women
Constant	8.7372	8.5497	8.3425	8.2314
	(0.0732)	(0.1093)	(0.0831)	(0.1262)
Schooling	0.0566	0.0629	0.0872	0.0844
	(0.0014)	(0.0023)	(0.0028)	(0.0048)
Age	0.0624	0.0607	0.0618	0.0612
	(0.0037)	(0.0054)	(0.0039)	(0.0055)
Age^2 / 100	-0.0558	-0.0630	-0.0515	-0.0603
	(0.0046)	(0.0068)	(0.0048)	(0.0069)
Part-time		-0.7108		-0.6952
		(0.0172)		(0.0177)
Adjusted R^2	0.37	0.42	0.28	0.38
F	887.35	713.85	599.11	601.17
N	4,601	3,954	4,601	3,954

Source: Own calculations based on the 1993 FQP survey.

Table 5.4 Reduced-form schooling equation

	Men		Women	
Constant	10.9014		12.7494	
	(0.6737)		(0.6200)	
Age	0.0676		0.0219	
	(0.0346)		(0.0322)	
Age^2 / 100	-0.1773		-0.1517	
	(0.0429)		(0.0403)	
Part-time dummy			-0.4720	
			(0.1019)	
Parents' Education	Father	Mother	Father	Mother
Primary	0.9507	0.8219	0.8390	0.8434
	(0.1097)	(0.1075)	(0.1079)	(0.1038)
Vocational lower secondary	0.9482	1.0911	1.0234	1.1183
	(0.1435)	(0.1739)	(0.1387)	(0.1616)
General lower secondary	2.2013	2.2226	1.5723	2.0340
	(0.2799)	(0.2287)	(0.2405)	(0.2088)
Upper secondary	3.1532	2.3097	2.0341	2.5853
	(0.2863)	(0.2820)	(0.2404)	(0.2590)
Vocational tertiary	1.9247	1.8753	1.8173	1.9009
	(0.3050)	(0.3674)	(0.2945)	(0.3322)
University or Grandes Ecoles	4.4695	1.7566	3.0686	2.9424
	(0.2482)	(0.3956)	(0.2332)	(0.3665)
Siblings	-0.2140		-0.1980	
	(0.0186)		(0.0185)	
Hausman t	1.0000 (0.0031)		1.0000 (0.0017)	
Basmann F	124.18 (0.0001)		99.43 (0.0001)	
F (B-J-B)	142.68 (0.0001)		186.01 (0.0001)	
R^2 (B-J-B)	0.0429		0.0912	
Adjusted R^2		0.31		0.35
F		137.41		136.48
N		4,601		3,954

Notes: Robust standard errors in parentheses. Marginal significance levels are reported under each t or F statistic. The parents' omitted educational level is 'No qualification'.
Source: Own calculations based on the 1993 FQP survey.

Following Harmon and Walker (1995), we proceed as follows. First, we compare OLS and IV estimates.[11] We then test for the endogeneity hypothesis using Hausman *t* statistics. These are obtained by including the residual from the schooling equation in the OLS earnings function. We also use Basmann's test for overidentification where the null hypothesis is that predetermined variables not included in the reduced form schooling equation have zero coefficients. As a final step, we examine the partial correlation coefficient associated with instruments in the reduced form equation as well as the corresponding F statistic. These statistics are refered to as R^2(BJB) and F(BJB).[12] The results are presented in Tables 5.3 and 5.4.

For men as well as for women, the exogeneity hypothesis is strongly rejected. Comparison of OLS and IV estimates shows that the former are downward biased, a result in line with those generally obtained in the literature. While the OLS estimate of the effect of schooling on annual wages is 5.66% (6.29%) for men (women), the IV estimate is 8.72% (8.44%). Note that while OLS estimates suggest the gender gap in the returns is in favour of women, IV estimates suggest it is in favour of men. Such a pattern has, however, not been confirmed when the 1995 Emploi survey has been used with father's occupation at the time the individual left school as an instrument (see endnote 7). OLS estimates suggested then that hourly wages increase by some 5.62% (6.53%) for men (women) with an extra-year of schooling while their IV counterparts suggested an increase of some 8.75% (9.63%).

SCREENING VERSUS HUMAN CAPITAL

Since Arrow (1973) and Spence (1974), the so-called screening hypothesis has argued that the returns to schooling reflect no productivity augmenting role for education, but only its role as a device for signaling to employers the innate capabilities of individuals. We first test for the existence of sheepskin effects, that is, 'bonus' returns for holding a qualification. We then turn on to see whether our data confirm predictions of the screening hypothesis.

Perhaps, the simplest way to see if sheepskin effects exist is to test the linearity of the earnings-schooling relationship. Table 5.5 reports estimation results based on the 1993 FQP as well as the 1995 Emploi surveys. The adopted specification includes experience and its square, the actual number of years of schooling as well as dummy variables for individuals' highest qualification, ranked according to the number of years that qualification typically requires. Thus, the coefficients on these dummy variables measure the 'bonus' return typical completion yields. As can be seen from Table 5.5, the linear hypothesis is strongly rejected, hence suggesting that these coefficients are not zero.

An alternative approach to measure sheepskin effects may consist in estimating a specification proposed by Park (1999) where regressors are experience and its square and interaction variables between schooling and qualifications. These are constructed by crossing a first set of dummy variables indicating the number of years individuals have spent at school and a second set indicating their highest qualification.

Table 5.5 Tests of the linearity hypothesis

	FQP 93		Emploi 95	
	Men	Women	Men	Women
Constant	10.2967	10.1089	2.9175	2.9173
	(0.0335)	(0.0540)	(0.0135)	(0.0150)
Schooling	0.0555	0.0567	0.0392	0.0377
	(0.0023)	(0.0038)	(0.0009)	(0.0010)
Gen. Lower Sec. (Age = 15)	0.1524	0.1441	0.1161	0.0781
	(0.0169)	(0.0260)	(0.0080)	(0.0074)
Voc. Lower Sec. (Age = 16)	0.0627	0.1060	0.0433	0.0559
	(0.0114)	(0.0204)	(0.0045)	(0.0053)
Upper Secondary (Age = 18)	0.1510	0.2105	0.1956	0.1983
	(0.0179)	(0.0257)	(0.0093)	(0.0081)
Undergraduates (Age = 20)	0.2593	0.2859	0.2893	0.3181
	(0.0236)	(0.0334)	(0.0084)	(0.0078)
Advanced Undergr. (Age = 22)	0.0999	0.1228	0.3819	0.4528
	(0.0282)	(0.0307)	(0.0123)	(0.0099)
Graduates (Age >= 23)	0.4849	0.4322	0.5254	0.6114
	(0.0314)	(0.0711)	(0.0103)	(0.0122)
Doctors (Age >= 26)	0.1257	0.2588		
	(0.0607)	(0.0998)		
Experience	0.0397	0.0327	0.0381	0.0309
	(0.0017)	(0.0023)	(0.0007)	(0.0006)
Experience Squared / 100	-0.0493	-0.0005	-0.0492	-0.0419
	(0.0035)	(0.0001)	(0.0014)	(0.0014)
Part-Time Dummy		-0.6993		-0.0943
		(0.0173)		(0.0043)
Fisher	305.35	274.27	2356.59	1915.45
Adj. R^2	0.41	0.44	0.42	0.44
N	4,395	3,835	29,082	24,683
F Linear	44.85	14.87	499.03	600.23
	0.0001	0.0001	0.0001	0.0001

Notes: Robust standard errors in parentheses. Marginal significance levels are reported under the F statistic associated with the linear hypothesis. The omitted educational level is 'Primary education'. In the Emploi survey, the Graduates group comprises Doctors.
Source : Own calculations based on the 1993 FQP and 1995 Emploi surveys.

Using the 1995 Emploi survey, we have considered eight categories: 1: Primary school (omitted group), 2: general lower secondary, 3: general upper secondary, 4: *baccalauréat*, 5: vocational lower secondary, 6: vocational high school graduates, 7: vocational tertiary and 8: university and *Grandes Ecoles*. Obviously, although less parcimonious than the one estimated in Table 5.5, the advantage of Park's specification is that it enables one to see whether the returns to qualifications change according to the number of years it takes individuals to attain them.

Instead of reporting the detail of the results we summarise them in Figure 5.2 for a sample of full-time male employees. For each qualification-schooling years combination, expected wages could be estimated from our earnings function. However, to account for opportunity costs, the reference group (10 years for primary school) has been assigned the sample average experience while individuals with greater numbers of years of schooling have been assigned equally lower numbers of years of labour market experience. Compared to the reference group, individuals who stayed longer at school have higher expected earnings but have incured foregone earnings equal to the number of extra-years of schooling times the reference group expected wage. Therefore, the returns to schooling they earn could be estimated by the ratio of their expected wage differential to the foregone earnings they have incured when compared to individuals in the reference group.[13]

Figure 5.2 reports these returns by distinguishing between individuals according to their highest qualification. It clearly shows how the returns to educational levels fall with the number of years spent at school to reach them. For instance, an upper secondary graduate would earn 9% more than the average individual who stopped schooling at the primary level if he completes the upper secondary degree within 11 years. The longer it would take him to complete it, the lower such a differential would be. The difference is even close to 0 for those who need more than 20 years to complete the upper secondary degree. This declining pattern is most likely to be due to the higher opportunity costs slow completion leads to. However, the curves for different qualifications never intersect each other. This implies that two individuals having spent the same number of years at school will earn equal returns only if both are successful in reaching a given qualification. These differentials are probably due to employers interpreting faster completion of a degree as a signal of higher ability.

It is very difficult to directly test the signaling hypothesis via the estimation of earnings functions.[14] It remains, however, possible to examine the accuracy of some of its predictions. Like Groot and Oosterbeek (1994), we are able to distinguish in the 1993 FQP survey the various components of schooling, that is, effective years (those typically required to obtain a degree), skipped years, repeated years, non-graduating years and unusual routing years. Indeed, such aspects of a person's educational record are very informative for employers since more rapid completion of a degree signals greater ability and should therefore lead to higher earnings while years spent in education without obtaining a degree should not increase earnings.

Figure 5.2 Returns to educational levels and years of schooling (men)

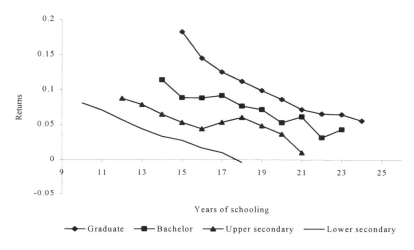

Source : Own calculations based on the 1995 Emploi survey.

Our results are reported in Table 5.6. They could be summarized as follows. The third specification which distinguishes between the various components of actual schooling is clearly preferable to those including the 'aggregate' actual number of years of schooling or the only effective number of years of schooling. Not only does it lead to a better fit, but F-tests (reported in Table 5.7) strongly reject its equivalence to each of the two other specifications.

This analysis allows also a richer interpretation of the earnings-schooling relationship. As expected, effective years of schooling have a positive effect on wages. This is in line with both human capital and signaling theories since these years increase human capital and/or provide a signal of higher ability. Note also that these returns are higher than the returns to actual years of schooling. One would indeed expect to observe higher returns if all years were successful for all individuals.

The results also suggest that non-graduating years have a positive effect on wages. This is in line with human capital theory since these years lead to an increase in individuals' human capital. However, the returns to dropout years are lower than the returns to effective years. An F-test of the equality of the coefficients associated with effective and non-graduating years indicates however that such a difference in the returns is statistically significant, particularly for women. This is another evidence for the existence of sheepskin effects. The screening hypothesis predicts that, compared to mere attendance for a number of years, graduation provides a stronger signal of ability and should therefore lead to higher earnings.

Table 5.6 Returns to components of schooling

	Women			Men		
	Eq. 1	Eq. 2	Eq. 3	Eq. 1	Eq. 2	Eq. 3
Constant	9.8466	9.9087	9.8745	9.3721	9.4124	9.3925
Actual (A)	0.0452			0.0563		
Effective (E)		0.0502	0.0523		0.0616	0.0667
Skipped (S)			0.0355			0.0621
Repeated (R)			0.0011			-0.0086
Detour (D)			0.0017			0.0067
Dropouts (N)			0.0277			0.0595
Age	0.0418	0.0395	0.0394	0.0640	0.0638	0.0613
Age^2/100	-0.0387	-0.0357	-0.0351	-0.0574	-0.0568	-0.0529
Adj. R^2	0.25	0.28	0.29	0.36	0.38	0.41
N	2988	2988	2988	3971	3971	3971

Source : Own calculations based on the 1993 FQP survey. A part-time dummy is included for women.

Table 5.7 F statistics for restrictions on coefficients

Restrictions		Women		Men	
	E=N	25.57	0.0001	2.81	0.0940
Eq 1 ⇔ Eq 3	E=-S=R=D=N	43.81	0.0001	77.51	0.0001
Eq 2 ⇔ Eq 3	S=R=D=N=0	8.12	0.0001	46.98	0.0001

According to human capital theory, one would expect repeated years to have no effect on wages if they do not lead to an increase in human capital or a slight positive effect if they lead to a more thorough understanding of what is taught. Our results for women are compatible with the hypothesis of no increase in human capital. However, for men, it seems that repeated years have a negative effect on wages. This result is in line with the screening hypothesis, which suggests that repeated years signal that the worker is of lesser ability than workers with the same effective schooling completed in standard time.

Examination of the coefficients associated with skipped years leads to similar conclusions. For women, skipped years have no significant effect on wages. As long as individuals are allowed to skip a year only when they could accumulate an amount of human capital equivalent to that accumulated by other individuals in standard time, our result is compatible with human capital theory. However, though significant at the 10% level only, the returns to skipped years seem to be positive for men. Such a positive effect could be interpreted in the screening framework as related to the signal of higher ability skipped years provide to potential employers.

Finally, unusual routing years have no significant effect on wages. This result is in line with the screening hypothesis since these detour years provide no useful information on ability to employers. Yet, it is also in line with human capital theory since detour years do not necessarily lead to an increase in the relevant human capital.

To sum up, the results in Table 5.6 suggest that there exist sheepskin effects and that repeated (skipped) years have a negative (positive) effect on males wages. Yet, they cannot be considered as strong evidence in favour of the screening hypothesis as it is not clear why there would be a signaling value in the returns to education for men, not for women.

CONCLUSION

Our results suggest that there are important differences between men and women and that endogeneity of schooling is the most serious source of bias. Our gender-based comparison of the evolutions over time of the returns to education shows that while the returns are systematically and persistently higher for men during the whole period in the private sector, the gender gap has gradually decreased in the public sector and became favourable to women in the early 1990s. While part-time and non-participation related selectivity biases for women seem to be very small, neglection of the endogeneity of schooling leads to a rather large bias since the use of instruments results in returns exceeding their OLS counterparts by more than two percentage points. Finally, our estimates also suggest that there exist significant sheepskin effects. Evidence for the screening hypothesis remains, however, mixed. On the one hand, the returns to qualifications seem to decrease with the number of years it takes individuals to pass them. On the other hand, only for men do repeated (skipped) years have a negative (slight positive) effect on earnings.

NOTES

1. See Guille & Skalli (1999) for a review of the French empirical literature.
2. As a result, by 1991, France has joined the leading group of countries (Germany, Switzerland and Japan) with respect to the schooling enrolment rates of 17–18 years olds (OECD, 1998). The schooling expectancy was 16.5 years for children aged 5 and 92% (84%) of the children aged 17 (18) attended school in 1996, while the OECD countries average was 84% (68%).
3. The proportions are 70%, 56% and 29% for the general, the technological and the vocational *Baccalauréat* respectively.
4. Note that this pattern is rather frequently observed. According to Buechtemann & erdier (1998), this is due to the low social value and the lack of recognition of vocational and technological secondary level degrees. Those joining universities after completion of vocational degrees are willing to avoid providing a signal of personal failure to achieve the higher academic levels, which are typically attended after the completion of general secondary degrees.
5. In France, employees do not pay as they earn. Instead, they generally receive gross wages (net of social security expenses) and declare annually their total household revenue to the tax authority. Tax calculation is then based on this declaration and depends on a large set of parameters such as the nature of earnings and the household structure.
6. See for example Ashenfelter & Ham (1979) who provide US evidence that the higher effect of schooling on earnings is mainly due to education having a greater effect on unemployment than on labour supply. See also Nickell (1979).
7. All the results we do not report are available upon request.
8. The distinction between the private and the public sector is motivated by our willingness to take account of differences in economic as well as institutional wage determinants. However, it is obvious that the sorting of individuals in both sectors is not random so that estimates might be biased if the employee-employers matching in both sectors is not taken into account. Since we do not address such an issue, our sector-specific regressions should be seen as leading to indicative results rather than to robust estimates.
9. According to Thélot (1997), women invest in education at least as much as men, but they are less likely to attend scientific university programmes or *Grandes Ecoles*.
10. Unemployed women have been ignored. Obviously, unemployment might also lead to a selectivity bias. Between 1982 and 1990, the number of unemployed women (men) has increased by 500,000 (200,000). For both men and women, education reduces the probability of unemployment - See Maruani (1996).
11. In the sequel, IV estimates refer to Two-Stage Least Squares.
12. The notation BJB refers to Bound-Jaeger-Baker (see Bound, Jaeger & Baker, 1993 and Harmon and Walker, 1995).
13. We are grateful to Josep Oliver, José-Luis Raymond and José-Luis Roig for suggesting this method.
14. See Layard & Psacharopoulos (1974).

REFERENCES

Arrow, K. J. (1973), 'Higher education as a filter', *Journal of Public Economics*, 2 (3), 193–216.

Ashenfelter, O. and J. Ham (1979), 'Education, unemployment and earnings', *Journal of Political Economy,* 87 (5), 99–116

Baudelot, C. and M. Glaude (1989), 'Les diplômes se dévaluent-ils en se multipliant?', *Economie et Statistique*, 225, 3–16.

Bound, J., D.A. Jaeger and R.M. Baker (1993), 'Problems with instrumental variables estimation when the correlation between the instruments and the endogenous explanatory variable is weak', *Journal of the American Statistical Association*, 90 (430), 443–50.

Buechtemann, C. F. and E. Verdier (1998), 'Education and training regimes : macro-institutional evidence', *Revue d'Economie Politique*, 108 (3), 291–320.

Card, D. (1999), 'The Causal Effect of Education on Earnings', in Orley Ashenfelter and David Card (eds), *Handbook of Labor Economics*, vol.3, Part. 7, 1801–63.

Ermisch, J. and R. Wright (1993), 'Wage Offers and Full-Time and Part-Time Employment by British Women', *Journal of Human Resources*, 28 (1), 111–33.

Groot, W. and H. Oosterbeek (1994), 'Earnings Effects of Different Components of Schooling : Human Capital versus Screening', *Review of Economics and Statistics*, 76 (2), 317–21.

Guille, M. and A. Skalli (1999), 'The Returns to Human Capital : A Review of the French Empirical Literature', in Rita Asplund and Pedro T. Pereira (eds), *Returns to Human Capital in Europe : A Literature Review*, Helsinki : ETLA, 85–123.

Harmon, C. and I. Walker, (1995), 'Estimates of the economic return to schooling for the UK', *American Economic Review*, 85 (5), 1278–86.

Jarousse, J.P. (1988), 'Working less to earn more: an application to the analysis of rigidity in educational choices', *Economics of Education Review*, 7 (2), 195–207.

Layard, R. and G. Psacharopoulos (1974), 'The screening hypothesis and the returns to education' , *Journal of Political Economy*, 84 (5), 985–98.

Maruani, M. (1996), 'L'emploi féminin à l'ombre du chômage' in Pierre Bourdieu (ed), *Les nouvelles formes de domination dans le travail*, Actes de la Recherche en Sciences Sociales, Paris : Seuil, 48–57.

Nakamura, A. and M. Nakamura (1983), 'Part-time and Full-time Work Behaviour of Married Women: A Model with a Doubly Truncated Dependent Variable' *Canadian Journal of Economics*, 16(2), 229-57.

Nickell, S. (1979), 'Education and Lifetime Patterns of Unemployment', *Journal of Political Economy,* 87(5), 117–31.

OECD (1998), *Education at a Glance*, OECD:Paris.

Park, J. H. (1999), 'Estimation of sheepskin effects using the old and the new measures of educational attainment in the current population survey', *Economics Letters*, 62(2), 237–40.

Spence, M. (1974), *Market Signaling*, Cambridge: Harvard University Press.

Thélot, Cl. (1997), *Repères et références statistiques sur les enseignements et la formation*, Paris : Ministère de l'Education Nationale, de la Recherche et de la Technologie.

6.   Germany

Charlotte Lauer
and
Viktor Steiner

INTRODUCTION

No consensus view has emerged from the empirical literature regarding the level of the return to education and its development over the past number of decades in Germany (see Lauer and Steiner, 1999 for a review of the empirical literature on this topic). Most recent studies for Germany do not focus explicitly on the relationship between education and wages, but rather on the wage structure or the wage distribution with respect to industrial sector (e.g. Fitzenberger and Kurz, 1996; Dustman and van Soest, 1998), gender (e.g. Gerlach, 1987; Prey, 1999) or region (Giles *et al.*, 1998), especially in comparisons of Western and Eastern Germany (such as Steiner and Wagner, 1998; Franz and Steiner, 2000). Only a few studies explicitly analyse the distribution of earnings in connection with the qualification structure (e.g. Bellman *et al.*, 1994; Weißhuhn and Clement, 1983 for the 1970s and the beginning of the 1980s). Moreover, the various studies differ with respect to the sample and the period observed, the specification and the estimation methods. As a result, they are hardly comparable and the results only hold within the specific framework adopted.

The aim of this study is twofold. First, it provides an overall assessment of the developments in the returns to education in West Germany over the period from 1984 to 1997. We restrict our analysis to West Germany, because changes in the East German wage distribution after unification differ fundamentally from West German wage developments in the 1990s (see Steiner and Wagner, 1998; Franz and Steiner, 2000). Secondly, it examines the extent to which the overall assessment depends on the specific framework adopted. To this end, we test for the sensitivity of the results in alternative contexts. By doing this, we hope to identify essential elements to be kept in mind for the interpretation of any study on the returns to education.

This study is organized as follows. The first part explores the basic relationship between education and wages. Following a brief descriptive overview, the estimation of standard Mincer wage equations provides the basis for bringing out the trend in the returns to education in West Germany since the mid-1980s. Then, we explore the sensitivity of these basic results to different specifications of the wage equation. First of all, the possible presence of cohort effects in the returns to education is analysed. Indeed, developments in the returns to education may result from time effects, but also from cohort effects or life-cycle effects. Secondly, we deal with the impact of the specification of the estimated wage function, focusing on the definition of the education variable, in quantitative terms (years of schooling) or qualitative terms (education levels), and on the definition of the other human capital variables. Furthermore, the sensitivity of the returns to the choice of the sample observed will be examined. In particular, it may be of interest to distinguish between full-time and part-time workers, between private and public sectors. Finally, the impact of the choice of the estimation method on the level of the returns to education will be analysed, particularly in selectivity issues and possible endogeneity of the schooling variable.

BASIC RELATIONSHIP BETWEEN EDUCATION AND WAGES

This study is based on data from the German Socio-Economic Panel (GSOEP). The GSOEP is a longitudinal household survey conducted on a yearly basis. In the first wave, in 1984, some 12000 in about 6000 households were interviewed. Detailed information about income, labour market status, education and various other socio-economic variables is collected. In addition to questions referring to the month preceding the date of the interview, the GSOEP also collects retrospective information on employment history over the entire life span from age 15. For the purpose of the analysis, the sample was restricted to West-German citizens. The self-employed, pensioners, military personnel, people still engaged in education or training were also excluded, as well as foreigners, whose educational background may fundamentally differ from that of German people.

The Qualification Structure in Germany

One specific feature of the German education system is that following primary education, pupils are directed into different types of schools, according to their abilities, where they may obtain secondary school-leaving certificates of different levels. Table 6.1 shows the qualification structure of West-German employees aged between 30 and 60 in 1984 and in 1997. The proportion of employees with no degree at all is close to zero. The large majority of West German employees (about two-thirds) holds a low or intermediate school degree (*Hauptschul-* or *Realschulabschluss*) assorted with an apprenticeship or a technical college degree (*Fachschule, Beamten-ausbildung, Gesundheitsausbildung*). Conversely, very few persons have a high school degree alone (*Abitur* or *Fachhochschulreife*). The bulk of high school (*Gymnasium*) leavers pursue their studies by completing an apprenticeship (particularly women) or higher education (particularly men). At the tertiary level, two-thirds of all employees have attended university or equivalent institutions, and only one-third the more practically oriented higher technical colleges (*Fachhochschulen*). Note the quasi-absence of short-track tertiary level institutions in Germany. The proportion of tertiary level graduates has increased from about 12% to some 18% between 1984 and 1997. Similarly, the proportion of high school graduates, especially those holding an additional vocational degree, as well as the share of master craftsmen has increased significantly, whereas lower qualified employees have become comparatively fewer. This points out the presence of an upward shift in the qualification structure over the period. Women are over-represented in the lowest educational categories (no vocational degree) and underrepresented at the tertiary level. However, the proportion of women with no vocational degree has decreased strongly.

Table 6.1 Qualification structure 1984 and 1997 (%)

	1984		1997		Total	
	Men	Women	Men	Women	1984	1997
No degree	0.0	0.3	0.0	0.1	0.1	0.1
Low or interm. school	10.0	29.6	6.0	14.5	16.9	9.4
Apprenticeship	55.6	51.9	47.4	55.6	54.3	50.7
Master	16.1	7.4	16.9	9.4	13.0	13.9
High school	0.1	0.3	1.1	0.8	0.1	1.0
High school + appr./tech.	4.2	2.0	6.6	6.8	3.5	6.7
Higher tech. college	5.4	2.6	8.2	3.1	4.4	6.1
University	8.6	6.1	13.4	9.0	7.7	11.6

Source: GSOEP 1984/97, own calculations.

Wage Developments since the Mid-1980s

In the following figures, individuals have been grouped into three broad educational categories: low education level with no degree or only a low or intermediate school degree; intermediate education level such as an apprenticehip, technical college, high school with or without apprenticeship/technical college; high education level with higher technical college or university.

Figure 6.1: Wage developments by education level.

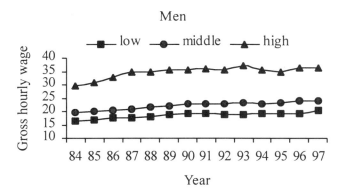

Men

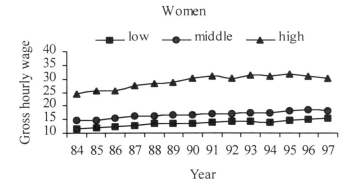

Women

Source : SOEP 1984-97, own calculations.

Figure 6.1 depicts the wage developments of employees aged between 30 and 60, where the real gross hourly wage is obtained by dividing the monthly nominal gross wage by the number of hours worked, and deflating it by the consumer price index. As can be seen from the graph, there is a huge gap between gross hourly wages of tertiary level graduates and the rest. Real gross hourly wages of unskilled and skilled workers have developed in a quite parallel way over the period. In relative terms, this means that the wage increase was somewhat stronger for the lower qualified (+25% for men and even about +33% for women). Men earn more than women at all education levels (see in Lauer 2000, an analysis of the origin of the gender wage gap).

These stylized facts tend to corroborate the view that education, especially higher education, yields a positive return. However, educational background is not the only factor influencing labour productivity and, hence, wages. Non school-based human capital is also expected to raise wages. In particular, labour market experience is likely to be a strong determinant of wages. Figure 6.2 shows the pattern of wages over the life-cycle, differentiated by education levels.

Figure 6.2 Age-wage profiles by education level.

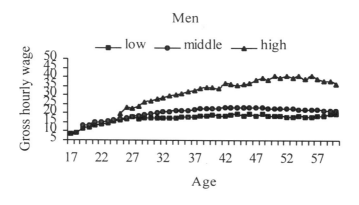

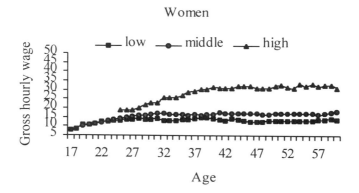

Source : SOEP 1984-97, own calculations.

Given that the length of studies differs across the education levels, the working careers associated with the various education levels start at different ages. Even at the beginning of their career, tertiary level graduates earn more than lower educated, although at this stage, the lower educated have a couple of years of working experience behind them. At all education levels, a concave shape can be observed. In a first stage, wages increase faster, then more slowly. The turning point is located at different ages across genders and across education levels. Generally speaking, it is earlier for women. This is probably due to the fact that women traditionally interrupt their working career owing to family duties and thus accumulate less human capital. Another observation is that the turning point is later for higher education levels. This implies that the educational wage premium becomes larger along with age.

Having described the most important stylized facts concerning the relationship between wages and education in Germany, we now turn to a more detailed analysis of the returns to education on the basis of empirical wage equations. Such an analysis makes it possible to estimate the returns to education while controlling for differing labour market experience.

Simple Estimates of the Returns to Education

To allow for changes in coefficients over time, the wage equation is estimated separately for each wave of the GSOEP. Since we are particularly interested in gender differences in estimated returns to human capital, we estimate the wage equation separately for men and women. The dependent variable is real gross hourly wage, defined as above. Years of schooling are derived from information on the highest completed educational or vocational degree by attaching a typical number of years to standardized educational levels. Following usual practice, labour market experience is defined as potential experience, that is, age minus years of schooling minus school starting age (6 years). To avoid an over-representation of the lower educated in the sample due to earlier career starting age, we focus on the population aged 30 to 60. All estimated coefficients are significant at the 1% level, and this simple model explains about 35-40% of the wage variance in the male sample and about 30% in the female sample.

The estimated returns to schooling are quite stable over time (the slight downward trend observable is hardly significant). We find a coefficient of about 0.08 for men and 0.10 for women, which corresponds to a return of about 8.3% for men and 10.5% for women per additional year of schooling. T-tests show that the gender differences with respect to the returns to schooling are highly significant (see Lauer and Steiner 2000 and Lauer 2000).

SENSITIVITY ANALYSIS

In the previous section, we followed the traditional approach for estimating empirical wage equations. This quite parsimonious model, applied to a specific sample, produced two main results regarding the returns to education: they have remained remarkably stable over time, and they are higher for women (about 10%) than for men (about 8%). Now, we explore the robustness of these results by estimating and testing alternative specifications of the wage function. We concentrate on four main questions. Firstly are there cohort effects in the returns to education? Secondly, does the level of return depend on the specification of human capital variables? Thirdly, are there notable differences across groups of workers in the returns to education? In particular, do the observed trend and gender differences depend on the sample chosen? Finally, is such a standard model subject to some estimation bias which might influence the level of return to education obtained?

Figure 6.3 Returns to education

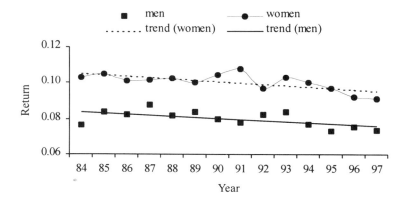

Source : SOEP 1984-97, own calculations.

Cohort Effects

In the reference model, we estimated the developments over time in average returns to education across all cohorts. This section aims at distinguishing between different effects which might influence the developments in the return to education:

- Time effects: by estimating the wage equations year by year, the standard approach intends to identify time effects. Indeed, changes in the returns to education since the mid-1980s may be attributable to the fact that the economic environment has changed, with phases of growth and recession, rising unemployment etc.
- Cohort effects: it may also be of importance to which birth cohort the observed individuals belong. For instance, a decrease in the return to

education may be due to the entry of baby-boomers generation in the labour market, which enhances job competition and drives wages down.

• Life-cycle effects: the age of the individuals observed in the period of time considered is essential. If the returns to education turn out to vary over the life-cycle, different cohorts should be compared at the same stage of their life. Otherwise, the differences may be wrongly attributed to cohort effects, whereas they only reflect life-cycle effects.

These effects are difficult to disentangle (see Heckman and Robb, 1985; Boockmann and Steiner, 2000). In fact, it is impossible to isolate them perfectly one from another, because the date of birth, the year and the age are inextricably linked in a linear relationship. Thus, it is impossible to observe two different birth cohorts at the same age and at the same year. However, by adopting different approaches, Figure 6.4 provide useful hints concerning possible cohort, life-cycle and time effects. Ideally, we wish we were able to examine each cohort over the whole life-cycle. In that case, we could run the regression separately for each cohort, while controlling for life-cycle effects by including a term for labour market experience and its square.

Nevertheless, if we can control for time developments within a cohort through year dummies, for instance, we cannot control for the fact that the cohorts would be observed in different periods in time. Here, there is an additional difficulty. Since we only have 14 years of observation, we can only catch one particular phase of the life-cycle for each cohort we want to observe. If the returns to education turn out not to be constant over the life-cycle, this may bias the estimated returns. Therefore, it seems essential to also analyse differences across cohorts at the same age.

In Figure 6.4a, we estimate the wage equation separately for different birth cohorts. In order to have a sufficient number of observations, we distinguish between only three cohorts: people born before 1945, people born between 1945 and 1955 and those born in 1955 or after. By doing so, we can compare the returns to education across different cohorts at a given year (reading the graph vertically) and follow the developments in the returns to education over the specific phase of the life-cycle corresponding to the period 1984 to 1997 for each birth cohort (reading the graph horizontally). Since we focus on the population aged between 30 and 60, the younger cohort is only represented in the second half of the observation period.

For men, the returns to education of the older cohort (born before 1945) and of the middle one (born between 1945 and 1954) have increased over the period, respectively from 8% (= [exp(0.077)-1] × 100) to 9.2% and from 8.3% to 10%. Women of the older cohort enjoy a particularly high increase in their returns to education (up to some 14%), which wanes somewhat at the end of the period. The increase in the returns of the middle female cohort over the period is the most pronounced, from 9% to 12%. For both men and women, the youngest cohort, aged 35 to 42 during this period, has the lowest returns to schooling. This is particularly obvious for women. Interestingly, the returns of the younger cohort are not increasing over the portion of the life-cycle observed.

Figure 6.4 Returns to education

a) by birth cohorts

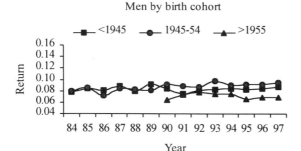

b) by age cohorts

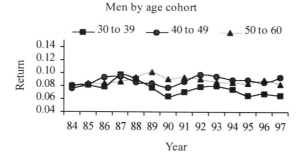

Figure 6.4 (continued) Returns to education

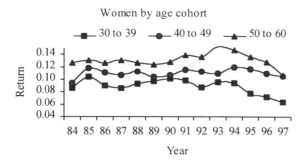

Women by age cohort

—■— 30 to 39   —●— 40 to 49   —▲— 50 to 60

Source : SOEP 1984-97, own calculations.

There are several interpretations for these developments. One interpretation would be that they depict the developments in the returns over the life-cycle: at the beginning of the life-cycle, male returns to education stagnate, in the middle of the life-cycle, they increase at a faster rate than at the end of their career. For women, the returns first stagnate, then increase strongly until the end of the career. The specific pattern for women could be attributable to the fact that many women interrupt their career in their prime years for family reasons and have not yet reaped the full benefit of their education at the first stage of their career, but catch up later. Following this life-cycle interpretation, men or women of the youngest cohort are assumed to experience the same developments in their returns when they attain a later stage of their working career as the older cohorts experience now. However, this interpretation is only valid if there are no cohort or time effects.

Another possible interpretation – which does not exclude the first one - would be that the return of the youngest cohort is lower not because it is at an earlier stage of the life-cycle, but because the returns have decreased across cohorts. This suggests that the returns of the youngest cohort will not be as high as that of the middle cohort when they reach the same stage of the life-cycle. An argument for this interpretation is that there are some jumps over the cohorts which are not explainable by life-cycle developments. For instance, the return to schooling of the youngest female cohort in 1997 should correspond more or less to the return of the 10-year older cohort 10 years earlier, that is, in 1987. However the latter (12.5%) is much higher than the former (7.7%). For men, the same is observable, although to a lesser extent. Therefore, we suppose that there are, in addition to life-cycle effects, cohort effects affecting the returns to education downwards, especially for women. One reason for this could lie in the strong educational expansion prevailing since the 1970s, which causes the supply of highly qualified individuals to increase at a faster rate than the demand.

In order to account for cohorts being at different stages of their life-cycle and test the hypothesis of cohort effects, we compare in Figure 6.4b the returns to education for different cohorts at the same age. Again, we selected three age groups: from 30 to 39, from 40 to 49 and from 50 to 60 years. Hence, the age cohort 30-39 in 1984 was born between 1945 and 1954, the age cohort 30-39 in 1985 corresponds to the birth cohort 1946-1955, and so on. Similarly, the age cohort 40-49 in 1984 is the birth cohort 1935-44, and the age cohort 40-49 in 1985 is the birth cohort 1936-45. Reading the graph horizontally, we can compare the returns to education for older (left) and younger (right) birth cohorts at a given age (but at different years). The defined birth cohorts are overlapping, so that the values reported are moving averages. Reading the graph vertically, you get the differences in the average return across age cohorts at a given year, i.e. across different birth cohorts.

For men, the birth cohort aged 50 to 60 in 1997 obtains about the same level of return to education as the cohort aged 50 to 60 in 1984 (about 8%). This general statement hides a first upward trend across birth cohorts with a peak at about 10.6% ([exp(0.100) - 1] × 100) in 1989 (birth cohort 1929-1939), followed by a downward trend for the younger cohorts between 50 and 60 years old. At age 40-49, however, some increase in favour of younger cohorts is observable: the return to education increased from less than 8% for the age cohort 40-49 in 1984 (birth cohort 1935-1944) to about 9.8% for the age cohort 40-49 in 1997 (birth cohort 1948-1957). At an earlier stage of the career (30-39 year-olds), the returns are clearly lower for younger cohorts: the return to education decreased from about 10.6% for the cohort aged 30 to 39 in 1987 (birth cohort 1948-57) to 6.7% for the cohort aged 30 to 39 in 1997 (birth cohort 1958-67).

For women, the differences between the age groups are much more pronounced: at each given year, it is apparent that the older the age group, the higher the return. This means that the increase in the returns to education over the life cycle is much more marked for women than for men. This confirms the observations drawn from Figure 6.4a. For women, the returns to education at age 40-49 remain fairly constant between the cohort aged 40-49 in 1984 and the cohort aged 40-49 fourteen years later. However, at an older age, the returns first remain stable, then increase significantly, and from 1993 the returns to education dropped sharply from 16.6% down to around 11.3%. At an earlier stage of the working career, a large decline across cohorts is observable, from about 11% to 6.6%. This decline is particularly pronounced from 1994 onwards, i.e. for birth cohorts born after 1955-64. The figure also shows that all age groups are affected by the decline in the returns to education since 1994, even if the decline is less pronounced for the middle-age group. This suggests that, in addition to cohort effects, time effects may have played a role in the decline of the female return to education.

MEASURE OF HUMAN CAPITAL

This section examines whether alternative specifications of the standard human capital wage function modify the findings. We focus on two issues: the definition of the education variable itself, and the specification of the other variables of the wage equation.

Education levels instead of years of schooling

In this section, we depart from the quantitative specification and allow education to affect wages in a non-linear way by including dummy variables for the highest completed educational or vocational degree in the earnings function. Here, we use the same categories as in the descriptive overview. The reference group consists of individuals without any degree or with only a low or intermediate school degree (*Hauptschul-* or *Realschulabschluss*). Holders of high school degree, with or without an additional vocational degree, have been grouped together. Hence, the wage equation we estimate here for each year from 1984 to 1997 is the following:

$$ln(Wage_i) = \alpha_0 + \alpha_1\ Apprenticeship_i + \alpha_2\ Technical\ college_i$$
$$+ \alpha_3\ High\ school_i + \alpha_4\ Higher\ technical\ college_i + \alpha_5\ University_i$$
$$+ \alpha_6\ Experience_i \quad + \alpha_7\ Experience_i^2 + u_i,$$

where the educational variables are dummies taking on the value 1 if the individual has the corresponding education level and 0 otherwise. The coefficients estimated from the regression represent the wage premium associated with the different education degrees compared to the reference group (no or only a low/intermediate school degree). For instance, individuals having successfully completed an apprenticeship earn an average $\exp[(\alpha_1) - 1] \times 100$ % higher hourly wage than a person without any vocational degree (reference group). The detailed results reported in Lauer and Steiner (2000) show that the higher the educational level, the higher the wage premium. For instance, the wage differential between individuals with a university degree and those with no vocational certificate amounted to about 70% for men and even 90% for women on average in the period.

However, one should take into account that the completion of the various educational degrees requires a different study duration. This affects the effective yearly return to education, since a longer period of studies implies higher opportunity costs due to a longer period of foregone earnings. The coefficients reported in Table 6.2 have been corrected for differing lengths of studies in the following way: the estimation coefficients have been divided by the time surplus needed to complete the degree concerned compared to the reference category, that is by the difference between the average schooling years of the category concerned and of the reference group.

The technical college degree yields by far the highest return, both for men and women. This is attributable to its short length of studies, e.g. compared to tertiary level studies. However, a decreasing trend is observable in the returns to technical college, particularly for women. The wage premium for employees with a high school diploma (with or without an additional vocational degree) has decreased sharply. This is particularly true for women, for whom the returns to high school dropped from 12.5% in 1984 to 7.4% in 1997. For men, this decrease only started in 1993, but is also quite strong (from 8-9% to less than 6%). As a result, a high school degree yields the lowest return at the end of the period, for both men and women, lower than the apprenticeship. This points out the importance of having a vocational qualification in Germany.

The returns to education are higher for women than for men in all educational categories except for holders of a higher technical degree. The trend in the return to higher technical college is constant over time for men, and slightly declining for women. This is mainly due to the fact that more and more women complete an apprenticeship prior to higher technical college studies, which increases the duration of studies. At the very end of the period, the returns to higher technical college are similar for both genders.

Table 6.2 Average return to educational degrees

	Apprentice	Technical college	High school	Higher technical college	University
		Men			
1984-1989	0.074	0.111	0.081	0.087	0.080
1990-1993	0.087	0.108	0.081	0.090	0.080
1994-1997	0.083	0.106	0.068	0.087	0.075
1984-1997	0.080	0.109	0.077	0.088	0.079
		Women			
1984-1989	0.111	0.137	0.104	0.107	0.097
1990-1993	0.106	0.128	0.091	0.092	0.103
1994-1997	0.094	0.120	0.082	0.094	0.092
1984-1997	0.104	0.129	0.094	0.099	0.097

Note: The reported returns are the simple averages of the estimated yearly returns over the period considered.
Source: SOEP 1984-97, own calculations.

Various measures of Non-School-based Human Capital

In the reference model, we used the typical potential experience, i.e. age minus years of schooling minus school starting age (6 years), as a measure for non-school-based human capital. This measure has the advantage of controlling for the individual's age as well as for the fact that potential working experience is expected to differ depending on the length of education. However, potential labour market experience is only a rough indicator of actual experience. Typically, it is a poor indicator of female labour market experience, since women tend to interrupt their working career to devote their time to family duties. Moreover, labour market experience is only one measure of an individual's productivity. A series of other variables may also be relevant. For this reason, we tested the effects of the following specifications of the wage equation on the returns to education:

- Reference model: this is the standard model, with potential experience and its square.
- Model 1: instead of potential experience, we use age and its square.
- Model 2: instead of potential experience, we use actual experience and its square.
- Model 3: instead of potential experience, we use actual full-time experience and its square.
- Model 4: in addition to potential experience, we include a variable for the duration of previous non-employment and its square.
- Model 5: in addition to model 4, we include a variable for previous unemployment and its square.
- Model 6: in addition to model 5, we include a variable for tenure with the current employer and its square, and a dummy variable for part-time work.
- Model 7: in addition to model 6, we include further control variables for firm size, industry branch and region of residence.

The variables designed to account for previous non-employment, previous unemployment and actual experience were constructed on the basis of the retrospective data on the employment status of the individuals from the age of 15 years contained in the GSOEP. Actual experience was constructed by adding the length of all full-time and part-time employment spells observed in the potential working career, that is after completion of initial training. Similarly, all spells of unemployment were added to build the "previous unemployment" variable. The variable for previous non-employment measures cumulated non-employment during the working career and was obtained by adding up all spells of unemployment, housekeeping, military service and other non-employment activities. The variables themselves, as well as a quadratic term and interaction terms, are included in the function in order to allow for non-linear experience effects. We include tenure with the current employer as a proxy for specific human capital acquired within the firm. Dummy variables were built for firm size, industry and region. For this part of the analysis, we concentrate on a single year, namely 1995, since we are mostly interested in the effect of adding further variables on the level of the returns to education rather than on the trend. In Table 6.3, the results of the schooling coefficients as well as of t-tests are reported. The latter test whether the alternative specifications differ with respect to the return to education from the reference specification where potential experience is used.

Table 6.3 Sensitivity of returns to education to different specifications of human capital variables other than schooling (1995)

	Return	Std Error	Men Obs.	R-Squared	t-test
Ref. model	0.073	0.003	1138	0.33	Ref.
Model 1	0.064	0.003	1138	0.30	-2.09
Model 2	0.071	0.003	1138	0.34	-0.60
Model 3	0.072	0.003	1138	0.35	-0.36
Model 4	0.071	0.003	1138	0.35	-0.50
Model 5	0.070	0.003	1138	0.37	-0.85
Model 6	0.068	0.003	1137	0.38	-1.26
Model 7	0.067	0.003	1135	0.47	-1.40
			Women		
Ref. model	0.097	0.006	722	0.32	Ref.
Model 1	0.088	0.005	722	0.31	-1.09
Model 2	0.098	0.005	722	0.34	0.14
Model 3	0.094	0.005	722	0.35	-0.40
Model 4	0.091	0.006	722	0.37	-0.69
Model 5	0.096	0.006	722	0.37	-0.13
Model 6	0.091	0.006	720	0.38	-0.70
Model 7	0.079	0.006	716	0.48	-2.18

Source: GSOEP 1995, own calculations.

Unless age is used as a proxy for labour market experience, male returns to schooling prove quite robust across the different specifications. For women, using age also reduces the return to schooling in a significant way. Using actual experience (total or full-time only) instead of potential experience does not change the results for men, and only slightly – but not significantly – for women. The same holds for model 4, which includes previous non-employment. Adding previous unemployment duration reduces the returns to schooling, but not dramatically. The same goes for the inclusion of tenure and the part-time dummy. However, the inclusion of a very large number of control variables for firm size, industry and region reduces the return to schooling significantly for women, so that gender differences are very small under this specification.

On the whole, male returns to schooling are not sensitive to the specification of the wage equation. Female returns are somewhat sensitive, especially with respect to controls for previous non-employment, as well as for industry, firm size and region.

Differences Between Subgroups of Workers

The returns to education may differ substantially across subgroups of workers. Here, we focus on the differences between full-time and part-time workers and between private and public sectors.

Figure 6.5 Returns to education

a) full-timers versus part-timers

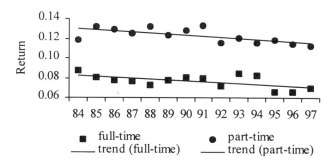

Full-time workers

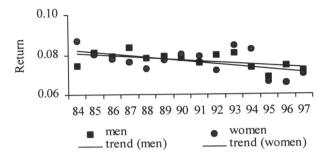

b) private versus public sector

Private sector

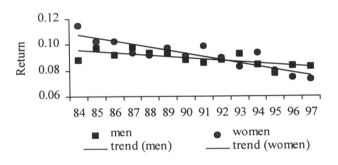

Public sector

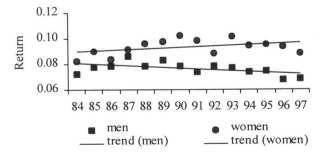

c) private versus public sector, full-time employees

Private sector, full-time

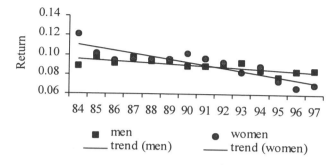

Public sector, full-time

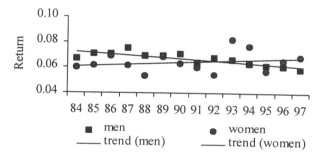

Source: GSOEP 1984-97, own calculations.

Although we used, in our basic model, hourly wage as the dependent variable and not monthly wage, for instance, the estimated returns to education may be affected by differences in working time. Part-time employment is a virtually non-existent phenomenon among men in Germany, but about 40% of our female sample work only part-time. Figure 6.5a represents the returns to education for part-time working women compared to those working full-time and gender differences among full-timers only. The results are striking. Overall, we found a return of about 10% for women in the reference model. However, this hides huge differences between full-timers and part-timers. Part-timers have a much higher return to education (around 13%) than full-time working women (around 8%). Hence, wage discrepancies between higher and lower educated workers seem larger among part-time workers. Interestingly, the returns to education for full-time workers are similar for men and for women. The slight downward trend seems comparable between part-time and full-time working women.

Furthermore, wage setting mechanisms are not the same in the public and in the private sector. Thus, the wage structure is expected to differ and so are returns to education. Figure 6.5b shows the estimated returns to education in the private and in the public sector. Again, the differences are remarkable. In the public sector, female returns to education tend to increase over the period, contrary to male returns, which decrease. As a result, the discrepancy between male and female returns has increased in favour of women. In the private sector, no such developments are observable. There, female returns to education have decreased significantly and more sharply than those for men. As a result, although female returns in the private sector were higher than for men at the beginning of the 1980s, they have become lower in the 1990s.

Figures 6.5a and 6.5b reveal marked differences between full-time and part-time workers, on the one hand, and between private and public sectors on the other hand. Figure 6.5c combine these effects and examine returns to education of full-time employees in the two sectors of the economy. The graph shows that the downward trend in female returns to education in the private sector is more pronounced if only full-time employees are taken into account (from 0.12 to less than 0.07). In the public sector, the level of the returns is significantly lower than in the case where all employees are considered, whether they work full-time or part-time. However, the upward trend in the returns to education of female full-time employees is more pronounced than that of employees overall.

On the whole, the choice of the sample of observation plays a crucial role concerning both the trend and the level of the returns to education. Therefore, returns to education can only be compared if the same sample is analysed.

ESTIMATION METHOD

So far, we have estimated our wage equations with OLS. However, much of the recent literature focuses on the estimation biases which may arise while estimating empirical wage equations (see Card, 1999). In particular, the issue of sample selectivity and the endogeneity of schooling are often mentioned as possible sources of biases.

Correcting for the Selectivity Bias of Participation in Employment

In the context of the estimation of wage functions, the individual decision to work determines whether we observe the person's wage in our data. If the factors influencing this decision were uncorrelated with those affecting individual wages, we could simply ignore the fact that not all wages are observed.

However, such an assumption is unlikely to hold in practice, especially for women, because women with higher market wages probably tend to participate more in the labour force. Hence, employed women are likely to be a self-selected group whose wages may not be representative of all women with given observed characteristics, which could bias estimated returns to education. This is called a sample selectivity bias (see Heckman 1979).

We apply a full maximum-likelihood procedure to correct for potential sample selection bias. We estimate the wage and the participation equations simultaneously. This procedure requires the availability of some credible instruments, that is variables significantly affecting labour force participation but having no direct effect on earnings. We test whether the standard specification is robust towards correction for selectivity bias, and whether the choice of the instruments matters. We estimate the following models for 1995:

- Reference model: no correction for selectivity bias.
- Model 1: we use marital status and the number of children below the age of 16 years as instruments for the selection equation.
- Model 2: we use household financial variables as exclusion restrictions (other net household income and the amount of monthly mortgage payments).
- Model 3: we use variables indicating whether mother and father were predominantly employed during childhood, and whether the person grew in a rural area, medium city or large city.
- Model 4: we use both marital status/number of children and household financial variables.
- Model 5: we include all variables together as exclusion restrictions.

In Table 6.4, we report the estimation results of the different models with respect to the return to schooling, the coefficient of the selectivity correction term λ and their respective standard errors. Additionally, we run two tests: a test of collinearity between the inverse Mill's ratio and the regressors of the regression (see Puhani, 2000), and a t-test to check whether the corrected coefficients of the various models significantly differ from the standard estimates without correction.

Estimation results from the selection equation show that most of the variables chosen as potential instruments are highly significant and have a strong effect on labour force participation. Being married or having children in the household, for instance, strongly reduces the probability of employment for women. For men, however, being married increases the probability of being employed, whereas the employment situation of the parents during childhood has no significant effect. Financial variables have a significant - though small - influence, since the higher other household income, the smaller the probability of being employed. Conversely, individuals in more highly indebted households are more likely to participate in the labour market.

Table 6.4 Sensitivity of the returns to education to selectivity bias (1995)

	Men						
	Return	Std Err	Lamda	Std Err	Obs	Collin Test[a]	t-test[b]
Ref. Model	0.073	0.003	-	-	1138	-	-
Model 1	0.074	0.003	-0.196	0.030	1138	0.14	0.07
Model 2	0.071	0.003	-0.189	0.021	1119	0.25	-0.60
Model 3	0.076	0.004	-0.119	0.142	868	0.84	0.49
Model 4	0.071	0.003	-0.171	0.021	1119	0.06	-0.50
Model 5	0.074	0.004	-0.170	0.023	851	0.08	0.07
	Women						
Ref. model	0.097	0.006	-	-	722	-	-
Model 1	0.081	0.007	-0.538	0.040	722	0.73	-1.70
Model 2	0.078	0,017	-0.439	0.034	705	0.43	-1.00
Model 3	0.087	0.008	-0.535	0.044	562	0.96	-0.91
Model 4	0.083	0.007	-0.403	0.037	705	0.25	-1.54
Model 5	0.085	0.007	-0.410	0.042	547	0.26	-1.21

Notes: [a] R^2 of the regression of the inverse Mill's ratio on the regressors of the main equation. [b] H_0: Return(model i) = Return(reference model).

For men, all estimations except for model 3 yield significant negative coefficients of the selectivity correction term λ, which suggests the presence of some selectivity bias. The coefficients range from -0.17 to -0.19. Nevertheless, the returns to schooling are not affected much by selectivity correction: the "corrected" coefficients are very close to the OLS estimates and the difference is negligible. For women, all correction terms λ have a negative and highly significant coefficient, ranging from -0.40 to -0.54. All models yield selectivity-corrected returns to schooling which are below the OLS return. However, the difference between the selectivity-corrected coefficient and the OLS coefficient is only significant (at the 10% level) in model 1, using marital status and the number of children as sole exclusion restrictions. For model 3, the collinearity test indicates that the instruments are rather weak. In model 5, where we also use marital status and number of children as exclusion in addition to other variables, the coefficient on λ is not significant. Therefore, the size and the significance of the selectivity correction term seems somewhat sensitive to the choice of instruments and this correction should therefore be used with care. Moreover, even if the λ turned out to be significant in most cases, overall we find no evidence for a sample selectivity bias with respect to the returns to schooling for men, and only rather small effects for women.

The preceding correction for selectivity bias makes no distinction whether women participate in full-time or in part-time employment. However, as we saw, the return to education is higher for part-time working women. Thus, it may be of interest to examine whether the coefficients estimated by OLS for women working part-time compared to full-time female employees are biased. Here, we adapt the two-step Heckman (1979) procedure and first estimate the selection equation by an ordered probit model, where the dependent variable is the probability of being either not employed, part-time employed, or full-time employed. This enables us to compute two selectivity correction terms, for part-time employment and for full-time employment, which we include as additional regressors in the second-step wage equations. We keep the five alternative models defined above, using the same exclusion restrictions, and compare them with OLS estimations for part-time and full-time workers, respectively.

As Table 6.5 shows, although the selectivity correction terms prove negative and significant for both part-time and full-time workers (except for model 3), there is not much difference in the schooling coefficients whether one corrects for sample selectivity or not. The corrected coefficients have the same order of magnitude as the OLS estimates, though the standard errors are relatively large.

Table 6.5 Sensitivity of the returns to education to selectivity bias correction by ordered probit (1995)

	Return	St. Err.	Lamda	St. Err.	Obs	Colin Test[a]	t-test[b]
	Part-time working women						
Ref. Model	0.119	0.008	-	-	378	-	-
Model 1	0.115	0.010	-0.116	0.010	378	0.42	-0.34
Model 2	0.106	0.009	-0.253	0.072	365	0.31	-1.08
Model 3	0.115	0.018	-0.485	0.694	312	0.95	-0.20
Model 4	0.113	0.009	-0.113	0.043	365	0.13	-0.53
Model 5	0.120	0.010	-0.105	0.052	301	0.15	0.09
	Full-time working women						
Ref. model	0.066	0.008	-	-	344	-	-
Model 1	0.058	0.009	-0.353	0.149	344	0.54	-0.73
Model 2	0.064	0.008	-0.113	0.055	340	0.05	-0.21
Model 3	0.070	0.016	0.281	0.709	250	0.94	0.22
Model 4	0.065	0.008	-0.162	0.045	340	0.15	-0.11
Model 5	0.063	0.009	-0.183	0.049	246	0.12	-0.22

Notes: [a] R^2 of the regression of the inverse Mill's ratio on the regressors of the main equation. [b] H_0: Return(model I) = Return(reference model).
Source: GSOEP 1995, own calculations.

Accounting for the Endogeneity of Schooling

Until now, we supposed that human capital variables are exogenous. Obviously, this may not be the case. Here, we examine the effect of allowing the schooling variable to be endogenous. This requires the availability of variables which affect educational attainment and, at the same time, have no direct effect on wages. Unfortunately, we do not dispose of indicators of learning ability, intelligence or motivation, which are undoubtedly essential factors affecting performance at school. However, the GSOEP does provide information about family background, which is likely to affect educational attainment. Here, we follow a two-stage instrumental variables (IV) procedure, where the schooling variable is first regressed on a set of explanatory variables and then instrumented by its predicted value in the second-stage wage equation.

Again, we test for alternative models using different instruments in order to inspect both the sensitivity of the return to education to the correction and to the choice of the instruments. We estimate the following models:
- Reference model: OLS estimation (i.e. schooling assumed exogenous).
- Model 1: the schooling variable is instrumented by the level of education of the mother and of the father, expressed in years of schooling.
- Model 2: the occupational position of the father when the individual was 15 is used as an instrument (not-employed/blue collar versus white collar, self-employed or civil servant).
- Model 3: both the educational degree and the occupation of the father are used.
- Model 4: dummies indicating whether the parents were predominantly employed during the individual's childhood, whether the person grew up with both parents, and whether the family lives in a rural or urban community serve as instruments.
- Model 5: all variables together.

Most of the variables chosen as instruments have a significant and strong effect on the level of educational attainment. The better educated the parents are, the higher the child's educational level tends to be. The educational level of the father seems to play a more important role than that of the mother, especially for women. The occupational position of the father also seems to be of crucial importance. Sons and daughters of civil servants have the best chances to become highly educated, followed by children of white-collar workers. For both genders, individuals whose parents are blue-collar workers or not employed have the worst educational prospects. Whether the person grew up with both parents or not seems to have a positive impact on males' educational attainment but no relevance for women. Altogether, these variables explain about 20% of the variance of schooling.

Table 6.6 Sensitivity of return to education: OLS versus IV with endogenous schooling (1995)

	Return	St. Err.	Men Obs.	R-Squared	t-test
Ref. model	0.076	0.003	1464	0.34	
Model 1	0.080	0.008	1026	0.10	0.38
Model 2	0.066	0.011	1138	0.04	-0.91
Model 3	0.077	0.008	1026	0.10	0.12
Model 4	0.148	0.046	868	0.02	1.54
Model 5	0.075	0.008	815	0.10	-0.17
			Women		
Ref. model	0.097	0.006	722	0.32	
Model 1	0.088	0.014	675	0.12	-0.60
Model 2	0.103	0.016	722	0.11	0.37
Model 3	0.093	0.013	675	0.14	-0.30
Model 4	0.112	0.060	562	0.08	0.26
Model 5	0.106	0.014	536	0.16	0.60

Source: GSOEP 1995, own calculations.

The results are somewhat sensitive to the choice of the instruments. However, the differences between the OLS and the instrumented returns to schooling are statistically insignificant in all models. This is sometimes due to the fact that the coefficients have the same order of magnitude (e.g. model 3 for men), or that the standard error is very large (e.g. model 4 for men or model 1 for women). Thus, no clear conclusion can be drawn from these estimations regarding the existence and even the direction of a supposed endogeneity bias. It is imperative to have better instruments at one's disposal if one intends to correct for the endogeneity of schooling.

CONCLUSION

Our empirical analysis has provided a broad assessment of the returns to education in West Germany over the past decades. In a first step, simple estimates of the returns to schooling based on standard Mincer equations showed that the returns to one additional year of schooling have remained remarkably stable since the mid-1980s. Women have significantly higher returns to schooling (about 10%) than men (about 8%). In a second step, we tested this specification in various ways, taking into account possible cohort effects, the choice of the sample, the definition of the human capital variables and different estimation methods.

Firstly, the analysis showed that the developments in the returns to education result from cohort and life-cycle effects in addition to time-effects. We found evidence that the returns to education are not constant over the life-cycle, especially for women. Evaluating the returns to schooling for different cohorts at the same age shows a significant decline in the returns to education across cohorts at age 30 to 39, and this decline is particularly pronounced for women since 1994. At the middle of the career (age 40-49), we found evidence for slightly increasing (men) or constant (women) returns across birth cohorts. Finally, at an older age (50 to 60), the returns to education are lower for younger cohorts, particularly for women beginning in 1994.

Secondly, we examined whether differences in the specification of human capital variables in the wage equation could alter the estimates of the returns to education. Departing from the quantitative measure of education, we analysed the returns to educational degrees. The higher the degree, the higher the wage premium. However, when we correct for the different length of studies associated with the various degrees, we find that the technical college degree yields the highest returns. Nevertheless, a downward trend is observable. The return to high school also declines at the end of the period. Our tests for alternative specifications of the other variables showed that the level of the return to schooling is quite robust. Only when we use age instead of labour market experience, the returns to education are somewhat lower. Female returns to education are somewhat sensitive to the inclusion of additional variables designed to capture previous non-employment or to control for the industrial and regional structure, but the difference from the simple specification is not really important.

Thirdly, the analysis reveals huge differences across subgroups of workers. The returns to education are much higher for part-time than for full-time working women. Taking full-time workers only, there are no significant gender differences: the return amounts to about 8% for both genders. Moreover, the differences between public and private sectors are also remarkable. In the public sector, female returns to schooling have increased somewhat over the period, whereas male returns have slightly decreased. As a result, female returns to schooling are significantly higher than male returns. Conversely, female returns decrease much stronger than male ones in the private sector. Thus, women have now lower returns to schooling than men. This trend is even more pronounced if one only considers full-time employees in the private sector.

Finally, we examined methodological issues and focused on the impact of possible selectivity and endogeneity biases on the level of the returns to education. The results were somewhat inconclusive and do not point to significant estimation biases. Whereas the selectivity correction term proved mostly significant, which points to the presence of selectivity bias, the returns to schooling were not affected by the selectivity correction in a significant way. The same results hold when we distinguish between selection into part-time and full-time employment. We adopted a similar approach to check for the endogeneity of schooling. Again, the results proved somewhat sensitive to the choice of the instruments to explain educational attainment and no conclusion can be drawn as to the size or even the direction of the supposed endogeneity bias.

On the whole, the simple estimates proved quite robust towards specification and estimation method. However, the overall assessment hides some more complex developments, that is huge differences between subgroups of workers or conjunction of time, life-cycle and cohort effects. Thus, studies on the returns to education in West Germany should be interpreted very carefully and one should be aware of the implications of the specific framework adopted.

REFERENCES

Bellmann, L., A. Reinberg and M. Tessaring (1994), 'Bildungsexpansion, Qualifikationsstruktur und Einkommensverteilung', in R. Lüdeke (ed), *Bildung, Bildungsfinanzierung und Einkommensverteilung II*, Berlin.

Boockmann, B. and V. Steiner (2000), *Cohort Effects and the Returns to Education in West Germany*, ZEW Discussion Paper 00-05, Mannheim.

Card, David (1999), 'The Causal Effect of Education on Earnings', in Orley Ashenfelter and David Card (eds), *Handbook of Labor Economics*, vol. 3, North-Holland, Amsterdam, 1801–63.

Clement W., M. Tessaring and C. Weißhuhn (1983), *Ausbildung und Einkommen in der Bundesrepublik Deutschland*, Beiträge zur Arbeitsmarkt- und Berufsforschung Nr. 80, Nürnberg

Dustman, C. and A. van Soest (1998), 'Public and Private Sector Wages of Male Workers in Germany', *European Economic Review*, **42**, 1417-1441.

Fitzenberger, B. and C. Kurz, (1996), *New Insights on Earnings across Skill Groups and Industries : an analysis based on the German Socio-Economic Panel*, University of Konstanz, CILE, Discussion Paper 1997-38.

Franz, W. and V. Steiner (2000), 'Wages in the East German Transition Process – Facts and Explanations', *German Economic Review*, **1** (2).

Gerlach, K. (1987), 'A note on Male-female Wage Differences in West Germany', *Journal of Human Resources,* **22**, 584-592.

Giles, C., A. Gosling, F. Laisney and T. Geib (1998), *The Distribution of Income and Wages in the UK and West Germany 1984-92*, The Institute for Fiscal Studies, London.

Heckman, J.J. (1979), 'Sample selection bias as a specification error', *Econometrica,* **47**, 153-161.

Heckman, J.J. and R. Robb (1985), 'Using longitudinal data to estimate age, period and cohort effects in earnings equations' in W.M. Mason and S.F. Fienberg (eds), *Cohort Analysis in Social Research – Beyond the Identification Problem*, New York.

Lauer, C. and V. Steiner (1999), 'Returns to Human Capital in Germany: Review of the Empirical Literature', in Asplund. R. and P. Pereira (eds), *Returns to Human Capital in Europe. A Literaure Review*, The Research Institute of the Finnish Economy, pp. 125-144.

Lauer, C. and V. Steiner (2000), *Returns to Education in West Germany – An Empirical Assessment*, ZEW Discussion Paper 00-04, Mannheim.

Lauer C. (2000), *The Gender Wage Gap in West Germany: How far do gender differences in human capital matter?*, ZEW Discussion Paper 00-07, Mannheim.

Prey, H. (1999), *Die Entwicklung der geschlechtsspezifischen Lohndifferenz in Westdeutschland 1984-96*, Forschungsinstitut für Arbeit und Arbeitsrecht and der Universität St. Gallen, Discussion Paper 57.

Puhani, P. (2000), 'The Heckman Correction for Sample Selection and its Critique', *Journal of Economic surveys,* **14**, 53-68.

Steiner, V. and K. Wagner, (1998), 'Has Earnings Inequality in Germany Changed in the 1980s', *Zeitschrift für Wirtschaftsund Sozial wissenschaften*, **118** (1), 29-54.

Weißhuhn, C. and W. Clement (1983), *Ausbildung und Einkommen in der Bundesrepublik Deutschland*, Beiträge zur Arbeitsmarkt- und Berufsforschung 80, Nürnberg.

7.   Greece

**Panos Tsakloglou
and
Ioannis Cholezas**

INTRODUCTION

The first attempts to estimate private returns to education in Greece go back to the 1960s (Leibenstein, 1967).   However, the subject has not been examined in as much a depth in Greece as in other European countries, in part due to data limitations. The existing studies which cover the period from the late 1950s to the early 1990s, rely on a variety of data sources which are not always representative of the entire labour force and/or consistent with each other.   Most of these use both standard Mincerian and cost-benefit techniques.[1]

The aim of the present study is to estimate private returns to education in Greece using a consistent source of data from three Household Budget Surveys (1974, 1987/1988 and 1993/1994). These are the only data sets available, which cover in a consistent way the entire labour force over the last twenty-five years and contain income and extensive labour market participation information.[2]

The structure of the chapter is the following. Section two presents the data used, section three reports the main estimates of earnings functions, while section four performs a number of sensitivity tests. Section five provides the conclusions.

DATA

The three Household Budget Surveys (HBSs) used in the paper were carried out by the National Statistical Service of Greece.[3] They cover the entire non-institutional population of the country and their sampling fractions are 3% for the 1974 HBS and 2% for the other two HBSs.   They contain detailed information about consumption expenditures, incomes and socio-economic characteristics of the households and their members. The income component reported in the surveys and used in the paper is 'earnings net of income taxes and social insurance contributions' which is well suited for the purposes of the paper. It includes wages, salaries, overtime payments, bonuses, holiday payments, and related benefits received from the main and secondary employer, normalized on a monthly basis.

Further, the surveys report the number of hours normally worked by each worker per week. Division of monthly income adjusted on a weekly basis by this figure yields "net hourly earnings" which is used as the dependent variable in our analysis. Due to the fact that during the periods of the surveys inflation was high in Greece, all earnings figures were expressed in mid-year prices (1974, 1988 and 1994, respectively).

Information on education is provided in grouped form in the HBSs – "highest level of education completed" – while there is no information on actual working experience and, thus, in line with many studies we calculate potential experience. The categorical variable "education" reported in the HBS is converted into a continuous one assuming that primary education lasts six years, lower secondary, upper secondary and technical tertiary education three years each and university education four years.

The samples consist of employees outside the agricultural sector aged 14–64. Thus, self-employed, employers, unpaid family members and apprentices are excluded. Males working less than 35 hours per week were also excluded from the analysis on the grounds that their less than full employment was probably involuntary. Further, two more small groups were excluded from the analysis. Firstly, persons who declared as "normal" working time more than 84 hours per week and, secondly, persons with incomes from self-employment as well as paid employment, since it is not possible to separate the proportion of their working time devoted to paid employment. Estimates of returns to education are reported separately for males and females, since it is believed that the two groups of workers follow different age-earnings paths – an assumption supported empirically by the data. The main characteristics of the three samples are reported in Table 7.1. In all surveys male workers enjoy higher average earnings than female workers. Between 1974 and 1988, average hourly earnings rose considerably for both males and females. In the case of the latter, the rise is particularly steep, 57.6%, and should be partly attributed to the enactment of "equal pay" legislation. Unlike the first sub-period, hourly earnings declined marginally during the second sub-period.. Throughout the period under examination the average education level of both male and female workers was rising and, in fact, in all surveys the average years of education were higher for female rather than male employees. The latter may be partly due to the fact that in all surveys the average female worker is younger than her male counterpart, as implied by the fact that, on average, females have lower potential experience than males or, perhaps, to selectivity bias, an issue investigated below.[4]

A more detailed picture of the evolution of the educational composition of the employees is provided in Table 7.2. In this table, each sample is subdivided into five groups according to the highest level of education completed. For both males and, particularly, females, the proportion of those with primary education or less declined spectacularly between 1974 and 1994, while the shares of tertiary and upper secondary education graduates rose constantly.

Before proceeding to the estimation of earnings functions, it is worth devoting a few words to the developments of the Greek economy during the period under examination, with emphasis on labour market developments. Before the first oil crisis, Greece was one of the fastest growing economies in the world. Incomes policies were used extensively, trade unions were under the firm control of the government, unemployment was low and there was a very high migration from the rural areas, both internal to the cities of Athens and Salonica and international to Western Europe (particularly Germany) and Australia. After the first oil crisis, which almost coincided with the collapse of a seven-year military dictatorship, the economy entered a period of relatively slow growth. Trade unions enjoyed new freedoms, there was a rise in union membership and militancy and the share of wages in Gross Domestic Product rose fast. International migration was halted and a considerable number of immigrants returned to Greece, especially after the second oil crisis and the recession that hit several West European countries.

Table 7.1 Basic descriptive statistics

		1974	1988	1994
Sample size	Males	2267	1860	2096
	Females	982	1191	1504
Mean net hourly earnings	Males	995.4	1203.8	1194.8
		(618.1)	(615.3)	(657.3)
	Females	706.4	1113.3	1068.4
		(617.4)	(787.2)	(722.4)
Average years of education	Males	7.83	9.96	10.15
		(4.27)	(4.30)	(4.07)
	Females	8.18	10.71	11.21
		(4.98)	(4.71)	(4.11)
Average years of potential experience	Males	23.19	21.54	21.75
		(12.80)	(12.43)	(11.97)
	Females	17.06	18.02	18.13
		(13.33)	(12.04)	(11.38)

Note: Standard deviations in parentheses

Table 7.2 Distribution of employees per level of education (%)

		1974	1988	1994
Primary not completed	All	12.7	4.2	4.3
	Males	11.0	3.5	4.6
	Females	16.7	5.3	3.9
Primary	All	44.9	31.5	23.1
	Males	48.8	34.1	25.8
	Females	35.9	27.3	19.5
Lower secondary	All	8.2	10.5	12.9
	Males	9.6	13.1	15.6
	Females	4.9	6.3	9.2
Upper secondary	All	24.8	34.7	35.3
	Males	22.1	32.8	34.3
	Females	31.0	37.7	36.6
Tertiary	All	9.4	19.2	24.4
	Males	8.5	16.5	19.8
	Females	11.5	23.4	30.8

Regarding education, in 1976 compulsory education was increased from six to nine years and, further, the first institutes of technical tertiary education were established. The 1980s were marked by Greece's accession to the, then, European Community (EC) and the first ever socialist governments in Greece's history. During the early years of the socialists' administration a number of redistributive measures were introduced – among them, generous increases in the minimum wage, wage indexation policies, etc – and, further, public sector employment expanded rapidly (a trend that had already started in the 1970s). Effectively, in the 1980s and the early 1990s the economy stagnated and unemployment rose almost continuously – it now stands at levels higher than the EU average. The macroeconomic history of this period is characterized by stop-and-go policies and, in the framework of these policies, incomes policies featured prominently.[5]

During the 1990s the economic climate changed drastically. Markets were liberalized, incomes policies were abandoned and, after the mid-1990s, the Greek economy started growing at satisfactory rates after a very long period. The other important development of the 1990s was the massive influx of legal and, particularly, illegal immigrants (mostly from Eastern European countries) in the Greek labour market. It has been estimated that in the late 1990s they were accounting for over 10% of the Greek labour force.

Even though detailed data do not exist, it is believed that the wages received by these immigrants are considerably lower than those received by the indigenous workers (Lianos *et al.,* 1996; Markova and Sarris, 1997). Finally, apart from the improvement in the average educational qualifications of the labour force that was mentioned earlier, another characteristic of the labour market during the period under examination is the continuous increase in female labour force participation, although the corresponding participation rate is still much lower than that encountered in most EU member states.

BASIC EMPIRICAL RESULTS

We start by estimating the standard Mincer (1974) equation based on net hourly earning, years of schooling, potential experience and a dummy variable for females working less than full time (less than 35 hours per week). The results are reported in Table 7.3. The coefficients of interest have the expected signs and are statistically significant. In all surveys returns to education are considerably higher for females than for males; 7.6% against 5.7% in 1974, 6.5% against 5.0% in 1988 and 8.6% against 6.3% in 1994. The relationship between log earnings and potential experience is bell-shaped for both sexes. Nevertheless, few workers are located in the descending leg of the curve. For example, in 1994 the turning point for males was 38.2 years and for females 37.3 years of potential experience. Taking into account that in the mid-1990s the median retirement age in Greece was around 57 years, it is not surprising to find that in the 1994 HBS only 10.6% of the males and 6.9% of the females are found in the descending leg of this curve.[6] Finally, the fact that the value of the constant term is higher for males, indicating that an individual with no schooling and potential experience need only be male in order to earn more, may be considered an indication of discrimination against females in the labour market.

Private returns to education declined between 1974 and 1988 and, then, rose again in 1994. The finding that returns to education declined between the 1970s and the 1980s is in line with the findings of a number of other studies (Kioulafas *et al.*, 1991; Lambropoulos, 1992; Lambropoulos and Psacharopoulos, 1992) which rely on different data sources. The interpretation offered in these studies is that the rapid expansion of the education system resulted in an increased supply of better educated workers, while at the same time slow economic growth contributed to a negligible rise in demand for such workers, thus producing a decline in returns to education.

Although these factors undoubtedly played an important role in the decline of private returns to education, this interpretation neglects a number of institutional factors. As noted earlier, throughout the 1980s incomes policies played an important role in Greece. Between 1981 and 1982 real hourly earning rose by 10.4% while productivity and GDP per capita were declining (IMF,1987, p.104).[7] At the same time, wage indexation policies were introduced. However, indexation was full only up to a particular wage level and less than complete above it. These developments coupled with high inflation rates lead to a very compressed wage structure. In the two years prior to the 1988 HBS severe austerity measures were introduced which reversed the earlier gains of wage and salary earners, but left the wage structure largely unchanged. As a consequence of this compressed wage structure, returns to education appear to decline substantially in the 1980s. These policies were reversed in the 1990s and, even though the education system continued to expand and economic growth continued to be anaemic, returns to education rose substantially between the late 1980s and the early 1990s.

Table 7.3 Private returns to education in Greece

		1974	1988	1994
Constant	Males	2.294	4.939	5.363
		(0.045)	(0.055)	(0.072)
	Females	2.059	4.769	5.066
		(0.053)	(0.059)	(0.095)
Years of schooling	Males	0.057	0.050	0.063
		(0.002)	(0.003)	(0.003)
	Females	0.076	0.065	0.086
		(0.004)	(0.004)	(0.006)
Potential experience	Males	0.068	0.053	0.068
		(0.003)	(0.003)	(0.005)
	Females	0.041	0.036	0.056
		(0.004)	(0.003)	(0.006)
Potential Experience^2/100	Males	-0.105	-0.073	-0.089
		(0.006)	(0.005)	(0.009)
	Females	-0.063	-0.046	-0.075
		(0.008)	(0.008)	(0.012)
Part time	Females	0.522	0.426	0.229
		(0.008)	(0.032)	(0.047)
Adjusted R^2	Males	0.358	0.310	0.274
	Females	0.433	0.437	0.248

Note: Standard Errors in parentheses.

The standard Mincer equation implies that each additional year of schooling has the same impact on the rate of return irrespective of the level or type of education. This assumption has been questioned in several empirical studies. In order to estimate rates of return to each separate level of education we use a model with dummy variables that take the value of (1), when a level is completed and (0) otherwise. Thus, the so-called extended Mincer equation takes the form:

$$lnW = a + \Sigma b_i L_i + cEXPER + dEXPER^2 + fPARTTIME + u$$

where the Ls are dummies for different levels of education: primary education not completed (control group), primary, lower secondary, upper secondary (general), upper secondary (technical), some years of tertiary, technical tertiary and university tertiary education.

Table 7.4 Private returns to education in Greece – educational levels

		1974	1988	1994
Constant	Males	2.496	5.114	5.577
		(0.051)	(0.089)	(0.081)
	Females	2.297	5.017	5.604
		(0.069)	(0.084)	(0.131)
Primary	Males	0.118	0.076	0.125
		(0.036)	(0.084)	(0.062)
	Females	0.180	0.107	-0.169
		(0.063)	(0.073)	(0.121)
Lower secondary	Males	0.232	0.275	0.309
		(0.045)	(0.089)	(0.069)
	Females	0.352	0.265	0.137
		(0.08i)	(0.093)	(0.137)
Upper secondary	Males	0.495	0.376	0.515
		(0.040)	(0.087)	(0.067)
	Females	0.674	0.495	0.412
		(0.066)	(0.082)	(0.132)
Upper secondary (technical)	Males	-	-	0.496
				(0.075)
	Females	-	-	0.493
				(0.148)
Some tertiary, no degree	Males	0.629	0.536	-
		(0.079)	(0.093)	
	Females	0.535	0.650	-
		(0.126)	(0.104)	
Tertiary technical	Males	-	-	0.706
				(0.074)
	Females	-	-	0.691
				(0.138)
Tertiary	Males	0.867	0.624	0.863
		(0.045)	(0.088)	(0.069)
	Females	1.151	0.816	0.827
		(0.070)	(0.081)	(0.137)
Potential experience	Males	0.068	0.057	0.071
		(0.003)	(0.003)	(0.005)
	Females	0.042	0.041	0.067
		(0.004)	(0.003)	(0.006)
Potential experience^2/100	Males	-1.108	-0.082	-0.097
		(0.006)	(0.006)	(0.009)
	Females	-0.073	-0.061	-0.107
		(0.008)	(0.008)	(0.013)
Part time	Females	0.476	0.406	0.194
		(0.045)	(0.034)	(0.049)

The corresponding results are reported in Table 7.4 and the implied average and marginal annual rates of return in Table 7.5. The clear conclusion that can be drawn from these estimates is that private returns to education in Greece are not a linear function of years/levels of education, i.e. the return to a year of schooling is not constant across the range of schooling years. This conclusion holds for all survey years, irrespective of the worker's sex. Unlike standard investment models, which assume that the rate of return is declining as the level of investment rises, the estimates reported in these tables imply that marginal private returns to schooling in Greece are increasing.

Table 7.5 Average and marginal returns per educational level (%)

		Primary	Lower secondary	Upper secondary	Tertiary
Average					
1974	Males	2.0	2.6	4.1	5.4
	Females	3.0	3.9	5.6	7.2
1988	Males	1.3	3.1	3.1	3.9
	Females	1.8	2.9	4.1	5.1
1994	Males	2.1	3.4	4.3	5.4
	Females	-	-	3.4	5.2
Marginal					
1974	Males	2.0	3.8	8.8	9.3
	Females	3.0	5.8	10.7	11.9
1988	Males	1.3	6.6	3.4	6.2
	Females	1.8	5.3	7.7	8.0
1994	Males	2.1	6.1	6.9	8.7
	Females	-	-	9.2	10.4

The rates of return to schooling reported in Table 7.5 are relatively high in comparison with estimates for other countries at a level of economic development similar with that of Greece, reported in Psacharopoulos (1985, 1994). Apart from this, most of the results of Table 7.3 are also reproduced in Table 7.4. The earning – potential experience profiles are bell-shaped for both sexes, the rates of return for most education levels were lower in 1988 than in the other two surveys and, in general, the results show that in the earlier surveys, for most levels of education, both average and marginal rates of return were higher for females than for males, but in the most recent survey the evidence is mixed.

Further, in the case of males returns to general education are higher than returns to technical education at comparable levels of the education system (upper secondary, tertiary), whereas in the case of females, this holds only for tertiary education.

SENSITIVITY TESTS

The estimates of returns to education derived from the basic Mincer equation reported in Table 7.3 were subjected to a number of alternative sensitivity tests. Four of these tests are reported in Tables 7.6 to 7.8, using the data of the 1994 HBS.[8]

Table 7.6 Selectivity Bias

	Probit	Mincerian
Constant	-1.433	4.795
	(0.096)	(0.136)
Years of schooling	0.096	0.099
	(0.006)	(0.007)
Potential Experience	0.053	0.061
	(0.006)	(0.005)
Potential Exp. sq./100	-0.135	-0.091
	(0.012)	(0.011)
Part time	-	0.002
		(0.0004)
Marital status	-0.441	-
	(0.052)	
No. of children below 6	-0.066	-
	(0.044)	
No. of children 6-13	-0.093	-
	(0.030)	
λ	-	0.092
		(0.060)

It is frequently argued that, in the case of females, returns to education derived from standard Mincerian models may be biased – probably overestimated – because the females that participate in the labour force are not representative of all females. In order to correct for such a potential selectivity bias, we estimated a two-step model along the lines proposed by Heckman (1979). In the first step, a probit model of the labour force participation probability of a female is estimated and, in the second step, the derived inverse Mills ratio is included in the earnings function as an additional explanatory variable in order to correct for the potential underlying bias caused by the non-random nature of the female participation. The corresponding estimates are reported in Table 7.6.

In addition to earnings and potential experience, marital status and number of children aged below 6 and aged 6 to13 are included in the probit model for

138

Education and Earnings in Europe

the purposes of identification. All the variables have the expected signs. The three additional variables appear to affect negatively the participation probability and are statistically significant, apart from the number of children below 6. However, when the inverse Mills ratio, denoted by λ, is included in the earnings function it turns out to be statistically not significant. Therefore, it can be argued that the estimates reported in Table 7.3 do not suffer from selectivity bias.[9]

It is often argued that age may be a more important determinant of earnings than potential experience, since it may be better able to capture elements of a worker's personality, such as maturity, that are valued by the employers. Moreover, in many award systems seniority plays a very important role. This is likely to be particularly true in the public sector and some large private sector corporations. For this reason in Table 7.7 the standard Mincer model is re-estimated using age instead of potential experience.

Table 7.7 Age instead of potential experience

	Males	Females
Constant	3.848	3.485
	(0.193)	(0.249)
Years of schooling	0.040	0.064
	(0.003)	(0.005)
Age	0.120	0.119
	(0.010)	(0.013)
$Age^2/100$	-0.122	-0.128
	(0.012)	(0.012)
Part time	-	0.208
		(0.047)
Adjusted R^2	0.280	0.248

The results differ substantially from the corresponding results reported in Table 7.3. The rates of return to schooling reported in Table 7.7 are lower by over two percentage points in comparison with those reported in Table 7.3 (declines, in relative terms, by 36.5% for males and 25.6% for females). As a result, even though in absolute terms the gap in the rates of return to education between males and females remains constant across models, in relative terms it rises considerably when we move from Table 7.3 to Table 7.7. Further, the estimates of Table 7.7 suggest that the peak of the age-earnings profile for male workers is reached at the age of 49.2, whereas for female workers it arrives earlier, at the age of 46.5.[10]

It is also argued that it may not be appropriate to mix public and private sector workers when estimating earnings functions, since the reward norms that are prevalent in the public sector may be different than those of the private sector. In the two most recent HBSs there is information on the worker's sector of employment. It should be noted, though, that in the HBS definition "public sector" includes, apart from government services, firms where the government held a controlling stake either directly or indirectly (utilities, banks and so on).

As noted earlier, public sector employment rose rapidly in the 1980s and, hence, it is not surprising to find that in 1994 38% of the workers in the sample were public sector employees. Estimates of returns to schooling for males and females disaggregated by sector of employment are reported in Table 7.8. A number of interesting points can be made with respect to these estimates. In both sectors returns to education are higher for females than for males. However, in the case of males these returns are higher in the private sector, whereas in the case of females they are higher in the public sector.

It should be noted, also, that for both sexes and for either sector these returns are lower than those reported in Table 7.3, thus calling into question whether it is appropriate to merge the two sectors when estimating returns to education. In addition, as noted earlier, the earnings/potential experience profiles are very different in the two sectors, with the private sector employees exhibiting far steeper profiles (particularly in the case of male employees).[11]

Table 7.8 Sector of employment

	Public		Private		Self-employed	
	Males	Female	Males	Female	Males	Female
Constant	5.861	5.578	5.362	5.327	6.030	5.933
	(0.128)	(0.150)	(0.929)	(0.132)	(0.130)	(0.261)
Years of	0.053	0.072	0.057	0.063	0.034	0.050
schooling	(0.005)	(0.010)	(0.005)	(0.009)	(0.006)	(0.014)
Experience	0.047	0.042	0.068	0.047	0.031	0.011
	(0.008)	(0.010)	(0.061)	(0.069)	(0.007)	(0.012)
Experience^2	-0.056	-0.061	-0.089	-0.064	-0.041	-0.021
/100	(0.014)	(0.021)	(0.011)	(0.014)	(0.012)	(0.022)
Part-time	-	0.326	-	0.017	-	0.424
		(0.052)		(0.078)		(0.136)
R^2 adj.	0.222	0.327	0.219	0.102		0.115

Normally, returns to education are assumed to be the outcome of increased productivity. The objection of a number of scholars to this argument is that increased productivity may not really be the result of increased education, but the result of other, perhaps unobserved factors, like higher ability. Therefore, education is only acting as a "screening device". Certainly, if valid, this hypothesis has serious implications for the estimation of social returns to education, but its implications for the estimated private returns to education are not clear.

In order to investigate the signalling value of education we estimate the standard Mincer equation for self-employed persons, who face no signalling effects. If their returns to education are lower than those of employees, then the latter are likely to receive higher returns due to the fact that their employer expects higher productivity based on their educational attainment; hence their education is, indeed, used as a signalling device.

The corresponding estimates are reported in Table 7.8 and they are statistically significantly lower than the relevant estimates of Table 7.3 for both males and females. Therefore, it can be concluded that education is used as a "screening device" in the Greek labour market and higher wages to those with higher educational qualifications may not be the result of higher productivity. This result is different than the corresponding results of other studies of the Greek labour market which test the "screening hypothesis" using alternative methodologies, such as Lambropoulos (1992) and Magoula and Psacharopoulos (1997).

For a number of reasons, the results in Table 7.8 should be interpreted with caution. On the one hand, the concept of income from self-employment used in the HBSs is "gross income". Therefore, taking into account that the Greek income taxation is progressive, the private rates of return to education derived from income data net of taxes for the self-employed would, probably, have been even lower than those reported in Table 7.8; hence the screening "scenario" appears to be even stronger.

However this claim may not be as strong as it looks at first sight. On the other hand, since the great majority of the self-employed work in unincorporated firms, it is likely that their reported incomes incorporate returns to both labour and capital; hence, a priori, we would anticipate them to have lower returns to education than persons in paid employment. Further, we attempted to restrict our comparison of returns to education of the self-employed to returns to education of private sector workers only, since it is in the private sector that wages are more likely to be more closely related to productivity, a line of argument also followed in Magoula and Psacharopoulos (1997). In this case the results were slightly different, since the "screening hypothesis" is not accepted in the sample of females but it is still not rejected in the sample of males.[12]

Finally, it should be noted that the estimates of returns to education reported so far do not take into account the impact of unemployment. As noted earlier, unemployment in Greece was rising rapidly during the period under examination and, further, it was particularly concentrated on women, younger persons and secondary education graduates. Therefore, leaving our results unadjusted for the probability of unemployment may bias a number of the study's conclusions (differential returns to males and females, trends, etc.). A rough attempt to provide such "corrected" rates of return to different levels of education for males and females is presented in Table 7.9. In this table, the estimates derived from Table 7.4 for each survey and level of education are multiplied by the employment probability corresponding to the relevant education level for male and female workers separately.[13]

Table 7.9 Average and marginal returns per educational level adjusted for unemployment (%)

		Primary	Lower secondary	Upper secondary	Tertiary
Average					
1974	Males	1.9	2.5	4.0	5.3
	Females	3.0	3.9	5.3	6.7
1988	Males	1.2	2.9	2.9	3.7
	Females	1.7	2.6	3.4	4.6
1994	Males	2.0	3.1	3.9	5.2
	Females	-	-	2.9	4.8
1974	Males	1.9	3.7	8.6	8.9
	Females	3.0	5.7	9.8	10.7
1988	Males	1.2	6.2	2.9	6.3
	Females	1.7	4.3	5.7	8.2
1994	Males	2.0	5.4	6.3	9.1
	Females	-	-	7.5	10.6

The estimates of Table 7.9 should be compared with those of Table 7.5. The differences between the estimates of the two tables are not very large. Naturally, the average rates of return reported in Table 7.9 are lower than those in Table 7.5, especially in the most recent surveys, when unemployment was higher. Rates of return to schooling were higher for females in the two earlier surveys, but the opposite is true in the 1994 HBS. The most interesting results, though, concern the marginal rates of return in the most recent survey. Because unemployment was particularly high among upper secondary education graduates – especially females – the adjusted marginal rates of return to tertiary education are higher than those reported in Table 7.5, thus, suggesting that from a private (or individuals) point of view tertiary education is an even more profitable form of investment than implied before.[14]

CONCLUSION

The aim of this chapter paper was to investigate several aspects of private returns to education in Greece using the data of three HBSs (1974, 1988 and 1994). Using standard Mincerian earnings functions it was shown that returns to schooling are higher for females than for males, that for both sexes they declined between 1974 and 1988 and then rose in 1994, when they stood at 6.3% for males and 8.6% for females. When returns to particular levels of education were examined, it was found that returns to education are increasing as the level of education rises.

A number of alternative sensitivity tests were also performed. The hypothesis of selectivity bias for the female members of the sample was not accepted, whereas when potential experience was replaced by age as an explanatory variable, the estimated returns declined by around two percentage points for both sexes. Returns to education were not found to be significantly different between public and private sector employees, but the corresponding age-earnings profiles were substantially different across sectors. Further, education was found to act as a screening device in the Greek labour market, at least in the case of male employees.

Finally, average and marginal rates of return adjusted for the probability of unemployment per level of education were not found to be considerably different than those estimated in the extended Mincer model although, in general, they were lower than the latter.

NOTES

1. Leibenstein (1967), Kanellopoulos (1982, 1985, 1986, 1997), Psacharopoulos (1982), Kioulafas *et al.* (1991), Lambropoulos (1992), Lambropoulos and Psacharopoulos (1992), Patrinos (1992, 1995), Patrinos and Lambropoulos (1993), Magoula and Psacharopoulos (1997); for a survey see Choleza and Tsakloglou (1999).
2. Another Household Budget Survey carried out in 1981/82 did not collect information for hours worked and, therefore, cannot be utilised for the purposes of the chapter.
3. Since the second and the third of these surveys were carried out mostly in 1988 and 1994, we will refer to them as the 1988 and the 1994 HBS, respectively.
4. Some estimates of Table 7.1 may seem paradoxical at first sight – especially the rather high average number of years of education and the fact that female workers appear to be better educated than male workers. The former is probably a consequence of the fact that Greece has the highest rate of self-employment in the EU and a very considerable proportion of the self-employed are farmers whose educational qualifications are substantially lower than those of the urban workers. The latter should be attributed to the fact that many of the better-educated males are self-employed in the non-agricultural sector of the economy.
5. For a survey of macroeconomic developments in Greece during the post-war period, see Alogoskoufis (1995).
6. Further disaggregation of the sample shows that it is especially the earnings-potential experience of private sector male workers that exhibits a steep bell-shaped pattern.

7. In 1982 marginal rates of return for secondary and tertiary education were the lowest recorded in any of the four HBSs available. These low rates of return should be attributed to the above policies.
8. Furthermore, the standard Mincer equation was also re-estimated (a) including in the concept of earnings incomes-in-kind provided by the employers, in order to account for the fact that a few employees received non-pecuniary as well as pecuniary remuneration (such as defined medical benefits or tranportation cost subsidies), (b) assuming that potential experience for males is equal to age-6-schooling-2, in order to account for the fact that all Greek males spend two years in the military under compulsory National Service, (c) assuming that university education lasts for 5 years, since studies in subjects such as engineering last for five years, in medicine for six years and a number of university graduates hold post-graduate degrees, and (d) interacting schooling with regional and locational dummies to allow the return to schooling to differ across these covariates. Under these specifications, returns to education appeared marginally lower: by 0.1% under (a), by 0.2% (males only) under (b), by 0.5% under (c) and by 0.1% under (d). Further, in (d) the great majority of the dummy variables turned out to be statistically not significant. Results available from the authors on request.
9. Similar results were also derived when the extended Mincer model was used. Further, note that the rate of return to schooling as estimated in Table 7.6 is higher, rather than lower, than that reported in the last column of Table 7.3.
10. In order to select between the two models, we employed a Davidson-McKinnon (1981) J-test for testing non-nested hypotheses. The test turned out to be inconclusive in the case of males but in the sample of female workers it rejected the model of Table 7.3 (with potential experience) in favour of the model of Table 7.7 (with age). This rejection has obvious implications for some of the results reported in the study.
11. It can be noted also that the dummy variable for female part-time employment is statistically significant for public sector workers but not for private sector workers. This may be due to a number of arrangements applicable to particular groups of female public sector workers but not to their private sector counterparts – for example, shorter working hours without loss of pay for mothers of young children. However, it may also raise some questions about the validity of the replies of some public sector workers (for example, teachers) to the question of "normal working hours" of the HBS.
12. The estimates reported in Table 7.8 are derived when the sample includes both self-employed and employers outside the agricultural sector. Even stronger results were obtained when the sample was restricted to the self-employed only. Further, note that even though all variables are statistically significant, they explain a very low proportion of the dependent variable's variance.
13. Employment probability rates are calculated from the samples of the HBSs and are slightly different than those reported regularly by the National Statistical Service of Greece.
14. The method adopted here rests on the assumption that there are no unemployment benefits. Taking into account that unemployment benefits in Greece are very low in value, almost flat and, normally, last for six months only (12 months in exceptional circumstances), this assumption is not particularly unrealistic. For example, in the 1994 HBS only 14% of the unemployed reported that they were receiving unemployment benefits.

REFERENCES

Alogoskoufis, G. (1995) 'The two faces of Janus: Institutions, regimes and macroeconomic policy in Greece', *Economic Policy*, 20,149–192.
Cholezas, I. and Tsakloglou, P. (1999) 'Private returns to education in Greece: A review of the empirical literature', in R. Asplund and P.

Telhado-Pereira (eds), *Returns to human capital in Europe: A literature review*, ETLA, Helsinki, 147–162.

Davidson, R. and McKinnon, J. (1981) 'Several tests for model specification in the presence of alternative hypotheses', *Econometrica*, 49, 781–793.

Heckman, J. (1979) 'Sample selection bias as a specification error', *Econometrica*, 47, 153–162.

IMF (1987), *International Financial Statistics Yearbook*, New York.

Kanellopoulos, C.N. (1982) 'Male-female pay differentials in Greece', *Greek Economic Review*, 4, 222–241.

Kanellopoulos, C.N. (1985) 'Individual pay differentials in Greece', *Spoudai*, **35**, 109–125.

Kanellopoulos, C.N. (1986) 'Incomes and poverty in Greece: Determining factors', Center of Planning and Economic Research Scientific Studies, 22, Athens (in Greek).

Kanellopoulos, C.N. (1997) 'Public-private wage differentials in Greece', *Applied Economics*, 29, 1023–1032.

Kioulafas, K., Donatos, G. and Michailidis, G. (1991) 'Public and private sector wage differentials in Greece', *International Journal of Manpower*, 12, 9–14.

Lambropoulos, H. (1992) 'Further evidence on the weak and strong versions of the screening hypothesis in Greece', *Economics of Education Review*, 11, 61–65.

Lambropoulos, H. and Psacharopoulos, G. (1992) 'Educational expansion and earnings differentials in Greece', *Comparative Education Review*, 36, 52–70.

Leibenstein, H. (1967) 'Rates of Return to Education in Greece', Economic Development Report, 94, Harvard University.

Lianos, T., Sarris, A.H. and Katseli, L.T. (1996) 'Illegal immigration and local labour markets: The case of Northern Greece', *International Migration*, 34, 449–484.

Magoula, T. and Psacharopoulos, G. (1997) 'Schooling and monetary rewards in Greece: Contributions to a debate', Athens University of Economics and Business, Department of Economics Discussion Paper No. 90 (forthcoming in *Applied Economics*).

Markova, E. and Sarris, A.H. (1997) 'The performance of the Bulgarian illegal immigrants in the Greek labour market', *Southern European Society and Politics*, 2, 57–77.

Mincer, J. (1974) *Schooling, experience and earnings*, Columbia University Press, New York.

Patrinos, H.A. (1992) 'Higher education finance and economic inequality in Greece', *Comparative Education Review*, 36, 298–308.

Patrinos, H.A. (1995) 'Socioeconomic background, schooling, experience, ability and monetary rewards in Greece', *Economics of Education Review*, 14, 85–91.

Patrinos, H.A. and Lambropoulos, H. (1993) 'Gender discrimination in the Greek labour market', *Education Economics*, 1, 153–164.

Psacharopoulos, G. (1982) 'Earnings and Education in Greece, 1960–1977', *European Economic Review*, 17, 333–347.

Psacharopoulos, G. (1985) 'Returns to education: A further international update and implications', *Journal of Human Resources*, 20, 583–597.

Psacharopoulos, G. (1994) 'Returns to investment in education: A global update', *World Development*, **22**, 1325-1343.update', *World Development*, 22, 1325–1343.

8. Ireland

Kevin J. Denny
and
Colm P. Harmon

INTRODUCTION

This chapter presents new estimates of the return to schooling for Ireland. Our results, broadly in line with earlier estimates, are reasonably robust to specification changes. The returns to education are in the region of 8% to 10% per year of schooling for men and 10% to 14% for women. However, when one controls for sample selection bias into employment it is found that this has the effect of lowering the estimated return for for women. We also control for ability in the wage equation and find some effect from ability but the dominant factor remains formal schooling.

THE EDUCATION SYSTEM IN IRELAND

The present education system has been largely shaped by policy changes from the late 1960s. In the 1966 the government announced a scheme whereby second level schools, which had relied to on individual fees, could receive a grant per pupil in return for eliminating fees. The majority of schools opted into the system although a significant number of schools stayed outside the new regime. Unlike the United Kingdom for example, these private schools still receive financial support from the state; the salaries of teachers are paid by the state irrespective of whether it is a private or state school. Other developments around this time include the raising of the minimum school leaving age from 14 to 15 in 1972. Also, a set of third level institutions called Technical Colleges in Dublin and Regional Technical Colleges elsewhere were established. These provide education at a sub-degree (diploma) level. However they do compete with universities in some areas (notably engineering and architecture). Means tested grants and scholarships were also put in place for third level education, which made tertiary education more accessible to people from low income households. These grants are implemented by local authorities but they are controlled by central government. In January 1996 fees for undergraduate third level education were abolished[1] and in 1998 the minimum school leaving age was increased to 16.

The educational system is split into primary, secondary and tertiary levels. Primary school typically begins at 5 even though the State does not compel children to start their formal education until the age of 6[2]. Thus, the first two years of primary school include what is regarded as pre-schooling in other countries. There is no state exam at the end of the primary cycle and no formal certification is required.

Post-primary education consists of secondary, vocational and community and comprehensive schools. Secondary schools cater for 61% of the age cohort with 26% and 13% of the cohort attending vocational and community schools respectively. Students tend to start post-primary education at 12 or 13 years. Students sit the Junior Certificate[3] after three years of secondary education. Those who remain study for a further two years and sit a set of exams called the Leaving Certificate. Some students elect to spend a 'transition year' after sitting their Junior Certificate and before starting the Leaving Certificate cycle. This year emphasizes less academic study and includes some job related experience. Both sets of exams are provided by the state and there is a common state-wide curriculum. They are broad based with a student typically taking about eight subjects in the Junior Certificate and about seven in the Leaving. Entry into third level courses depends on performance in the Leaving Certificate examinations. Partly in response to criticism that the Leaving Certificate was excessively "academic" in orientation and perhaps suited to those not intending to pursue further education a Leaving Certificate Applied Program (LCAP) was introduced in 1992. This provide a more vocational aspect to an otherwise very academic schooling system.

Following the refom to school fees introduced in 1967, participation rates in secondary schools increased dramatically with the numbers sitting the Junior Certificate exam close to 100% in the 1990s, and those taking the Leaving Certificate exam reaching 90%. This was largely led by a striking increase in the early 1970s where the numbers attending secondary school have doubled.

The third level sector encompasses the universities, the technical colleges, teacher training colleges and private colleges. There are about 100,000 students attending third level education, with the universities accounting for about 54 % and technical colleges accounting for 36 %. Along with the publicly funded colleges, there are a growing number of private colleges, mainly involved with the provision of business and professional training. The higher education system has seen rapid expansion in the last two decades, for example there was 18,500 students attending third level in 1965 compared to more than 100,000 at present. The OECD (1996) show that the growth in participation in third level education from the mid 1980s has been higher in Ireland than most European countries[4]. The introduction of a means-tested third level grant system, the general restructuring already outlined and the high retention rates at second level has fuelled the demand for higher education. The growing demand for places in college has out stripped the number of places available and this has led some students to look for a college places elsewhere, mainly the UK. In 1996 there were 7,000 Irish students attending third level colleges in the UK.

The Leaving Certificate is the main selection point in the Irish education system. Results in the exam determines access into third level education via a "Points system". Based on their best six subjects in their Leaving Certificate students are allocated points on the basis of the grades they receive in their exam. Most subjects can be taken at one of two levels and the points awarded are higher for papers taken at the higher level. Application for third level education is by a centralsied system whereby a student indicates a set of 10 preferences. Following the release of the Leaving Certificate results, offers are made to students based on their points score and the minimum points necesssary for entry to a particular course. These points thresholds vary significantly across subjects and, to a lesser extent, across institutions. Entry to third level is, as a result, highly competitive and there is a widely held view that it puts a very high degree of pressure on students and an excessive emphasis on exam performance.

A relatively recent development has been the expansions of less academic, third level courses. These include Post Leaving Certificate (PLC) courses which typically last one or two years leading to a diploma. These courses are available to students who have completed the senior cycle and equip their students with vocational and technological skills necessary for employment and access to further education, mainly in the   Institutes of Technology. Vocational Training at third level comes mainly through the above-mentioned PLCs and apprenticeships and job placements within college courses. Apprenticeships operate through providing the individual experience in a trade, for example, engineering, construction, and carpentry.

DATA

The data sets used in this analysis are two household surveys carried out by the Economic and Social Research Institute (ESRI) in 1987 and the International Adult Literacy Survey (IALS) which was administered by 13 governments[5] in association with the European Union, the OECD and UNESCO between 1994 and 1996. However, we also use the ESRI's School Leavers Survey (SLS) to provide us with a measure of changes in the return to education over time. This data source is of limited interest as it samples school leavers one year after leaving secondary school. So many of the individuals will still be in full time education (i.e. in third level education). The 1987 ESRI survey contains information on 3,294 households, generating information on over 6,500 adults. The IALS consists of a sample of 2,423 individuals.

The surveys are comprehensive datasets comparable to those used in microeconometric research in other countries. They and the IALS contain data on the number of years schooling and the highest level of education attained. The IALS does not contain contain detailed income data but groups income into five income bands, which makes the estimation of the standard earnings function slightly complicated. Under the assumption that the continuous but unobserved variable, earnings, is log-normally distributed. One can use maximum likelihood methods to estimate the standard Mincer earnings equation. This is preferable to ad hoc procedures such as using the mid-points of the wage bands.

The IALS is an unique data set in that it gives us a measure of functional literacy, so one can include some measure to control for ability bias in the wage equation. However some caution is warranted here. These tests, while partly cognitive in nature, are not designed to be general tests of intelligence or cognitive ability and should not be interpreted as such. Hence including the test scores as covariates in earnings equations is not equivalent to, for example, much of the American research which uses tests of *pre-market ability* since individuals in the IALS survey take the test at different ages and different levels of education. The literacy level is measured on three scales: prose, document and quantitative. Prose literacy is the knowledge required to understand and use information from texts, such as newspapers, pamphlets and magazines. Document literacy is the knowledge and skill needed to use information from specific formats, for example from maps, timetables and payroll forms. Quantitative literacy is defined as the ability to use mathematical operations, such as in calculating a tip or compound interest. In order to provide an actual measure of literacy each individual was given a score for each task, which varied depending on the difficulty of the assignment.

RESULTS

Returns to Education

Table 8.1 shows standard Mincer wage equations for male and females with the dependent variable measuring gross hourly earnings. The results show that the returns to each additional year of education for men range from 9% to 11% and the return varies from 10% to 14% for women. These estimates are higher than previous estimates, which estimate the return to schooling for men at around 8 percent (see Denny and Harmon, 1999; Callan and Wren, 1994; and Denny *et al.*, 1999). The returns are higher for women and are decreasing over time. There is no clear pattern to the returns to education for men from Table 8.1.

However, one can examine, albeit in a limited way, trends in the returns to schooling by examining estimated returns from the 1986–1995 School Leaver Surveys. The sample here is all those in employment having left secondary school one year prior to sampling. This clearly is not ideal given the potential selection into employment of this sample.

However other studies have shown this to be more of a problem for girls than boys (see Denny and Harmon, 2000). The estimated return to a year of schooling for boys and girls is plotted in Figure 8.1 for the 1986–1995 period, along with the estimated linear trend for the series of returns. The return to secondary school is very volatile and pro-cyclical. There is a marked downturn in estimated returns between 1986 and 1988 when the economy was in a recession and accordingly a recovery in the mid-1990s as the economy improved. The return is higher for women than it is for men.

Table 8.1   Returns to Education-Mincer equations

	1987		1995 (IALS)	
	Males	Females	Males	Females
Years of schooling	0.097	0.142	0.115	0.109
	(0.005)	(0.008)	(0.011)	(0.013)
Potential experience	0.064	0.049	0.073	0.062
	(0.003)	(0.004)	(0.008)	(0.010)
Experience squared	-0.001	-0.001	-0.110	-0.110
	(0.007)	(0.01)	(0.016)	(0.022)
Part-time dummy		0.016		0.291
		(0.042)		(0.074)
Constant	-0.298	-0.849	-0.439	-0.214
	(0.070)	(0.111)	(0.166)	(0.177)
Sample Size	1171	754	530	430

Notes: Robust Standard errors in parenthesis. Experience squared multiplied by 100.

Returns to Experience

The return to potential experience in Table 8.1 is estimated at 6% to 7% for men, almost two percentage points higher than the return for women. Figure 8.2 graphs this relationship for 1994, which exhibits the concave pattern we expect, that earnings increase with on-the-job experience but at a diminishing rate. At the peak of the curve, at 30 year's experience a man's earnings has increased by 120%, whereas a woman's earnings has only increased by 80%. Obviously, using potential experience for women may bias the results, as one is not taking account of absences from employment because of child care or other interruptions. We examine the extent of the bias by comparing actual and potential experience for the 1994 data in the same graph (Figure 8.3). The differential at 30 years experience has now decreased to almost 20% when actual experience is used.

Figure 8.1   *Returns to a years schooling one year after secondary school*

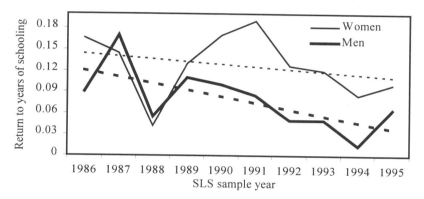

Figure 8.2   *Returns to experience, 1994*

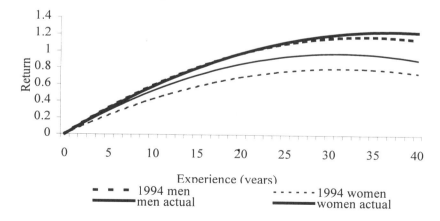

EXTENSIONS

Sensitivity Analysis

This section examines how the returns to education varies with different specifications of the wage equation. Our base model (1) contains potential experience, its square and years of education. The female wage equation also includes a part-time dummy. The results are shown in Table 8.2. Specifications (2)–(5) experiment with the definition of experience and with the definition of the dependent variable. There is little change in the parameter of interest, the returns to education, for men and women whether actual or potential experience are used (compare specifications 1 and 3). However, using age instead (and age squared, specification 2) does yield a significant and noticeable difference, causing a drop of almost two percentage points in the return for both sexes. While including age as the control is less in the spirit of the Mincer model it has the advantage that is likely to be measured acurately. By contrast experience or potential experience are more prone to measurement error and this can bias not just its own coefficient but those of other variables including that on education. Adding a quadratic for years unemployed to our base model in specification (4) slightly lowers the return for both sexes. It can be seen that some of the results are sensitive to whether the dependent variable is specified as gross or net: using net wages lowers the estimated return to education from 9% to 7% for men and from 14% to 11% for women. Given that income tax is progressive this is what one would expect qualitatively.

In Table 8.2 we also add some control variables to specification (1). In specification (6) we include six regions in the Mincer equation, which basically are the cities in Ireland and the default region being everywhere else. The results show that hourly earnings are significantly higher in most regions with the exception of Limerick for men and Limerick and Cork for women. Specification (7) includes some family characteristics, for example marital status and number of children under 14 in the household. We find that being married increases earnings by about 30% for men and over 7% for women. The number of children in the household has not a significant effect on earnings. Specification (8) includes some broad industry dummies, with the default industry being agriculture. All industries have a large positive wage premium over agriculture.

Specification (9) includes all the above-mentioned control variables. We find that the inclusion of all the control variables reduces the returns to education for men by one percentage point, which brings the return closer to previous estimates. However, the coefficient on education for the female wage equation is altered substantially when we add the industry dummies causing a return to decrease by two percentage points. In general, we find that the returns to education are fairly robust to specification changes; the difference in the return to schooling between specification (6) and (9) is in the region of 1% for men and 3% for women. Experimenting with the dependent variable and the definitions of experience also shows some instability in the returns to education. Moreover, the alternative specifications yield some sizeable differences in the returns to experience for both sexes.

Table 8.2   Sensitivity of results, 1987

	Men			Women		
	Exper.	Exper.2	Years of schooling	Exper.	Exper.2	Years of schooling
(1) Potential experience	0.069	-0.105	0.091	0.051	-0.087	0.139
	(0.003)	(0.007)	(0.004)	(0.004)	(0.010)	(0.006)
(2) Age	0.112	-0.112	0.071	0.081	-0.084	0.119
	(0.006)	(0.008)	(0.004)	(0.009)	(0.012)	(0.006)
(3) Actual experience	0.067	-0.099	0.089	0.062	-0.105	0.13
	(0.003)	(0.007)	(0.004)	(0.004)	(0.012)	(0.006)
(4) Years unemployed	0.072	-0.111	0.081	0.051	-0.087	0.135
	(0.003)	(0.007)	(0.006)	(0.004)	(0.010)	(0.007)
(5) Net wages	0.055	-0.082	0.071	0.031	-0.052	0.106
	(0.003)	(0.005)	(0.005)	(0.003)	(0.008)	(0.006)
(6) Region	0.067	-0.104	0.088	0.052	-0.089	0.138
	(0.003)	(0.007)	(0.005)	(0.004)	(0.011)	(0.008)
(7) Family	0.046	-0.072	0.084	0.046	-0.079	0.136
	(0.003)	(0.008)	(0.004)	(0.005)	(0.012)	(0.006)
(8) Industry	0.061	-0.093	0.086	0.042	-0.076	0.112
	(0.003)	(0.007)	(0.004)	(0.004)	(0.012)	(0.006)
(9) All	0.043	-0.065	0.081	0.04	-0.074	0.111
	(0.003)	(0.008)	(0.005)	(0.005)	(0.011)	(0.007)

Notes: The female wage equation also includes a part-time dummy. See Table 8.1 for sample sizes. Robust standard errors are in parenthesis. Experience squared multiplied by 100.

Controlling for Ability

The earnings differences across groups and education levels not only reflect the earnings effect of education but also the effects of other characteristics of these groups, such as ability. Therefore, not controlling for ability may introduce bias in the returns to education. We examine the extent of this bias by exploiting the ability information that is available in the IALS data.

The ability measure in the IALS is a measure of functional literacy. However, it is clear from the study design that the definition of literacy contains a significant cognitive element.[7] Literacy is measured on three scales: prose, document and quantitative. In order to provide an actual measure of literacy each individual was given a score for each task, which varied depending on the difficulty of the assignment. Scores for each scale ranges from 0–500, and it is these measures that are used in the regression analysis.

Table 8.3 is taken from Denny *et al.* (1999). The wage equations are estimated for men only and the dependent variable is the log of gross hourly earnings. Specification (1) estimates the standard wage function without any ability measures. The return to a year of education is 8%. Specification (2) includes the three literacy variables directly, which causes the return to schooling to fall to 7%; however the difference is not significant. Quantitative literacy has the biggest effect. Specification (3) simply focuses on the quantitative literacy variable and is significant without altering the coefficient on education.

Table 8.3   Controlling for ability, 1995 IALS

	(1)	(2)	(3)	(4)	(5)
Years of schooling	0.082	0.070	0.069	0.070	0.069
	(0.012)	(0.013)	(0.002)	(0.013)	(0.013)
Document literacy		-0.002			
		(0.002)			
Prose literacy		0.000			
		(0.002)			
Quantitative literacy		0.003	0.002		
		(0.002)	(0.001)		
Functional literacy				0.023	
				(0.009)	
Schooling × functional					0.002
literacy					(0.001)
Log likelihood	-722.1	-722.1	-722.5	-723.0	-722.9
N	451	541	541	541	541

Notes: The model also includes age and age-squared, firm size and regional location dummies. Robust standard errors in parenthesis.

A combined measure of functional literacy takes the place of the separate literacy variables in specification (4). It is computed by the first principal components from the three test score vectors: one for each document, prose and quantitative literacy. This variable is rescaled to have a mean of zero and standard deviation equal to one. Since the 'factor loadings' (the weights attached to each component) are very similar it is in effect an average of the three. It can be seen that functional literacy has a positive effect on earnings. To get an idea of the size of the effect, consider variations in the measure for an individual at the median level of functional literacy. An individual at the first quartile earns approximately 6% more than one at the median whereas an individual at the third quartile is worth 4.7% over the median.[6] In the final specification (5) schooling is interacted with functional literacy. The results are significant and suggest that the returns to education are increasing in the functional literacy variable.

CONCLUSION

This chapter contains estimates of the returns to education for Ireland using several microeconomic datasets principally for 1987 and 1994. Standard estimation of Mincer earnings equations by OLS gives returns for males of around 9-10% for males and around 14% for females. The higher return for females is consistent with a lower (albeit rising) participation rate in the labour market. The evidence from one of our datasets, the 1994 IALS, is somewhat at variance with these estimates giving a return which is slightly higher for males (11% compared to 10%). It is not clear what accounts for this difference. It is difficult to say anything about trend in returns with two datapoints, however looking at data on school leavers suggest that the return is pro-cyclical at least for people just out of school.

Turning to the returns to potential experience it can be seen that it is higher for men than for women. Care needs to be taken in interpreting this figure since the gap between actual and potential experience is likely to be greater for females due to interruptions in employment. For the same reason the measured variation in this variable for women is likely to understate the true variation.

Several alternatives to the basic specifications were considered. Controlling for potential sample selectivity bias in the estimates for females (no such selectivity bias arises with males) causes a fall in the return of about 2 percentage points bringing it pretty close to the estimates for males. Extensions to this analysis allowing for selectivity into part time employment adds little to the analysis.

Replacing potential experience with actual experience in employment is of little consequence but using age as the control does matter, generating lower returns for both men and women by about 2 percentage points. Using wages net of payroll taxes generates lower returns as we would expect with a progressive tax system.

The main other set of results of interest is when we relax the traditional Mincer assumption of modelling human capital as simply years of education completed. Replacing it when the highest level of education completed is consistent with there being significant premia (or 'sheepskin effects') associated with completing particular levels of education. Moreover inferring the average return to years of education associated with a particular level of education shows higher average returns from higher levels of education.

In the last seven years the Irish economy, following a long recession, has experienced spectacular growth averaging 9% per annum. It will be interesting to see whether future research for this period shows a significant change in the returns to education.

NOTES

1. This policy change only applied to full-time students.
2. About 55% of 4 year olds and almost 99% of 5 year olds are attending primary school.
3. This exam was known as the Intermediate Certificate until 1992.
4. OECD (1996), p 130 .
5. The countries involved were Australia, Canada, Belgium, Germany, Ireland, Netherlands, New Zealand, Sweden, Switzerland (French and German speaking),   United   Kingdom, United States, Poland. It is very similar to the large National Adult   Literacy   Survey collected by the National Council for Educational Statistics (NCES) in the US in 1992.
6. See Denny et al (1999) for more on this.

REFERENCES

Breen, Richard, Damian Hannan and Richard O'Leary (1995), "Returns to Education: Taking account of Employers' Perceptions and use of their Educational Credentials", *European Sociological Review*, Vol. 11, No.1, pp59 –75.

Callan, Tim and Anne Wren (1992), " Male-Female Wage Differentials Analysis and Policy Issues", Dublin E.S.R.I. *General Research Series no. 166.*

Callan, Tim and Colm Harmon (1997), "The Economic Return to Schooling in Ireland", mimeo, ESRI.

Denny,K., C. Harmon and S. Redmond (1999), "Cognitive Skills and the Labour Market-Evidence from the International Adult Literacy Survey", mimeo, Department of Economics, University College Dublin

Denny, K and Colm Harmon (2000), "The Impact of Education and Training in the Labour Market Experiences of Young Adults", IFS working paper no. W00/08.

Denny, K., C. Harmon, D. McMahon and S. Redmond (2000), "Literacy and Education in the Irish Labour Market". Economic and Social Review.

OECD (1996), *Employment Outlook*, Paris: OECD

9. Italy

Giorgio Brunello, Simona Comi and Claudio Lucifora

INTRODUCTION

There is agreement among economists and policy makers that investment in human capital is key for economic development and growth (OECD, 1998). The standard economic approach to the analysis of the decision to invest in education (and training) is that individuals and households compare their expected benefits and costs from the investment. For each individual, the optimal investment in human capital, measured for instance by the optimal number of years of schooling, is obtained when expected marginal benefits and expected marginal costs are equal (see Card, 1995).

Governments can affect individual decisions by influencing both the costs and the benefits of education. In an economy, the outcome of the interactions of heterogeneous agents who invest in education to increase their human capital can be measured by average educational attainment and by the labour market returns to education. Usually a distinction is drawn between private and public returns to education, with the former including the returns appropriated by the single individuals and the latter including the positive externalities of individual investment.

The purpose of this chapter is to provide an update of the empirical evidence on the private returns to education in Italy. We build on previous research that is reviewed in a companion study (see Brunello *et al.*, 1999a). The chapter is organised in seven sections. We start with a brief description of the Italian schooling system. Next, we introduce the empirical model and the estimates based on ordinary least squares (OLS). Section three considers our results in the light of the European evidence and section four looks at the evolution of the returns to education over time. Estimates based on the method of instrumental variables are presented in section six. The remaining two sections are devoted respectively to estimating the returns to different educational levels and to the evaluation of the labour market returns to education for selected groups.

Education and Earnings in Europe

THE ITALIAN SCHOOLING SYSTEM

The Italian schooling system has been shaped over the years by a number of important reforms. Following the 1922 educational reform, primary school (*scuola elementare*) became compulsory for children aged 6 to 11. Secondary school was divided into two distinct tracks, academic and vocational, and only students belonging to the academic track were allowed to enter tertiary education.

The reform of compulsory lower secondary school (*scuola media*) of 1962 established the school-leaving age at 14, adding to primary school three further years of compulsory and comprehensive education. The 1969 reform eliminated restrictions to access to university and allowed graduates of vocational secondary schools to enrol. Primary school was reformed again in 1990, when the new curricula[1] approved in 1985 were fully implemented. Combined with the ageing of the Italian population, one of the main effects of this reform was to increase the teacher/pupil ratio, thus providing jobs for an increasingly large excess supply of primary schoolteachers.

Two (and three) year diplomas were also introduced in 1990 as an alternative to traditional tertiary education. Finally, the compulsory leaving age was raised from 14 to 15 in 1999, a change to be effective from the year 2000. A drastic reform of the whole system, from primary to upper secondary, is currently being discussed in the Italian Parliament.

In the Italian schooling system exams are normally taken at age 14 (*esame di scuola media inferiore*) and further education is then a matter of choice. In 1995 approximately 91.1% of the relevant cohort stayed on and attended formal education, either at school or at vocational schools, while the rest entered the labour market searching for a job. For those continuing education there is another leaving exam, usually after five years of upper secondary school (*scuola superiore*). This exam (known as *esame di maturità*) is mostly taken at age 19. The pass rate is currently about 94%. Many students, however, drop out of school before reaching the final exam. In 1995 about 66.7% of individuals aged 19 obtained an upper secondary school diploma and among the latter only 68.4% continued by enrolling in a tertiary institution. The university system includes both undergraduate (usually four years) and postgraduate studies (doctorate).

Educational attainment in Italy, measured by the percentage of individuals with upper secondary education, was 68.5% in 1992, much lower than the OECD average (84.8%). Attainment measured by tertiary education was even lower (10.2% in Italy, compared to 20.8% in the OECD). An alternative measure of performance of the education system is the percentage of graduates in the population at theoretical age of graduation. This percentage is again significantly lower in Italy than in the OECD average: less than 70% of individuals at theoretical age of graduation completed upper secondary education in Italy in 1992, compared to about 85% in the OECD average.

This difference is partly explained by the high dropout rate in the Italian system. According to a study by ISTAT (1999), in of a cohort of 1000 individuals completing compulsory school, only 925 individuals enrol in upper secondary schools. Among them, 610 pass the final exam after five years and 401 enrol in a university course; only 160 individuals graduate. The importance of dropouts in the Italian system can also highlighted by looking at enrolment rates in schools by individuals aged 16 and 17. While in Italy only six and a half teenagers out of ten are still in school at 16; this proportion is close to nine in the OECD average.

EVIDENCE FROM SIMPLE ESTIMATES

We start our empirical investigation of the returns to education in Italy by estimating a standard Mincer equation, that associates the log of individual earnings to years of schooling, potential experience (defined as age minus years of schooling minus 6) and its square.

Our data are drawn from the Survey of Household Income and Wealth of the Bank of Italy (SHIW). The SHIW survey is based on a random sample of approximately 8000 households per year, and is available from 1977 annually and at odd years after 1987.[2] It contains information both on households (family composition) and on individuals. This information includes the highest completed school degree,[3] gender, age, potential and actual work experience, net yearly earnings, average weekly hours of work and number of months of employment per year.[4] It also contains information on family background (the education, age, occupation and sector of parents). There are no other nationally representative surveys in Italy that cover the same range of information. We restrict our sample to non-agricultural employees aged from 14 to 65. Furthermore, we consider only males working full time and females working both full time and part time.[5] In Table 9.1, we report for two selected years the summary statistics of the main variables used in the empirical analysis[6]. Average age is around 36 years for females and close to 40 for males, with some evidence of an ageing (sample) female population over the years. Years of schooling, measured as the number of years required to complete the highest attained degree, are higher on average for females (11 years) than for males (10 years). Both these factors contribute to the observed lower potential labour market experience of females (19 years) compared to males (23 years).

Turning to job attributes, as one might expect, blue-collar occupations are under-represented among females (between 30 and 40%). Part-time work is still a rather marginal phenomenon (around 10%). Males tend to work longer hours (on average) than females, even when we exclude part-time workers. They are also more likely to be located in the northern regions of Italy. Males have significantly higher yearly (net) earnings, but the gender gap in earnings

Education and Earnings in Europe

is significantly reduced when hourly wages are considered. In the reminder of this chapter we shall use the information contained in the SHIW dataset to investigate the relationship between hourly wages, education and labour market experience, and to address a number of issues related to the measurement of the returns to education.

Table 9.1   Selected variables and their means in SHIW, 1989 and 1995

	1989		1995	
	Females	Males	Females	Males
Age	36.19	39.21	37.38	38.99
	(10.49)	(10.97)	(10.26)	(9.09)
Years of schooling	11.15	9.80	11.10	10.07
	(3.84)	(3.79)	(3.57)	(3.61)
Potential experience	19.04	23.40	20.27	22.91
	(11.57)	(12.24)	(11.21)	(12.07)
Blue-collar	0.32	0.48	0.36	0.53
	(0.49)	(0.49)	(0.48)	(0.49)
Part time	0.08		0.13	
	(0.27)		(0.34)	
North	0.63	0.52	0.64	0.57
	(0.48)	(0.49)	(0.47)	(0.49)
No. of hours worked	37.06	40.75	34.12	40.39
	(7.37)	(4.89)	(9.39)	(7.29)
Net annual earnings	16163.37	19424.87	19153.93	24366.47
	(5059)	(7054.89)	(7991.48)	(10297.2)
Net hourly wage	9.94	10.18	13.42	13.53
	(5.68)	(3.51)	(7.68)	(6.42)
Gross hourly wage	12.88	13.24	n.a	n.a
	(7.79)	(5.49)		
Gross yearly earnings	20888.21	24140.17	n.a	n.a
	(7283.51)	(10699.56)		
Number of observations	2235	3937	2326	3441

Notes: n.a: not available.

The standard specification we consider is

$$ln(\, w_i\,) = \alpha + \beta S_i + \gamma_1 X_i + \gamma_2 X_i^2 + \varepsilon_i,$$

where *ln(w)* is net log hourly wages, *S* is years of schooling (in years); *X* is potential experience and ε is the error term. The subscript *i* refers to individuals ($i = 1, \ldots, N$). This specification can be obtained from standard human capital theory and is based on the assumption that individuals accumulate human capital both at school and in the labour market (see Willis, 1986 for a derivation). It is based on a number of simplifying assumptions: first, the relationship between log wages and years of schooling is linear; second, there is no complementarity between the accumulation of human capital in the labour market and educational attainment. We will relax some of these assumptions in a later section of this chapter.

Ordinary least squares estimates for 1995 are presented in Table 9.2 The regression for females also includes a part-time dummy, taking the value 1 if the employee is working part-time and 0 otherwise, while only males working full time are considered. Based on these estimates, the marginal return to a year of education is 6.2% for males and 7.7% for females. Moreover, conditional on schooling, one additional year of potential labour market experience increases hourly wages by 4.1% for males and by 3.6% for females.

AN INTERNATIONAL COMPARISON

The natural question to ask is whether the estimated marginal return to a year of schooling in Italy is high or low in a comparative perspective. In this section, we compare our results with those obtained for other 14 European countries, using a similar specification and methodology. Despite the pressures from economic integration, limited labour mobility within Europe suggests that observed differences in educational attainment and in the costs and returns to education across Europe can be persistent.

On average, returns to education in Europe are close to 0.072 for males and to 0.079 for females (see Christensen and Westergaard-Nielsen, 1999). As shown in Table 9.2, returns to schooling in Italy are below the European average. Before drawing any conclusion, however, it is important to assess to what extent the observed difference is due to different measurement criteria or to genuine lower returns to education in Italy with respect to the European average. An important measurement problem is that the estimated returns to education in Table 9.2 are based on net wages rather than on gross wages, as is the case in most other European countries.

To check whether using net rather than gross wages significantly affect our estimates we fit our equation on both gross and net hourly wages (i.e. including and excluding direct taxation).[7] Table 9.3 presents the results. It turns out that returns based on gross wages are approximately 20% and 13% higher with respect to net wages, respectively for males and for females. Assuming that the difference between estimates of returns based on net and gross wages is relatively constant over time, the adjusted 1995 estimate of the marginal returns to schooling turns out to be 0.074 for males and 0.087 for females. These numbers are very similar to the European average.

Table 9.2   OLS estimates of returns to education (year of schooling), 1995

	Men	Women
Education	0.062	0.077
	(0.001)	(0.002)
Potential Experience	0.041	0.036
	(0.001)	(0.002)
Potential Experience^2	-0.0005	-0.004
	(0.00003)	(0.00005)
Part time		-0.047
		(0.023)
N	3441	2326
R-squared	0.40	0.37

Notes: Standard errors in parentheses.

Table 9.3   Returns to education: Gross and net hourly wages, 1989

	Males		Females	
	Gross	Net	Gross	Net
Education	0.048	0.040	0.052	0.046
	(0.001)	(0.001)	(0.002)	(0.001)
Potential experience	0.030	0.026	0.024	0.023
	(0.001)	(0.001)	(0.002)	(0.002)
Potential experience squared	-0.0003	-0.0003	-0.0002	-0.0003
	(0.00003)	(0.00002)	(0.00005)	(0.00004)

Notes: standard errors in parentheses.

While estimated returns based on gross wages are close to the European average, educational attainment, measured by the percentage of individuals aged 25 to 64 who have at least upper secondary education, is lower than average (see OECD, 1997). How do we explain this?[8] Using a standard human capital model (see Card, 1995), the optimal level of schooling is obtained by equating the marginal return to the marginal cost of schooling. When individuals are homogeneous, similar returns to education can be consistent with different levels of educational attainment if a) marginal returns are similar and b) either the intercept or the slope coefficient of the marginal cost function are higher in the country with lower attainment. When individuals are heterogeneous, similar returns and different attainment can be accounted for if the country with lower attainment has a larger share of individuals with higher marginal costs and/or steeper marginal cost functions.

Using this framework, the finding that Italy has both lower educational attainment and (marginal) returns to education (conditional on age) that are not significantly different from the European average could be accounted for by the fact that a relatively larger share of the relevant population has higher marginal costs or faces steeper marginal cost functions. Recall that these costs include both monetary outlays by individual households, non-pecuniary costs and the opportunity costs of delaying labour market entry. While comparative evidence on the costs of education is limited, further research in this area is important, especially when increasing the educational attainment of the labour force is considered to be a national priority.

THE EVOLUTION OF RETURNS OVER TIME

An interesting question is whether the estimated returns to education have varied significantly over time. To investigate this issue, we estimate Mincer earnings equations for each year between 1977 and 1995. The results are displayed in Table 9.4.

Results confirm that returns are higher for females than for males over the entire sample period. In Figure 9.1 we plot these by gender, the returns have not changed much over the period, with the exception of 1993 and 1995, when they have increased significantly, especially among female employees.

A closer inspection of the figure reveals the presence of a mild downward trend in the returns to education up to the late 1980s for females and of a mild upward trend during the same period for males. Since Italy has experienced during the same period a similar trend in the overall structure of wage differentials, the described pattern might capture the contribution of the schooling wage premium to the overall dispersion of wages.

In previous work (see Brunello *et al.* 1999b), we have taken a more detailed look at the dynamics of returns to education by estimating earnings equations separately for the private and the public sector. Our results suggest that, while returns to education have remained more or less constant in the private sector, they have increased in the public sector, especially in the early 1990s, because of very favourable renewals of wage contracts (see Brunello and Dustmann, 1996). The empirical evidence also suggests that these wage increases have not been spread out evenly among different educational groups, but have mainly affected the relative payoff of higher education.

Table 9.4   Estimates of the Returns to Education, 1977-1995

	Males			Females		
	Education	Exp	$Exp^2_{(a)}$	Education	Exp	$Exp^2_{(a)}$
1977	0.049	0.046	-0.03	0.062	0.068	0.07
	(0.002)	(0.002)	(0.004)	(0.004)	(0.009)	(0.01)
1978	0.041	0.047	-0.06	0.057	0.078	-0.08
	(0.002)	(0.002)	(0.004)	(0.004)	(0.008)	(0.01)
1979	0.039	0.048	-0.06	0.054	0.067	-0.07
	(0.002)	(0.002)	(0.005)	(0.004)	(0.007)	(0.01)
1980	0.041	0.044	-0.06	0.050	0.032	-0.03
	(0.002)	(0.002)	(0.004)	(0.004)	(0.008)	(0.01)
1981	0.039	0.044	-0.06	0.051	0.037	-0.03
	(0.002)	(0.002)	(0.004)	(0.004)	(0.008)	(0.01)
1982	0.040	0.040	-0.05	0.048	0.032	-0.03
	(0.001)	(0.002)	(0.003)	(0.003)	(0.007)	(0.009)
1983	0.045	0.036	-0.04	0.052	0.03	-0.02
	(0.001)	(0.001)	(0.003)	(0.003)	(0.006)	(0.008)
1984	0.041	0.041	-0.05	0.046	0.047	-0.05
	(0.002)	(0.002)	(0.004)	(0.002)	(0.006)	(0.008)
1986	0.042	0.040	-0.05	0.046	0.051	-0.05
	(0.001)	(0.001)	(0.002)	(0.002)	(0.004)	(0.006)
1987	0.049	0.032	-0.04	0.052	0.043	-0.04
	(0.001)	(0.001)	(0.002)	(0.002)	(0.004)	(0.005)
1989	0.041	0.026	-0.03	0.045	0.031	-0.02
	(0.001)	(0.001)	(0.003)	(0.001)	(0.003)	(0.005)
1991	0.046	0.033	-0.04	0.059	0.045	-0.04
	(0.001)	(0.001)	(0.002)	(0.001)	(0.004)	(0.005)
1993	0.062	0.044	-0.05	0.086	0.058	-0.05
	(0.001)	(0.001)	(0.003)	(0.002)	(0.005)	(0.006)
1995	0.062	0.041	-0.05	0.077	0.046	-0.03
	(0.001)	(0.001)	(0.003)	(0.002)	(0.005)	(0.006)

Notes: Figures in parentheses are standard errors. (a) Coefficients and standard errors of experience squared are divided by 100.

In the international literature explaining the current increase in wage differentials by education and skills, a lot of emphasis has been placed on the role played by skill-biased technical change (see Card and Lemieux, 1999 for a recent review). By shifting the relative demand of educated labour relative to available supply, the argument goes, skill-biased technical change has increased the economic returns to education. A potential problem with this story in our context is that skill-biased technical change should have affected the marginal returns to skill both in the private and in the public sector. Our evidence suggests, however, that returns have increased only in the public sector. Skill-biased technical progress should also have increased educational attainment. While attainment did increase in Italy, especially among teenagers, the percentage of individuals in the relevant age group with a college degree has remained disappointingly flat since the mid-1970s.

We infer from this that the observed increase in the returns to education could be induced by institutional factors rather than by market forces. Clearly, more empirical research on the relationship between technical progress and the economic returns to education is necessary before reaching a satisfactory explanation of the current trends.

Figure 9.1   Returns to education over time

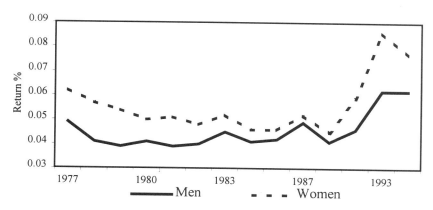

ESTIMATES BASED ON INSTRUMENTAL VARIABLES

So far, we have presented empirical estimates based upon ordinary least squares. These estimates, however, face two important problems. First, when years of schooling are measured with error, they are biased toward zero (*attenuation bias*). Second, education is not randomly assigned to individuals but is the result of choice that depends, among other things, on unobserved individual ability (see Card, 1999).

The measurement of years of schooling in our data is clearly exposed to error because we lack information on completed years and observe only the last completed degree. Individuals with the same completed degree, however, could have spent a significantly different number of years in education. One reason is repetition by students being failed. Another reason, especially relevant among college students, is that enrolment can continue even after the prescribed duration of the course. In practice, many students in Italy take a few years longer than the required minimum to complete a degree. Last but not least, dropouts have typically spent time in education without completing a degree. Another source of bias is the use of potential experience in the earnings equation. Potential experience is defined as age minus years of schooling minus 6 (starting age of school in Italy) and depends on measured years of schooling. To avoid this bias, we will use in this section age instead of potential experience.

One way to deal with measurement errors and the endogeneity of education is to estimate using instrumental variables. The identification of valid instruments is a thriving industry, which has been recently reviewed by, among others, Card (1999) and Ashenfelter *et al.* (1999). The requirements for an instrument to be valid are that it should be correlated with educational choice but not correlated with wages conditional on schooling. A class of candidates used in the literature is given by quasi-natural experiments associated to policy interventions and to reforms of the educational system. Examples in this literature include the compulsory schooling laws discussed by Angrist and Krueger (1991) and Harmon and Walker (1995).

An important reform in the Italian context is Law 910 of December 1969, which extended the possibility of enrolment in college to individuals with completed secondary education, independently of the track (general or vocational) chosen in secondary school. Since expected age of completion of secondary school is in general 18–19 years, this opportunity was mainly open to cohorts born from 1951 onwards.

We capture this educational reform with the dummy *REFORM*, equal to 1 for individuals born from 1951 onwards and to 0 otherwise. A rough indication of the impact of the reform can be obtained by comparing the percentage of 19-year old individuals enrolling in college shortly before and shortly after the reform. It turns out that enrolment rates were 16.3% of the relevant population for individuals born in 1949 and 27.3% for those born in 1952. At the same time, the percentage of high school graduates enrolling in college was 54% for the 1949 cohort and 66% for the 1952 cohort. Higher enrolment in college after the reform, however, had a rather limited impact on the percentage of college graduates in the population at theoretical age of graduation, partly because the percentage of irregular students (*fuori corso*), who stay in college longer than the number of years required to complete the curriculum, increased sharply for the cohorts enrolling since the early 1970s. Hence, the increase in the number of college students after the reform was accompanied by a reduction in the efficiency of the college system and by an increase in the average time required to complete the degree.

When we compare educational attainment of individuals in our sample born before and after 1951, we find that the percentage of college graduates increased only marginally, at least compared to the consistent increase in the percentage of individuals graduating from junior and upper secondary schools. This suggests that the dummy *REFORM* picks up both the exogenous reform of December 1969 and the general increase in the level of schooling achieved by the population who went to school during the economic boom of the late 1950s and later.

An additional potential instrument is a measure of individual risk aversion. To illustrate its relevance for the schooling decision, consider the following extension of the human capital model discussed by Card (1995). Let earnings y be defined as

$$y_i = e^{\lambda S_i}$$

where i is for the individual and $\lambda \leq 1$ is a parameter, and define individual utility as

$$U_i = u_i(y_i) - \phi(S_i)$$

where u is the utility attached to income and ϕ is the disutility attached to investment in schooling.[9] When the individual maximize her utility, the optimal choice of schooling is given by

$$u'\lambda e^{\lambda S_i} = \phi'(S_i)$$

where the prime denotes first derivatives. Using a first order Taylor approximation of u' and exploiting the second order conditions for a local maximum one obtains $\partial S / \partial ARA < 0$, where ARA is the coefficient of absolute risk aversion. An increase in the measure of absolute risk aversion ARA reduces the marginal utility of income from schooling, thus reducing the selected years of school, without affecting the marginal returns to schooling.

Our measure of risk aversion is based on a specific question included in the 1995 wave of SHIW. The question asks how much the interviewed household head is willing to pay (the maximum amount of money) to participate in a lottery offering a fixed premium in the event of success and the loss of the invested capital in the event of failure. The question is framed so as to yield a natural measure of absolute risk aversion that we compute following the definition used by Guiso and Paiella (2000).

We select from our data the sub-sample of male household heads older than 29 and younger than 65 who are working full time for the full year and estimate using both OLS and by IV, where *REFORM* and *ARA* are the instruments. Results are presented in Table 9.5. Absolute risk aversion that varies among individuals is a valid instrument if it affects the choice of schooling without influencing the returns to schooling, conditional on education. This is unlikely to be true, however, because absolute risk aversion varies with household income and wealth,[10] both of which are correlated with current earnings. We avoid this problem by regressing ARA on household income and financial wealth and by taking the residuals as our instrument. By construction, these residuals measure the component of absolute risk aversion that is orthogonal to household assets. Guiso and Paiella (2000) find that ARA, conditional on wealth, varies significantly by region of birth and age.

Table 9.5 OLS and IV estimates of returns to education: 1995

	OLS	IV
Education	0.048	0.068
	(0.002)	(0.029)
Age	0.041	0.049
	(0.010)	(0.014)
Age-squared	-0.0003	-0.0004
	(0.0001)	(0.0001)
F-test on instruments (P-value)		0.0149
N		0.658 [1]
R-squared		
	1762	1762
	0.29	0.24

Notes: Degrees of freedom in parentheses. Instruments for schooling in IV: REFORM, ARA. The data used in the estimation is for male heads of households only.

As it happens for current smoking as an instrument of education, the problem remains that risk aversion could be caused by education itself[11]. We test instrument validity using the Sargan test[12]. This test verifies whether the instruments play a direct role in explaining log wages, not just an indirect role, through predicting educational attainment. If the test fails, one or more of the instruments are invalid and ought to be included in the explanation of log wages (Deaton, 1999). An important requirement is also that the selected instruments should be correlated with the endogenous variable. We test this by computing the F-statistic on the excluded instruments in the reduced form schooling equation, as suggested by Bound *et al.* (1995).

The table shows that the Bound test always rejects the null hypothesis of no correlation between education and additional instruments. Moreover, the Sargan test never rejects the null hypothesis of no misspecification. We find that the estimated returns to education based on instrumental variables are about 42% higher than the estimated returns based on OLS. Hence, estimates based on OLS carry a large downward bias, a typical finding in this literature.

EDUCATIONAL CHOICES AND THE RETURNS TO DIFFERENT TYPES OF SCHOOLS

The accumulation of human capital is not necessarily a smooth, linear and (almost) continuous process and returns need not to be the same across different types of school. In some schooling systems an additional investment in education does not necessarily lead to the award of a degree, and hence might not grant additional labour market returns. Similarly, as suggested by the 'credentialism' hypothesis, in the presence of heterogeneity what really matters is the type of school rather than the overall number of years spent in formal education.[13]

Table 9.6 Returns to education using educational dummies

	Males	Females
Junior High	0.207	0.187
	(0.016)	(0.033)
High School	0.376	0.451
	(0.017)	(0.032)
Tertiary education	0.656	0.782
	(0.026)	(0.037)
Age	0.064	0.047
	(0.003)	(0.005)
Age^2	-0.0005	-0.0003
	(0.00004)	(0.00007)
Adjusted-R^2	0.40	0.38
Observations	3385	2085

Notes: Excluded dummy: primary school.

We investigate these issues by using educational dummies rather than years of schooling in our earnings regressions. In particular, we first look at education achievements by broad levels: primary, junior high, high school and tertiary education. Second, we address the issue of 'credentialism' by distinguishing among types of school (for instance, vocational or general, scientific or humanistic) within each educational level. Results of OLS estimates that use educational dummies rather than years of schooling are reported in Table 9.6.

The estimated coefficients of the educational dummies reported in the table should be interpreted as differentials with respect to the baseline return accruing to individuals with no school or with only primary school. This pattern of estimated returns by educational level confirms that there is a monotonic (positive) relationship linking returns to education to the highest level of education attained.

We pursue further the issue of "credentialism" by using a larger set of dummy variables, which allows us to distinguish not only among school levels but also among different types of secondary and tertiary education. The interpretation of the estimated coefficients is in terms of the additional return that the combination of educational level plus school type grants to the individual with respect to the reference category (compulsory schooling in our case). Our main sets of results (OLS estimates) are reported in Table 9.7. The returns to formal education are estimated with hourly wages. [14]

We find that returns to different levels of schooling are in general higher for females than for males and increase with the number of years spent in education. Focusing on upper secondary education and on hourly earnings, there is evidence of significant variation in the returns from different school types. This variation is substantially reduced when we use monthly earnings. Short-term tertiary and tertiary education yield much higher returns than upper secondary school. Among tertiary degrees, medicine, that requires more years of schooling, leads to higher returns in terms both of hourly and of monthly wages. Apart from medicine, it is often the case that the very high returns measured on the basis of hourly wages are significantly reduced when we use monthly earnings. This is especially true of degrees in the humanities. Finally, we notice that traditionally male-dominated degrees, such as engineering, yield to females the highest returns. The reverse does not appear to be true for males who graduate in female-dominated areas (such as the humanities).

Table 9. 7 Returns to different types of school: 1995

Type of school	Hourly wage			
	Males		Females	
	Coef.	St. err.	Coef.	St. Err.
Vocational School	0.14	0.021	0.20	0.031
High-school	0.23	0.012	0.32	0.017
Vocational	0.15	0.031	0.24	0.037
Technical (1)	0.24	0.013	0.25	0.023
Licei (2)	0.24	0.030	0.31	0.040
Liceo Artistico (3)	0.36	0.067	0.31	0.076
Teacher College(4)	0.33	0.055	0.43	0.023
Other	0.21	0.067	0.24	0.073
Short term tertiary	0.35	0.071	0.47	0.077
Medicine	0.44	0.228	0.76	0.185
Economics and Statistics	0.42	0.228		
Political science	0.35	0.228	0.13	0.213
Humanities			0.19	0.369
Other	0.33	0.086	0.49	0.096
Tertiary	0.50	0.021	0.65	0.025
Mathematic	0.52	0.048	0.66	0.050
Agriculture & Veterinary	0.32	0.102	0.63	0.369
Medicine	0.60	0.097	0.75	0.165
Engineering	0.44	0.045	0.80	0.261
Architecture	0.47	0.131	0.70	0.213
Economics and Statistics	0.45	0.050	0.60	0.099
Political science	0.33	0.102	0.57	0.140
Law	0.65	0.074	0.56	0.088
Humanities	0.62	0.045	0.67	0.031
Others	0.55	0.078	0.50	0.083

Notes: Standard errors in parentheses. (1)Technical high school diploma;(2) Italian secondary school specialising in classical, scientific or foreign languages studies. (3) Italian secondary school specialising in art subjects.(4) Teacher training college.

LABOUR MARKET CHOICES AND RETURNS TO EDUCATION: EVIDENCE FROM SELECTED GROUPS

Besides differences in the returns to education arising from observed and unobserved characteristics, another source of differences across individuals is related to their labour market choices - choices that might not be independent of their educational attainment.[15] An important issue addressed in this section deals with the endogenous distribution of individuals – and their related characteristics – across groups. Most often choices made in the labour market are not independent from individual characteristics and (*ex-post*) group composition cannot be taken as randomly assigned. In this context an appropriate methodology should be used to control for the presence of non-random sampling across groups and for the existence of selectivity bias.

Hereafter, we investigate the returns to education for different groups of individuals based on their labour market choices. In particular, we focus on whether they work full time or part time, whether they are employed in the public or in the private sector and finally whether they reside in a developed high-wage region or in a relatively underdeveloped low-wage region.[16]

Women and Part-time Work

In the previous section we estimated the returns to education of female employees by using a sample of full-time and part-time females and by introducing a part-time dummy to control for differences in hourly wages. Our estimates there suggest that female part-timers earn a lower hourly wage than females working full time (the hourly wage is 4.4% lower on average). There are, however, at least two difficulties with the above approach. First, female participation to the labour market is non-random as women select themselves into working based on the wage they expect to earn.[17] Second, when the participation choice is made, the decision to work part time or to work full time is also taken. To deal with selectivity, we look both at the decision to participate and at the choice between not participating, working full-time and working part-time. In the former case we use a probit equation as in the conventional two-step approach *à la* Heckman (1979). In the latter case – to account for the multiple choices made – we replace the simple probit model with an ordered probit as in Ermisch and Wright (1993).[18] In practice, endogenous selectivity is treated by estimating an auxiliary probit (simple or ordered) equation, where family background characteristics and unearned income are used as identifying variables.

The first column of Table 9.8 reports the estimates based on correcting both for endogenous labour market participation choices[19] and for endogenous education, using the instruments discussed in section six. Results show that selectivity bias is a relevant issue. The coefficient associated to the inverse Mills ratio is positive and statistically significant, suggesting that females who have actually chosen to participate in the labour market earn higher wages than randomly assigned females. Interestingly, the estimated returns to schooling marginally increase after correcting for selectivity.

Notice that the coefficient associated to the inverse Mills ratio is a positive function of the covariance of the error terms in the earnings and in the selection equation. A positive coefficient implies that a shock to the selection equation that increases female labour market participation also increases conditional log earnings. This suggests that observed combinations of earnings and participation are traced out by labour demand shocks.

Table 9.8 Returns to education with endogenous selection. females, 1995

		IV
	Heckman (1)	Two-step ordered probit[a] (2)
Education	0.071	0.072
	(0.005)	(0.005)
Age	0.064	0.064
	(0.007)	(0.007)
Age^2	-0.0005	-0.0005
	(0.000)	(0.000)
Part-time dummy	-0.155	-0.078
	(0.025)	(0.041)
Selectivity term (λ)	0.107	0.098
	(0.041)	(0.042)

Notes: Figures in parentheses are standard errors. (a) As in Ermisch and Wright.

The second column in the table reports the estimates based on correcting also for the decision to work part time. Here too we find that selectivity effects are statistically significant and attract a positive sign. Therefore, females who have chosen to be employed full time earn higher hourly wages than randomly assigned females.

Public versus Private Sector

In most industrialized countries the public sector plays a relevant role in the economy. In some countries – Italy is one of them – the share of the public sector in total employment is over 20% and the state is the largest employer of highly educated people (teachers, doctors, scientists, etc.). Moreover, the rules that govern pay determination in the public sector are significantly different from those prevailing in the private sector. Therefore, not only individual characteristics (i.e. education) but also the rewards to these characteristics are likely to vary across the private and public sectors.

Needless to say, the allocation of individuals to the private and the public sector cannot be taken as randomly distributed: both observed (education, gender, etc.) and unobserved individual characteristics (risk aversion, motivation, etc.) influence the distribution of employment across sectors.

We estimate the returns to education in the public and the private sector separately for males and females working full time. To account for endogenous selectivity, we estimate an auxiliary probit equation that relates this allocation to educational attainment, a polynomial in age and two dummies that capture whether the father and the mother of the individual were employed in the public sector. The endogeneity of education is handled by using two-stage least squares, that is by replacing education with the predicted value from a regression on the full set of available instruments, as discussed in detail in section six of this chapter. The final estimate is based on the Heckman two-step procedure. The results are in Table 9.9.

Table 9.9 Returns to education in the public and private sectors

	IV and Heckman			
	Private		Public	
	Males	Females	Males	Females
Education	0.050	0.059	0.043	0.52
	(0.004)	(0.011)	(0.005)	(0.010)
Age	0.049	0.039	0.049	0.029
	(0.004)	(0.014)	(0.005)	(0.014)
Age^2	-0.0004	-0.0003	-0.0004	-0.0001
	(0.00006)	(0.0001)	(0.00007)	(0.0001)
Selectivity	0.176	-0.029	0.027	-0.011
term	(0.023)	(0.098)	(0.050)	(0.101)
Observations	2110	839	1007	958

Notes: Figures in parentheses are standard errors.

We find that, while the returns to education are higher for females than for males in either sector, the returns to age are higher for males. Both returns to education and to age are higher in the private sector, independently of gender. Lower expected returns to education and age in the public sector are consistent with an equilibrium allocation of individuals to sectors if the public sector provides additional returns that are not captured by these regressions. Obvious candidates are higher job protection, lower effort and substantially more favourable pension benefits (see Brunello and Rizzi, 1993).

CONCLUSION

In this chapter we have provided an update of the empirical evidence on the private returns to education in Italy. In conclusion, we emphasize three results that we believe warrant additional research. First, we have shown that, while returns to education in Italy (based on gross wages) are in line with the European average, educational attainment is generally much lower (particularly at secondary and tertiary levels). How can these findings be reconciled? Building on a simple human capital model, where the optimal level of schooling is given by equating the marginal return to the marginal cost of education, we have speculated that either marginal costs are steeper in Italy or that a larger share of the population involved in human capital investment faces high marginal costs in Italy than in the European average. An important implication of our results is that explanations of the lower educational attainment of the Italian labour force relative to the European average should focus more on costs than on returns.

Second, we have examined whether the estimated returns to education have varied significantly over time. The evidence is that returns have not changed much over the period 1977 to 1995, with the exception of 1993 and 1995, when they have increased significantly, especially among female employees. Quite interestingly, the observed increase in the returns to education has been almost completely driven by higher returns to education in the public sector. Assuming that skill-biased technical change has been an important factor in shifting out the marginal returns to education, an important question for future research is why these shifts have only affected returns in the public sector of the economy.

Third and last, we have confirmed the usual finding in the international literature that accounting for measurement error in years of schooling and/or for the endogeneity of educational choices by using instrumental variables significantly increases the returns to education with respect to estimates based on OLS methods.

While we have tried to cover many issues, important aspects of the relationship between education and earnings have not been considered. To mention only two, we have not considered the effect of educational attainment on earnings *growth* and we have ignored unemployment as an important labour market outcome. These topics are left to future research.

NOTES

1. Primary school education is now aimed at promoting initial cultural literacy and the full development of individual pupils, with an emphasis on interaction with families and the social community.
2. In 1985 the survey was not carried out.

3. Standard and not actual years of formal schooling are recorded. Since students who fail to reach a standard have to repeat the year, the actual number of years is likely to be underestimated.
4. Our definition of the net hourly wage is: (net yearly earnings)/(months worked) * (weekly hours worked)*4; net yearly earnings are after deduction of direct taxation.
5. The inclusion of females working part-time is motivated by the fact that in some European countries over 50% of females hold a part-time job. In Italy, this percentage falls to 10%.
6. We have excluded from Table 2 employees whose wage information was missing. In some cases, the sample may slightly differ because of the higher non-response rate to some survey questions (i.e. family background).
7. This can be done for wave 1989 of the SHIW data, because gross wages in that wave have been carefully estimated at the individual level. We use the data kindly provided by Dino Rizzi of the University of Venice, who has estimated individual gross wages by adding expected income taxes to individual net wages in the 1989 SHIW wave.
8. We consider here for simplicity only the European average and ignore the important variations of educational outcomes within Europe.
9. Card uses a *CARA* specification for u(..).
10. See the evidence in Guiso and Paiella (2000).
11. See the discussion in Fersterer and Winter Ebmer (2000)
12. The Sargan test is an over-identification test for instruments validity with an asymptotic chi-squared distribution and degrees of freedom equal to the number of over-identifying restrictions.
13. In principle, both the information on the 'actual' number of years spent in school as well as the (minimum) 'standard' number of years necessary to obtain a certain type of degree achieved would be desirable, because many students, in Italy, take more years than formally stated to complete their studies (i.e. when they fail, they have to repeat a year). The difference between the two measures would be an (indirect) indicator of both student 'quality', as well as of school selectivity. Unfortunately, the 'actual' number of years spent in school is not available in the SHIW dataset.
14. In particular, 87% of employed females with a university degree (versus 64% of males) work in the public sector. Among them, 80% (versus 61% for males) are schoolteachers.
15. It is fair to note that, at least in the long run, unexplained differentials in returns ought to be eliminated by the working of market forces, and that the differences which persist should depend only on productivity differentials. However, given the time required to eliminate the unbalances between supply and demand for any given group of individuals, differences in returns may well persist over time. Furthermore, it should be stressed that other factors, irrespective of productivity, may introduce differences in returns to education. These include preferences, taste for discrimination, market segmentation and other factors originating from imperfect information and non-competitive forces.
16. Another example, not discussed in this chapter, is allocation of employees to different firm sizes (see Brunello and Colussi, 1998).
17. Non-working females supplying zero hours might choose not to work because the market wage is lower than their reservation wage.
18. In the first stage of the ordered probit we assign the value 0 to non-participation, 1 to part-time work and 2 to full-time employment.
19. Although the model could be identified parametrically by functional form (assuming normality), we also impose additional exclusion restrictions (i.e. family background and unearned income), which are assumed to determine labour market participation but not wages.

REFERENCES

Angrist, J. and Krueger, A. (1991) "Does Compulsory School Attendance Affect Schooling and Earnings?" *Quarterly Journal of Economics*, 106 (4), pp. 979-1014

Ashenfelter, O., Harmon, C. and Oosterbeek, H. (1999), "A Review of Estimates of the Schooling/Earnings Relationship: with tests for Publication Bias", *Labour Economics*, Vol. 6, pp. 453-70.

Bound, J. Jaeger and D. Baker, R. (1995), "Problems with Instrumental Variable Estimation when the Correlation between the Instruments and the Endogenous Explanatory Variables is Weak", *Journal of the American Statistical Association,* June, pp. 442 –50.

Brunello,G. and Rizzi, D. (1993), "I differenziali retributivi nei settori pubblico e privato in Italia. Un'analisi cross-section. *Politica Economica,* June, pp. 339-66.

Brunello, G. and Dustmann, C. (1996), "Public and Private Sector Wages: a Comparison between Germany and Italy", in INSEE, *Comparaisons Internationales de Salaires*, Paris, 85-107.

Brunello, G. and Colussi, A. (1998), "The Employer Size-Wage Effect. Evidence from Italy", *Labour Economics*, 5 (2), pp. 217-30.

Brunello, G. and Miniaci, R. (1999) "The Economic Returns to Education in Italy", forthcoming in *Labour Economics: an International Journal*

Brunello, G., Comi, S. and Lucifora, C. (1999a), "The returns to education in Italy. A review of the Applied Literature" Chapter 9 in R. Asplund and P.T. Pereira *Returns to Human Capital in Europe. A Literature Review,* ETLA, Helsinki.

Brunello, G., Comi, S. and Lucifora, C. (1999b), "The Returns to Education in Italy: A new look at the Evidence" *FEEM Working Paper 101/99* .

Card, D. (1995), "Earnings , Schooling and Ability Revisited", *Research in Labor Economics,* JAI Press: Greenwich, Conn. and London, Vol. 14, pp. 23-48.

Card, D. (1999), "The causal Effect of Education on Earnings" in O. Ashenfelter and D. Card (Eds.) *Handbook of Labor Economics*, Volume 3, Amsterdam: Elsevier North-Holland.

Card, D. and Lemieux, T., (1999), Can Falling Supply Explain the Rising Return to College for Younger Men? A cohort Based Analysis, mimeo, University of California at Berkeley.

Christensen, J.J. and Westergaard-Nielsen, N. (1999) " The Returns to Education in Europe: Evidence from the PURE Countries", mimeo Aarhus University, *Centre for Labour Market and Social Research.*

Deaton, A. (1997) *The Analysis of Household Surveys,* Johns Hopkins University Press for the World Bank, Baltimore .

Ermisch, J. and R. Wright (1993), "Wage Offers and Full-Time and Part-time Employment by British Women", *Journal of Human Resources*, 28, 111–33.

Fersterer, J. And Winter-Ebmer, R. (2000), "Smoking, Discount rates and returns to Education", *IZA Working paper 126*, Bonn.

Guiso, L. and Paiella, M. (2000), "Risk Aversion, Wealth and Financial Market Imperfections", mimeo, Ente Einaudi, Rome.

Harmon, C. and Walker, I. (1995), "Estimates of the Economic Return to Schooling for the UK", *American Economic Review*, 85 (5), pp. 1278-86.

Heckman, J. (1979), "Sample Selection Bias as a Specification Error", *Econometrica*, 47 (1), pp. 153-61.

ISTAT(1999) *Lo stato dell'università – I principali indicatori,* Indicatori statistici, No.1.

OECD (1997), *Education at a Glance*, Paris.

OECD (1998), *Education Policy Analysis*, Paris.

10. The Netherlands

Jeroen Smits, Joop Odink and Joop Hartog

INTRODUCTION

In an earlier study (Hartog *et al.*, 1999), we presented an overview of the empirical literature on the rate of return to education in the Netherlands. An important conclusion of that study was that the rate of return in terms of the gross hourly wage of Dutch males was about 11% in 1962 and decreased steadily since then to about 7% in 1985. Between 1985 and 1989 it remained stable. The returns computed on the bases of the net hourly wage were somewhat lower than those on the bases of the gross hourly wage, and, in the early 1980s, the rate of return for females seemed to be somewhat lower than for males. Estimates of returns to education using instrumental variables techniques (to control for ability bias and endogeneity of schooling) were somewhat higher than estimates using ordinary least squares regression.

The main aim of this study is to increase the body of knowledge on returns to education in the Netherlands with new empirical evidence, using comparable datasets, for the period 1986-1996. We start with the estimation of standard Mincerian earnings equations (the log of the hourly wages regressed on years of education, potential experience and potential experience squared) for male and female Dutch workers in the years 1986, 1988, 1990, 1992, 1994 and 1996, using the OSA panel data sets. We discuss both the (changes in) the returns to education and the (changes in) the returns to potential experience in this period. After that, the existing long-term time series on the rate of return in terms of the gross hourly wages for Dutch males is extended to 1995, on the basis of data from the 1995 Structure of Earnings Survey. We also compute comparable figures for Dutch females, for the years 1989 and 1995.

Then, we present the results of a number of analyses on the 1996 wave of the OSA panel, in which the effect of alternative specifications of the earnings equation on the coefficient of the educational variable is tested. We replace potential experience and potential experience squared by age and age squared and by actual experience and actual experience squared. Separate models are estimated for the private and the public sectors, and we consider the effect of adding extra variables to the equation, like region, urbanization, the presence of a partner, and the social status of family background. We also test whether the selective non-participation of women influences the estimated returns to education for them. And, finally, we present estimates of the returns to educational levels and fields for the Netherlands.[1]

DATA

For most of the analyses presented in this chapter, we use the data from the OSA panel, a panel survey that is biannually conducted by the Dutch Organisation for Strategic Labour Market Research (Organisatie voor Strategisch Arbeidsmarkt Onderzoek), or OSA. The first wave of this OSA panel was held in 1985 and subsequent waves were held in 1986, 1988, 1990, 1992, 1994 and 1996. This survey pertains to individuals aged 16 to 64, and contains detailed information on (changes in) labour market situation and education. The number of respondents is approximately 4500.

Besides the OSA panel we will also use data from the 1989 and the 1995 Structure of Earnings Survey of the Dutch Central Bureau of Statistics. The survey will be used to extend the long-term time series on returns to education in the Netherlands, which previously covered the period 1962-1989, and to estimate comparable figures for women. For the estimation of this time series, Hartog *et al.* (1993) used the Structure of Earnings Surveys held in 1962, 1965, 1972, 1979, 1985 and 1989. Until 1979, the Structure of Earnings Survey was a large cross-sectional employer survey in which information on gross earnings, educational level, sex, age, and industry of employees was gathered. In the 1985 and 1989 versions, the same information was obtained by gathering additional educational information for a sub sample of the yearly 'Wage Survey'. This is an employer survey in which normally no questions on education is asked. The 1995 version of the Structure of Earnings Survey was created by combining information at the individual level of three different data sources: the 1995 'Employment and Wages Survey', the 1995 'Insured Persons Register', and the 1994 to 1996 'Labour Force Surveys'. The number of respondents in the Structure of Earnings Survey was very large in the period 1962 to 1979, about 10 000 in 1985, 30 000 in 1989, and 140 000 in 1995.

RESULTS

Returns to Years of Education

Tables 10.1 and 10.2 present the coefficients from standard Mincerian earnings equations for male and female employees in the Netherlands. The estimates are based on the OSA data for the years 1986, 1988, 1990, 1992,

1994 and 1996. The dependent variable in all cases is the natural logarithm of the net hourly wage. Independent variables are the number of years of education completed after primary education,[2] potential experience (age-years of education-12), and potential experience squared. The analyses for the males are restricted to full-time workers, defined as persons working more than 34 hours per week. The analyses for the females apply to all salaried workers. In the analyses for the females, a dummy variable is added to indicate whether (1) or not (0) the woman works part-time (34 hours or less in a week). Self-employed workers are excluded from the analyses.

Table 10.1   Mincer models for net hourly wages of Dutch males

| | Net hourly wages | | | | | |
	1986	1988	1990	1992	1994	1996
Constant	1.626	1.645	1.744	1.866	1.811	1.843
	(0.034)	(0.032)	(0.028)	(0.028)	(0.028)	(0.029)
Education	0.058	0.061	0.054	0.056	0.063	0.063
	(0.003)	(0.003)	(0.003)	(0.003)	(0.002)	(0.002)
Experience	0.046	0.049	0.053	0.047	0.053	0.051
(Potential)	(0.003)	(0.003)	(0.002)	(0.002)	(0.002)	(0.002)
Experience	-0.067	-0.073	-0.084	-0.070	-0.080	-0.072
squared*	(0.006)	(0.006)	(0.006)	(0.005)	(0.005)	(0.005)
Adjusated-R^2	0.368	0.404	0.444	0.441	0.513	0.497
Observations	1367	1389	1448	1432	1367	1423

Notes: Standard errors in parenthesis.* Parameter multiplied by 100.
Source: OSA 1986 to 1996

Tables 10.1 and 10.2, and also Figure 10.1, show that the average rate of return to one extra year of education for the males is around 6% in the second half of the 1980s. The returns are lower in 1990 (about 5.4%) and then go upward to about 6.3% in 1996. For the females the returns are also about 6% in the second half of the 1980s. After 1990 they show a downward trend to about 5.1% in 1996. The coefficient on the dummy for women working part-time is not significant.

The OSA data sets for the years 1994 and 1996 contain, besides information on the net earnings of the respondents, also information on their gross earnings. For these years, the coefficients of the schooling variables of Mincerian models with the gross hourly wage as dependent variable are presented in Table 10.3 and in Figure 10.1. For the males, the return in terms of the gross wages was 7.3% in 1994 and 7.5% in 1996. For the females these figures were 6.4% and 5.6%, respectively. So, for the males the gross returns are about 1% higher than the net returns whereas for the females the difference is about 0.5%.

Table 10.2   Mincer models for net hourly wages of Dutch females

	Net hourly wages					
Year	1986	1988	1990	1992	1994	1996
Constant	1.521	1.584	1.708	1.867	1.876	1.916
	(0.049)	(0.044)	(0.038)	(0.038)	(0.037)	(0.041)
Education	0.062	0.060	0.060	0.053	0.057	0.051
	(0.006)	(0.005)	(0.004)	(0.004)	(0.004)	(0.004)
Experience	0.045	0.044	0.041	0.034	0.037	0.041
(Potential)	(0.004)	(0.004)	(0.003)	(0.003)	(0.003)	(0.003)
Experience	-0.078	-0.071	-0.068	-0.056	-0.057	-0.063
squared*	(0.011)	(0.009)	(0.008)	(0.008)	(0.007)	(0.008)
Part time	0.026	0.036	-0.008	0.023	0.033	0.013
	(0.026)	(0.024)	(0.023)	(0.022)	(0.021)	(0.022)
Adjusted-R^2	0.256	0.315	0.315	0.253	0.325	0.280
Observations	782	803	893	959	928	1029

Notes: Standard errors in parenthesis. * Parameter multiplied by 100.
Source: OSA 1986 to 1996.

Figure 10.1   Returns to education in the Netherlands 1986-1996

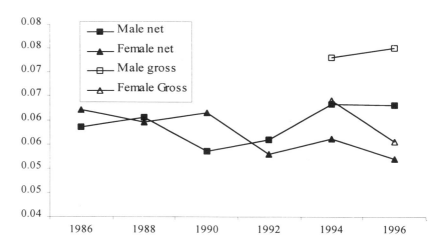

Source: OSA 1986 to 1996.

Table 10.3   Mincer models for gross hourly wages of males and females

| | Males | | Females | |
	1994	1996	1994	1996
Constant	2.076	2.082	2.159	2.207
	(0.038)	(0.037)	(0.046)	(0.048)
Education	0.073	0.075	0.064	0.056
	(0.003)	(0.003)	(0.005)	(0.005)
Experience (potential)	0.058	0.056	0.040	0.046
	(0.003)	(0.003)	(0.004)	(0.004)
Experience squared*	-0.086	-0.076	-0.055	-0.076
	(0.007)	(0.007)	(0.009)	(0.009)
Part ime			-0.003	0.000
			(0.026)	(0.026)
Adjusted-R^2	0.448	0.472	0.306	0.254
Observations	1287	1338	850	949

Notes: Standard errors in parenthesis. * Parameter multiplied by 100.
Source: OSA 1994 and 1996.

Table 10.4   Returns using net and gross wages: males and females, 1996

| | Males | | Females | |
	Net wage	Gross wage	Net wage	Gross wage
Constant	9.474	9.718	9.583	9.827
	(0.029)	(0.036)	(0.067)	(0.078)
Education	0.061	0.073	0.068	0.079
	(0.002)	(0.003)	(0.007)	(0.008)
Experience (potential)	0.050	0.055	0.022	0.027
	(0.002)	(0.003)	(0.006)	(0.006)
Experience squared*	-0.070	-0.075	-0.031	-0.041
	(0.005)	(0.007)	(0.013)	(0.015)
Part time	-	-	-0.665	-0.674
			(0.037)	(0.043)
Adjusted R^2	0.494	0.465	0.310	0.292
Observations	1421	1335	1030	951

Notes: Standard errors in parenthesis. * Parameter multiplied by 100.
Source: OSA, 1996.

Table 10.4 shows the returns based on the net and gross yearly earnings for the year 1996. For the males, there is little difference between returns based on hourly wages and those based on yearly earnings. That is no surprise given the fact that the returns to the hourly wages are for full-time workers only. For the females, the differences are much larger, with the returns to yearly earnings about 2% higher than those based on hourly wages.

Returns to Experience

All of the estimates above show decreasing returns to potential experience. When the number of years of potential experience increases, the returns first rise and subsequently fall. In Figure 10.2 and Table 10.5 the rates of return to selected numbers of years of potential experience are presented for males and females in 1996. The returns for the males are higher than those for the females and reach their maximum at a higher experience level.

Table 10.5   Returns to potential experience: males and females, 1996

Potential experience	Returns males	Returns females
5 years	0.240	0.188
10 years	0.443	0.343
15 years	0.611	0.467
20 years	0.743	0.560
25 years	0.838	0.621
30 years	0.898	0.650
35 years	0.922	0.647
40 years	0.911	0.612
45 years	0.863	0.546
50 years	0.779	0.449

Source: OSA 1996.

Table 10.6   Returns to 10 years of potential experience and maximum of potential experience curve for males and females

	Returns males	Returns females	Maximum males	Maximum females
1986	0.393	0.367	34.3 years	28.4 years
1988	0.421	0.372	33.7 years	31.1 years
1990	0.448	0.341	31.8 years	30.1 years
1992	0.397	0.281	33.2 years	29.9 years
1994	0.449	0.313	33.1 years	32.7 years
1996	0.443	0.343	35.8 years	32.1 years

Source: OSA 1986 to 1996.

Figure 10.2 Returns to potential experience in the Netherlands in 1996

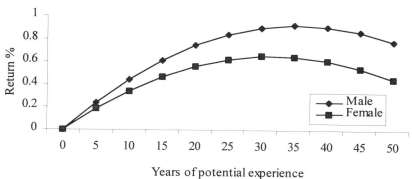

Table 10.6 shows for the period 1986 to 1996 the rate of return to 10 years of potential experience and the number of years of potential experience at which the maximum is reached. In each year, the rate of return to 10 years of potential experience is substantially higher for the males than for the females. For the males, the returns to 10 years of potential experience were higher in 1994 and 1996 than in the 1980s. For the females these returns were highest in 1986 and 1988. The maximum of the experience curve for men lies at around 33 years of potential experience. For women it lies somewhat lower.

Long-term Trend

In our review of the Dutch empirical literature on returns to education, we considered a time series computed by Hartog *et al.* (1993) on the returns to education in terms of the gross hourly wage of Dutch males in the period 1962 to 1989. For this study we have extended this series to 1995, using data from the Structure of Earnings Survey conducted in 1995. Furthermore, we have used data from the 1989 and 1995 Structure of Earnings surveys to compute a comparable series for women. The results of these analyses are presented in Figure 10.3. A difference with the other results presented in this chapter is that, for reasons of comparability with the earlier results, the figures presented in Figure 10.3 are computed on the basis of all working males and females, and that for the females no indicator variable for working part time is used.

For the males, the coefficient of years of education in 1995 has a value of 0.074, which means that the stabilization of the long-term trend between 1985 and 1989, found by Hartog *et al.* (1993), to a large extent continues in the first half of the 1990s. For the females, the coefficient of years of education has the same value in 1989 and 1995. In both years the rate of return to education is 6.6%. In 1995, the difference in rate of return to education between males and females is a little less than 1%.

Figure 10.3   Long-term trend in returns to education in the Netherlands

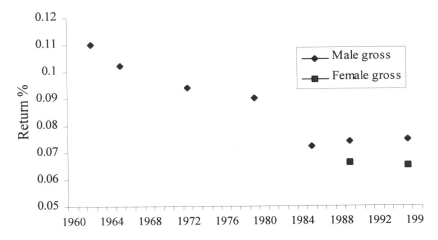

Source: Structure of Earnings Survey: 1962, 1965, 1972, 1979, 1985, 1989 and 1995.

Alternative Specifications of the Earnings Equation

In Tables 10.7 to 10.11, the coefficients of a number of alternative specifications of the Mincerian model are presented, estimated on the basis of the OSA data for the year 1996. Model I in Tables 10.7 and 10.8 is the baseline model from Tables 10.1 and 10.2, with education in years, potential experience and potential experience square, and, for the females, a dummy indicating part-time employment. In Model II, potential experience and potential experience squared are replaced by age and age squared. In Model III they are replaced by actual experience and actual experience squared, and in Model IV by age, age squared, actual experience and actual experience squared. In all three alternatives, the coefficient on the education variable is lower than in Model I, for both the males and the females. The difference is largest in the models with age, but it is also substantial in the model with actual experience. The education coefficient in the models with both age and actual experience do not differ much from those in the models with only age. For the males, the effects of age and actual experience are decreasing in this model. For the females, the effect of age is also decreasing but the effect of actual experience is linear.

Models V and VI are separate models for the private and public sector. For the males, the returns to education are about 1.5% higher in the private sector than in the public sector. For the females, the returns are somewhat higher in the public sector. Model VII tests whether the returns to education for men are different if they are computed on the basis of all male employees instead of only the full-time workers. This does not seem to be the case. The coefficient of education of Model VII is only a little lower than that of Model I.

Table 10.7   Effects of potential experience, actual experience, age, working part-time, and difference between private and public sector for males in 1996

Model	I	II	III	IV	V	VI	VII
Constant	1.843	0.7416	1.998	1.258	1.775	2.083	1.844
	(0.029)	(0.091)	(0.026)	(0.136)	(0.036)	(0.056)	(0.030)
Education	0.063	0.045	0.057	0.042	0.068	0.053	0.062
	(0.002)	(0.002)	(0.002)	(0.003)	(0.003)	(0.004)	(0.003)
Experience	0.052				0.055	0.038	0.051
(Potential)	(0.002)				(0.003)	(0.005)	(0.002)
Experience	-0.072				-0.077	-0.049	-0.069
squared*	(0.005)				(0.006)	(0.010)	(0.005)
Age		0.081		0.046			
		(0.005)		(0.009)			
Age		-0.079		-0.030			
squared*		(0.006)		(0.011)			
Experience			0.048	0.018			
(Actual)			(0.002)	(0.004)			
Experience			-0.075	-0.049			
squared*			(0.005)	(0.009)			
Part time							0.033
							(0.023)
Adjusted-R^2	0.497	0.492	0.466	0.501	0.482	0.470	0.465
Obs.	1423	1423	1416	1416	1039	384	1579
Selection	>34 hours	>34 hours	>34 hours	>34 hours	Priv. >34	Pub. >34	All

Notes: Standard errors in parenthesis. * Parameter multiplied by 100.
Source: OSA 1996.

To find out whether the returns to schooling in the Netherlands differ between different parts of the country, Table 10.9 presents the coefficients of Mincer models with dummy variables for region and with interaction terms between education and region. Models I and III show that in the most densely populated and industrialized mid-western part of the Netherlands, called the Randstad (the omitted reference category in Table 10.9), the hourly wages are higher than in the North (Groningen, Friesland, Drenthe), the East

Education and Earnings in Europe

(Overijssel, Gelderland, Flevoland) and the South (Zeeland, Noord-Brabant, Limburg) of the country. Only the wages of females in the North of the country do not differ significantly from those in the Randstad.

Table 10.8   Effects of potential experience, actual experience, age, and difference between private and public sector for females in 1996

Model	I	II	III	IV	V	VI
Constant	1.916	0.821	2.022	0.022	1.891	2.018
	(0.041)	(0.121)	(0.037)	(0.022)	(0.063)	(0.059)
Education	0.051	0.037	0.042	0.040	0.047	0.049
	(0.004)	(0.004)	(0.004)	(0.004)	(0.007)	(0.005)
Experience	0.041				0.044	0.035
(potential)	(0.003)				(0.005)	(0.004)
Experience	-0.063				-0.067	-0.055
squared*	(0.008)				(0.012)	(0.010)
Age		0.078		0.065		
		(0.007)		(0.009)		
Age		-0.083		-0.078		
squared*		(0.009)		(0.011)		
Experience			0.041	0.015		
(actual)			(0.004)	(0.005)		
Experience			-0.067	-0.007		
squared*			(0.010)	(0.012)		
Part time	0.013	0.006	0.058	0.022	-0.050	0.031
	(0.022)	(0.022)	(0.022)	(0.022)	(0.035)	(0.030)
Adjusted-R^2	0.280	0.295	0.286	0.323	0.265	0.229
Obs.	1029	1030	1024	1024	429	600
Selection	All	All	All	All	Private	Public

Notes: Standard errors in parenthesis. * Parameter multiplied by 100.
Source: OSA 1996.

Adding the dummies for region to the equation does not affect the coefficient of the educational variable. Moreover, none of the interaction effects between education and region are significant. This finding indicates that there are no substantial differences in returns to education among the Dutch regions.

Table 10.10 presents coefficients of Mincer models with indicators of the social status of the respondents' parents when they were 12 years of age: whether (1) or not (0) the main breadwinner has completed secondary or a higher education ('high education parent'), whether or not the main breadwinner was working in a non-manual occupation ('high occupation parent'), and two dummies indicating whether or not the educational and occupational information of the parent was missing ('education parent missing' and 'occupation parent missing'). Models I and III only contain main effect parameters; Models II and IV contain main effect parameters and parameters for the interaction between education and parental education and occupation.

Table 10.9   Effects of region for males and females in 1996

	Males, model		Females, model	
	I	II	III	IV
Constant	1.876	1.872	1.943	1.951
	(0.030)	(0.033)	(0.042)	(0.048)
Education	0.062	0.063	0.052	0.050
	(0.002)	(0.004)	(0.004)	(0.006)
Experience	0.052	0.052	0.041	0.041
(potential)	(0.002)	(0.002)	(0.003)	(0.003)
Experience	-0.072	-0.073	-0.064	-0.063
squared	(0.005)	(0.005)	(0.008)	(0.008)
Region North[b]	-0.084	-0.042	-0.035	0.050
	(0.022)	(0.044)	(0.033)	(0.076)
Region East[b]	-0.044	-0.052	-0.064	-0.101
	(0.017)	(0.034)	(0.026)	(0.063)
Region South[b]	-0.051	-0.047	-0.057	-0.110
	(0.017)	(0.035)	(0.026)	(0.058)
Region North × Education		-0.008		-0.015
		(0.008)		(0.012)
Region East × Education		0.002		0.006
		(0.006)		(0.010)
Region South × Education		-0.001		0.009
		(0.006)		(0.009)
Part time			0.015	0.017
			(0.022)	(0.023)
Adjusted R^2	0.503	0.502	0.284	0.284
Observations	1422	1422	1027	1027

Notes: Standard errors in parenthesis.
[a] Parameter multiplied by 100.
[b] Reference category for region is Randstad.
Source: OSA 1996.

Only the coefficient of parental occupation for the males is significant. Having a parent with a non-manual occupation has a significantly positive effect on their hourly wage. None of the interaction effects with education is significant. This indicates that in the Netherlands the rate of return to education does not depend on the social status of one's family background.

Table 10.11 presents the coefficients of models with a number of extra
control factors. There are dummy variables indicating whether or not the
respondent works in the public sector ('public sector'), has a partner ('with
partner'), and lives in a large city ('large city'). The models also contain the
indicators of the social status of the respondents' parents when they were 12
years of age and the dummies for region. Finally, work experience of the
respondent is measured with both potential experience and potential
experience squared and actual experience and actual experience squared.

*Table 10.10   Effects of parental education and occupation for males and
females in 1996*

	Males, model		Females, model	
	I	II	III	IV
Constant	1.833	1.846	1.881	1.889
	(0.033)	(0.035)	(0.047)	(0.052)
Education	0.061	0.059	0.050	0.049
	(0.003)	(0.003)	(0.004)	(0.006)
Experience	0.051	0.051	0.041	0.041
(potential)	(0.003)	(0.003)	(0.003)	(0.003)
Experience	-0.071	-0.071	-0.064	-0.064
squared*	(0.005)	(0.005)	(0.008)	(0.008)
High education parent	0.017	-0.021	0.011	-0.102
(breadwinner)	(0.026)	(0.061)	(0.037)	(0.099)
Education parent missing	0.002	0.003	0.018	0.019
	(0.015)	(0.015)	(0.024)	(0.024)
High occupation parent	0.047	0.024	0.029	0.028
(breadwinner)	(0.014)	(0.029)	(0.021)	(0.047)
Occupation parent missing	0.025	0.026	0.068	0.067
	(0.028)	(0.028)	(0.040)	(0.040)
Education parent × Education		0.006		0.018
		(0.008)		(0.014)
Occupation parent × Education		0.004		0.000
		(0.005)		(0.007)
Part time			0.018	0.018
			(0.023)	(0.023)
Adj. R-squared	0.501	0.500	0.281	0.280
Observations	1423	1423	1029	1029

Notes: Standard errors in parenthesis. * Parameter multiplied by 100.
Source: OSA 1996

Table 10.11   Effects of several control factors simultaneously, males and females in 1996

	Males	Females
Constant	1.886 (0.035)	1.913 (0.049)
Education	0.061 (0.003)	0.042 (0.004)
Experience (potential)	0.032 (0.005)	0.027 (0.005)
Experience squared	-0.025 (0.012)	-0.051 (0.010)
Experience (actual)	0.011 (0.005)	0.018 (0.005)
Experience (actual) squared	-0.036 (0.011)	-0.018 (0.013)
Public sector	0.007 (0.015)	0.067 (0.021)
With partner	0.143 (0.018)	0.027 (0.025)
High education parent	0.019 (0.025)	0.003 (0.036)
Education parent missing	0.004 (0.015)	0.021 (0.023)
High occupation parent	0.050 (0.014)	0.023 (0.020)
Occupation parent missing	0.015 (0.027)	0.049 (0.039)
Region North[b]	-0.100 (0.022)	-0.029 (0.033)
Region East[b]	-0.055 (0.017)	-0.061 (0.025)
Region South[b]	-0.058 (0.017)	-0.054 (0.026)
Large city	-0.038 (0.013)	0.009 (0.020)
Part time		0.015 (0.023)
Adjusted R^2	0.533	0.319
Observations	1415	1021

Notes: Standard errors in parenthesis. [a] Parameter multiplied by 100, [b] Reference category for region is "Randstad"
Source: OSA 1996

For the males, having a partner, having a parent working in a non-manual occupation, and living in the Randstad, leads to significantly higher hourly wages, whereas living in a large city has a significant negative effect on their wages. For the females, the wages are significantly higher in the public sector and significantly lower in the East and the South of the country. With all these control factors in the model, the coefficient of education for the males is only slightly reduced. For the females, this coefficient is about 1% lower than in the model without control factors.

One last observation is that in the Netherlands the hourly wages of persons working part time on average are not lower than those of full-time workers. Only in Model III of Table 10.8, the dummy for working part-time has a significant effect, and there the effect is positive, indicating higher net hourly wages for women working part time.

Selective non-participation of women

Table 10.12   Mincer models for Dutch females with and without Heckman control factor (Lambda) for participation selectivity bias

Model	I	II[a]	III	IV[b]	V	VI[c]
Constant	1.916	1.892	2.044	2.029	1.758	1.960
	(0.041)	(0.054)	(0.056)	(0.059)	(0.057)	(0.115)
Education	0.051	0.053	0.047	0.050	0.061	0.054
	(0.004)	(0.004)	(0.005)	(0.006)	(0.006)	(0.008)
Experience (Potential)	0.041	0.041	0.033	0.032	0.053	0.051
	(0.003)	(0.003)	(0.004)	(0.005)	(0.005)	(0.006)
Experience Squared[d]	-0.063	-0.065	-0.050	-0.050	-0.087	-0.071
	(0.008)	(0.008)	(0.010)	(0.010)	(0.014)	(0.018)
Part-time	0.013	0.008				
	(0.022)	(0.024)				
Lambda		0.034		0.057		-0.155
		(0.050)		(0.037)		(0.070)
Selection	All	All	Part time	Part time	Full time	Full time
Observations	1029	1029	702	702	327	327

Notes: Standard errors in parenthesis.
[a] Standard probit selection model.
[b] Ordered probit selection model: part-time workers.
[c] Ordered probit selection model: full-time workers.
[d] Parameter multiplied by 100.
Source: OSA 1996.

Returns to Educational Levels and Sectors

Table 10.13 shows the coefficients of Mincerian models for male and female workers with the years of schooling variable replaced by dummies for educational levels. The reference group is primary education only. In Models II and IV, the coefficients of the dummies of the levels are divided by the number of years of schooling it normally takes after primary education to complete the level. These coefficients show the returns to one year of education for persons with that level as highest level completed.

Table 10.13   Wage equations with dummy variables for educational level[a]

	Males		Females	
	Total returns	Returns per year	Total returns	Returns per year
Constant	1.946	1.942	2.032	2.032
	(0.030)	(0.030)	(0.045)	(0.045)
Lower secondary vocational	0.091	0.023	0.017	0.004
(VBO)	(0.022)	(0.005)	(0.041)	(0.010)
Lower secondary general	0.237	0.059	0.140	0.035
(MAVO)	(0.026)	(0.006)	(0.039)	(0.010)
Intermediate secondary general	0.274	0.055	0.146	0.029
(HAVO)	(0.039)	(0.008)	(0.054)	(0.011)
Upper secondary general	0.412	0.069	0.273	0.045
(VWO)	(0.035)	(0.006)	(0.068)	(0.011)
Upper secondary vocational	0.318	0.042	0.222	0.030
(MBO)	(0.025)	(0.003)	(0.039)	(0.005)
Higher professional	0.535	0.059	0.427	0.047
(HBO)	(0.026)	(0.003)	(0.042)	(0.005)
University	0.705	0.064	0.675	0.061
	(0.035)	(0.003)	(0.072)	(0.007)
Experience (potential)	0.051	0.051	0.039	0.039
	(0.002)	(0.002)	(0.003)	(0.003)
Experience squared[b]	-0.074	-0.074	-0.063	-0.063
	(0.005)	(0.005)	(0.008)	(0.008)
Part-time			0.021	0.021
			(0.022)	(0.022)
Adjusted R^2	0.540	0.540	0.314	0.314
Observations	1423	1423	1029	1029

Notes: Standard errors in parenthesis.
[a] Reference category for education is primary schooling only.
[b] Parameter multiplied by 100.
Source: OSA 1996.

The returns to one year of schooling vary among schooling levels, with rather low returns to lower and upper secondary vocational schooling. At each level, the returns for the males are higher than those for the females. For the males, the returns to each year invested in education are highest for individuals who started to work after completing upper secondary general education and for the ones who finished university. For the females, the returns are highest for the years invested in university education.

In Tables 10.14 and 10.15, education is split up further according to four educational sectors: (1) general education (preparing for further study), (2) technical and agricultural education, (3) economic and administrative education, and (4) social, medical, and personal care education. Table 10.14 presents separate coefficients for the main educational levels and for the sectors. In Table 10.15, each level sector combination is represented by a dummy variable. Columns I and II are total returns and returns per year.

Table 10.14   Explanation of log net hourly wages in 1996 with separate dummy variables for educational level and field

	Males		Females	
	Coef.	Std. err.	Coef.	Std. err.
Constant	1.827	(0.033)	1.923	(0.066)
Educational level				
Primary	Reference category			
Lower secondary	0.210	(0.024)	0.110	(0.038)
Upper secondary	0.397	(0.026)	0.256	(0.043)
Lower tertiary	0.663	(0.032)	0.474	(0.050)
Upper tertiary	0.818	(0.040)	0.731	(0.078)
Educational field				
Technical	Reference category			
General	0.107	(0.017)	0.132	(0.052)
Economic/administrative	0.084	(0.024)	0.066	(0.053)
Social/medical/personal care	-0.069	(0.025)	0.091	(0.049)
Experience (potential)	0.051	(0.002)	0.037	(0.003)
Experience squared*	-0.074	(0.005)	-0.059	(0.008)
Part time			0.019	(0.023)
Adjusted-R^2	0.541		0.300	
Observations	1399		1010	

Notes: Standard errors in parenthesis. * Parameter multiplied by 100.
Source: OSA 1996.

Table 10.15   *Dummy variables for level and field combinations*[a]

	Males		Females	
	I	II	I	II
Constant	1.928	1.928	2.052	2.052
	(0.030)	(0.030)	(0.047)	(0.047)
Lower secondary general	0.237	0.059	0.138	0.035
	(0.026)	(0.006)	(0.039)	(0.010)
Lower secondary Technical	0.091	0.023	-0.028	-0.007
	(0.022)	(0.005)	(0.090)	(0.022)
Lower secondary economics/administration	0.094	0.023	-0.049	-0.012
	(0.057)	(0.014)	(0.065)	(0.016)
Lower secondary social/medical/personal care	0.085	0.021	0.042	0.011
	(0.091)	(0.023)	(0.044)	(0.011)
Intermediate secondary general	0.276	0.055	0.142	0.028
	(0.039)	(0.008)	(0.054)	(0.011)
Upper secondary general	0.412	0.069	0.269	0.045
	(0.035)	(0.006)	(0.068)	(0.011)
Upper secondary technical	0.305	0.041	0.127	0.017
	(0.027)	(0.004)	(0.082)	(0.011)
Upper secondary economics/administration	0.394	0.052	0.228	0.030
	(0.035)	(0.005)	(0.049)	(0.007)
Upper secondary social/medical/personal care	0.242	0.032	0.225	0.030
	(0.046)	(0.006)	(0.041)	(0.006)
Non-university tertiary technical	0.576	0.064	0.349	0.039
	(0.033)	(0.004)	(0.109)	(0.012)
Non-university economics/administration	0.612	0.068	0.342	0.038
	(0.049)	(0.005)	(0.077)	(0.009)
Non-university social/medical/personal care	0.470	0.052	0.439	0.049
	(0.033)	(0.004)	(0.043)	(0.005)
University technical	0.677	0.062	0.577	0.052
	(0.050)	(0.005)	(0.158)	(0.014)
University economics/administration	0.843	0.077	0.885	0.080
	(0.058)	(0.005)	(0.158)	(0.014)
University social/medical/personal care	0.631	0.057	0.633	0.058
	(0.053)	(0.005)	(0.087)	(0.008)
Adj R-squared	0.546	0.546	0.307	0.307
Observations	1399	1399	1010	1010

Notes:[a] Reference category for education is primary education. [b]Parameter multiplied by 100.

The figures show that for both males and females, the returns to general education are higher than the returns in the other educational sectors. The group of pupils who do not continue to further education after finishing general education may be a selected group, which, for example, may consist of pupils who received a good job offer. For the males, economic-administrative education comes in the second place and the returns in the care-sector are the lowest. For the females, the care-sector comes second and the returns to technical education are the lowest.

CONCLUSIONS

Given the results of the new analyses of the rates of return to education in the Netherlands, a number of interesting conclusions can be drawn. First, we have extended the existing long-term time series on returns to education in terms of the gross hourly wages of Dutch males on the basis of new data for 1995 and we have computed comparable rate of return figures for females in the years 1989 and 1995. Our results show that for the males, the stabilization of the trend between 1985 and 1989 has continued after 1989. In 1995, the rate of return to education for Dutch males is 7.4%, which is only 0.2% higher than in 1985. Compared to the large decrease from 11% in 1962 to 7.2% in 1985, the increase after 1985 is very small. For the females, the rate of return to education in terms of the gross hourly wage remained stable between 1989 and 1995 at about 6.6%.

Second, we have made a more detailed analysis of the trend in returns to education computed on the basis of the net hourly wage for males and females in the period from 1986 to 1996. For both males and females, this rate of return was about 6% in 1986. For the males the returns decreased slightly to less than 5.5% in 1990, increasing to 6.3% in 1995. For the females, the returns decreased somewhat over this period to 5.1% in 1996.

Third, the rate of return to potential experience was found to be substantially higher for males than for females. The maximum of the experience curve lies for males around 33 years of potential experience and for females at about 31 years of potential experience.

Fourth, several alternative specifications of the earnings equation were tested. If age or actual experience is used instead of potential experience, the coefficient of the educational variable is lower than in the model with potential experience. The rate of return to education for the males is higher in the private than in the public sector. For the females, the returns are somewhat higher in the public sector. Adding controls for region, urbanization, social status of family background, or for having a partner has very little effect on the male's education coefficient. The effect of the female's education decreases by almost 1% when all these control factors are in the model. Controlling for selection bias with regard to the labour force participation of females leads to a small decrease of the rate of return to education for full-time working females.

Finally, we have tested the effect of using educational levels and sectors instead of years of education. The returns to one year of schooling were found to differ rather much among the levels. At each level, the returns are higher for males than for females. The returns are highest for the years invested in university education and – for the males – also in upper secondary general education. With regard to educational sectors, the returns are higher for general education than for vocational education. Within vocational education, males have the highest returns to economic-administrative education. Females have relatively high returns in the care sector.

NOTES

1. Information about the Dutch educational system can be found in our earlier study (Hartog *et al.*, 1999).
2. The number of years completed after primary education was coded as follows: lower secondary (VBO and MAVO) four years; senior general secondary (HAVO) five years; upper secondary pre-university (VWO) six years; upper secondary vocational (MBO) seven and a half years; higher professional (HBO) nine years; university elevn years.

REFERENCES

Hartog, Joop, Hessel Oosterbeek and Coen Teulings (1993), 'Age, wages and education in the Netherlands', in Johnson, P. and K. F. Zimmermann (eds.), *Labour markets in an ageing Europe*, Cambridge: Cambridge University Press, pp. 182–211.

Hartog, Joop, Joop Odink and Jeroen Smits (1999), 'Private returns to education in the Netherlands', in Asplund, R and P. T. Pereira (eds.), *Returns to human capital in Europe: A literature review*, Helsinki: ETLA, pp. 209–226.

11. Norway

Erling Barth
and
Marianne Røed

INTRODUCTION

This chapter gives an overview of the rates of return to years of education in Norway from 1980-1995[1]. Changes in the return to education typically arise from three sources: changes in the demand for educated workers, changes in the supply of educated workers or from the institutional features of wage formation. Internationally, a rising return to education has been attributed to increasing demand for highly educated workers, particularly as a result of technological change (see for example Freeman and Katz, 1995). For Norway, Hægeland *et al.* (1999) find very little change in the return to education between 1980 and 1990 and argue that the supply expansion has been at least as great as the increase in demand. However, Kahn (1998) attributes the relative stability of the wage distribution between 1980 and 1991 to the recentralization of the bargaining system.

An important feature of the Norwegian economy is the large public sector, with large transfers and consequently a relatively high level of taxes. A particular feature of this chapter is that we also consider the effects of taxes and transfers on the private returns to education. There are a number of studies that analyse the distributional effects of the tax system in Norway. None of these, however, consider the effect on the wage distribution, but rather study the effect of taxes and transfers of the income distribution (see, for example, Thoresen, 1995). Below, we estimate the rate of returns to education in terms of net and disposable income compared with the estimated rate of return in terms of gross income.

Previous studies of the returns to human capital in Norway are reviewed in Barth and Røed (1999). This chapter provides a comprehensive study over time, using identical specifications from comparable data sets. We also undertake several specification tests, some of which have not previously been done on Norwegian data. These specification tests include accounting for omitted variable bias from other human capital variables, more flexible functional forms, and endogenous labour supply for women and endogenous schooling choice. We also consider briefly the returns in terms of income versus wage rates.

The chapter is organized as follows. The next section describes the data. In section three, we report and discuss the comparative results over time. Section four reports the results of several specification tests. Section five analyses the role of taxes and transfers for the returns to education, and the last section concludes.

THE DATA

The analysis is limited to wage earners aged 16 to 67 years. The sample of males is limited to full-time workers (greater than or equal to 30 hours per week). The sample of females includes part-timers, with a dummy variable to account for part-time female workers. The *wage variable* is calculated as reported monthly/weekly/hourly gross wage, divided by the number of reported weekly hours. The individuals are asked to report their *usual* level of wages and hours – including usual level of overtime. The *level of education* is based on a three-or-five digit code of highest completed education. In the surveys from 1980 to 1987, the variable is coded from self-reported completed education (three-digit code). In the surveys from 1989 and onwards, the educational variable is merged from administrative registers (five-digit code). Two types of Norwegian surveys are used:

1. *The Norwegian Survey of Organizations and Employees (NSOE).* The 1989 survey was conducted among Norwegian employers and employees by the Institute for Social Research and Statistics Norway. The sample is a self-weighted sample of all wage earners in Norway in 1989. Both employers (managers, staff managers and union representatives) and employees were interviewed. In 1993 the same individuals were interviewed again by Statistics Norway. In addition, the sample was expanded with employees hired by the employers in the period 1989 and 1993 in such a way as to make the sample representative of wage earners in 1993.

2. *The Level of Living Surveys (LLS)* is an ongoing project at Statistics Norway, surveying a sample of the Norwegian adult population. In 1980 the sample was limited to the 16 to 79 age range, and the sample was drawn among households. Subsequently, the samples have comprised individuals. The LLS is a panel survey, adding young persons in every wave. Every LLS contains about 5000 individuals, comprising around 2500 wage observations. Since the NSOE repeated many questions from the LLS, the two types of surveys may be used together and comparatively over time.

RATES OF RETURN TO EDUCATION 1980-1995

Table 11.1 reports the basic Mincer ordinary least squares (OLS) results. The estimates are based on both LLS and NSOE. We find that the estimates for the economy as a whole range from 4.28% to 5.95% over the whole period. There seem to have been a rise in the returns to education in the early 1980s, followed by a decline and levelling out in the 1990s. All in all, there is not much movement in the estimated returns to education in Norway over this period. When we consider men and women separately, we find that the returns to education were higher for women than for men during the 1980's, but that the rates of return have converged in the 1990's.

The figures reported here concur with those found in other Norwegian studies. Summarizing a number of studies, Barth and Røed (1999) report figures in the same range for this period, both from the same and from different data sources, when similar simple estimation techniques are used. The novel feature here is that we make comparative analyses with identical specifications over all these years. The average rate of return to education for the 15 years is 5.1%, calculated from the simple Mincer regressions. This figure is low compared to similar figures from other countries reported in this book.

In general, wage dispersion has been fairly stable in the Norwegian economy. Internationally, the price of skills has been rising in many major countries (see, for example, OECD, 1996). Changes in the wage distribution have been interpreted and explained by changes in *demand, supply and wage-setting institutions* (Freeman and Katz, 1995; Kahn, 1998). In this section, we briefly discuss the recent development of the rate of return to education in Norway in light of the development in the interaction between underlying market forces and wage-setting institutions.

Since the wage-setting regime varies considerably between the public and private sectors, it is useful to consider the price of skills in these two sectors separately. In Figure 11.1 we illustrate the development of the returns to education for men in the private and public sector.[2] We find that the returns to education increased in the early 1980s, particularly in the private sector.[3] This was followed by a period with wage compression in both sectors, which was particularly strong in the public sector. In the last two years of our analysis, returns to education have increased sharply in the private sector, while the public sector has continued to experience wage compression.

We now consider the development in wage-setting institutions. In the private sector, wage-setting was highly centralized at the end of the 1970s. In the first half of the 1980s, however, wage-setting was rather decentralized with industry bargaining and a large proportion of wage increases being determined at the local level. In the last half of the 1980s, when Norway faced declining oil prices and historically high levels of unemployment, the bargaining system was recentralized and wage moderation was the main policy of all parties involved. Wage drift was very limited, sometimes by agreement and even by law. In the 1990s, the bargaining system again allows for more local adjustments in the private sector. In the public sector, the wage-setting system has been highly centralized throughout the whole period. There was a reform around 1991 allowing for some local adjustments in wages. However, the central parties are still by and large in control of the wage structure in this sector.[4]

Table 11.1 Returns to education in Norway, 1980 to 1995.

Year		All	Men	Women
1980	Return to Schooling	0.043	0.037	0.054
	Standard error	(0.003)	(0.003)	(0.004)
	Sample size	1914	1047	867
1983	Return to Schooling	0.060	0.056	0.066
	Standard error	(0.003)	(0.003)	(0.005)
	Sample size	1927	1048	879
1987	Return to Schooling	0.050	0.045	0.058
	Standard error	(0.003)	(0.003)	(0.004)
	Sample size	2018	1002	1016
1989	Return to Schooling	0.049	0.048	0.052
	Standard error	(0.002)	(0.002)	(0.003)
	Sample size	3804	1985	1819
1991	Return to Schooling	0.054	0.053	0.056
	Standard error	(0.003)	(0.004)	(0.004)
	Sample size	1826	938	888
1993	Return to Schooling	0.048	0.047	0.049
	Standard error	(0.002)	(0.002)	(0.003)
	Sample size	3443	1789	1654
1995	Return to Schooling	0.055	0.057	0.053
	Standard error	(0.003)	(0.004)	(0.003)
	Sample size	1851	919	932

Notes: All regressions include years of experience and experience squared. Regressions for women include a dummy for part-time (less than 30 hrs). Experience is calculated as age-16-education.

Education and Earnings in Europe

Figure 11.1 Rates of return to education for males by sector

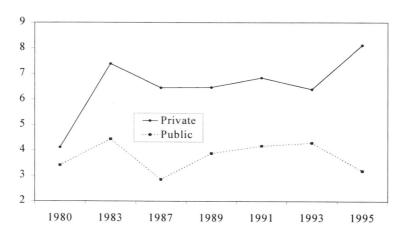

Turning now to *market forces*, Norway has experienced a boom in the supply of higher education over the period studied here. The number of persons in the Norwegian population aged 16 to 67 years with higher education (more than 12 years duration) increased dramatically from around 350000 in 1980 to well above 600000 in 1995. In 1995, 30% of wage earners had higher education. However, in line with international developments, there has been a significant increase in the demand for highly educated workers during the same period. The number of employed persons with higher education doubled from below 300,000 in 1980 to around 600000 in 1995 (Barth and Røed, 1999).

A measure of labour market tightness is unemployment. Between 1980 and 1983 the market for higher education was tight, while unemployment rose for groups with lower education. Demand side pressures worked in the direction of higher returns to education. The bargaining system was decentralized, allowing market pressures to be translated into changes in wages, particularly in the private sector. During the mid 1980s, the unemployment rate of persons with lower skills fell, and it is possible that the combined supply and demand side forces contributed to lower returns to education.

After 1987, when the economy entered a serious recession, the system of wage determination became highly centralized. Implicit in the agreement over wage moderation was an idea that low-paid workers should be relatively protected from the restraint. This contributed to the stability in the following years as well as a reduction in the returns to education. At the same time unemployment for highly educated workers soared for the first time.

Beginning at the end of the 1980s, the supply of educated workers increased rapidly.

Table 11.2 Returns to education and on-the-job-training variables, 1989

	Model 1 Mincer experience	Model 2 Reported experience	Model 3 Reported experience	Model 4 Reported experience	Model 4 Reported experience
Constant	4.100	4.115	3.732	3.714	3.778
	(0.013)	(0.013)	(0.052)	(0.052)	(0.052)
Women	-0.183	-0.166	-0.172	-0.171	-0.156
	(0.008)	(0.008)	(0.009)	(0.009)	(0.010)
Experience	0.022	0.023	0.011	0.009	0.007
	(0.001)	(0.001)	(0.002)	(0.002)	(0.002)
Experiece^2/100	-0.036	-0.039	-0.017	-0.015	-0.014
	(0.002)	(0.003)	(0.004)	(0.004)	(0.004)
Age squared			0.024	0.026	0.021
			(0.003)	(0.003)	(0.003)
Age squared/100			-0.027	-0.028	-0.023
			(0.004)	(0.004)	(0.004)
Seniority				0.003	0.003
				(0.001)	(0.001)
Training					0.032
					(0.004)
Education	0.050	0.049	0.046	0.045	0.042
	(0.002)	(0.002)	(0.002)	(0.002)	(0.002)
Adjusted R^2	0.364	0.360	0.370	0.374	0.386
Sample size	3802	3802	3802	3802	3802

Notes: All coefficients significant at 1% level. Education squared and seniority squared (unreported) were not significantly different from zero.

In the 1990s, the institutional wage restraint was still very strong in the public sector, in particular for the highly educated workers. Thus when the labour market turned in 1993, it was the educated workers in the private sector who gained the most. This may indicate that the market pressure raising returns to education in other countries is also at work here, but only translates into wage increases in the private sector because of the still highly centralized bargaining system in the public sector. It remains to be seen how the public sector reacts to the widening gap between the returns to education in the two sectors.

SPECIFICATION TESTS

Our results so far have been based on a simple OLS Mincer equation. In this section we undertake some specification tests in order to assess the quality and interpretation of the coefficients reported above.[5] We start by considering potential omitted variable bias by introducing other measures of human capital in the analysis. Next, we test the implicit assumption of a constant rate of return across years of education by employing a more flexible functional form. In the last subsection, we run a simple two-stage least squares (2SLS) model to test for endogenous schooling.

The Returns to Schooling and other Forms of Human Capital

In Model 1 in Table 11.2 we first report the standard Mincer equation for 1989. The return to education is estimated to 5.0%. In the next column, we use reported experience instead of the constructed "age minus 16 minus years of education". This is a better measure of actual labour market experience. The estimated returns to education fall slightly to 4.9%. In the next column, we control for both experience and age. Two things happen: the first is that the coefficients for the age variables are large and significant, actually larger than the experience coefficients. Obviously, age and experience are highly correlated, but the result still indicates that there is more to the experience wage profile than just the years accumulated in the labour market. There may be some cohort effect or other factors that are correlated with age rather than years in the labour market and which affects individual wages as well. Good panel data is required in order to attempt to identify the effect of age, cohort and experience more carefully, of course. The second thing that happens is that the returns to education drops to about 4.6% per year.

In the next model, we include seniority as well. This depresses the coefficient by a further 0.5%, resulting in a return education of 4.5%. In the last model, we introduce a measure of on-the-job training requirements in the present job, measured in years.[6] This gives a high return. Due to the fact that education is positively correlated with ojt, the estimated rate of return to education drops to 4.2% after the introduction of on-the-job-training requirements.

In general, we conclude that the estimated coefficient for education drops by 0.5 to 0.9 percentage points when controlling more carefully for other human capital variables. This exercise also shows that one of the channels for higher wages for more educated persons is through more on-the-job training and experience. It seems reasonable to argue that it is the estimated coefficient in Model 1, which is the "gross" of all on-the-job training influences that is important for school choice and thus reflects the rate of return on investment in one more year of schooling. The estimates in Model 5, however, reflect the pricing of education in the market, given the level of on-the-job training.

Linear Returns to Education

In this section we calculate the returns to education separately for each year of completed education. Table 11.3 reports the results.

Table 11.3 Returns to education, categorical model. All wage earners 1995. Dependent variable: log(wage)

	Employment share	Model 1 Coefficient	Standard error	Model 2 Coefficient	Standard error
Schooling		0.055	0.003		
9 years	14.7			-	-
10 years	38.2			0.069	0.020
11 years	9.1			0.156	0.026
12 years	22.4			0.202	0.021
13 years	5.5			0.334	0.031
14 years	9.5			0.301	0.025
15 years	2.9			0.365	0.040
16 years	7			0.339	0.028
17 years	2.2			0.591	0.044
18 years	2.8			0.476	0.039
19 years	0.1			0.846	0.183
20 years	0.2			0.349	0.129
Adjusted R^2		0.355		0.367	
Sample size		1851		1851	

Notes: Both models include experience (Mincer), experienced squared, gender and part-time dummies (women only).

A test of the flexible specification versus the constrained model reported in Model 2 barely fails to reject a hypothesis of equal returns to each year at a significance level of 5% (p-value of 0.0544). According to the point estimates, the return to education is relatively low for workers with 14, 16 and 18 years of education. Also the group with the highest level of education (Ph.D. level, comprising only 0.2% of the sample) has a low return to education.

There appears to be some differences in the estimated returns to education across groups. However, with the sample size that we are dealing with here, we are not able to reject the hypothesis of linear returns. We conclude that larger sample sizes are required to sort out potential significant differences between year-groups of education.

Endogenous Schooling

It may well be that years of schooling is correlated with the earnings potential. Internationally, this problem has received a lot of attention. See for example, Card (1999) and Harmon and Walker (1995). The only two papers dealing with this issue on Norwegian data are Hægeland, Klette and Salvanes (1999) and Raaum and Aabø (2000). Hægeland et al. (1999) use a two-stage model to control for schooling choice. Their central identifying variable is region of birth. In accordance with most of the international evidence using the instrumental variable approach, they find that the OLS estimates are slightly downward biased. Raaum and Aabø (2000) use extremely good register based twins-data, comprising all sibling pairs in the Norwegian economy. Also in accordance with international evidence from twin studies, they find that the OLS estimates are upward-biased rather than downward-biased when comparing within-twin-pair estimates with the standard OLS estimates.

In order to check if our own results in Table 11.1 are incorrect, we have undertaken a 2SLS estimation of schooling and wages. We use 1995 data, as these contain rather good information on family background. We ran a first stage regression of the level of schooling, including all the exogenous variables in the model (age and gender) as well as a variety of variables reflecting the parents' age, occupation, education and job attachment. In the second stage, we regress wages on gender, age and the predicted value of years of schooling (reported in Table 4 as 2SLS).

Table 11.4 Returns to education in Norway, 1995. Two stage least squares estimator, endogenous variable is schooling

	Coefficient	Standard Error
OLS	0.055	(0.003)
OLS, include instruments	0.053	(0.003)
2SLS	0.060	(0.006)
R^2	0.258	
Hausman test	0.0068 (0.006)	
Basman test of over-identifying restrictions	P-value = 0.5138	

The first line of Table 11.4 gives the standard OLS estimate. The second line reports the standard OLS estimate when all instruments are included as regressors. The estimated rate of returns falls only slightly from 5.45 to 5.30%. The following lines report statistics from the 2SLS regressions. The reported estimate of the rate of return to education is about half a percentage point above the OLS estimate, indicating a negative, but small bias in the OLS estimates. This observation is in line with Hægeland *et al.* (1998), who use a different model (more flexible specification and other identifying variables). However, the reported Hausman test indicator, which may be thought of as a measure of the correlation between ε and u, is not significantly different from zero at conventional levels of significance. This indicates that the selection issue is not significant in this model. The advantage of 2SLS over the multivariate probit specification of Hægeland *et al.* (1999) is that simple tests of the over-identifying restrictions are available for the 2SLS specification. The Basman test reported in the table indicates that the instruments are valid, and not significantly correlated with the wage variable.

Observe that we only check our 1995 result against potential selectivity bias. It may well be the case that selectivity issues are of greater importance in the early 1980s, with a smaller proportion of the population with high education, than in the 1990s with a larger proportion of the population with higher levels of education. However, Hægeland *et al.* (1999) find that the consequences of including selection control are no different between 1980 and 1990.

THE EFFECT OF TAXES AND TRANSFERS

Income versus Wage

Since our tax data refers to income rather than to wage rates, we have to analyse the influence of taxes and transfers on the rate of return to education in terms of income rather than in terms of wage rates. At a first glance, it may seem reasonable to use income differentials rather than wage differentials when calculating the returns to education. After all, income is what we live off. However, the choice of working hours may be endogenous, and if chosen freely, it will be chosen such that the value of the marginal utility of out-of-work time equals the wage rate. It is thus not appropriate to use income, but rather to use the wage rate, since this is actually the parameter of the indirect utility function.

Since income equals the wage rate times the hours worked the elasticity of income with respect to education equals the sum of the elasticity of wages with respect to education and the elasticity of hours with respect to education. According to Table 11.5, the estimated returns to education in terms of hourly wages is 5.2%. The effect on hours of a one-year increase in education equals 3.3%, yielding an elasticity of income of 8.5%. We have ignored the fact that 'hours' is potentially endogenous, and we should thus interpret the coefficients with appropriate caution.

We have also conducted the same analysis for a sample of full-time working, married or cohabiting men. The reason for this is to facilitate comparisons with the results in the next section, where the role of taxes and transfers is analysed. The elasticity of working hours with respect to education is much smaller for married men, and the difference between the effect on income and wage is thus smaller for this group.

Table 11.5 Income versus wage rates, 1995

	All wage earners		Men (full time and married)	
	Sample Mean	Coeff. On schooling	Sample Mean	Coeff. on schooling
Hourly Wage (survey question)	4.62	5.2	4.75	4.9
Hours of Work (survey question)	3.55	3.3	3.72	0.7
Annual Wage Income	12.12	8.5	12.42	5.6
Observations	1299		414	

Notes: The return to education is the parameter from a log wage/income/hours equation, including controls for seniority, experience, experience squared and gender.

Gross versus Net Income

In this section we use linked data from tax registers. The data includes figures for the gross household income from work (*GHI*), total amount of taxes paid by the household (*HT*), gross income from work (*GI*) and disposable income (*DI*) for the individual. Disposable income is net of taxes and includes transfers as well.

In order to calculate net income from work (*NI*) for each of our respondents, we have calculated the average tax rate for each household *ATR* = *(HT/GHI)*, and then deducted this tax rate from gross income from work. We have *NI = GI(1 - ATR)*, where we note that the tax rate is calculated individually for each household. The average tax rate in the sample is slightly below 30%.

The first line of Table 11.6 shows the coefficient from a regression of the tax rate on years of education (including seniority, gender and experience). The figure 0.54 thus means that, given a level of experience, gender and seniority, a person with one year more of education should expect an average household tax rate which is 0.54% higher. This is thus an estimated "gross" measure of the progressiveness of the tax system, summing up both the expected effect of education on wages, household income and the tax rate.

The next line of Table 11.6 shows different measures of the rate of return to education. The first line shows the rate of returns calculated in terms of gross income. The figures 5.6 and 5.8 should be compared to the estimated figures of 8.5 and 5.6 from the survey questions in Table 11.5.[7]

Table 11.6 Gross versus net income, 1995

	All Wage Earners		Men	
	Sample mean	Coef. on schooling	Sample mean	Coef. on schooling
Tax Rate	28	0.54	28	0.74
Gross income	12.25	5.6	12.37	5.8
Net income	11.91	4.8	12.02	4.7
Disposable income	11.90	4.4	11.98	5.1
Observations	1299		414	

Moving down to the estimated rate of return in terms of net income, we find that the tax system tends to depress the rate of return from education in Norway by about 0.8–0.9 percentage points. This is probably mainly due to the progressiveness of taxes, even though effects of the relationship between the income of spouses may have an effect here as well.

The next line shows disposable income. When we look at the whole population of wage earners, the rate of return in terms of disposable income is even smaller, 4.4%. The difference between 5.6 and 4.4% indicates a strong effect of the total system of taxes and transfers on individuals' returns to education. The difference between 4.8 and 4.4 indicates that transfers are in favour of the least educated. However, when we look at married full-time working men, we find the same effect when comparing gross income to disposable income (5.8 versus 5.1%), but the difference between our calculated net income and disposable income goes in the other direction. Unfortunately, the shift to disposable income involves two changes. One is that the person's own amount of taxes is deducted, not the average household tax. The other is that transfers are included as well. It is thus difficult to give a clear interpretation of this result.

With the caution that this is only a partial analysis, ignoring potential feedback effects of the behavioural impact of taxes, we conclude that the system of taxes and transfers tends to compress income variation, and reduces the private rate of return to education. The effect is, however, not very large; our estimates suggests something in the range of 0.5 to 1.2 percentage points. Since the level of returns is rather low in the first place, the relative effect is substantial. About one-fifth of the return to education in terms of income is sliced off by the system of taxes and transfers.

CONCLUSION

In an international perspective, Norway has low returns to education. Our average estimate over the period from 1980 to 1995 is 5.1% per year of education. There are no consistent changes in the overall rate of return over this period, a fact that we attribute to the combined influences of supply, demand and changes in the wage setting system. The most recent developments in the private sector may, however, give an indication of future rising rates of return in Norway.

Our specification tests are informative, in that they support the use of simple Mincer equations when giving broad assessments of the returns to education in Norway. Using better specifications, more flexible functional forms or instrument variable methods to estimate the rate of returns seem to add very little. Of course, this statement is only valid when working with fairly broad questions, using survey data with a limited number of observations. If the questions we raise are of a more specific nature, such as the return to a particular type of education, more data is required. With respect to the endogenous characteristic of education, we obtain similar results as elsewhere, but it seems that the effect of accounting for such biases is small in Norway. Using the instrument variables approach changes the estimates very little for Norway, but we note the results of Raaum and Aabø (2000) who find considerably smaller rates of returns within twin pairs.

The system of taxes and transfers tends to depress the rate of return. We find that taxes and transfers subtract between 0.5 and 1.2 percentage points from the private rate of return to education in Norway, *cetaris paribus*.

What are the consequences of the relatively low rates of return to education? First of all, the obvious consequence is a more compressed income distribution. Next, we would expect incentives to higher education to be distorted. So far, however, it seems that the enrolment of students by and large has been constrained by capacity. Norway has experienced a considerable boom in higher education over the twenty years or so, and is now located among the OECD countries with the highest enrolment rates. High levels of student support may account for the high enrolment rates. There may be signs now, however, that enrolment is on the decline at the university level, and that we have reached a point where the capacity exceeds applications. In such a regime, the private returns to education may be crucial.

Migration could also be a consequence of differences in the wage structure between Norway and other countries. So far, this has not been an issue, however there are significant cultural and other barriers to migration in Europe.

Of course, employers' behaviour should be taken into account as well. Low skill prices mean that employers are less selective when they choose what qualifications to use for what purposes. This may lead to a deadweight loss. On the other hand, if it is true that there are spillovers from education, it may very well be sensible to "subsidize" knowledge-intensive activities through low skill prices.

NOTES

1. For an overview of previous studies for Norway, see Barth and Røed (1999). The Norwegian part of the PURE project is financed by the Norwegian Ministry of Education and the Norwegian Ministry of Administration in addition to the TSER-funding. Thanks to Bernt Bratsberg, Torbjørn Hægeland and Oddbjørn Raaum for comments on earlier drafts.
2. The numbers underlying the figure as well as the same numbers for women are available from the authors on request.
3. The results for 1980 should be interpreted with some caution, because the translation from educational codes to years of education is somewhat cruder for the 1980-survey than for the later surveys. We thus tend to believe that the figures reported here slightly overstates the increase in the rates of return to education in the beginning of the eighties
4. This is due to both small nominal wage increases, a small share set aside for local bargaining and consistent egalitarian wage increases at the central level.
5. We also experimented with controls for endogenous labour supply for females using Heckman's lambda. But since the coefficient for Mill's ratio turned out insignificant, and (consequently) the effect on the estimate of the rate of return was very small, we have chosen not to report this exercise in more detail.
6. The *ojt* variable is constructed from a question about the "average length of time if would take to teach someone with your qualifications but who are new to the job, to do your job properly". See Barth (1997) and Schøne (2000).
7. We find that for all wage earners, income figures calculated from survey questions tend to produce a higher estimated rate of return than the register data. Since the estimates for full-time males are quite consistent across definitions of income, we conclude that the difference arises from the estimated effect of education on hours for women or part-time workers. Since this is not our main focus here, we leave this question for now.

REFERENCES

Barth, E. (1997), "Firm-specific seniority and wages", *Journal of Labor Economics*, 15(3), 495-506.

Barth, E. and M. Røed, (1999), " The Return to Human Capital in Norway, A review of the Literature", in R. Asplund and P. Pereira (eds.), *Returns to Human Capital in Europe*, ETLA Helsinki: Taloustieto Oy.

Card, D. (1999), "The Causal Effect of Education on Earnings", in O. Ashenfelter and D. Card (eds.), *Handbook of Labor Economics,* Vol. 3B, Amsterdam: Elsevier.

Freeman, R. and L.Katz (eds.) (1995), *Differences and Changes in Wage Structures*, NBER Comparative Labor Market Series, Chicago: The University of Chicago Press.

Harmon, C. and Walker, I. (1995), "Estimates of the economic return to schooling for the UK", *American Economic Review*, 85(5), 1278-1286.

Hægeland, T., T. J. Klette and K. G. Salvanes (1999), "Declining returns to education in Norway? Comparing estimates across cohorts, sectors and over time", *Scandinavian Journal of Economics,* 101(4), 555-576.

Kahn, L. (1998), "Against the wind: bargaining recentralisation and wage inequality in Norway 1987-91", *Economic Journal*, Vol.108, 603-645.

OECD (1996), Employment Outlook, OECD.

Raaum O. and T. Aabø (2000), "Earnings and educational attainment:The role of family background studied by a large sample of Norwegian twins", *Nordic Journal of Political Economy* (forthcoming).

Schøne P. (2000), "Analysing the effect of training on wages using combined survey-register material", *International Journal of Manpower* (forthcoming).

Thoresen, T. (1995), "The Distributional Impact of the Norwegian Tax Reform Measured by Disproportionality", Discussion Papers no.146, Statistics Norway.

12. Portugal

Pedro Telhado Pereira
and
Pedro Silva Martins

INTRODUCTION

Returns to education are an important policy instrument. They allow researchers and policy-makers to perceive how important is the role played by education in terms of enhancing an individual's wage perspectives. In fact, and following the Mincer (1974) framework, the coefficients obtained can be interpreted as the internal rate of return or the average marginal return to one year of education.

In this chapter we employ the Mincer methodology and focus on the returns to education in Portugal, during the 1982–1995 period. This was a time when this country witnessed many changes in both its education system and its broader economic framework. It was also a period which followed a very turbulent time, associated to the 25 April 1974 revolution, when both the education and the economic systems undergone very serious structural changes. It is therefore relevant to realize what implications these events had upon the financial return to education, if any.

Previous evidence for Portugal suggested that "OLS estimates of the return to education are broadly in line with results for other Western economies, although they are marginally at the upper end of the scale" – Vieira (1999). In fact the survey by Pereira and Lima (1999) and the meta-analysis by Pereira and Martins (2000b) outline that previous studies (including Psacharopoulos, 1981; Kiker and Santos, 1991 and Hartog *et al.*, 1998) obtained Mincer coefficients ranging between 7.3 and 10.8 % (men), 8 and 11.1 % (women) and 6.2 and 10 % (all).

Our work is structured as follows. We start by briefly outlining the main events in the Portuguese education system during the last 70 years. We then describe the datasets we use and unfold our main results, considering schooling both linearly and in terms of different educational levels. We then assess the robustness of these results by considering extra regressors and addressing the impact of selectivity biases. The last section summarizes and concludes. Other analysis, such as those based on instrumental variables or quantile regressions, are available elsewhere, such as in Vieira (1999) and Pereira and Martins (2000a), respectively.

THE PORTUGUESE EDUCATION SYSTEM

The Portuguese education system was very unstable during the 70 year period we cover. There were several reforms throughout these years, in accordance with the different approaches towards the role of education and each period's predominant social values. We divide this epoch into four different sub-periods: 1926–55 (a period of 'regression'), 1956–73 ('growth'), 1974–1982 ('rupture') and 1983–1995 ('consolidation').

The first period is associated with the most backward posture of the Salazar regime. Education was not deemed as relevant for the country's social and economic welfare. Instead, it was regarded as a useful instrument only to the extent that it instilled patriotism and respect for the 'traditional values' among the youth. The compulsory level of education was reduced in 1929 from 5 to 3 years.

Students completing primary education (four years) could then follow the academic path, taking the first and second cycles of secondary education (of five and two years, respectively), after which they could attend university, should they pass their entrance examinations. Alternatively, and also after completion of primary school, students could follow a technical, labour-market-focused stream. In this case, students would take a first cycle (the 'preparatory cycle') of two years and then a second cycle of three or four years.

From 1956 onwards, and until early 1974, a new approach sets in (the 'growth' period). This change is due to the period of extraordinary economic growth that other Western European countries were experiencing, together with the recognition that the low human capital endowment of Portugal's labour force would be a serious drawback in any attempt to catch up. Illiteracy levels were 68% in 1930, 60% in 1940 and 49% in 1950. These levels corresponded to those that prevailed in most developed Western European countries during the mid-19th century.

The major institutional changes of this period were the increase of the compulsory level of schooling from three to four years (only for boys) in 1956, to four years (boys and girls) in 1960, and to six years in 1964. More importantly, both the number and quality of schools increased significantly.

Concerning the above-mentioned change in the minimum schooling, one cannot but remain suspicious about the true compulsory nature of such laws (illiteracy among children aged 7-11 in 1930 exceeded 30%, for instance.) Since the Portuguese population was rather poor and working mostly on agriculture, it was difficult for parents to forego the help their children could provide them. Moreover, some parents might not attach too much relevance to the benefits of such simple skills as reading, writing and counting.

It was then, when more reforms were about to be put into practice (including a further increase of the compulsory minimum level of schooling), that a military coup erupted, overthrowing the 48-year-old dictatorship. The third period of the Portuguese education system ('rupture') starts then and coincides with the first eight years of the new democratic regime.

One of the first measures taken was abolishing the technical stream of the lower secondary level (the three or four years taken after completion of primary and preparatory cycles). This branch of the education system was regarded as incompatible with the revolution goals of equality. This incompatibility resulted from the alleged perpetuation of unwanted blue-collar/white-collar divisions between those who moved on to university and those who only took upper primary/lower secondary technical courses.

Simultaneously, administrative problems connected with the political instability of 1975 led to the introduction of an extra year at secondary school before accession to university so as to postpone the entrance of a new cohort of students. This was necessary apparently also because the previous years' growth in enrolment at secondary schools was causing too much pressure for university entrance.[1]

Because it was facing capacity constraints, the department of education introduced in 1978 the so-called 'Numerus Clausus' system, whereby a maximum number of vacancies for each university was earmarked. Admission became then dependent not only on successfully passing the entrance examinations but also on getting good enough marks in relative terms.

The fourth and last period ('consolidation') started with the 1983 reform. Its most relevant achievement was to reorganize the technical branch, this time at the upper secondary level. Students who wished to focus on a more job-related type of learning would take a three-year course, after having completed nine years of academic-oriented education. Unlike in the second period (1956–1973), for some of the courses available then, students graduating from these technical courses could move on to university. Anyway, this branch turned out not to be too successful since the academic path was overwhelmingly preferred by prospective upper secondary students.

The last event alluded to in this short survey is the 1986 framework law which has been regulating the Portuguese education system up until now. It organizes the schooling system into a basic level, with a new compulsory minimum level of nine years; a secondary level of three years (including the just described technical branch); and a superior level, which comprizes both universities (which award 4, 5 or 6 year degrees) and polytechnic institutes (which confer 3 year degrees, usually more technical).

The second main feature of this law is that it allowed private universities to operate and expand. This was regarded as an important step towards a freer education system, in the sense that it would decrease the state's involvement in the higher education system. In fact, from then on, private universities have mushroomed, both in terms of students enrolled and of degrees awarded.[2]

Throughout this and the previous period, enrolment rates in all levels of education kept increasing, accounting for the rise in the number of students (15% of total population in 1960 and 23% in 1991, while only 5% in 1926[3]). Nevertheless, illiteracy has not disappeared yet, as the last census (performed in 1991) alarmingly points to an 11% figure.

Thus, the main institutional changes in the educational system which are likely to have had a direct impact at the labour market in terms of returns to education are the following: compulsory level reduced from five to three years in 1929; focus on the technical stream of lower education (7th, 8th and 9th year of schooling) from the early 1950s onwards; compulsory level raised to four years (boys only) in 1956; to four years (boys and girls) in 1960; to six years (both genders) in 1964; lower secondary technical schools abolished in 1975; 'Numerus Clausus' system implemented in 1978; upper secondary technical education introduced in 1983; compulsory level further increased to nine years in 1986; private universities allowed to operate on a larger scale in 1986.

THE DATASETS

The main data-set used is 'Quadros de Pessoal' (Personnel Records). Every year, all firms, either private or public, must fill in a table that asks for data concerning every employee and also detailed firm-specific information. Other distinguishing features of 'Quadros de Pessoal' are its broad time coverage (since the late 1970s until the present) and its panel nature.

In our research, we used samples from 1982 up until 1995, each one with information for approximately 50000 workers and their firms.[4] We dropped those observations for which no information on earnings, hours worked or schooling attainment was available.

Another dataset which we draw upon is the European Community Household Panel (ECHP), issued by the Eurostat. This covers most Western European countries and includes information from a large number of socio-economic questions asked to all members of each household surveyed.[5] However, information on the educational achievement of each individual is not very detailed.

In this work, we used the 1994 cohort of the ECHP. This wave includes information for more than 12500 individuals for Portugal. Approximately one third of them are workers for whom we have information on earnings and schooling attainment.

Another issue one should mention is the procedure adopted for the imputation of schooling years. Since data concerning education are available in educational levels only, in order to compute Mincer estimates a correspondence has to be made between such education levels and the associated number of schooling years. We tackled this by assuming that individuals needed the minimum required years of schooling to achieve their degrees and that they did not attended further years of schooling.

Preliminary Analysis of Data

In Table 12.1 we present some descriptive statistics of our samples for the extreme years (1982 and 1995) and for each gender. The variables outlined here refer to the workers' age, education, experience, tenure, earnings and hours worked. The two snapshots presented describe the evolution of these variables throughout the thirteen-year period covered in our survey.

Table 12.1 Descriptive statistics, 1982 and 1995

	1982		1995	
	Men Mean	Women Mean	Men Mean	Women Mean
Educ[a]	4.89	4.92	6.26	6.89
Age	36.12	32.65	36.85	33.83
exp[b]	25.20	21.71	24.59	20.94
Tenure	8.79	7.85	8.13	7.00
D4[c]	0.59	0.57	0.46	0.38
D6[c]	0.13	0.12	0.23	0.24
D9a[c]	0.05	0.07	0.10	0.12
D9t[c]	0.06	0.05	0.03	0.02
D11/D11a[c]	0.03	0.04	0.09	0.14
D11t[c]			0.01	0.01
D14[c]	0.01	0.01	0.01	0.02
D17[c]	0.01	0.01	0.03	0.03
htot[d]	192	175	179	166
remtot[e]	21891	14804	131444	93797
remth[f]	116.15	91.43	742.95	602.67
Observations	24827	11726	24526	13373

Notes:
[a] years of education; [b] years of experience; [c] dummy variable taking value 1 for individuals with x schooling; [d] hours worked per month; [e] total wage per month (in the year's escudos) [f] hourly wage (in the year's escudos);

Analyses of the dummy variables associated to specific educational levels are useful as they explain how the distribution of schooling levels evolved during the time period considered. We see that the overwhelming majority of individuals who held a four-year degree is attenuated, from 59% (57%) of the 1982 men (women) sample to 46% (38%) in 1995. The proportion of men (women) who held less than four years of schooling also falls abruptly during this 13-year period, from 12% (13%) to 3% (3%). All the remaining educational levels, associated to a larger number of schooling years, see their share rise, the exception being the technical lower secondary degree, which was extinct in the mid-1970s. The most notable examples are the upper primary degree (from 13% to 23% for men, and from 12% to 24% for women) and the tertiary academic degree (from 1% to 3%, for both genders).[6] Other features of the data are the decreasing number of average hours worked, from 192 (175) in 1982 to 179 (166) in 1995 for men (women) and the relative stability of variables such as age (36 for men and 33 for women), experience (25 and 21) and tenure (9 and 8).

Table 12. 2 Average real wages per schooling level and deciles [a]

Education	1982	1986	1991	1995	% diff [b]
4	96677	80855	93787	96042	-0.1%
9	146796	122130	141904	132443	-0.8%
11	153356	124502	142494	144370	-0.5%
16	264548	235929	303087	328658	1.7%
Mean (men)	120570	102005	125575	131444	0.7%
Mean (women)	81537	72659	86477	93797	1.1%
Deciles	1982	1986	1991	1995	% diff [b]
0.1	53370	45326	54367	52000	-0.2%
0.5	90118	73572	82095	85000	-0.4%
0.9	179503	154573	191746	203075	1.0%

Notes:
[a] 1995 prices; [b] yearly growth rate (1982-1995)

Real wages in our sample proved also stable (see Table 12.2). Since the period covered includes some high inflation years (especially 1982 –1985 and 1989–1991), the high growth rate implicit in nominal wages proves elusive. However, we were surprised by the low or even negative real growth rates we found for many levels in our samples. The latter situation applies to the lower educational levels and the first and fifth deciles. Only the academic tertiary degree-holders' class and the individuals at the nine decile of the wage distribution see their real earnings increase during the period considered.[7]

In order to compare our two data-sets, we present descriptive statistics concerning the ECHP working individuals (see Table 12.3). These allow us to perceive what kind of sample biases may we find in the previous data-set as it disregards the self-employed and public servants.

Table 12.3 Descriptive statistics, ECHP

Men (N = 2436)	Mean	Std.Dev.	Min	Max
Education	6.025	3.894	0	16
Age	38.664	12.994	17	75
Experience	26.639	14.264	0	66
Hours	44.360	7.712	35	96
Wage	124193	101175	1277.9	1816000
Women (N = 1692)	Mean	Std.Dev.	Min	Max
Educations	6.602	4.583	0	16
Age	38.154	11.457	17	78
Experience	25.551	13.337	1	72
Hours	38.671	9.502	2	90
Wage	105411	77747	1500	532000
Part-time	0.145	0.352	0	1

RETURNS TO EDUCATION

Linear Cefficient

In the simplest Mincer equation specified for men, only those working full time (35 hours or more per week) were considered. A slightly different equation was estimated for women to control for part-time working (via a dummy variable taking value 1 for women working less than 35 hours and value 0 for the remaining). All working women were considered, regardless of their number of hours worked.

In Figure 12.1 we show the different values of the education coefficients for each gender sub-sample and for the entire sample and for each one of the 13 years covered.[9] Table 12.4 present the underlying figures plus the results for the other regressors and their standard errors. Men see their returns rise from 0.102 in 1982 to 0.115 in 1993, when they then tumble to 0.107 in 1995. Women followed a similar path, as they start from 0.108 in 1982, moving up to 0.114 in 1993, and then fall to 0.108 in 1995. A similar pattern is found for the entire sample as returns increase from 0.107 in 1982 to 0.117 in 1993 and then fall to 0.109 in 1995.

Figure 12.1   Education coefficients, 1982–1995

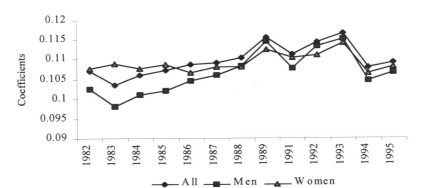

Table 12.4a   Mincer regressions, selected years

All	1982	1987	1991	1995
Educ	0,107	0,1091	0,1111	0,109
	(0,0008)	(0,0007)	(0,0007)	(0,0007)
exp	0,0598	0,0616	0,0508	0,0487
	(0,0006)	(0,0006)	(0,0006)	(0,0007)
exp2	-0,0007	-0,0007	-0,0006	-0,0005
	(0,0000)	(0,0000)	(0,0000)	(0,0000)
Constant	3,0961	3,8634	4,4914	4,8191
	(0,0092)	(0,0096)	(0,0095)	(0,0105)
Observations	36553	37395	41026	43463
R-squared	0,43	0,45	0,42	0,37

Notes: Standard errors in parentheses. All coefficients are significative at 1%

One should not necessarily conclude that the increasing trend uncovered for the 1982–1993 period is reverted from then on. In fact, after the 1993/1994 'break', the increase in returns to education resumes in 1994 as coefficients for 1995 are always larger than in 1994, regardless of the sub-sample considered. This reversal in the upward trend witnessed from 1982 to 1993 is most likely due to the change in the coding of the education variable. However, before data for the subsequent years are made available, one can only speculate about this matter. In any case, fitted lines for the returns in the

1982–1993 period suggest an average increase of between 0.05% and 0.16% per annum, which drops to a range between 0.02% and 0.09% should we also include 1994 and 1995.

We have also followed an alternative Mincer specification, where we do not impose a unitary hour elasticity of earnings. The results for this new specification are depicted in Figure12.2. We see that there are no apparent changes as far as the entire sample and the women-only sub-sample are considered. However, returns to education for men are lower than those we obtained before.

Table 12.4b Mincer regressions, selected years

Men	1982	1987	1991	1995
Education	0.1024	0.1059	0.1076	0.1065
	(0.0009)	(0.0009)	(0.0009)	(0.0009)
Experience	0.0636	0.0658	0.0564	0.0541
	(0.0007)	(0.0008)	(0.0008)	(0.0009)
Experience^2	-0.0008	-0.0008	-0.0007	-0.0006
	(0.0000)	(0.0000)	(0.0000)	(0.0000)
Constant	3.1398	3.8903	4.5346	4.8598
	(0.0105)	(0.0121)	(0.0123)	(0.0139)
Observations	24827	23534	24246	24526
R^2	0.47	0.46	0.42	0.38
Women	1982	1987	1991	1995
Education	0.1076	0.108	0.1103	0.1079
	(0.0014)	(0.0011)	(0.001)	(0.001)
Experience	0.0497	0.0533	0.0415	0.0426
	(0.0011)	(0.001)	(0.0009)	(0.0009)
Experience^2	-0.0006	-0.0007	-0.0005	-0.0005
	(0.0000)	(0.0000)	(0.0000)	(0.0000)
Part-time worker	0.1747	0.1948	0.2015	0.2745
	(0.01)	(0.0083)	(0.0079)	(0.0083)
Constant	3.0903	3.8677	4.4835	4.7751
	(0.0169)	(0.0146)	(0.0137)	(0.0149)
Observations	11726	13861	16780	18937
R^2	0.39	0.47	0.46	0.43

Notes: Standard errors in parentheses. All coefficients are significative at 1%

Figure 12.2 Education coefficients, alternative specification, 1982– 1995

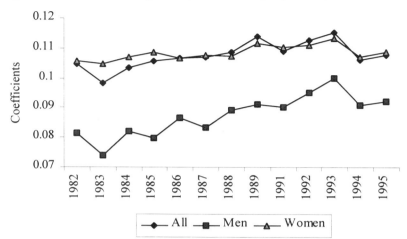

*Table 12.5 Mincer regressions, "alternative specification" ***

	All		Men		Female	
	1982	1995	1982	1995	1982	1995
Educ	0.1048	0.1076	0.0815	0.0921	0.1058	0.1086
	(0.0008)	(0.0007)	(0.0009)	(0.001)	(0.0014)	(0.001)
Exp	0.0605	0.0492	0.0607	0.0508	0.0499	0.043
	(0.0006)	(0.0007)	(0.0007)	(0.0008)	(0.0011)	(0.001)
Exp2	-0.0008	-0.0006	-0.0008	-0.0006	-0.0006	-0.0005
	(0.0000)	(0.0000)	(0.0000)	(0.0000)	(0.0000)	(0.0000)
Lnh	0.7855	0.7518	-0.7694	-1.499	0.7569	0.8461
	(0.0085)	(0.0091)	(0.0285)	(0.0471)	(0.0131)	(0.0122)
Part					-0.0285	0.1783
					(0.0149)	(0.0115)
Const.	4.2297	6.1064	12.5664	17.9429	4.3796	5.5693
	(0.046)	(0.0483)	(0.1521)	(0.247)	(0.0715)	(0.0644)
Obs.	36553	43463	24827	24526	11726	18937
R^2	0.46	0.4	0.45	0.39	0.53	0.49

Notes: Standard errors in parentheses.

Table 12.6 Regression results, ECHP

	All	Men	Women
	Coef.	Coef.	Coef.
Educatiom	0,0935	0,0942	0,0932
	(0,0029)	(0,0037)	(0,0046)
Experience	0,0573	0,0615	0,0519
	(0,0030)	(0,0036)	(0,0052)
Experience^2	-0,0007	-0,0008	-0,0007
	(0,0001)	(0,0001)	(0,0001)
Part-time worker			0,2589
			(0,0510)
Constant	4,8141	4,8122	4,7884
	(0,0487)	(0,0579)	(0,0849)
R^2	0,2373	0,2651	0,226
No. of observations	4128	2436	1692

The explanation for this gender difference lays at the very different hour elasticities of wages between men and women. While the first present negative values, regressions for the latter resulted in coefficients above 0.75 – see Table 12.5. This means that the hourly wage is slightly lower for women who work more hours, while for men both the hourly and monthly wage decrease with the number of hours worked.

Finally, the comparison with estimates using the ECHP data-set supports our previous findings – see Table 12.6 – as the estimated return obtained is around 0.094 (at the lower bound of the interval obtained with the 'Quadros de Pessoal' data-set for 1994).

Educational levels dummies

The following step was to relax the assumption of a single marginal rate of return, thus acknowledging there might be different financial rewards to specific educational levels. We therefore run the same Mincer equations described above except for the education years regressor which was replaced by a set of (seven) dummies, representing the different educational degrees one can obtain at the Portuguese education system. Dummy variables taking value 1 if the individual's highest level completed was, respectively, the lower primary, upper primary, lower secondary (academic branch), lower secondary (technical branch), upper secondary, tertiary (vocational) and tertiary (academic) educational levels were entered in the regressions in place of years of schooling.[10]   For the years of 1994 and 1995, we also distinguished between the academic and technical branches of the upper secondary levels. The results are presented in Figures 12.3 and Figures 12.4.

One can immediately notice the expected rankings in the pay-off to different levels. Furthermore, the time trends associated to different levels are not similar: The two upper levels (tertiary degrees) see their reward increase across the entire period, while there is some stability at the upper secondary degree and the lower secondary technical degree. For instance, the academic tertiary level (d17) increases its pay premium with respect to the dropped level (less than four years of schooling) from 350% to 450% (for both men and women). The remaining degrees, from the lower secondary academic degree to the lower primary degree see their financial reward fall. An example is the upper primary level (d6), whose premium falls from 55% to 38% (men) and from 49% to 38% (women).

Figure 12.3 Returns to educational levels, Men, 1982–1995

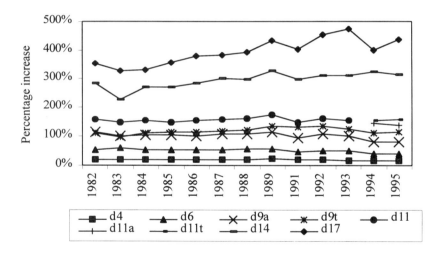

Figure 12.4: Returns to educational levels, Women, 1982-1995

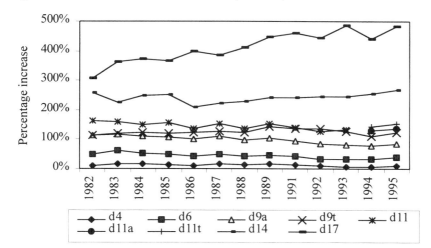

Another important result that comes out from this analysis is that a lower secondary technical degree pays always more than its academic counterpart. Moreover, the former type seems to have resisted the erosion that is conspicuous for its academic counterpart: As far as men are concerned, while returns to the academic branch amounted to 112% in 1982, they are only 79% in 1995. On the other hand, the technical branch, for men, had a pay-off ranging 112% in 1982 and it remained at that level in 1995.

Some conclusions might be drawn. First, the marginal yearly return from the first level (lower primary education) is rather low. According to our samples, for every year and for both genders, such return is never above 4%. This suggests that those who stopped at that level obtained a low financial return with respect to the individuals who did not reach such degree. However, this conclusion should be somewhat softened since we know that the latter group (used to perform the comparison) includes individuals who remained close to obtaining the degree (e.g. having studied for three years, and not finishing the fourth) or who also obtained the basic skills taught at that level (reading and writing, for instance).

Table 12.7 goes a step forward in this analysis as they present the marginal returns associated to upgrading from one level to the following, in terms of the school hierarchy.[11] The figures reported in the first column of Table 12.7 indicate the percentage wage increases associated to a higher level of education, while before we displayed the coefficients obtained in the Mincer regressions (where education entered in years). The figures in the second column were derived from the first column, corresponding to the implicit yearly rate of return from upgrading from one level to the next.

Table 12.7 Marginal returns of educational levels, selected years

Men		1982		1986		1991		1995	
Level	Base	a	b	a	b	a	b	a	b
d4	d0	20%	5%	19%	4%	19%	5%	15%	4%
d6	d4	29%	14%	27%	13%	23%	11%	20%	10%
d9a	d6	37%	11%	31%	10%	31%	9%	29%	9%
d9t	d9a	0%	0%	8%	8%	19%	19%	19%	19%
d9t	d6	37%	11%	41%	12%	56%	16%	53%	15%
d11	d9a	21%	10%	27%	13%	28%	13%	33%	15%
d14	d11	49%	14%	51%	15%	60%	17%	74%	20%
d17	d11	77%	12%	89%	14%	103%	15%	125%	18%

Women		1982		1986		1991		1995	
Level	Base	a	b	a	b	a	b	a	b
d4	d0	11%	3%	11%	3%	14%	3%	11%	3%
d6	d4	34%	16%	29%	13%	25%	12%	24%	11%
d9a	d6	44%	13%	42%	12%	38%	11%	35%	10%
d9t	d6	44%	13%	57%	16%	67%	19%	61%	17%
d9t	d9a	0%	0%	11%	11%	21%	21%	20%	20%
d11	d9a	23%	11%	17%	8%	22%	11%	27%	13%
d14	d11	35%	11%	31%	10%	43%	13%	55%	16%
d17	d11	55%	9%	111%	16%	134%	19%	147%	20%

Notes: [a] Comparison drawn in absolute terms; [b] Comparison per year

A second conclusion has to do with the pattern of marginal returns as one moves from a lower to a higher level. For men, the results pertaining to the 1980s suggest constant marginal returns to schooling,[12] while the 1990s are better characterized by increasing marginal returns. Results for women suggest decreasing marginal returns in 1982, a mixed pattern in 1986 and, as for men, increasing marginal returns in the nineties.

A final result would be that holders of technical levels (lower secondary degrees) have seen their reward increase with respect to their academic-branch counterparts. While in the beginning of the period covered each diploma had similar average returns, the situation reversed from then on and the differential has widened ever since, ranging between 19% (men) and 21% (women).

A tentative interpretation of this result is that after a few years during which such technical skills were no longer provided by the education system, they became increasingly scarce, and thus their return surpassed the one of the academic branch. Our results suggest then that the political decision to drop this technical branch was unwise.

Sensitivity to Different Specifications

An important issue that arises when one is researching returns to education is the extent to which the estimates obtained are robust. There are different types of other regressors which one would want to consider when estimating a wage equation since one knows that pay policies may differ considerably throughout industries, regions, bargaining regimes, occupation, hierarchy levels and other features.

However, this is liable to criticism should one still wish to interpret the education coefficients as a return to education. Since education might influence many of the just-mentioned characteristics, which then also influence one's earnings, accounting for such variables would necessarily bias the impact of education upon earnings.

Table 12.8 Education coefficients, Extra regressors

	1982	1986	1991	1995
No extra regressors	0.107	0.1086	0.1165	0.109
	(0.0008)	(0.0007)	(0.0007)	(0.0007)
Regions	0.098	0.0992	0.1012	0.1
	(0.0007)	(0.0007)	(0.0007)	(0.0007)
Bargaining regime	0.0945	0.0954	0.1006	0.0988
	(0.0007)	(0.0007)	(0.0007)	(0.0007)
Ownership	0.0925	0.0894	0.1003	0.1008
	(0.0007)	(0.0007)	(0.0007)	(0.0007)
Firm size	0.096	0.097	0.1008	0.0995
	(0.0007)	(0.0007)	(0.0007)	(0.0007)
Firm age	0.107	0.1086	0.1111	0.1094
	(0.0008)	(0.0007)	(0.0007)	(0.0007)
All variables	0.0851	0.0844	0.0899	0.0878
	(0.0007)	(0.0007)	(0.0007)	(0.0007)
All variables: men	0.0803	0.0802	0.0857	0.0847
	(0.0008)	(0.0008)	(0.0009)	(0.0009)
All variables: women	0.0869	0.0824	0.0893	0.0876
	(0.0013)	(0.0011)	(0.001)	(0.001)

Bearing this in mind, we consider different types of firm characteristics: the region where it is based, the bargaining agreement in place, the firm ownership (private, including being held by nationals or foreigners, and

Education and Earnings in Europe

public) and the firm size (number of workers) and firm age. Each type of characteristics was added separately to the base specification mentioned in the previous section. A final specification drew together all the firm characteristics mentioned above. We report in Table 12.8 the resulting Mincer coefficients.As expected, the education coefficients fall when one considers extra regressors. However, such decrease is not very large as it only on a few occasions exceeds 10% and, on aggregate, is always less than 15%, regardless of gender or year. When one adds all the regressors, returns to education fall by around 20% and never do they decrease by more than 25%.

Table 12.9 Returns to education, private and public-owned sectors

	1982		1995	
Private	Men	Women	Men	Women
Educ	0.0865	0.0947	0.0944	0.0988
	(0.001)	(0.0015)	(0.001)	(0.0011)
Exp	0.0582	0.046	0.0486	0.0382
	(0.0007)	(0.0011)	(0.0009)	(0.001)
Exp2	-0.0008	-0.0006	-0.0006	-0.0005
	(0.0000)	(0.0000)	(0.0000)	(0.0000)
part		0.1726		0.2953
		(0.0103)		(0.0086)
Const.	3.246	3.1636	4.9671	4.8543
	(0.0109)	(0.0174)	(0.0144)	(0.0155)
Obs.	20154	9910	20947	16313
R^2	0.4	0.35	0.33	0.41
	1982		1995	
Public	Men	Women	Men	Women
educ	0.0876	0.0909	0.103	0.0996
	(0.0017)	(0.004)	(0.0028)	(0.0047)
Exp	0.0439	0.0336	0.0526	0.0519
	(0.002)	(0.0038)	(0.0031)	(0.0042)
Exp2	-0.0005	-0.0004	-0.0005	-0.0005
	(0.0000)	(0.0001)	(0.0001)	(0.0001)
part		0.2174		0.2464
		(0.0286)		(0.029)
Const.	3.7471	3.7529	5.1799	5.1081
	(0.0335)	(0.0663)	(0.0541)	(0.0844)
Obs.	3465	995	1829	720
R^2	0.44	0.37	0.44	0.47

We also consider whether there were differences across the private and the state-owned sectors. We used the information available on the private or public nature of firms and regressed separate equations for each type –see

Table 12.9. Here we found some gender differences, as returns to education tend to be larger in the public sector for men, while for women the opposite situation applies.

Selectivity Bias

The principle of comparative advantage suggests there should be some correlation between the decision to participate in the labour market and the size of the reward for education investments. If this were the case, then not accounting for such choice would provide an unrepresentative estimate of the latter measure.

This problem is relevant only for women, since the share of working age men who do work is extremely high. We computed such figures for the ECHP dataset (see Table 12.10) where it can be seen that in the 30–50 age cohorts, the percentage of working women is roughly half of the one of men (80%).

Table 12.10 Participation rates - ECHP

	Sex	
Age group	Male	Female
15-20	23%	5%
20-30	47%	37%
30-40	82%	48%
40-50	76%	37%
50-60	53%	31%
60-65	17%	6%

In order to deal with the potential selectivity problem, we employed the Heckman two-stage method - see Table 12.11. We used as identifiers the women's number of children and living status (such as living with a partner or with partner and children). The rationale for this is that such characteristics should influence the participation of women in the labour market but not their performance and thus their wages.

Our results show that, in empirical terms, selectivity bias are unimportant. The associated lambda proved not significant and the corrected return is not significantly different from the one obtained in the straightforward specification.

Table 12.11 Selectivity biases

	Heckit		Probit		OLS
Educ	0.092		0.079		0.091
Exp	0.048				0.048
Exp2	-0.001				-0.001
Part	0.419				0.423
Const	4.791		-4.707		4.820
Age			0.232		
Age^2			-0.003		
Children			-0.122		
WPT[a]			-0.345	**	
WPC[b]			-0.203	***	
WC[c]			0.133	***	
WPR[d]			0.042	***	
Lambda	0.023	***			
R^2					41.3%
N			3514		1039

Notes:
* not significant at a 1% confidence level
** not significant at a 5% confidence level
*** not significant at a 10% confidence level
[a] with partner
[b] with partner and children
[c] with children
[d] with parents

CONCLUSION

We addressed in this chapter the size and time trend of returns to education in Portugal, a country that has undergone several changes at both its education system and its overall economy since the mid–1970s. These have not prevented Portugal from severely lagging behind most Western countries in terms of the schooling achievement of its population. Two examples of this should suffice: 80% of its working age people do not hold more than nine years of schooling (OECD, 1998); 10% of its 1991 population were still unable to read or write.

Bearing in mind this background, we addressed the financial dimension of the schooling decision, in terms of the rewards associated to holding further education – the Mincer returns to schooling. We covered a 13–year period

(1982–1995) by drawing on samples from 'Quadros de Pessoal', an extensive matched employer-employee data-set. Other issues were covered by using the 1994 wave of the ECHP.

Robust evidence was found that the returns to education in Portugal are high, above 9% in all cases, and have been increasing. Moreover, no sizeable gender differences were found. Given the increase in the supply of more schooled individuals, a more than proportional increase in demand should have been driving these results. Preliminary evidence (see Pereira and Martins, 2000c) supports this interpretation.

On the other hand, very contrasting evidence was found as to the pay-off to different educational levels. Higher degrees (upper secondary and above) not only consistently boast high returns as they have seen such returns increase during the period covered. Lower degrees face the opposite situation: low and decreasing pay-off. Besides, our results suggest that the returns at the higher levels have been increasing also in marginal terms.

More specifically, the men's results pertaining to the eighties suggest constant marginal returns to schooling, while the 1990s are better characterized by increasing marginal returns. Results for women suggest decreasing marginal returns in 1982, a mixed pattern in 1986 and, as for men, increasing marginal returns in the nineties.

Also concerning educational differentiation, the comparison between the situations faced by the academic and the technical branches of the lower secondary level led us to conclude that the political decision to drop the latter level was misguided. In fact, individuals who had obtained such skills (which naturally became scarcer since only recently has a similar branch been reintroduced) witnessed a significant relative increase of their earnings with respect to their academic branch counterparts.

Finally, analysis of the sensitivity to extended specifications concluded that returns do not fall by much. We made use of several firm-specific data which 'Quadros de Pessoal' makes available and noticed only a slight decrease of returns. With respect to differences between the private and the public-owned sectors, we got mixed evidence: returns to education for men are higher in the public sector than in the private sector while the opposite applies for women. Selectivity bias, with respect to the participation of women in the labour market, also showed that there are no reasons to suspect that estimates of returns to education for women are misleading on account of their lower participation rates.

NOTES

1. The decision to abolish the technical stream also probably contributed to this phenomenon, since students could no longer obtain at the secondary school those skills that the labour market rewarded. Moving on to university became the only option available in order to acquire such skills.

2. Only recently, at the end of the 1990s, does this mushrooming trend seem to be reversing. This is probably explained by the increase in the supply of vacancies at public universities, which crowds out potential applicants to their private counterparts.
3. These figures refer to the share of the total Portuguese population who were attending school at the time.
4. The exception is the year of 1990, which was not available. Sampling problems also cast some doubts on the accuracy of the results obtained with the 1983 sample.
5. Only individuals who are at least 17 years old are surveyed.
6. This percentage is downward biased as the 'Quadros de Pessoal' data-set does not consider the self-employed, a category which includes a disproportionately large share of university-degree-based workers (e.g. lawyers, doctors, architects).
7. Another feature is the large gender wage differential, averaging approximately 45%.
8. The small differences between net and gross earnings might be related to problems in computing such figures, which lead some individuals to end up presenting gross values, even when asked about net wages.
9. It should be pointed out that these coefficients cannot be immediately interpreted as the average marginal increase in earnings on account of an extra year of schooling, which corresponds to $e^{\beta}-1$. However, for small values of β the difference between the two is very small. Only for β's higher than .15 (and all our coefficients are smaller than that) will the difference between $e^{\beta}-1$ and β be higher than 0.01.
10. This means that, for each individual, only one dummy variable takes value 1, while all the remaining take value 0.
11. We try to follow the path one student could have taken along its schooling achievement. We thus disregard comparisons such as upper secondary technical level with the lower secondary academic level or tertiary academic degree with the tertiary non-academic degree as these are not pairs of degrees which could be achieved sequentially.
12. An exception is the transition from the lower to the upper primary education levels, when a sizeable increase is witnessed.

REFERENCES

Hartog, Joop, Pedro Pereira and José Vieira (1998) 'Changing returns to education in Portugal during the 1980's and early 1990's: OLS and quantile regression estimators', Discussion Paper, Tibergen Institute.

Kiker, Bill and Maria Santos (1991) 'Human capital and earnings in Portugal', *Economics of Education Review*, 10, 187–203.

Mincer, Jacob (1974), *Schooling, experience and earnings*, National Bureau of Economic Research, US.

OECD (1998), *Education at a glance – OECD indicators*, Paris, France: Centre for Educational Research and Innovation.

Pereira, Pedro and Francisco Lima (1999), 'Wages and human capital: evidence from the Portuguese data', in Rita Asplund and Pedro T. Pereira (eds), *Returns to human capital in Europe: a literature review*, Helsinki, Finland: ETLA/Taloustieto Oy., pp 259–278.

Pereira, Pedro and Pedro Martins (2000a) 'Does education reduce wage inequality? Quantile regressions evidence from fifteen European countries', Discussion Paper 120, IZA, Bonn.

Pereira, Pedro and Pedro Martins (2000b) 'A meta-analysis of returns to education in Portugal', mimeo, Faculdade de Economia da Universidade Nova de Lisboa.

Pereira, Pedro and Pedro Martins (2000c) 'Explaining the increase in returns to education in Portugal', mimeo, Faculdade de Economia da Universidade Nova de Lisboa.

Psacharopoulos, George (1981) 'Education and the structure of earnings in Portugal', *De Economist* 129, 532–545.

Vieira, José (1999) 'Returns to education in Portugal', *Labour Economics* 6, 535–541.

13. Spain

Fernando Barceinas-Paredes, Josep Oliver-Alonso, Jose Luis Raymond-Bara and Jose Luis Roig-Sabaté

INTRODUCTION

Education is the most direct form of investment in human capital that individuals may undertake. The estimation of the private returns on that investment is one of the most widely studied topics in labour economics, giving rise to a huge empirical literature. Our objective is contributing to this literature from the perspective of the Spanish case.

The Spanish economy has undergone a rapid process of structural change during the last two decades. One of the factors underlying this change is the improvement in the quality of labour. Although the educational level of the Spanish population is lower than the European average, during the last two decades an important increase in the stock of human capital of the labour force has taken place. While the share of the labour force holding post-compulsory qualifications in 1980 was 14.5%, this share rose to 35.3% in 1998. It was in the 1980s when a huge public financial effort made available post-compulsory education to larger sections of the schooling age-population through public supply or publicly subsidised private supply. This increase has affected both male and female population, but in the last case the effect has been stronger. This has had as a result a growing female participation in all the cohorts.

The fact that the Spanish economy has been suffering since the beginning of the 1980s the highest unemployment rate in Europe is probably not neutral to the explanation of the increasing demand for education. A reduction in private opportunity costs of further education and the differentials both in wages and job probability in favour of those with higher education has, probably, led to a rise in the decisions to continue into higher education for a growing proportion of youth.

A large stream of Spanish evidence has been published for the last 10 years. The availability of different microdatasets during those years has made possible progress in the field. Several conclusions can be drawn from this literature. Firstly, returns to education, when years of schooling is used as independent variable, tend to show a range of values between 5 and 7%. These figures reflect different weights from gender and sector. Also, higher returns for women than for men and higher returns for private than for public sector is a common finding. Secondly, when using qualifications as independent variable, results tend to show linearity. Thirdly, return differentials between compulsory and higher education tended to increase during the 1980s. Fourthly, those authors trying to test for signalling effects have only found evidence of weak signalling.

Our results tend to confirm those findings for different samples. Moreover, they show robustness to different specifications departing from the basic Mincerian model. However, we find a difference in the level of returns. In our case, returns take values around 8%. Most of the previous Spanish evidence is drawn from data of 1990 or 1991. Our results for 1994 and 1995 would imply a slight increase in the returns to education during the first half of the 1990s. This is a remarkable result given the growth in the supply of educated workers during the period.

The datasets used were the Household Budget Survey 1990/1991 (HBS 1990/1991) that offers information about all members of 20000 households, especially in those aspects related to qualifications attained, annual net income, as well as their employment status. Unfortunately, information about hours worked is not available. The Continuous Household Budget Survey (CHBS 1985–1996) is a quarterly survey with a sample based on 3000 households. Variables are the same as those in the HBS 1990/1991, but are provided only for the head of household. The Household Budget Survey 1980 (HBS 80) has the same structure as the CHBS but with a sample of 24000 households. The Wage Structure Survey 1995 (WSS-95) is a employer survey of 175 000 wage earners, which contains an important amount of characteristics related to each worker (qualification, tenure, type of contract, type of job, sector, firm size, and so on). Wages are gross and net and they are provided on an hourly, monthly and annual basis. Finally, the European Household Panel 1994 (ECHP-94) offers information about 8000-surveyed households. Basic personal characteristics are provided for each individual as well as labour market status. For the employed, information is given on gross and net wages, and worked hours. This survey provides information about educational level, and also on age-leaving education, which allow us to approximate 'real' years of schooling.

All surveys were purged dropping those observations with wages below minimum wage, younger than 18 years and older than 65 years and, in ECHP 94, individuals whose approximated 'real years of schooling' were evidently atypical. In the case of male observations, only full-time workers were included in the used samples. For female workers both full- and part-time workers made up the samples but a control dummy is included.

In order to make easier the comparability of surveys, all the considered wages were reconverted to gross wages before taxes and social security payments. This process was carried out with a specific program and according to the information from the taxable units. Our work makes new contributions to the Spanish evidence. In the first place, we have compiled a homogeneous database in terms of wage definition. In this sense all estimations are run using gross wages as dependent variable. Most of the Spanish literature is based on a definition of net wage close to the concept of 'take home income'. So our results are more clearly interpretable in terms of the effect of human capital on productivity. In the second place, new contributions are made on three topics. Firstly, we control for endogeneity of schooling by using instrumental variable estimators. The results show stability of the results under conditions specified later in the text. Secondly, we introduce the effect of unemployment on returns to education under different hypothesis by using an internal rate of return approach whose results are consistent with those obtained from a standard Mincerian specification using qualification dummies. Finally, we test sheepskin effects by estimating the effects on returns to education of repeated years to get a degree, and we present several tests in order to demonstrate the validity of the human capital theory versus the signalling theory.

The next section describes the education system. The third section establishes the cross-section and time series results of returns to education from a basic Mincerian model. After that, we test in the fourth section the robustness of the basic model results by introducing different controls on that model. Section five introduces the effect of unemployment on returns. In section six, the possibility of signalling and sheepskin effects is tested with different procedures. The seventh section addresses the problems of schooling endogeneity and instrumental variable estimations. The main conclusions drawn from the previous work are given in the final section.

THE EDUCATIONAL SYSTEM IN SPAIN

The Spanish non-university education system was recently reformed by the General Organic Act of the Education System (LOGSE) of 1990. This new system implies two additional years of compulsory education from 14 to 16 years of age and strengthening. A first cohort of students under the new system should have completed the whole cycle in year 2000. The individuals included in the datasets used in this work studied under the previous systems. This is the reason why we concentrate the explanation on the previous system. The Education General Act of 1970 structured for the first time the whole education system, establishing a general compulsory level for all students until the age of 14.

The compulsory level, General Basic Education (EGB), was an eight-year cycle for all pupils from 6 to 14 years. It includes primary and lower secondary education. Those students who did not succeed had the option to go to first grade of vocational training. Students who completed successfully EGB could take either upper secondary or vocational training.

Upper secondary education (BUP) was composed of two core courses and a third in which students had to take an option between sciences and humanities. This cycle was completed by a fourth course for students wishing to go on tertiary education called Course of University Guidance (COU) in which students had to opt among four fields: science and technology, biology and health, social sciences and, finally, humanities and foreign languages. After passing this course students had to sit an exam for university admission. After completing BUP another possibility was to enter the second level of vocational training.

Vocational training had two levels. The first one (FPI) implied two years and was compulsory and free for all students who did not take the BUP option. After completing this first level those wishing to do so could continue to the second level (FPII). As has been mentioned this was an option also for students that had completed BUP. The second level might take two or three years depending on the field of specialization.

Tertiary education was organized in two options. Short-cycle degrees with a more professional profile took three years. Long-cycle degrees taking five years had a more academic profile. In technical degrees the legal requirement might imply an additional year.

PRIVATE RETURNS TO HUMAN CAPITAL: A MINCERIAN FRAMEWORK

In this section we deal with the main results obtained from a parsimonious Mincerian model estimated by OLS, with years of education and quadratic on potential experience as independent variables and logarithm of hourly gross wages (including all social security payments) as dependent variable. We use a sample of full-time workers from ECHP-1994 and WSS-1995 but exclude all workers reporting earnings below the minimum wage in annual terms. Table 13.1 shows the results obtained using years of schooling in 1994 and 1995, with values ranging between 7.5 - 10%. From these results, three main simple facts can be pointed out. Firstly, full-time male and female workers have returns to schooling around 8% per annum. Secondly, full-time female returns are slightly higher than men's. And, finally, when in the WWS-1995 part-time female workers are controlled for, female returns are still higher than in the previous case.

Table 13.1   Returns to schooling (%)

	Men	Women[a]	Women[b]
ECHP-94	7.46	8.29	8.28
WSS-95	8.20	8.27	10.02

Notes: The returns are in % of gross hourly earnings.
[a] only full time.
[b] all the sample controlling for part time.

The fact that we are working with an employer survey (WWS-1995) and a household survey (ECHP-1994) may produce some distortions in the comparability of working hours. The latter may be behind the dissimilarities in the results obtained for men. Because we might grant a higher reliability in wages and working time data to employer surveys, returns to education for full-time male workers in Spain in the mid Nineties must be slightly higher than 8%. For women, rates of return estimates depend on the inclusion of a dummy variable that controls for the part-time (which accounted for 15% of the female working population during this period). While full-time female workers show almost the same return to schooling in both years and surveys (8.29% in 1994 and 8.27% in 1995), when part-time is controlled for a quite important difference appears: from 8.28% in 1994 to 10.02% in 1995. Again, since 10.02% comes from a sample that was addressed to employers this result seems to be more reliable.

Generally speaking, it seems that the similarity between full-time male and female rates and the differences between returns to schooling when female part-time is controlled for, could be explained by the following reasons. Firstly, dissimilarity between sample sizes used in both surveys: while the WSS-1995 includes 118027 observations for males and 30769 for females, in the ECHP-1994 we have only 2181 for males and 848 for females. The second explanation concerns the sample selection bias that arises when we look at the various samples of working women only. There is a further discussion of this issue below.

The only Spanish data set that allows estimation of our mincerian equations for a series of years to track the evolution of returns through time is the CHBS 1985–1996. This source presents two limitations. First, the necessary data on earnings is only given for head of households and on annual basis (no information on hours of work), and, secondly, sample size is rather small.

We tested whether the results obtained using the CHBS 1985-1996 were consistent with those obtained from larger samples by looking at the heads of households only. There are some years for which CHBS and the other larger samples have information on the heads of households. These larger samples of heads of households are available in two data sets: HBS-1990/91 and ECHP-1994. The returns obtained from samples of male head of households for annual earnings were 6.9% in 1990 and 7.2% in 1994. These returns are almost identical to those found using the CHBS samples for the same years. Therefore, one should be reasonably confident on the consistency of the results obtained using the CHBS series. That is, it is possible to claim that there are not big differences between the return for heads of households and the return for the whole population. Additionally, HBS-1980/81, which has exactly the same characteristics as CHBS, except for a larger sample, was included in the time series.

Figure 13.1   Rates of return to education: 1980–1996

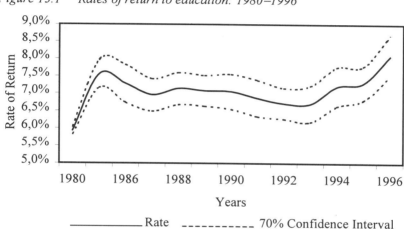

Estimated equations rates of return to schooling are graphed in Figure 13.1. The time profile of returns shows three phases: an increase from 1980 to 1985, a slight decreasing trend from 1985 to 1993 and, finally, a rapid increase from that year until 1996, last year of the sample. Altogether, the range of returns runs from 5.9% in 1980 to 8.1% in 1996. In order to test the equality of coefficients over time, temporal dummies with schooling interactions were included in the equation. Only in one case the coefficient was not significant and the test about structural change showed statistical significance. It should be mentioned that variations in returns over time seem to be related to the GDP cycle. Therefore, these small changes in rates of return may reflect differences in demand for human capital depending on cyclical sensitivity.

The rather stable pattern of returns to schooling takes place in a period with a steady increase in the average level of qualification of the labour force, as shown in Figure 13.2. Certainly, many factors could help to explain these changes. For example the decrease in the numbers without formal education is related to demographic changes particularly in relation to the agricultural sector. However the most important one is the increase in the supply of education by the public sector. In any case, the most important feature that appears in this increasing average level of schooling and the stability (and even a certain increase) in returns to education is that demand for more educated people has even overtaken supply. Probably, both the technological change and the tertiaritation that the Spanish economy has undergone in the last 20 years could explain this match between supply and demand.

Figure 13.2   Per capita years of schooling of the labour force

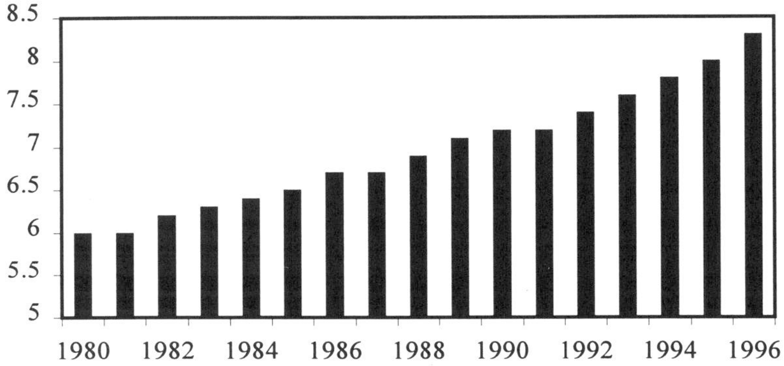

Notes: The figures are for the heads of households
Source: Labour Force Survey.

VARIATIONS ON THE BASIC MODEL

Qualifications as an Explanatory Variable

The use of qualifications as explanatory variable allows us to test the linearity hypothesis, which underlines the years of schooling approach. Marginal rates of return for each level of education are shown in Table 13.2. Patterns from both datasets look very similar. We find growing returns as we move up the educational ladder, specially from primary to upper secondary. On the other hand, the returns show a relative stability in the university cycles. Furthermore, a common feature to all four estimates is a larger jump of returns in two levels, namely upper secondary and and upper vocational.

Female returns tend to be higher than male returns, and in this sample differentials increase with qualification. This is not the case for ECHP-94 where the opposite tends to be the case. Figures 13.3 and 13.4 show the evolution of wage premiums to number of years required for the completion of each degree, in general and vocational paths. Clearly, rewards increase with higher qualifications, while after eight years of schooling the linear approximation could be adequate.

Table 13.2   Marginal rates of return (%)

	ECHP-1994		WSS-1995	
	Men	Women	Men	Women
Primary	1.0	2.8	1.2	3.7
Lower secondary	3.8	4.4	3.5	5.2
Upper secondary	9.6	9.6	10.3	12.4
Short university cycle[*]	10.2	11.0	9.3	8.0
Long university cycle[*]	10.0	9.1	11.2	14.6
Primary	1.0	2.8	1.2	3.7
Lower secondary	3.8	4.4	3.5	5.2
Upper vocational	7.0	6.9	8.6	10.5
Years schooling	7.4	8.3	8.2	10.0

Notes: *In this case, the six real years of schooling required to obtain the university degree was divided in 3.5 years to short University cycle and 2.5 to long university cycle. The return is % of gross hourly wages.

Figure 13.3   Wage premium: general path, reference is no schooling

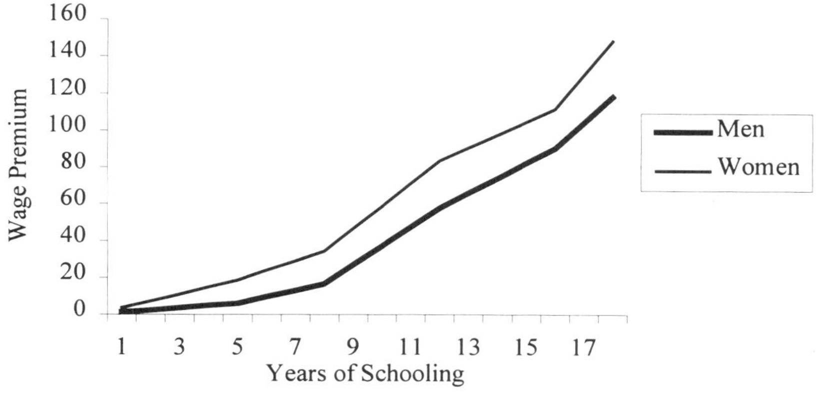

Notes: The wages, taken from the WSS-1995, are gross hourly wages.

Figure 13.4   Wage premium: vocational path, referenc is no schooling

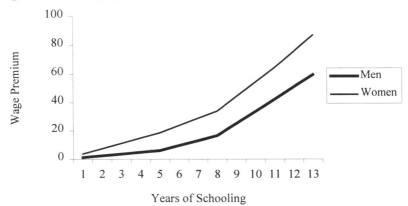

Notes: The wages, taken from the WSS-1995, are gross hourly wages.

Other Forms of Human Capital

Human capital theory considers other forms of human capital investment than schooling. Experience and tenure increase human capital accumulation along the life cycle. It should be taken into account that the most common measure of experience is potential (as a difference between age and years of schooling). This definition of experience should not be a serious problem in the case of men. However, for women the approach is more ambiguous because of their discontinuities in the labour market. In the Spanish case, only a few previous works have used tenure (see Cañada, 1993; De la Rica and Ugidos, 1995; Ullibarri, 1996; Garcia *et al.*, 1997; and Salabarria and Ullibarri, 1997). Other works use age instead of experience (see Lassibille, 1994; Garcia *et al.*, 1997; Oliver *et al.*, 1998; Lassibille and Navarro, 1998).

Moreover, two points should be added to those discontinuities in relation to the use of a cross-section. Firstly, we should expect female attachment to labour force to increase with education. Secondly, we are dealing with different generations in the sample. In the Spanish case, a clear generational break took place in the last 20 years in terms of labour market attachment of female working-age population.

WSS-1995 provides information on tenure. This information has allowed us to qualify potential experience as the 'experience up to current job'. That is, the number of years that go from leaving school until the current job. It should be reminded that this definition of experience is also potential. But, on the other hand, this approach allows us to consider experience and tenure separately. In the specification that includes both previous experience and tenure the rates of return to education show a slight decrease in relation to the standard Mincerian specification. The rate for men decreases from 8.2% to 7.4% and the rate for women from 10.0% to 8.3%.

As the specification of both previous experience and tenure is quadratic to calculate their returns we need to do it for a certain number of years. Table 13.3 shows returns to experience and tenure for 1, 5, 10, 20 and 30 years of previous experience and tenure. Three points are worth mentioning from these results. Firstly, returns to education are far higher than returns to experience and tenure. Secondly, returns to both experience and tenure are higher for women but decrease at a faster rate probably reflecting a different life cycle in the labour market. In addition, it should be noticed that differentials are much larger in tenure than experience. Finally, returns to tenure are more important than returns to experience.

Table 13.3 Return to other forms of human capital (%)

	Men	Women
Returns to previous experience		
Years of experience		
1	1.8	2.6
5	1.6	2.2
10	1.4	1.7
20	1.0	0.8
30	0.5	-0.1
Returns to tenure		
Years of tenure		
1	4.1	7.9
5	3.7	6.7
10	3.2	5.2
20	2.1	2.2
30	1.1	-0.7

Notes: The dependent variable is the gross hourly wage from WSS-95.

Additional Control Variables and Selection Bias

Earnings functions with additional control variables coming from three different surveys have been estimated. From the HBS-1990/1991 sector and regional dummies were taken, while from the ECHP-94 regional dummies were used. Finally, from the WSS-95 we used sector, job contract (fixed term versus non-fixed term), company ownership (private or public) and plant size. Table 13.4 summarizes our results. As expected, a clear and common feature appears: rates of return slightly go down. Using the highest number of control variables a maximum reduction appears in WSS-95, with near 2 points less (from 8.2% to 6.5%). These results seem to show that larger reductions are related to the introduction of choice variables. In this sense, the larger reduction observed in the case of WSS–1995 would be due to the fact that all the variables included refer to job characteristics, and therefore endogenous choice variables. In fact, the change in job characteristics is one of the mechanisms through which the more educated achieve higher wages, so some of these estimates tend to underestimate the real return to education. (Mincer, 1974).

Table 13.4   Rates of return to education with additional variables. Men (%)

HBS-90/91: annual gross wage						
Rate of Return	7.0	6.8	7.0	6.8	7.0	6.7
Sectors		X		X		
Regions			X	X		X
Regions *schooling					X	X
Adjusted R^2	0.39	0.40	0.40	0.41	0.40	0.41
ECHP-94: hourly gross wage						
Rate of Return	7.5	6.6	7.3	6.6	8.6	7.6
Sectors		X		X		
Regions			X	X		X
Regions *schooling					X	X
Adjusted R^2	0.34	0.38	0.36	0.40	0.36	0.40
WSS-95: hourly gross wage						
Rate of Return	8.2	7.6	8.1	7.4	7.5	6.5
Contract		X				X
Ownership			X			X
Size of Firm				X		X
Sector					X	X
Adjusted R^2	0.38	0.42	0.39	0.47	0.43	0.53

An interaction between regions and schooling has been used, searching for different rates of return among regions. Overall, results are relatively stable to such inclusion with figures ranging from 6.3% to 7.3% in 1990–1991 and from 6.1% to 8.6% in 1994. Despite that, the null hypothesis that all regions share a common return to education is statistically rejected.

Another modification in our parsimonious Mincerian model has been the correction of female sample selection bias, using Heckman's two-step approach, but·with some modifications, because we try to separate the decision to participate from the probability of being employed. For women, employment probability is related to some household and personal characteristics, but it is also a situation conditioned by the decision to enter the labour market. To tackle these two different process, we estimated two different probits, the first one aimed at obtaining the probability of entry into the labour market, while the second one allows us to know the female employment probability. Both models yielded expected results with respect to behaviour variables.

When controlling for selection bias returns are slightly lower than when no selection bias control was used. That is, for ECHP-94 (with hourly wages as independent variable), returns vary from 7.45% to 7.38% depending on whether or not part time is controlled for, whereas when selection bias is not controlled for returns were 8.29% and 8.28% respectively.

These results allow us to reconsider the female returns obtained using the more simple Mincerian framework. The sample selection bias, which clearly affects both the rate of female participation in the labour market and their probability to be employed, has an increasing impact on female returns.

Private and Public Sector Samples

As suggested in the first section there are clear differences between male and female returns when sector is considered, with a higher return in private than in public. For instance, using gross yearly wages, differences in men are higher than 1 percentage point (from 6.06% in public sector to 7.12% in private one), while for females the difference reaches 1.5 points (from 5.71% in private sector to 7.26% to public sector). The same pattern arises when gross hourly wages are taken into account, but with lower differentials between both sectors: from 6.43% to 6.89% for males and no differences for women.

For males, both phenomena (higher returns in private sector and a decreasing pattern between yearly and hourly wages) can be explained by differences in the process of wage determination between sectors. Whereas in the private sector men show higher dispersion in hourly wages and in the number of hours worked, in the public sector these differences tend to be lower.

Hourly and Yearly Wages

Returns to schooling from hourly wages can only be estimated using the 1994 and 1995 surveys. Since these datasets are rather new, most empirical work on returns for Spain uses yearly wages. This element leads us to estimate returns with the same data purging process but with different wage definitions, yearly and hourly.

Additionally, a second aspect related to the definition of number of hours worked suggests the necessity to discuss differences between hourly and yearly returns. First of all, it should be mentioned that the hours of work variable we use in our simple Mincerian model is defined as number of hours in collective bargaining agreements. However, that number of hours may not necessarily be the actual working time, because sickness and absenteeism provoke a non-negligible impact on them. Table 13.5 shows the number of hours worked by educational level and from it two important features appear.

Table 13.5   Yearly male hours worked, by educational level

Level	Real	Bargained	Difference (%)
1	1.664	1.757	-5.3
2	1.675	1.764	-5.0
3	1.624	1.754	-7.4
4	1.671	1.733	-3.6
5	1.651	1.747	-5.5
6	1.670	1.745	-4.3
7	1.671	1.727	-3.2
8	1.655	1.718	-3.6
All	1.655	1.750	-5.4

Firstly actual hours are lower than bargained ones and, secondly the difference is higher the lower the educational level. In any case, only when actual hours of work are considered the Card (1999) decomposition of returns to education appears. As Card has shown for the USA, approximately two-thirds of returns to education of annual wages observed in the 1990s can be explained by the effect of hourly wages, while the rest is accounted for by hours per week and weeks per year of work. In the Spanish case the estimation of the actual number of hours worked for the higher level of education is not reliable and this can explain that the Card decomposition does not follow the expected pattern. Results with both definitions of wages (hourly bargained and yearly) are shown in Table 13.6.

Results suggest that the definition does not matter in relation to returns. This conclusion is clear for men in the ECHP-94 and holds also in the WSS-95 for both men and women. Only in the female sample from ECHP-94 a slight difference appears in the University cycles (long and short) in favour of hourly wages, but this result probably has to do with the small sample used.

Table 13.6   Rates of return to education by levels and years in relation to no schooling (%, gross yearly and hourly wages)

| | ECHP-94 | | | |
| | Men | | Women | |
Levels	Yearly	Hourly	Yearly	Hourly
Primary	0.82	0.98	2.82	2.79
Lower secondary	1.81	2.05	0.07	0.08
Upper secondary	4.3	4.58	2.69	2.87
Upper vocational	3.54	3.94	2.2	2.59
Short university cycle	5.29	5.66	3.92	4.55
Long university cycle	6.23	6.43	4.84	5.30
Years	7.46	7.46	7.37	8.29

Notes: Female part-time controlled for.

UNEMPLOYMENT AND RETURNS TO EDUCATION

In the previous sections the estimation of returns to education was carried out assuming that individuals have the same unemployment probabilities. In addition, it seems quite clear that unemployment could have affected both the demand for higher levels of education and rates of return to education. Table 13.7 shows unemployment rates by level of education and age, obtained from the LFS samples. Individuals younger than 30 have not been included due to comparability problems in terms of job search information.

As it can be seen we have had a high, persistent and not equally distributed unemployment. This fact probably affects previous rates of return estimates. The effect of unemployment can appear through two ways: by modifying the opportunity cost of education and by affecting future earnings since differently qualified people have different probabilities to enter and to leave unemployment. For these reasons, when unemployment is taken into account returns may be subject to a non-negligible impact.

The effect of unemployment on returns to education has not been almost treated in the literature. Rather the focus has tended to be on the effect of education on unemployment. However, it is obvious that education affects the probabilities to be unemployed and the duration of unemployment spells and, as a result, average life-cycle incomes and, therefore, their respective rates of return to education. In this sense, the number of contributions, which analyse the first approach, is not very extensive. We should mention specially Ashenfelter and Ham (1979), Nickell (1979) and Groot and Oosterbeek (1992). In this literature, the forgone earnings are included in the estimation of returns to schooling, but some dissimilarities in the treatment appear. A fundamental difference is introduced in Ashenfelter and Ham with respect to the other authors. Ashenfelter and Ham aim to disentangle the importance of voluntary and involuntary unemployment on unemployed hours, whereas in the case of Nickell and Groot and Oosterbeek unemployment is basically seen as involuntary. This means that non-pecuniary benefits may arise from a situation of unemployment that should be taken into account. Even though a part of unemployment should be considered voluntary, in the Spanish case we can assume that most of it is involuntary. Therefore we exclude non-pecuniary benefits from the calculation without much cost.

From this point of view, our approach tries to introduce the effect of unemployment on both, costs and benefits, by using the internal rate of return (IRR). This system has three stages. Firstly a probit model estimates the probability of being unemployed, taking into account different qualifications and ages. Secondly an earnings equation is run with the sample of wage earners, controlling for selection bias. Finally, the age-earnings profiles are derived taking into account both the probabilities of being employed and the unemployment benefits, and the IRR is calculated. The age-earnings profiles are calculated according to the formula

$$\widetilde{Y} = (\exp\{\hat{Y} + \tfrac{1}{2}\hat{\sigma}^2\}) * f(x) + b * \left[1 - f(x)\right]$$

where $\hat{Y}$ is the fitted earning value, $f(x)$ is the employment probability, b is the unemployment benefit and σ is the standard error of the regression. We also assume that unemployment benefits are 60% of the last wage that the unemployed received. The proportion of the unemployed population receiving benefits in any particular year were 42.9% in 1990, 57.8% in 1994 and 62.9% in 1995. Finally, the wage has been estimated using the forecasted value according to age and qualification. Because we are interested in private returns, unemployment benefits are considered. If we were interested in the social returns unemployment benefits would not have been considered.

Figure 13.5a and 13.5b   Unemployment effects on return to education.

(a) Age-earnings profile without unemployment

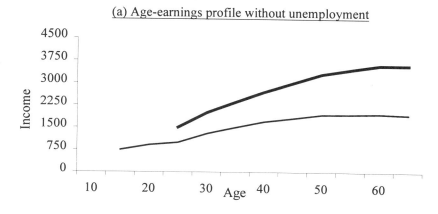

(b) Age-earnings profile with unemployment

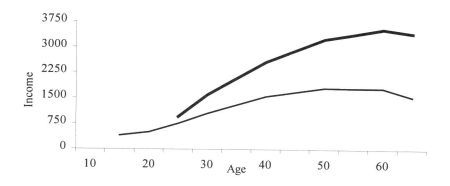

From a conceptual point of view, the effects of considering the unemployment probabilities in the evaluation of the rates of return to education can be seen in Figure 13.5. The age-earnings profiles without unemployment effect are shown in panel (a), and the unemployment effect on the age-earnings profiles is shown in panel (b). The figure shows that when unemployment probabilities are taken into account, and comparing two educational levels (university level is the bold line), two different effects appear. Firstly, the opportunity cost of remaining in the educational system becomes smaller. Secondly, the extra income of the more educated population increases because the effect of unemployment is more intense for less educated people (see Table 13.7). Consequently, the IRR that corresponds to panel (a) is 10.8%, whereas for panel (b) it is 14.3%.

Education and Earnings in Europe

Table 13.7   *Unemployment rates by educational qualifications (%, men)*

	All	30 to 44 years	45 to 65 years
LFS-90			
Illiterates	15.9	17.0	14.1
Primary	10.5	8.8	6.5
Lower secondary	14.4	7.1	4.9
Upper secondary	11.7	6.2	4.5
Lower vocational	17.0	7.8	6.5
Upper vocational	10.0	5.2	2.3
University (SC)	5.6	2.6	3.2
University (LC)	6.9	4.3	1.1
Total	11.8	8.0	7.6
LFS-94			
Illiterates	25.8	32.5	21.7
Primary	17.8	17.2	11.6
Lower secondary	24.0	16.3	8.4
Upper secondary	17.2	9.6	6.5
Lower vocational	24.1	14.5	10.7
Upper vocational	17.4	9.7	8.4
University (SC)	9.0	5.5	2.4
University (LC)	10.8	5.6	2.9
Total	19.5	14.8	12.0
LFS-94			
Illiterates	24.87	29.0	21.5
Primary	16.26	16.7	10.8
Lower secondary	21.51	14.8	9.2
Upper secondary	15.49	8.7	6.5
Lower vocational	20.22	10.6	6.9
Upper vocational	14.46	7.7	7.6
University (SC)	9.7	6.2	2.7
University (LC)	10.4	6.4	2.0
Total	17.63	13.4	11.1

Table 13.8   Returns to education relative to compulsory level (%, men)

	Standard	IRR	Unemployment	Unemployment and benefit
HBS-90 (annual wages)				
Upper secondary	7.0	6.9	7.3	6.9
Lower vocational	6.9	6.8	6.9	6.6
Upper vocational	6.9	6.7	8.6	7.8
University short cycle	7.7	7.6	9.2	8.5
University long cycle	8.1	8.1	9.8	9.2
ECHP-94 (hourly wages)				
Upper secondary	9.7	10.1	14.8	11.6
Upper vocational	7.0	6.9	10.5	8.1
University short cycle	9.4	9.6	14.2	11.4
University long cycle	10.1	10.5	14.3	12.1
WWS-95 (hourly wages)				
Upper secondary	10.3	10.7	15.2	12.8
Lower vocational	12.8	13.7	20.3	16.7
Upper vocational	8.6	8.7	13.2	10.9
University short cycle	9.2	9.4	13.1	11.1
University long cycle	10.2	10.5	13.8	12.0

Notes: The WSS-95 is an survey of employers, it does not, therefore contain unemployment information. Consequently it was not possible to control for the bias due to selection into employment. We applied the probabilities of being employed derived from EPA-95 in order to calculate the age-earnings profile and obtain the IRR.

The results from using this approach are shown in Table 13.8. Here we compare returns under three different assumptions: firstly, no unemployment effect (by dummy coefficients and by IRR); secondly, taking the unemployment effect into account but not including benefits and, finally, including benefits. Results show that if unemployment effect is not included, differences between the IRR approach and the standard econometric procedure through coefficients are negligible. However, as it was expected, rates of return increase considerably when employment probability is included in the calculation. For example, the rate of return to university long cycle increases by 1.1 percentage points in 1990/1991, 4.2 percentage points in 1994 and 3.6 percentage points in 1995. There are similar changes in the return to education when benefits are included in the regression. Obviously, the largest increases are obtained in 1994 and 1995 because the unemployment rates for these years are higher than for 1990.

It is important to note that the most important modification occurs in upper vocational returns. However, despite that change in the upper vocational returns, the rate continues to be the lowest one, except for 1990/1991 when the upper vocational return with probability to be employed and unemployment benefits is higher than the lower vocational and upper secondary rates. To summarize, when we consider the employment probability the rates of return increase by, on average, 16% in 1990/1991, 46% in 1994 and 43% in 1995. But, when unemployment benefits are included these increases go down to 8%, 17% and 20% respectively.

SIGNALLING AND SHEEPSKIN EFFECTS

The screening hypothesis (Spence, 1973; Stiglitz, 1975) states that education primarily acts as a screening device for workers as opposed to enhancing their productivity. In any case, it is possible to claim that education could have two effects on returns: a direct one by increasing productivity and an indirect one in signalling innate or pre-existing ability. Therefore, if we are interested in rates of return to educational investment it will be important to know the signalling weight. In the following paragraphs, a set of procedures is employed to test the signalling hypothesis: comparisons of rate of return to schooling between screened *versus* unscreened groups and life-cycle wages profile of differently qualified people.

Screened Versus Unscreened Rate of Return Method

First we compare rates of return of a particular sub-sample of the population as a theoretically unscreened group with other theoretically screened sub-samples. Sometimes, the comparison of the rates of return to schooling between self-employed (unescreened group) and wage earners (potentially screened group) has been suggested as a way to test signalling versus human capital models. However, due to the lack of reliability of the data, in our case this approach has not been considered. This approach is based on the comparison of rates of return between private (competitive and, therefore, unscreened group) and public sector (non-competitive and, therefore, screened group). If signalling theory is correct, then non-competitive sectors should show higher rates of return than competitive sectors do. This is because in the first situation productivity is less important and signalling is more likely to occur.

Table 13.9 shows results from earnings equations with a sample from public and private sectors, based on HBS-1990/1991 and ECHP-94. Some authors consider that sector choice is not random. Thus, results from separated estimations by sector could have a specification bias (Arabsheibani and Rees, 1997). To tackle this problem, Heckman's procedure has been applied in two stages. However, in the ECHP-94 case the *lambda* coefficients were not significant, so we preserve the model without selection bias correction. The rates of returns to education based on HBS-90/91 are higher in the private than in the public sector, while rates of return based on ECHP-94 are very similar, suggesting that a strong version of signalling theory must be rejected.

Table 13.9   Earnings function by sector (men)

	HBS-90/91 [Annual wages]		ECHP-94 [Hourly wages]	
	Private	Public	Private	Public
Constant	12.9	13.2	6.0	6.3
	478.6	*106.6*	*104.1*	*64.1*
Schooling	0.1	0.1	0.1	0.1
	27.9	*15.0*	*19.4*	*15.5*
Experience	0.1	0.0	0.0	0.0
	35.5	*15.7*	*11.8*	*5.5*
Experience²	-0.0007	-0.0004	-0.0005	-0.0004
	-27.9	*-11.7*	*-7.5*	*-3.5*
Lambda	-0.2	0.1		
	-4.4	*1.5*		
Adjusted R²	0.4	0.4	0.3	0.3
Obervations	7192	2551	1612	569

Notes: White robust t-statistic in italics.

Return to Tenure and Qualifications Groupings Method

A second procedure is based on the comparisons of life-cycle return profile of differently qualified people. That is, signal theory suggests that the educational process acts only as a 'filter', separating individuals with higher innate ability (with higher educational level) from the rest. But, when employers increase their knowledge about the 'true' productivity of their employees (as a result of their experience) these differences must decrease. Alternatively if those differences increase signalling theory must be rejected.

To test the signalling theory we use two different methods. The first method is the P-test, proposed by Psacharopoulos (1979). According to the weak version of this test, employers pay initially higher wages to more educated workers. In the strong version, these differences persist throughout the life cycle. If screening hypothesis is correct, then we should find a convergent profile once employers have adjusted wages of higher educated people to their *true* productivity. Otherwise, if a divergent profile of wages between different levels of education is found, then signalling theory must be rejected. Table 13.10 shows estimations of earning functions by qualifications.

Table 13.10   Earning functions by educational qualifications, WSS-95

	Compulsory	Upper secondary	Lowe vocationa	Upper vocational	Short cycle	Long cycle
Constant	6.89	7.17	7.0	7.19	7.50	7.68
	1000.00	*599.20*	*462.8*	*750.50*	*542.70*	*582.20*
Tenure	0.04	0.05	0.0	0.05	0.05	0.06
	61.00	*43.30*	*33.2*	*41.50*	*27.50*	*27.80*
Tenure^2	-0.04	-0.08	-0.0	-0.08	-0.07	-0.11
/100	*-19.60*	*-21.40*	*-14.6*	*-20.80*	*-13.60*	*-14.90*
Experience	0.02	0.02	0.0	0.02	0.02	0.03
	24.80	*13.20*	*10.5*	*14.50*	*13.30*	*15.30*
Exp.^{2}	-0.00	-0.01	-0.0	-0.02	-0.02	-0.02
/100	*-13.40*	*-2.40*	*-2.5*	*-4.40*	*-2.80*	*-2.40*
Adjusted-R^2	0.35	0.28	0.4	0.37	0.28	0.27
Observations	33208	12709	579	9961	6329	7058

Notes: White robust t-statistic in italics. The dependent variable is the male gross hourly wage.

First of all, it should be noticed the strong significance of the 'tenure' coefficients, and their positive sign. This is *prima-facie* evidence against the strong hypothesis. As can be observed, the 'compulsory upper secondary university long cycle' pattern shows a divergent process in the profile income-tenure. That is, workers with a higher degree of education have higher wages and similar returns to tenure than the less educated ones even when employers have had the possibility to see their 'true' productivity.

A second test, also suggested by Psacharopoulos (1979), is based on comparing the mid-to-early career earnings ratio for different sectors as years of schooling increase. A compatible behaviour with signalling theory should show a steady decrease and higher ratios in non-competitive than in competitive sectors (Cohn *et al.*, 1987). The result of this method is presented in Table 13.11. Results, based on samples from HBS-90/91 and WSS-95, do not support the signalling hypothesis. In the HBS-90/91 sample, the hypothesis that the non-competitive sector (public sector) has higher ratios than the competitive sector has not been proved. Moreover, the required decreasing pattern of this ratio is not clear, either.

Table 13.11   Income ratios at the middle and beginning of careers

	\multicolumn{6}{c}{Years of schooling}					
	8	10	12	13	16	18
Sector						
Manufacturing	1.6	1.7	1.6	1.7	1.7	1.7
Utilities	2.1	2.1	2	1.9	1.7	2.1
Construction	1.6	1.8	1.5	1.7	1.7	1.6
Traded	1.7	1.9	1.8	1.9	1.9	1.7
Hotels	1.5	1.4	1.5	1.2	1.8	1.4
Transport	1.6	1.7	1.6	1.8	1.5	1.5
Financial	1.2	1.7	1.4	1.7	1.6	1.5
Business	1.7	1.8	2.1	1.7	1.9	1.9
Public	1.4	.1.3	1.3	1.2	1.3	1.2
Private	1.3	1.2	1.4	1.2	1.3	1.7
Other	1.6	1.7	1.6	1.8	1.4	1.5

Notes: Results are based on samples drawn from both the WSS-95 (income in the middle and at the beginning of their career is attributed to tenures greater than eight years and lower than three years, respectively) and the HBS-90/91 (income in the middle and at the beginning of their career is attributed to ages higher than 35 and 45 years old and lower than 25 years, respectively).

In summary, it seems quite clear that a strong version of signalling theory must be rejected in the Spanish case. Our results confirm those reached by other Spanish studies (see Lassibille, 1994; Corugedo, 1998; Blanco and Pons, 1999). Our work suggests that a weak impact of signalling should be considered. Then, it is not possible to assert that the signalling hypothesis does not contain some elements of truth. However our empirical evidence shows that signalling can explain only a small part of return differentials at most.

Sheepskin Effect

Another form of signalling is the so-called sheepskin effect (Layard and Psacharopoulos, 1974; Park, 1999), which can be tested by comparing the effect on wages coming from 'actual' schooling years needed to attain a certain qualification. Several authors have argued that some degree of signalling could appear if people with qualifications earn more that those without them, but with the same amount of years of schooling. Note though that higher wages are likely to reflect higher productivity if individuals with higher abilities are more likely to obtain higher qualifications (Layard and Psacharopoulos, 1974). According to this interpretation, qualification acts as a proxy of ability (as a 'credential'), or as a proxy for benefit accruing from educational investment. Nevertheless, it is important to note that we have no information to determine the precise reason to explain why some individuals require more years to obtain a qualification (for instance, whether it is due to less ability or because the individual studied part time while working). In this sense, it is not possible to assert whether the sheepskin effects imply signalling. So, in this part of the work we are only concerned with establishing if sheepskin effects exist.

Following Park (1999), the specification used to estimate this effect is

$$\ln W = \alpha_0 + \alpha_1 X + \sum_{i \in I} \sum_{j \in J} \beta_{ij} D(level = i) * D(S = j) + \eta$$

Where X is a set of control variables, S is the number of years of schooling, I is a set of indicator variables for each level of schooling. The individual components i of the vector I are broken down as follows: compulsory (3), upper secondary (4), lower vocational (5), short university cycle (6) and long university cycle (7). The vector $J = \{8,9,21\}$ is also a set of indicator variables for total years of schooling. $D(level=i)$ is a dummy variable that takes value 1 when individual has attained the level of education i. In addition, $D(S = j)$ is also another dummy variable which takes value 1 if the individual has years of schooling equal to j. Finally, the parameter η is a random disturbance term. To illustrate, $D413$ represents a dummy variable equal to 1 for individuals with upper secondary level and 13 years of schooling. From 1970 onwards, the number of official years of schooling required to obtain each qualification are as follows (the numbers in brackets indicate the number of years required under the previous system): BUP and COU is the sum of three different levels, that is, Lower Vocational with 10 years, BUP with 11 years (10 years) and COU with 12 years (11 years). Short University Cycle, on the other hand, needs 15 years (14 years), while Long University Cycle demands 17 years, (16 years). Rates of return to education are calculated according to:

$$\frac{\widehat{W}_{i,j} - \widehat{W}_{3,8}}{n * \widehat{W}_{3,8}},$$

where each of the wage parameters are predicted values. The parameter n represents the number of years of education between the minimum compulsory level (3, 8) and (i, j).

Data used for this analysis comes from ECHP-94. The experience variable was calculated using average men values obtained from the sample. Then, this average experience was assigned to individuals with eight years of schooling (compulsory level). From this experience, each additional year of education was subtracted to build different predicted values. Figure 13.6 shows rates of return to education for upper secondary, short university and long university cycles. Results point to a negative influence of returns when more years of schooling are needed. For instance, those individuals who finish their university long cycle studies after 16 years of schooling have a rate of return of 15.6%. This rate decreases to 15.1% if they need 17 years and it goes down even more, to 11.9%, if the total amount of years needed is 18.

Figure 13.6   Sheepskin effects (hourly gross wages, men)

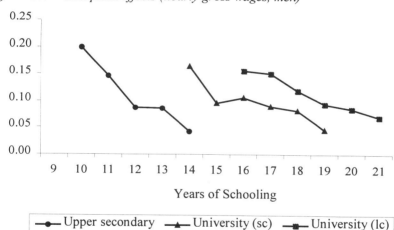

The profile is clearly decreasing until a low rate of return of 6.9% with 21 years of schooling (see Corugedo, 1998). This decreasing pattern of returns appears because additional schooling years imply higher opportunity costs and, at the same time, a shorter payback period. In addition, it is also possible that individuals who finalize their studies in a shorter period are more skilful and have a higher productivity and, therefore, obtain higher rates of return. It should be noticed, again, that extra years of schooling could reflect interrupted process connected with work, illness or familiar responsibilities, as well as less ability to achieve qualification. Nevertheless, we have no information about these different causes.   An initial signal effect clearly appears when sheepskin is considered. But this effect may only reflect a weak signal if individuals with the same qualification tend to earn similar wages along the life cycle.

ENDOGENEITY AND INSTRUMENTAL VARIABLES

As it is well known, OLS estimates of returns to education are biased if explanatory variables in earnings equations are not exogenous. The most common problem that arises from endogeneity is the 'ability bias'. It appears because the error term from the Mincerian earnings equation reflects, among other factors, innate ability of individuals. If the more skilful people are those who obtain higher qualifications, the random disturbance and the regressor (that is, years of schooling) will be correlated, and estimates will be inconsistent. Instrumental variables is an ordinary procedure to deal with this problem. However, adequate instruments must be found, that is, instruments related to years of schooling but not correlated with the random disturbance.

We have chosen 'age' *(E)* as the most adequate instrument for the Spanish case, because the important change of our educational system had a higher impact on younger than on older generations. Several factors have raised the average level of education of new generations: increasing public educational supply, its growing extension to young population and increasing compulsory age. Hence our instruments are independent of individuals' innate ability. The functional form adopted includes a quadratic in age and some spline terms. That is

$$S_i = \varphi_0 + \varphi_1 E + \varphi_2 E^2 + \delta_1[D_1(E - E_1)] + \delta_2[D_2(E - E_2)] + \ldots + \delta_m [D_m(E - E_m)]$$
$$+ v_i,$$

where

$$D_j = 0 \quad \text{if} \ \ E \le E_j$$
$$D_j = 1 \quad \text{if} \ \ E < E_j \quad \text{to} \quad j = 1, 2, \ldots m.$$

This approach requires correct selection of E_j. To do so, a stepwise process was followed. In the first step, all possible values of E_1 were used and the final value was selected according to the best adjusted model. In a second step, with a fixed E_1 an identical processes were followed using all possible values of E_2 ($E_2 > E_1$), and so on. This procedure shows that the instrument defined is adequate, because growing supply of schooling is related to increasing years of schooling. That is, instruments are correlated with the regressor. At the same time, it seems reasonable to expect that innate ability has not changed in the last 50 years. This assumption implies that instruments chosen are independent from the random disturbance.

Results from OLS versus IV are shown in Table 13.12. The IV estimates are presented in three different forms. The first one is the standard IV estimate, the second one consists in correcting for differences in individual specific coefficient and self-selection bias by employing a method proposed by (Garen, 1984), which is applicable when the choice variable is continuous. Finally, the third one is based on a split sample instrumental variable (SSIV)

(Angrist and Krueger, 1995), which uses one-half of a sample to estimate parameters of the first stage equation. First-stage parameters estimates are then used to construct fitted values and second-stage parameters estimates in the other half a sample. This approach was applied only to the WSS-95 sample, because it contains a large number of observations.

Table 13.12   Earnings equations: OLS versus instrumental variables (men)

	OLS		IV		IV Garen		SSIV	
	Coef.	t-stat.	Coef.	t-stat.	Coef	t-stat.		
[HBS-90/91. Annual gross wage (9743 observations)]								
Constant	13.09	711.8	12.90	201.7	12.95	207.2		
Schooling	0.07	67.1	0.08	12.7	0.08	11.7		
Exp.	0.05	41.7	0.05	40.1	0.05	39.5		
Exp.^{2}/100	-0.06	-29.4	-0.07	-24.3	-0.06	-23.8		
Adjust-R^2	0.39		0.38		0.40			
Sargan			2.50	5.99*				
Hausman			82.40	7.82*				
Bound (F)			151.80					
[ECHP-94. Hourly gross wage (2181 observations)]								
Constant	13.55	296.2	5.67	24.0	5.64	25.2		
Schooling	0.07	29.3	0.09	3.5	0.10	3.9		
Exp.	0.04	13.0	0.05	7.6	0.05	7.6		
Exp.^{2}/100	-0.04	-8.0	-0.06	-3.8	-0.06	-3.9		
Adjust. R^2	0.34		0.32		0.36			
Sargan			0.20	5.99*				
Hausman			26.30	7.82*				
Bound (F)			35.40					
[WSS-95. Hourly gross wage (118027 observations)]								
Constant	6.04	932.9	6.03	255.5	6.11	258.3	6.01	167.8
Schooling	0.08	242.6	0.08	30.6	0.07	26.3	0.07	20.2
Exp.	0.05	124.5	0.06	123.0	0.06	117.5	0.06	75.2
Exp.^{2}/100	-0.06	-76.9	-0.07	-72.3	-0.07	-70.4	-0.07	-42.7
Adjust. R^2	0.38		0.38		0.40		0.15	
Sargan			26.08	9.49*				
Hausman			846.30	7.82*				
Bound (F)			972.50					

Notes: * indicates chi-squared critical values at the 5% level.

Reliability of IV versus OLS was tested using Sargan test. This test implies a rejection of the null hypotheses only with WSS-95 estimations, as a result of the large number of observations (118027). As it is well known, if the test is consistent, the standard hypothesis test approach gives an asymmetrical treatment to the type I error (erroneous rejection of a true null hypothesis) versus the type II error (erroneous acceptance of false null hypothesis). When the sample size increases, the probability of error type II error tends to zero; meanwhile the probability of type I error is constant at the significance level selected. Consequently, if the significance level does not fall as the sample size increases, a large sample size means a greater probability of rejection of the null hypothesis. In the limit, all the models and constraints would be rejected to the extent that they constituted a simplified representation of reality. In the Hausman test, high values of χ^2 statistics implied the rejection, in all cases, of the null hypothesis of exogeneity of the education variable. Finally, F-statistic Bound (Bound et al., 1995) test of the excluded regressor suggests that the instrument used is correct.

Looking at the IV results, there is no substantial change from those obtained with OLS, but there are slightly higher values for HBS-90/91 and ECHP-94, and slightly lower values for WSS-95. This implies that in the Spanish case the ability bias seems to be not very important and that differences between OLS and IV estimates do not follow a clearly identifiable pattern. This contrasts with a common finding in the empirical literature that shows higher rates of return obtained by IV rather than OLS. However, as Card (1999) has suggested, in some cases IV estimator do not represent sample average returns to education but those from particular groups, far away from the sample average, and strongly correlated with used instruments.

CONCLUSIONS

The main conclusions of this work could be grouped in the following items:

1. Global returns to education

(i) Regarding private returns to education in terms of hourly wages, our findings suggest estimates of around 8% per year. This result is fairly robust to different samples used in this work and to different estimation methods.

(ii) The historical evolution of returns to education from 1980 until 1996 shows a certain increasing trend in spite of the increase in the human capital stock of the Spanish population. In fact, in 1980, the estimated rate of return was 6% per year and the average years of schooling of the labour force was six. On the other hand, in 1996, the estimated rate of return to education was 8% and per capita years of schooling of the labour force increased to 8.3 years. The rate of return to education has increased by 33% and this figure has been accompanied by a 45% increase in the human capital stock of the Spanish labour force. In other words, the race between human capital demand and supply has shown a certain advantage for the demand side, which translates to an increase in the returns to education, despite the large increase in the supply of educated labour.

(iii) When evaluating the returns to education it is important to consider the various employment probabilities associated with different educational levels. We find that as the educational level increases, the unemployment probabilities become smaller. This relationship may represent an important link, which permits the more educated individuals to take full advantage of their high educational level. In this case, the returns to education tend to be around 2 percentage points higher than the 8% rate of return that we get when we assume that the unemployment rate is similar among different educational levels.

(iv) The returns to education by sex are relatively similar when both samples (males and females) are considered in a homogeneous way; in particular, considering full-time workers and dropping anomalous observations.

(v) With respect the private and public sector the returns to education appear to be slightly higher for the former, a result that could be a consequence of wage-setting mechanisms for civil servants in the public sector.

(vi) When we consider other forms of human capital different from schooling, we find returns to previous experience of between 2% and 0.5%, and returns to tenure in the range of 1% to 4%.

2. Returns to education and educational level

(i) Education in Spain seems to show increasing returns, in the sense that the returns to an extra year of education manifest a tendency to grow when the number of years of education increases. However, after eight years of schooling, corresponding to lower secondary, the increase in the returns to education becomes moderate. In fact, an upper limit must exist, because otherwise, from an individual point of view, there would be no incentives to stop the accumulation of human capital.

(ii) Investment in university education gives a greater return than investment in vocational education. This could be a consequence of the way in which the vocational path is selected (in some cases the vocational path is selected as a second option) and can reflect differentials in innate ability of the individuals. It could also be considered to be a by-product of the relative failure of the vocational path in Spain.

3. Is education only a filter device?

If education is a filter, social returns to education would be much lower than private returns and the whole educational system would be considered inefficient and a wasted screening mechanism that absorbs a disproportionate amount of resources. We have dedicated important efforts to discriminate between the human capital hypothesis and the screening hypothesis. Our results indicate certain signalling when the individual enters the labour market (weak signalling) but there is no evidence that this is so over time. So, high private educational return could be considered as an indication of a high social return. In other words, if there is no screening, or if the screening hypothesis does not explain a significant part of the wage differentials, then investing in human capital could be a profitable activity from an individual is as well as public or social point of view.

4. Methodological questions.

Traditionally, the estimation of the educational returns by OLS to Mincer-type equations has been submitted to the criticisms of ability and endogeneity bias, since schooling would be correlated with the random disturbance term that would include the unobservable individual ability. In our case, the estimates by IV, when the sample is adequately purged, become similar to those obtained by OLS. An explanation of why in some cases both methods could produce important differences is suggested taking the Spanish case as a reference.

References

Alba-Ramirez, A. (1993): "Mismatch in the Spanish labour market. Overeducation?," *The Journal of Human Resources,* XXVIII, 2, pp. 259–278.

Alba-Ramirez, A., and M. J. San Segundo (1995): "The return to Education in Spain," *Economics of Education Review,* 14 (2), pp. 155–166.

Angrist, J. D., and A. B. Krueger (1995): "Split-sample instrumental variables estimates of the return to schooling," *Journal of Business and Economic Statistics,* April, 13 (2), pp. 225–235.

Andrés, J., and J. Garcia (1991): "El nivel de estudios como factor explicativo del desempleo, de los ingresos y de la movilidad laboral," *Economía Industrial,* 278, pp. 13-22.

Arabsheibani, G., and H. Rees (1997): "On the weak versus the strong version of the screening hypothesis," *Economics of Education Review,* 17 (2), 189–192.

Arrow, K. J. (1973): "Higher education as a filter," *Journal of Public Economics,* 2, pp. 193–216.

Ashenfelter, O., and J. Ham (1979): "Education, unemployment, and earnings," *Journal of Political Economy,* 87 (5), pp. S99–116.

Blanco, J.M., and E. Pons (1998): "Evidencia empírica de la teoría del capital humano y la hipótesis de señalización en el mercado de trabajo español," in *VII Jornadas de la Asociación de la Economía de la Educación*, Isabel Castillo et al. (coordinadores). AEDE y Universidad de Cantabria. Santander.

Bound, J., D. A. Jaeger, and R. M. Baker (1995): "Problems with instrumental variables estimation when the correlation between the instruments and the endogenous explanatory variables is weak," *Journal of the American Statistical Association* June, 90 (430), pp. 443–450.

Brown, S., and J. G. Sessions (1999): "Education and employment status: a test of the strong screening hypothesis in Italy," *Economics of Education Review*, 18 (4), pp. 397–404.

Cañada, J. A. (1993): "Educación y disparidad salarial en España y Francia," I Simposio sobre igualdad y distribución de la renta y la riqueza, *Mercado de Trabajo y desigualdad IV*, Fundación Argentaria.

Card, D. (1999): "The causal effect of Education on Earnings", in O. Ashenfelter and D. Card (editors) *Handbook of Labour Economics*, Vol. 3A, North-Holland.

Cohn, E., B. Kiker, and M. Mendes de Oliveira (1987): "Further evidence on the screening hypothesis," *Economics Letters*, 25 (3), pp. 289–294.

Corugedo, I. (1998): "La hipótesis del capital humano y del credencialismo: una comprobación empírica para España," *HPE*, monografias *Educación y Economía.*

De la Rica, S., and A. Ugidos (1995): "¿Son las diferencias en capital humano determinantes de las diferencias salariales observadas entre hombres y mujeres," *Investigaciones Económicas*, XIX (3), pp. 395–414.

Garen, J. (1984): "The return to schooling: a selectivity bias approach with a continuous choice variable," *Econometrica*, 52 (5), pp. 1199–1218.

Groot, W., and H. Oosterbeek (1992): "Optimal Investment in Human Capital Under Uncertainty," *Economics of Education Review*, 11 (1), pp. 41–49.

Harmon, C., and I. Walker (1995): "Estimates of the Economic Return to Schooling for the United Kingdom," *The American Economic Review*, December, 85(5), pp. 1278–1286.

Hernandez, P.J. (1996): "Segregación ocupacional de la mujer y discriminación salarial," *Revista de Economía Aplicada*, 4 (11), pp. 57–80.

Lambropolous, H. S. (1992): "Further evidence on the weak and the strong versions of the screening hypothesis in Greece," *Economics of Education Review*, 11 (1), pp. 61–65.

Lassibille, G. (1994): "La distribución de rentas de los asalariados y de los trabajadores por cuenta propia: un test de las teorías del filtro y del capital humano," *Hacienda Pública Española*, 131, pp. 109-116.

Lassibille, G., and L. Navarro (1998): "The Evolution of Returns to education in Spain 1980–1991," *Education Economics*, 6 (1), pp. 6–9.

Layard, R., and G. Psacharopoulos (1974): "The screening hyphotesis and the return to education," *Journal of Political Economy*, 82 (5), pp. 985–998.

Mincer, J. (1974): *Schooling, experience and earnings.* Columbia University Press New York.

Nickell, S. J. (1979). "The effect of unemployment and related benefits on the duration of unemployment," *Economic Journal* 89(353), pp. 34–49.

Oliver, J., J. L. Raymond, J. L. Roig, and A. Roca (1998): "Función de ingresos y rendimiento de la educación en España," *Papeles de Economía Española*, 77, pp. 115-132.

Park, J. H. (1999). "Estimation of Sheepskin Effects Using the Old and New Measures of Schooling in the CPS". *Economic Letters*, 62 (12), pp. 237–240.

Pons, A. (1998): "El papel de la educación en la determinación de ganancias: diferencias entre el sector público y el sector privado," in *VII Jornadas de la Asociación de la Economía de la Educación*, Isabel Castillo *et al.* (coordinadores) AEDE y Universidad de Cantabria. Santander.

Psacharopoulos, G. (1981): "Returns to education: An Updated International Comparisons," *Comparative Education,* 17 (3), pp. 321-341,

Psacharopoulos, G. and R. Layard (1979): "Human Capital and Earnings: British Evidence, a critique", *Review of Economic Studies*, 46 (3), pp. 485–503.

Rosen, S. (1977): "Human capital: a survey of empirical research," in Ronald Ehrenberg (ed.) *Research in Labor Economics,* Volume 1, Greenwich Connecticut: JAI Press.

San Segundo, M. J. (1997): "Educación e ingresos en el mercado de trabajo español," *Cuadernos económicos de ICI,* 63, pp. 105–123.

Salabarría, A., and M. Ullibarri (1997): "¿Trabajar en ocupaciones "femeninas" reduce los salarios?" Documento de trabajo 9706, Universidad Pública de Navarra.

Spence, M. (1973): "Job market signalling," *Quarterly Journal of Economics*, 87 (3), pp. 355–374.

Stiglitz, J.E. (1975): "The theory of "screening", education, and the distribution of income," *American Economic Review* 65 (3), pp. 283–300

Tucker III, I.B. (1986): "Evidence on the weak and the strong version of the screening hypothesis in the United States," *Economics Letters*, 21 (4), pp. 391–394.

Ullibarri, A. M. (1996): "Diferencias salariales entre el sector público y privado, por nivel educativo y sexo," Documento de trabajo 9606, Universidad Pública de Navarra.

Vila, L. E., and J. G. Mora (1998): "Changing return to education in Spain during the 1980s," *Economics of Education Review,* 17 (2), pp. 173-178.

14. Sweden

Mahmood Arai and Christian Kjellström

INTRODUCTION

This chapter deals with estimation of returns to schooling in Sweden. Based on standard methodology and the standard literature[1] in this field, we aim at presenting estimates of returns to education that are as comparable as possible across countries in the PURE project. This chapter provides condensed replicated and updated results covering returns to schooling and experience from 1968 to 1996 using available data. We also present some new results considering the impact of attained diploma on earnings (the sheepskin effect) as well as across field-variation in returns to schooling with various levels of education.

We briefly describe the Swedish education system and summarize our main empirical findings on returns to human capital in Sweden. The differences in the estimated return on education over time and between gender might in part be due to differences in the return to different types of education. Another reason might be the way in which the private and public sectors reward educational attainment. Moreover, there have been changes in the progressive national income tax rate during the period we study, implying that various measures of wages (gross or net earnings) would affect the return to schooling differently.

There is an extensive debate in the literature about different types of bias in the estimated coefficients using ordinary least squares. The problem is that we observe wages only for those who work. Sample selection bias arises when factors determining participation are correlated with wages. This is especially important when it considers women. Another source of bias is the endogeneity of schooling as well as failure to control for ability and measurement error in the human capital variables. We deal with these sources of biases in returns to schooling given the possibilities our data offer.

The remainder of the chapter is as follows. The next section outlines the main features of the Swedish education system and the system of funding. The datasets are thereafter presented. Results from estimating standard Mincer equations and sensitivity analyses regarding importance of the model specification, selectivity, and omitted variables etc. are reported in the two sections that follow. The chapter is concluded with some general remarks.

EDUCATION SYSTEM - HISTORICAL PERSPECTIVE

Primary Education[2]

In 1950, the Swedish parliament decided to extend compulsory schooling to nine years. The primary aims of the educational reform were to promote equality of opportunity, and to facilitate the transition to both upper secondary and post-secondary schools. Up to 1991, the comprehensive school had been compulsory from the age of seven. Since 1991 parents have been given the opportunity of letting their children start school when they are six years old but this opportunity is seldom used.

The majority of the comprehensive schools in Sweden are public. Only a small minority of the children attend private/independent schools (around 2% in 1994/1995). These non-public schools are subject to the same rules concerning fees and curriculum as the public schools. They also receive public funding.[3] Class sizes do not systematically differ across public and non-public schools.

The proportion of the pupils who leave the comprehensive school with a diploma, that is attain a grade in every subject, is around 95% (somewhat lower in public schools than in private schools). An explanation for this high figure is that the school authorities have an obligation to allocate special assistance to pupils who have difficulties in achieving the requirements. Lately, there has been a tendency towards an increased number of dropouts.

Secondary Education

Upper secondary schooling is free of charge. However, the independent schools covering around 10% of the pupils are allowed to charge fees in certain cases. The majority of the compulsory school-leavers go on to secondary level studies that are voluntary. About 98% of the compulsory school-leavers attained upper secondary school in 1996/1997. About 80% of those who started their upper secondary school in 1993 completed their education within four years. The admission to upper secondary education is based on grade point averages.

The upper secondary education system has been subject to several changes. The upper secondary school, technical school and vocational education were brought together in a joint upper secondary school in the 1970 school reform. The vocational education was organized in two-year programmes, whereas the remaining programmes were three or four years. In the 1991 school reform, the municipalities were obliged to offer upper secondary schooling to all students younger than 20 years old. The programmes were also reorganized into 16 national programmes. The old system of two-year programmes were all transformed to three-year programmes that fulfil the general admission requirements for further higher education.

Tertiary Education

The 1968 Commission on Higher Education (U68) ended in the 1977 reform of the higher education system when a uniform system for tertiary education was introduced. The five most important elements of this reform were:

1. Some earlier non-academic programmes, such as nursing, child care education and education in the fine arts (around 50 000 students) were incorporated to higher education. Thus, there is no longer a difference between university and non-university tertiary education.
2. Study programmes were organised in five wide sectors: technical; administrative, economic and social work; health; teacher training; information, communication and arts.
3. Higher education was organised either in the form of study programmes that vary in length from one year to five and a half years, or single-subject courses. Whereas the study programmes lead to a degree, the single-subject courses offer both the possibility of combining courses for a full degree or just a certificate upon completion of a course.
4. An administrative authority on the national level became responsible for admission to all higher education. The applicants had to fulfil the general requirements of having completed upper secondary school or by being 25 years of age with at least four years of work experience. Proficiency in Swedish and English must correspond to the last year of upper secondary school. In addition, many study programmes/single-subject courses had specific requirements that applicants also had to meet. Furthermore, to overcome the large inflow of students to faculties with unrestricted admission, it was decided that admission to study programmes should be based on grade-point averages from upper secondary school. A special higher education aptitude test was available for those without upper secondary schooling.
5. The Government decided to establish new university colleges. To attract new groups of students several new institutes of higher education were located outside the traditional university regions. Another argument for decentralizing higher education was that regional universities would have positive employment effects.

The educational policies of the 1980s and 1990s have been characterised by the expansion of higher education. There are at present 11 universities, 32 university colleges of technology, 23 colleges of health sciences and 7 colleges of fine art in Sweden. The majority of the university colleges are state-run, but there are also some semi-private institutions. Education at the universities is free of charge, except for a small obligatory fee to the student union. Nevertheless, there are still major regional differences in educational levels among the population. Therefore, Parliament decided to increase the capacity of the higher education system by 68 000 students between the years 1997 and 2000.

In 1993, the universities and university colleges were given increased autonomy when they were given the opportunity to decide the admission and degree requirements, as well as programmes and single-subject courses to offer. Furthermore, a new financing system was introduced. The system up to 1993 was based on the costs of providing courses, whereas the system since 1993 is based on the number of degrees awarded.

The graduation rate within seven years among university entrants in study programmes/single subject-courses, for the academic year 1989/1990, is 54% (59% for women and 48% for men). Excluding students in single-subject courses, the graduation rate within seven years among first-year students in study programmes in 1989/1990 is 65% (72% for women and 56% for men).

The System of Funding

The total expenditure on compulsory education was 4925 million Euro (or 5313 Euro per child) in 1995, whereas the total expenditures on upper secondary education was 2069 million Euro (or 6686 Euro per student). The expenditure on tertiary education amounts to over 3300 million Euro (research included) of which 30% consists of research grants by research councils etc.

Child allowance per child was 951 Euro per year in 1995. This amount is paid for all children under the age of 16. For full-time students between 16 and 20 who are attending upper secondary school the study allowance is 713 Euro per year, which corresponds to the same monthly amount as the child allowance but is not paid for the summer vacations. For those above 20 who study (full time or part time) at the upper secondary school level the study assistance comprises both a study grant and a subsidized student loan. However, a student has to apply for this study allowance, which is obtainable for a maximum of six terms.

The study allowances for students at universities and university colleges are identical as that for students who study in the upper secondary school, the only exception being that the study allowances are obtainable for a maximum of 12 terms instead of six terms. Students in higher education and those who are above 20 years of age who study in the upper secondary school are eligible to a maximum yearly grant of 1827 Euro (1995). The yearly amount of the student loan was 4745 Euro in 1995. These amounts, however, are reduced according to the student's income. Notice that the parents' income or wealth does not affect the eligibility to these amounts. Moreover, the Swedish study assistance system also consists of special adult study assistance for unemployed or low-educated people, boarding grants and travel discounts.

Since 1989, repayment of the student loans is income-related (4 percent of total labour income two years earlier. The interest rate, which is set by the Government for one year at a time, was 6% in 1995. The Swedish study assistance system is funded by taxes. In 1995, the total expenditure for study assistance amounted to around 1000 million Euro, of which 80% consists of costs for secondary and post-secondary assistance.

DATA

We used the Swedish Level of Living Surveys (SLLS)[4] from 1968, 1974, 1981, and 1991 and the Household Market and Nonmarket Activities Surveys (HUS) from 1984, 1986, 1993 and 1996 to investigate levels and changes over time in the return to investments in human capital.[5] SLLS contain about 6000 randomly sampled people between ages 16 and 75 (18–75 for 1991). The non-response rate has increased over time, from 9% in 1968 to roughly 20% in 1991.

Data from HUS contain information on both the household and the individuals who make up the household. The 1984 survey was based on a stratified cluster sample of people aged 18–74, and of over 2300 households to which these individuals belong. This survey was followed by smaller surveys in 1986, 1988 (considerably smaller), 1991, 1993 and 1996. As a complement to those who were re-interviewed, a supplementary sample was added. This supplementary sample consists of those who became adult members of existing households and as well as a new random sample of households. For some of the years, only individuals in the new supplementary samples were asked questions on, for example, work experience and years of schooling. For the rest, we had to construct these variables by using information from previous years. The non-response rate is about 20%.

On one occasion, namely when the importance of omitted ability variables is examined, we used data from the Individual Statistics (IS) projects.[6] These data consist of two nationally representative samples (age cohorts) of pupils born in 1948 and 1953. The samples cover basically all individuals born on the fifth, fifteenth and twenty-fifth of each month during these years. The data sets include information on scores in achievement test scores in Swedish, English and mathematics, school marks in Swedish, English and mathematics, and scores from three intelligence tests representing the verbal, spatial, and reasoning factors of intelligence. Data were collected in 1961 and

1966 when the respondents were between 12 and 13 years of age. Information on highest educational level and yearly earnings in 1993 are from registers (utbildningsregistret and ÅRSYS) provided by Statistics Sweden.

GENERAL RESULTS

Descriptive statistics for the main variables in our analysis are reported in Tables 14.1a and 14.1b. The wage dispersion measured as the standard deviation of log hourly earnings decreases over time. Comparing the male and female wages, we find that the decline in wage dispersion for women is much larger than for men. The average number of years of schooling has increased by almost four years from 1968 to 1996. Consequently, the number of years of work experience has declined for men. However, due to increased female labour participation, the number of years of work experience has instead increased by two and a half years for women during 1986–1991. For men, the average number of years with current employer is 10 years in 1991. This figure has been rather constant over time. For women there has been an increase from six years in 1968 to 10 years in 1991. This might be the effect of increased generosity of the parental leave system during this period which enables mothers as well as fathers to be on leave for a period of over one year. Another important factor is the expansion of the public child care system. The proportion of women working less than 35 hours has been between 40 and 50% for all years.

Since information on actual years of work experience is missing for some respondents in the HUS surveys, we restrict ourselves to potential work experience (age minus six minus years of schooling) for these years. We return to the consequences of using different measures on work experience in the sensitivity section.

Tables 14.2a and 14.2b report the OLS estimates of standard wage equations for 1968, 1974, 1981, 1984, 1986, 1991, 1993 and 1996. The explained variation in log hourly wages by years of schooling, and experience, is highest in 1968 and drops by around 20 percent by 1991. For instance, the adjusted R-squares have declined from about 40 (30) percent for men (women) in 1968 to about 30% (25%) in 1991. The figures obtained from HUS show a continued fall in the explained variation. Results indicate a decline in the schooling coefficient from about 8% in 1968 to about 4% (3%) for men (women) in 1996.

The main decline took place between 1968 and 1974, falling from 8% to 5%. Results for the period from 1974 to 1996 do not indicate any major change in returns and the estimates of returns are roughly unchanged.

Table 14.1a   Descriptive statistics, standard deviation in italics

Men	1968	1974	1981	1984	1986	1991	1993	1996
Log of gross hourly earnings	2.43	3.00	3.67	3.87	4.08	4.45	4.56	4.67
	0.39	*0.33*	*0.30*	*0.29*	*0.29*	*0.31*	*0.30*	*0.28*
Schooling (years)	8.71	10.18	10.72	11.25	11.35	11.77	12.21	12.56
	2.86	*3.53*	*3.49*	*3.54*	*3.46*	*3.30*	*83.36*	*3.40*
Work exp. (years)	22.07	21.76	19.84			19.57		
	13.94	*13.81*	*12.94*			*12.44*		
Potential exp. (years)					23.24	23.88		23.99	25.13
					12.14	*11.97*		*12.01*	*11.42*
Seniority (years)	9.82	10.98	9.70			10.32		
	10.70	*11.80*	*9.33*			*9.99*		
Observations	1691	1232	1636	715	761	1507	831	728

Source: SLLS (1968, 1974, 1981, 1991) and HUS (1984, 1986, 1993, 1996)

Table 14.1b   Descriptive statistics, standard deviation in italics

Women	1968	1974	1981	1984	1986	1991	1993	1996
Log of gross hourly earnings	2.09	2.71	3.48	3.69	3.92	4.24	4.39	4.49
	0.46	*0.37*	*0.27*	*0.28*	*0.33*	*0.24*	*0.31*	*0.25*
Schooling (years)	8.71	9.80	10.29	10.79	11.06	11.51	12.07	12.54
	2.71	*3.00*	*3.15*	*3.23*	*3.15*	*2.90*	*3.19*	*3.22*
Work exp. (years)	14.39	14.29	15.33			16.86		
	11.47	*10.74*	*10.68*			*10.82*		
Potential exp. (years)					23.52	24.07		24.21	25.97
					13.11	*12.71*		*12.58*	*11.48*
Seniority (years)	6.01	6.94	7.77			9.62		
	7.08	*8.37*	*7.24*			*9.12*		
Part time %	0.38	0.44	0.49	0.53	0.49	0.41	0.42	0.38
Observations	1139	1177	1603	819	841	1605	1027	805

Source: SLLS (1968, 1974, 1981, 1991) and HUS (1984, 1986, 1993, 1996)

Table 14.2a   OLS log earnings equation estimates

Men	1968	1974	1981	1984	1986	1991	1993	1996
Schooling	0.076	0.050	0.044	0.050	0.052	0.041	0.046	0.039
	0.003	*0.002*	*0.002*	*0.003*	*0.003*	*0.002*	*0.003*	*0.003*
Actual Exp.	0.045	0.035	0.027			0.026		
	0.002	*0.002*	*0.002*			*0.002*		
Actual Exp.^{2}/100	-0.072	-0.054	-0.039			-0.037		
	0.004	*0.004*	*0.004*			*0.004*		
Potential Exp.				0.030	0.028		0.027	0.022
				0.003	*0.003*		*0.003*	*0.003*
Potential Exp.^{2}/100				-0.036	-0.035		-0.032	-0.026
				0.006	*0.006*		*0.006*	*0.006*
Adjusted-R^2	0.406	0.328	0.306	0.368	0.358	0.305	0.376	0.265

Table 14.2b   OLS log earnings equation estimates

Women	1968	1974	1981	1984	1986	1991	1993	1996
Schooling	0.082	0.052	0.038	0.045	0.044	0.037	0.041	0.031
	0.004	*0.003*	*0.002*	*0.003*	*0.040*	*0.002*	*0.003*	*0.003*
Actual Exp.	0.042	0.033	0.022			0.018		
	0.003	*0.003*	*0.002*			*0.002*		
Actual Exp.^{2}/100	-0.074	-0.058	-0.034			-0.026		
	0.008	*0.007*	*0.004*			*0.004*		
Potential Exp.				0.014	0.013		0.016	0.008
				0.003	*0.003*		*0.003*	*0.003*
Potential Exp.^{2}/100				-0.012	-0.015		-0.019	-0.007
				0.005	*0.006*		*0.005*	*0.004*
Part time	0.070	0.054	0.035	0.039	0.073	-0.002	0.049	0.004
	0.024	*0.019*	*0.012*	*0.018*	*0.021*	*0.011*	*0.018*	*0.017*
Adjusted-R^2	0.308	0.237	0.229	0.207	0.146	0.247	0.186	0.146

Notes: Standard errors are in italics beneath the reported coefficient. The model included an intercept term that is not reported here.
Source: SLLS (1968, 1974, 1981, 1991) and HUS (1984, 1986, 1993, 1996)

During the same period, we have two periods of sharp increases in the relative supply of labour with higher education, first in early 1970s and second in the early 1990s. While the increase in supply in the early 1970s was accompanied by a sharp fall in returns to schooling, the increase in supply in the early 1990s left the returns to schooling almost unchanged. Hence, we can rule out the simple supply argument. However, the data is consistent with the argument that there was a significant compression of the wage structure over the period, a trend that has been well documented for Sweden. Further research is needed to explain changes in returns to education.

Table 14.3   *OLS log earnings equation estimates*

	1968		1974		1981		1991	
	Men	Women	Men	Women	Men	Women	Men	Women
Schooling	0.075	0.081	0.049	0.051	0.043	0.037	0.040	0.036
	0.003	*0.004*	*0.002*	*0.003*	*0.002*	*0.002*	*0.002*	*0.002*
Actual Exp.	0.042	0.037	0.030	0.027	0.023	0.018	0.024	0.017
	0.002	*0.004*	*0.002*	*0.003*	*0.002*	*0.002*	*0.002*	*0.002*
Exp.^{2}/100	-0.069	-0.067	-0.050	-0.050	-0.036	-0.029	-0.035	-0.028
	0.004	*0.008*	*0.004*	*0.007*	*0.004*	*0.005*	*0.005*	*0.004*
Seniority	0.007	0.014	0.009	0.013	0.008	0.009	0.005	0.001
	0.002	*0.005*	*0.002*	*0.003*	*0.002*	*0.003*	*0.002*	*0.002*
Seniority^2/100	-0.011	-0.024	-0.013	-0.020	-0.009	-0.016	-0.009	-0.003
	0.005	*0.016*	*0.004*	*0.006*	*0.007*	*0.008*	*0.007*	*0.006*
Part time		0.081		0.062		0.038		-0.001
		0.024		*0.019*		*0.011*		*0.011*
Adjusted R^2	0.412	0.316	0.344	0.251	0.324	0.239	0.307	0.251

Notes: Standard errors in italics below reported coefficient, intercept not reported.
Source: SLLS (1968, 1974, 1981, 1991)

The estimated coefficients on work experience for men (women) in 1968 (1968 and 1974) imply a much faster wage growth during the first years of work than the parameters for later years imply. The return to five years of actual work experience for men is about 20% in 1968 and about 10% in 1991, with the main fall between 1968 and 1974. The return to 40 years of work experience is about 60% and 40%, respectively. Corresponding figures for women are somewhat lower. The return for women with five years of work experience is about 20% in 1968 and about 10% in 1981 and 1991. The return to 40 years of work experience, in turn, is about 50% in 1968 and 30% in 1991. The estimated parameters of work experience imply that in the years

1968, 1974, 1981 and 1991, wages peaked in the range of 30 to 35 years of work experience for men and between 28 and 35 years for women. Furthermore, we estimate a model that includes both work experience and seniority. The results in Table 14.3 indicate that seniority has a small effect on earnings. The estimates for 1991 imply that 10 years of seniority raises the wages of men (women) by approximately 4% (1%), while 10 years of experience raises the wages of men (women) by approximately 20% (14%). A similar pattern is found for the remaining years, but at somewhat higher levels.

SENSITIVITY ANALYSIS

Gross versus Net Wages, and Actual versus Potential Work Experience

In the following sections, unless otherwise stated, we use cross-sectional data from the 1991 wave of the Swedish level of living survey. Table 14.4 outlines the descriptive statistics for actual and potential experience as well as net and gross wages. Mean and standard deviation of actual work experience are somewhat lower than the corresponding measures for potential work experience. For men the mean actual experience is two years less than mean potential experience. The corresponding difference for women is around five years. The measure of potential experience for women is however quite unreliable due to non-participation of women, especially in the older cohorts.

Table 14.4   Descriptive statistics

	Log of gross hourly earnings	Log of net hourly earnings	Actual work experience (years)	Potential work experience (years)	Age
Men	4.45	4.12	19.57	21.47	39.24
St. dev.	*0.31*	*0.29*	*12.44*	*12.44*	*11.61*
Women	4.24	3.95	16.86	22.15	39.66
St. dev.	*0.24*	*0.26*	*10.82*	*12.99*	*12.01*

Source: SLLS (1991).

Nevertheless, the estimated coefficient on schooling and experience are not particularly sensitive to the different measures of work experience (Tables 14.5a and 14.5b). The main difference is that return to actual experience is higher than returns to potential experience for women. Moreover, using estimates on potential work experience imply that wages peak at later stages in the working life (see Tables 14.6a and 14.6b). An alternative and rather crude measure of work experience is age. Using age as a proxy for experience yields considerably lower estimates on the return to schooling, and somewhat higher estimates on the return to work experience (see Tables 14.5a and 14.5b).

Table 14.5a OLS log earnings equation estimates – SLLS 1991

Men	Log (gross hourly wage)			Log (net hourly wage)		
Schooling	0.041	0.041	0.033	0.035	0.035	0.028
	0.002	*0.002*	*0.002*	*0.002*	*0.002*	*0.002*
Actual Exp.	0.026			0.024		
	0.002			*0.002*		
Actual Exp2/100	-0.037			-0.036		
	0.004			*0.004*		
Potential Exp.		0.027			0.026	
		0.002			*0.002*	
Potential Exp.^{2}/100		-0.038			-0.038	
		0.005			*0.004*	
Age			0.036			0.037
			0.004			*0.004*
Age^2/100			-0.032			-0.036
			0.005			*0.005*
Adjusted-R^2	0.305	0.296	0.282	0.272	0.267	0.256

Table 14.5b OLS log earnings equation estimates – SLLS 1991

Women	Log (gross hourly wage)			Log (net hourly wage)		
Schooling	0.037	0.038	0.033	0.034	0.035	0.031
	0.002	*0.002*	*0.002*	*0.002*	*0.002*	*0.002*
Actual Exp.	0.018			0.018		
	0.002			*0.002*		
Actual Exp2/100	-0.026			-0.031		
	0.004			*0.004*		
Potential Exp.		0.015			0.013	
		0.002			*0.002*	
Potential Exp.^{2}/100		-0.018			-0.019	
		0.003			*0.004*	
Age			0.024			0.023
			0.003			*0.003*
Age^2/100			-0.022			-0.024
			0.004			*0.004*
Part time	-0.002	-0.008	-0.008	0.016	0.013	0.013
	0.011	*0.011*	*0.011*	*0.012*	*0.012*	*0.012*
Adjusted-R^2	0.247	0.231	0.232	0.181	0.165	0.167

Using net wages instead of gross wages results in about 10% lower estimates of the schooling coefficient, but produces basically the same magnitude of the coefficients on actual work experience, potential work experience and age. The human capital variables better explain the variation in log of gross hourly wage than the variation in log of net hourly wage.

Table 14.6a Return to work experience (actual and potential)

Work experience	Men		Women	
	Actual	Potential	Actual	Potential
10 years	0.22	0.23	0.15	0.13
20 years	0.37	0.39	0.26	0.23
30 years	0.45	0.47	0.31	0.29
Peak (years)	35	36	35	42

Notes: The dependent variable is the logarithm of net hourly wages
Source: SLLS (1991)

Table 14.6b Return to work experience (actual and potential)

Work experience	Men		Women	
	Actual	Potential	Actual	Potential
10 years	0.20	0.22	0.15	0.11
20 years	0.34	0.37	0.24	0.18
30 years	0.40	0.44	0.26	0.22
Peak (years)	33	34	29	34

Notes: The dependent variable is the logarithm of net hourly wages
Source: SLLS (1991)

Selectivity and Endogeneity of Schooling

We start by examining whether the returns to human capital for women are sensitive to sample selection. The decision to participate in the labour market may not be independent of earnings and educational length. Thus, using a sample of employed women to estimate the return to schooling with OLS will probably produce biased estimates. To deal with this problem we use Heckman's two-step selection model. We use a standard wage equation including predicted probabilities of participation. The participation equation is an ordered probit model where the labour market status variable is treated as an ordinal discrete variable. The explanatory variables in this model are county, years of schooling, age, aged squared, marital status, household size and number of children in the household. Results of these estimations, presented in Table 14.7, indicate no major changes compared with the standard OLS estimates of the single wage equation.

To deal with the endogeneity problem regarding the schooling decision we use an IV procedure. Several instruments have been proposed in the literature. Our data allow us to replicate some of these estimations. We use the number of siblings, parental education and a smoking dummy as instruments.

We use two models. In the first model we use number of siblings and parental education as instruments. The Hausman test strongly rejects the hypothesis of exogeneity. As expected, and in line with previous results, the reported IV estimates of return to schooling in Table 14.8 are much higher than comparable OLS estimates.

The second model is specified as the first model, but also includes a measure constructed using age and years of smoking as a basis. The dummy for smoking D_{smoke} is defined as follows:

$$D_{smoke} = 1 \text{ if } \frac{age-16}{smoking} < 1.2$$

$$D_{smoke} = 0 \text{ if } \frac{age-16}{smoking} > 1.2 \text{ or if } smoking = 0,$$

where *smoking* is the number of years the individual has smoked. This construction is assumed to capture time preferences for different individuals at an early age. The idea is that a smoker might have a higher discount rate than a non-smoker. A higher discount rate would then mean higher weight for current income and thus lower propensity to invest in schooling.

Table 14.7   Estimated returns to schooling for women

	No selectivity correction			Selectivity correction		
	Total	Part-time	Full-time	Total	Part-time	Full-time
Schooling	0.037	0.036	0.036	0.034	0.038	0.032
	0.002	*0.003*	*0.002*	*0.002*	*0.004*	*0.003*
Experience	0.018	0.016	0.018	0.017	0.017	0.016
	0.002	*0.003*	*0.002*	*0.002*	*0.003*	*0.002*
Experience²/100	-0.027	-0.026	-0.026	-0.024	-0.027	-0.020
	0.004	*0.007*	*0.005*	*0.004*	*0.007*	*0.005*
Part time	0.000			0.007		
	0.011			*0.011*		
Lambda				-0.046	0.020	-0.093
				0.022	*0.033*	*0.027*
Observations	1661	671	990	1661	671	990

Source: SLLS (1991)

In the reduced form, the coefficient on the smoking dummy proved to be negative and significant. However, despite this fact, the coefficient on schooling in the wage equation drops only marginally. Interestingly, in this specification, the Hausman test for the female sample does not reject the hypothesis of exogeneity.

Table 14.8   OLS and IV estimates, controlling for endogeneity

	Men			Women		
	OLS	IV[a]	IV[b]	OLS	IV[a]	IV[b]
Schooling	0.041	0.056	0.054	0.037	0.047	0.044
	0.002	*0.006*	*0.006*	*0.002*	*0.005*	*0.005*
Experience	0.026	0.025	0.025	0.018	0.017	0.018
	0.002	*0.002*	*0.002*	*0.002*	*0.002*	*0.002*
Experience^2/100	-0.037	-0.032	-0.032	-0.026	-0.024	-0.024
	0.004	*0.005*	*0.005*	*0.004*	*0.004*	*0.004*
Part-time				-0.002	0.009	0.006
				0.011	*0.012*	*0.012*
Hausman test[c]		✓ 1%	✓ (1%)		✓ (5%)	✕
Observations		1507			1605	

Notes:
[a] Instruments: number of siblings and parental education.
[b] Instruments: number of siblings, parental education and a dummy for early, smoking.
[c] ✓ Indicates significance at the 1% or 5% level, as noted in parentheses and ✕ indicates insignificance.
Source: SLLS (1991)

Private versus Public Sector

Another issue is the extent to which wage differentials exist between the private and the public sectors, and if these differences reflect differences in the way in which the private and public sectors reward educational attainment. The system of wage negotiations as well as security of employment might differ between the two sectors.

Table 14.9 reports the estimated returns to schooling by gender and sector. Returns to schooling for men and women are higher in the private sector than in the public sector. Moreover, the gender gap is more or less the same in the two sectors. This is in spite of the fact that the proportion of women in the public sector is higher than the proportion of men. As indicated by the adjusted-R^2 of the regression, the human capital variables explain more of the variance in log hourly wage in the public sector compared to the private sector. Although we do not report it here, this is a pattern repeated in the earlier years for which we have data, and, in fact, the difference is much smaller in 1991 compared to earlier years. This difference between 1991 and the earlier years more than likely reflects the administrative wage-setting criteria in the public sector that existed in those years. These criteria were based on workers' education, experience and seniority, and were somewhat relaxed from 1991 onwards.

Table 14.9   Public and private sector estimates of the return to education

	Men		Women	
	Private	Public	Private	Public
Schooling	0.053	0.038	0.047	0.034
	0.003	*0.003*	*0.004*	*0.002*
Actual Exp.	0.028	0.027	0.022	0.016
	0.002	*0.003*	*0.003*	*0.002*
Actual Exp.^{2}/100	-0.040	-0.034	-0.036	-0.021
	0.005	*0.007*	*0.007*	*0.005*
Part-time			-0.037	0.023
			0.020	*0.012*
R-square (adjusted)	0.328	0.381	0.241	0.282
Observations	1081	426	624	981

Source: SLLS (1991)

Region and Family Background

The distribution of educational attainment may differ between regions, which implies that the estimated return to schooling could be in part due to regional differences. For instance, if workers with education S_1 live in region A and workers with education S_2 live in region B, the return to schooling may catch regional differences in earnings and not only the effect of schooling on earnings.

Inter-regional differences in educational attainment could to some extent be explained by differences in family background and accessibility of education. There is a strong correlation between parental education and their children's highest completed educational levels. Individuals from worse off family backgrounds are less likely to pursue higher education. This group might have lower ability, stronger distaste for education, or limited economic support.

We include controls for regions and family background. We distinguish between seven different regions (aggregate of municipalities) based on population density. However, controlling for regions and family background does not substantially improve the fit of the model and the estimates on schooling are only moderately affected.

Ability Bias

As suggested in the schooling literature the estimated return to education might be biased upwards due to the omission of relevant variables such as ability. To examine this issue we have used two datasets (the individual statistics project), which contain several measures of intelligence and scholastic achievement collected when the respondents were between the ages of 12 and 13. The measures include school marks in mathematics, Swedish and English, as well as scores from intelligence tests and national achievement tests.

The intelligence tests represent the verbal (choosing the opposite of a given word from four choices), spatial (finding the three-dimensional object that can be made from a flat piece of metal from four alternatives) and reasoning (completing a specific number series) factors of intelligence. Since we found that measures associated with mathematics are the most important ones, we restrict our model to include scores from the intelligence test associated with mathematics (number series). A potential source of selectivity bias is that missing data on ability are systematically related to ability, in the sense of tolerating individuals absent from school on the days of testing. Therefore, we also estimate a model that includes school marks (dummies) in mathematics on samples that include missing observation on test scores. Since we do not have information on hourly wage, work experience, or working hours, we restrict our attention to men. In this way we avoid the problems caused by gender differences in labour supply.

Tables 14.10a and 14.10b report the estimates. As expected, the estimated wage premium for education falls when ability is controlled for. Generally, the reductions in magnitudes are in the range of 10% to 20% . Moreover, it does not matter whether we use marks in mathematics or results from the intelligence test.   Furthermore, omitting individuals with missing observations on test scores hardly affect the results. The estimated wage premiums are more or less the same in samples that also includes individuals with no information on scores from the intelligence tests.

Screening and the Sheepskin Effect

In addition to increasing individual productivity a diploma might serve as a signal of higher innate productivity. Individuals who receive a diploma would therefore have both higher wages and lower risks of being unemployed compared to those who do not complete a degree. Table 14.11 displays the results from estimating the system proposed by Park (1999). The wage equation here differs from the standard Mincerian approach in that it includes an interaction term for years *and* level of schooling, as well as the usual part time dummy.

We distinguish between seven different educational levels, but only report results for some of these levels. For instance, the college (longer post secondary education) sheepskin effect ($\beta_{post-secondary,15} - \beta_{upper-secondary,15}$) is 8% for men and 11% for women. The figure for high-school (longer upper secondary schooling) sheepskin effect ($\beta_{upper-secondary,12} - \beta_{compulsory,12}$) is eight percent for men and four percent for women, but note that no figures in the table turn out to be significantly different from zero.[7]

We have good reasons to expect that the signal of higher innate productivity attenuate in value with work experience. The employers' knowledge about the workers' productivity improves with work experience, that is, the sheepskin effect would be more pronounced in early age cohorts. Otherwise, if the sheepskin effect remains with work experience, the causal relationship between earnings and educational degree may reflect ability differentials and not sheepskin effects. However, excluding all individuals older than 35 years from the samples does not change the results. This is not surprising since the Swedish educational system is very much based on piecewise examination and the system offers possibilities of certifying passed courses. Lack of a formal diploma might just be a matter of missing the formal application for the diploma or sometimes due to some small courses missing for the degree.

Table 14.10a   OLS log earnings equation, omitted ability bias estimates

Comprehensive (9-10 years)	Sample 1 Reference category			Sample 2 Reference category	
Upper secondary school	0.024	0.017	0.020	0.033	0.027
(up to two years)	*0.019*	*0.019*	*0.019*	*0.018*	*0.018*
Upper secondary school	0.158	0.131	0.129	0.168	0.136
(greater than two years)	*0.020*	*0.020*	*0.020*	*0.019*	*0.019*
Post secondary school	0.215	0.185	0.183	0.229	0.196
(less than 3 years)	*0.023*	*0.023*	*0.023*	*0.021*	*0.021*
Post secondary school	0.407	0.356	0.346	0.419	0.355
(at least three years)	*0.020*	*0.021*	*0.021*	*0.019*	*0.020*
Controls:					
Number series	✗	✓	✗	✗	✗
School marks	✗	✗	✓	✗	✓
Adjusted-R^2	0.199	0.213	0.214	0.203	0.219
Observations		3967		4442	

Notes: Standard errors in italics, the intercept is not reported. For the controls reported above a ✗ indicates that it was not included in the model estimation, and a ✓ indicates the opposite. The estimates are for men only
Source: IS project, 1948 cohort

Table 14.10b OLS log earnings equation, omitted ability bias estimates

Comprehensive (9-10 years)	Sample 1 Reference category			Sample 2 Reference category	
Upper secondary school	0.037	0.030	0.030	0.038	0.030
(up to two years)	*0.016*	*0.016*	*0.016*	*0.015*	*0.015*
Upper secondary school	0.148	0.122	0.118	0.149	0.121
(greater than two years)	*0.019*	*0.020*	*0.020*	*0.019*	*0.019*
Post secondary school	0.230	0.198	0.194	0.235	0.200
(less than 3 years)	*0.019*	*0.019*	*0.019*	*0.018*	*0.019*
Post secondary school	0.396	0.355	0.341	0.399	0.346
(at least three years)	*0.018*	*0.019*	*0.020*	*0.018*	*0.019*
Controls:					
Number series	×	✓	×	×	×
School marks	×	×	✓	×	✓
Adjusted-R^2	0.174	0.184	0.184	0.175	0.184
Observations		3456		3644	

Notes: See the notes to table 14.10a. The estimates are for men only.

Source: IS project, 1953 cohort

Table 14.11   The sheepskin effect, model due to Park (1999)

	Conditional on schooling	Men (age interval)		Women (age interval)	
		18 - 65	18 - 35	18 - 65	18 - 35
Shorter upper sec. schooling diploma relative to compulsory schooling as highest diploma	11	0.035 *0.094*	0.079 *0.152*	0.022 *0.047*	0.077 *0.203*
Longer upper sec. schooling diploma relative to compulsory schooling as highest diploma	12	0.082 *0.126*	0.117 *0.216*	0.042 *0.079*	
Shorter post-sec. schooling diploma relative to longer upper sec. schooling as highest diploma	14	0.136 *0.072*	-0.048 *0.116*	0.005 *0.052*	0.024 *0.080*
Longer post-sec. schooling diploma relative to longer upper sec. schooling as highest diploma	15	0.078 *0.090*	-0.005 *0.134*	0.111 *0.088*	0.124 *0.213*
Observations		1507	603	1605	630

Source: SLLS (1991)

CONCLUSION

Our main findings are as follows. The returns to schooling in Sweden is among the lowest in Europe and this also holds true with respect to almost all other dimensions of wage dispersion. Overall, the sensitivity analysis does not imply a major revision of the OLS results is required, although the IV estimates yield substantially higher estimates. We also find no sheepskin effects, as estimated by controlling for completed diplomas. When we include various measures of ability the returns fall by between 10% and 20%. Furthermore, we find that there are significant differences in returns to schooling across various fields of study within each education level indicating heterogeneity in schooling.

With regards to the development of rate of returns to schooling over time, the main change in this rate took place during the period between 1968 and 1974, falling from 8% to 5%. This is consistent with the argument that wage compression took place as a result of wage compression policies in Sweden.

NOTES

1. For this reason, we skip detailed references to earlier literature and refer to Willis (1986), Card (1999) and Chapter 1 of this book and the references therein for the review of the related literature. For a review of the previous Swedish studies see our earlier paper within this project (Arai and Kjellström, 1999).
2. Source: see for example Richardson (1998).
3. This is also the case for upper secondary schooling.
4. Levnadsnivåundersökningarna (LNU).
5. For a detailed description of SLLS see Erikson and Åberg (1987) and Fritzell and Lundberg (1994). For a detailed description of HUS, see Klevmarken and Olovsson (1993) and Flood, Klevmarken and Olovsson (1997).
6. A more detailed description of the datasets and purposes of the IS project is given in Svensson (1971) and Härnqvist and Svensson (1973).
7. Antelius (2000) report some sheepskin effect based on a specification without control for part time work, and no distinction between shorter and longer university education.

BIBLIOGRAPHY

Antelius, Jesper (2000), Sheepskin Effects in the Returns to Education: Evidence on Swedish Data, Working Paper, FIEF, No. 158.

Arai, Mahmood and Christian Kjellström (1999), 'Returns to Human Capital in Sweden', in Asplund, R. and P. T. Pereira (eds) *Returns to Human*

Capital in Europe – A Literature Review, ETLA, Taloustieto Oy, pp. 299–324.

Card, David (1999), 'The Causal Effect of Schooling on Earnings', in Ashenfelter, O. and D. Card (eds), *Handbook of Labor Economics*, Volume 3A, Elsevier, Amsterdam.

Erikson, Robert and Rune Åberg (1987), *Welfare in Transition. A Survey of Living Conditions in Sweden 1968–1981*, Clarendon Press, Oxford.

Flood, Lennart, Anders Klevmarken and Paul Olovsson (1997), *Houshold Market and Nonmarket Activities (HUS)*, Volume III–VI, Department of Economics, Uppsala University.

Fritzell, Johan and Olle Lundberg (1994), *Vardagens villkor – Levnadsförhållanden i Sverige Under Tre Decennier*, Brombergs Förlag, Stockholm.

Härnqvist, Kjell and Allan Svensson (1973), 'A Swedish Data Bank for Studies of Educational Development', *Sociological Microjournal*, 7, pp. 35–42.

Klevmarken, Anders and Paul Olovsson (1993*)*, *Houshold Market and Nonmarket Activities – Procedures and Codes 1984–1991*, Volume I–II, The Industrial Institute for Economic and Social Research, Almqvist & Wiksell International, Stockholm.

Park, Jin H. (1999), 'Estimation of Sheepskin Effects Using the Old and the New Measures of Educational Attainment in the Current Population Survey', *Economics Letters*, 62, pp. 237–240.

Richardson, Gunnar (1998), *Svensk Utbildningshistoria – Skola och Samhälle Förr och Nu*, Studentlitteratur, Stockholm.

Svensson, Allan (1971), *Relative Achievement – School Performance in Relation to Intelligence, Sex and Home Environment*, Almquist & Wiksell.

Willis, Robert (1986), 'Wage Determinants: A Survey and Reinterpretation of Human Capital Earnings Functions', in Ashenfelter, O. and R. Layard (eds), *Handbook of Labor Economics*, Elsevier Science Publishers BV, pp. 525–602.

15. Switzerland

Bernhard A. Weber, Aniela M. Wirz and Stefan C. Wolter

INTRODUCTION

The aim of this study is to give an overview on what we know about private rates of return to education in Switzerland. One of the main issues is the level and the time stability of returns to education in the 1990s. In order to test the robustness of our estimates we present results of a variety of alternative specifications and estimation methods. Heterogeneity is another issue. The question here is, how representative the empirical findings are and if we can identify groups with diverging rates of return to education. In the last section we finally raise the question if there is a link between actual wages and wage expectations of young people confronted with the choice whether to continue their education on the tertiary level or to remain on the secondary II level.

THE EDUCATIONAL SYSTEM IN SWITZERLAND

With its 26 cantons, Switzerland has an especially developed federal structure, which is also reflected in its educational system. In fact Switzerland has 26 school systems, which are only partially regulated by the central government or co-ordinated between the cantons. Figure 15.1 gives a simplified picture of the educational system in Switzerland.

Early childhood education (ISCED 0) is optional in Switzerland. In 1995 however every canton offered at least one year of early childhood education. On average early childhood education lasted 1.8 years in 1995.

At the age of 6 or 7 children start compulsory schooling at the *primary level of education* (ISCED 1). With the exception of specialized schools or separate classes for children with mental disabilities, behavioural disorder or language difficulties, there is no selection process at this stage. Depending on the canton the duration of primary education varies between four and six years. At the *lower secondary level* of education (ISCED 2) most cantons have schools with two to four different performance levels. In 1995 about one-third of the pupils in Switzerland went to a school with "basic-requirements", which prepare for intellectually less demanding apprenticeships. Two-thirds went to schools with "extended requirements", which prepare for longer studies or intellectually more demanding apprenticeships. The normal duration of compulsory schooling (primary and secondary I) is nine years.

Education at the *upper secondary level* usually starts at the age of 15 or 16. There are mainly two different types of education. In 1995 20% of the 19-year-olds had completed a *general education* of four years' duration and had therefore obtained a university admission certificate (A levels). The admission to general education is very selective, the admission criteria being exams and previous schooling performance. Within general education a certain specialisation is possible (i.e. ancient and modern languages, maths, economics, teacher training).

A majority of 66% of the juveniles in 1995 had completed an *apprenticeship* of between two and four years. The average duration was about three and a half years for men (note that all apprenticeships have a duration of full years) and three years for women. An apprenticeship in Switzerland typically combines on-the-job training in a firm (between three and four days per week) with a theoretical education (between one and two days per week) in a vocational school. This organisational form is also common in Germany and Austria and is called the "dual-system of vocational education". Since an apprenticeship is legally based on a private contract between a training firm and the apprentice, the selection process takes place on the labour market. Hence there are a lot of potential selection criteria like the schooling performance or individual characteristics. On the other hand factors like the general economic situation or the firms' expected costs and benefits of an apprenticeship have an impact on the demand for apprentices.

In Switzerland the total diplomation rate for training during *more than one year* at the upper secondary level was 86.6% in 1995. The remaining 14.2% either made a short one-year apprenticeship (SAPS) or left the educational system right after compulsory schooling. Between 6% and 10% of the juveniles did not complete an education at the upper secondary level at all in 1995.

At the tertiary level of education we can distinguish three types of education. On the one hand there are *universities*, which confer academic degrees. In 1995 the university diplomation rate was 7% (ISCED 6). According to a rough estimate around 30% of those with a degree make a doctorate (ISCED 7). Pupils with an A level have the right of admission to every university in Switzerland. The universities, which are run by the cantons, are free to set up further admission criteria (for instance entrance examinations), to admit students without A-level diplomas. Only recently universities have started to restrict entry for studies in medicine (numerus clausus). It is not planned so far to generally restrict entry to university however.

At the non-university tertiary level (ISCED 5) there are two types of education, which lead to more than 800 different types of diplomas or degrees. *Higher vocational colleges (HVC)* last on average about two years (full time). Since only final examinations are regulated either by the cantons or the central government this educational category is very heterogeneous. Many different private and public schools offer full- and part-time training to prepare for the exams. The admission criteria are a completed apprenticeship of at least two years' duration and another two years of experience on-the-job. The diplomation for HVC was 23.5% in 1995. *Higher business and administration or technical colleges (HBTC)* lasted on average about three years (full time). In general these colleges were run by the cantons. The admission was very selective and regulated by entrance examinations. In 1995 the diplomation rate for this type of education was 3.9%. Since then, these institutions were transformed into *Universities of Applied Science (UAS)*, still run by the cantons but regulated by the confederation. The studies have now a minimal duration of three years, leading to a bachelor diploma.

METHODOLOGY AND DATA

Our estimates of rates of return to schooling are based on *statistical earnings functions* of the form

$$\ln W_i = \beta_0 + \beta_1 {}^*S_i + \beta_2 {}^*EXP_i + \beta_3 {}^*EXP_i^2 + \beta_4 {}^*Z_i + u_i$$

where $\ln W$ is the natural logarithm of the gross hourly wage rate, S is completed years of schooling, EXP represents years of potential labour market experience, Z is a vector of other factors potentially affecting wages and u is a random disturbance term reflecting unobserved ability characteristics and the inherent randomness of earnings statistics. This formulation, which is known in the literature as the *Mincer equation* is very popular in economics of education, since the coefficient β_1 under certain assumptions can be interpreted as private rate of return to schooling (Mincer, 1974).

The estimates presented in this study are based on the Swiss Labour Force Survey (SLFS), which is the main data source for labour-market-related questions in Switzerland. Since 1991 the SLFS has been produced annually by the Swiss Federal Statistical Office. The sample, which is collected by telephone, numbers between 16 000 and 18 000 observations per year (in 1995 it was 32 000) and is representative of the adult population (greater than 14 years-of-age) permanently living in Switzerland.

The available information on earnings, paid holidays and working hours per week allows us to calculate an hourly wage rate. In the analysis of time trends salaries for teachers were omitted because their working time (including preparation time) has only been reported since 1995. In the more detailed analysis for 1995 teachers are included. Years of schooling are deducted from the highest educational level achieved by imputing the theoretical number of years of full-time education necessary to attain a certain degree.

Figure 15.1   The Swiss educational system (1995)

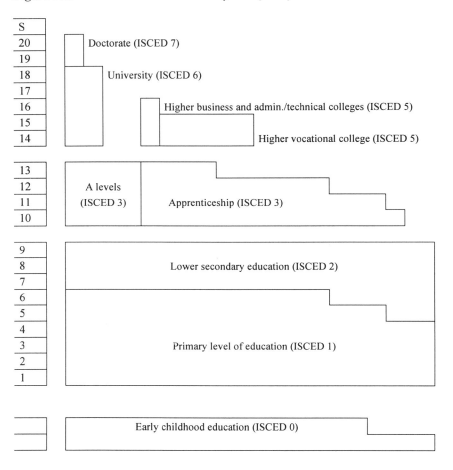

RETURNS TO SCHOOLING IN THE 1990s

Table 15.1 shows that the returns to schooling have remained quiet stable in the 1990s for both men and women. Testing for a linear time trend in a pooled sample of all available years reveals no significant changes of the schooling coefficient. The estimates of absolute levels of educational returns may be biased by the fact that teachers are not in the sample. As an analysis for 1995 reveals, including teachers would raise women's returns to education above those of men.[1]

Table 15.1   Wage equation (gross hourly wages)

		Men				Women		
	S		Adj-R^2	N	S		Adj-R^2	N
1992	.091	(.0026)	.382	3305	.078	(.0042)	.135	2821
1993	.088	(.0026)	.349	3403	.083	(.0042)	.163	2850
1994	.087	(.0026)	.356	3380	.079	(.0041)	.145	2865
1995	.092	(.0020)	.353	6066	.089	(.0034)	.146	5257
1996	.087	(.0026)	.373	3082	.080	(.0041)	.164	2763
1997	.088	(.0026)	.371	3104	.082	(.0038)	.169	2799
1998	.088	(.0025)	.362	3155	.084	(.0037)	.191	2864
1999	.088	(.0023)	.368	3417	.079	(.0035)	.177	3203
1992-1999	.089	(.0009)	.365	28912	.083	(.0014)	.164	25422

Notes: Teachers are excluded (their hourly wage can be measured for 1995 to 1999 only); women: including a part-time dummy (<38h per week); men: only full-time workers (≥ 38h).

ROBUSTNESS AND SENSITIVITY OF ESTIMATES

Selection bias

In this section we check to what extent estimates of the average private rate of return to schooling are sensitive to selectivity. First we look at the selectivity of labour-market participation using a traditional two-step estimation procedure following Heckman (1979). Then we look at the selectivity between non-labour-market participation, part-time or full-time labour-market participation using an ordered probit in the first step of the Heckman's procedure following the methodologies described by Ermisch and Wright (1993). Since the sample of men is restricted to full-time working men and labour market participation of men is very high these analyses are done for women only.

The estimation result of the wage equation correcting for simple labour market participation selection (Table 15.2) shows that the hypothesis of a random sample underlying the OLS estimation can not be maintained. The coefficient of the inverse Mill's ratio in the wage equation turns out to be significant and negative. It indicates that there is a selection bias and that women with lower wages are also more likely to participate in the labor market. A further anaylsis of the data reveals that this effect is dominated by women of foreign nationality, who tend to receive lower wages, and also by women with no or low household income besides their own salary who have a higher participation rate. Taking into account this selectivity the fit of the model, however, is not significantly improved and the rate of return to schooling decreases only slightly.

Table 15.2   Wage equation for women (1995), selectivity correction by probit and ordered probit employment equation

	Heckman two-step		Ordered probit			
			Part-time workers		Full-time workers	
	OLS	Sel. corr.	OLS	Sel. corr.	OLS	Sel. corr.
S	.086	.079	.105	.096	.075	.070
	(.004)	(.004)	(.007)	(.007)	(.004)	(.004)
Adj.-R^2	.121	.133	.131	.152	.173	.189
N	4672	4672	1880	1880	2577	2577

Notes: Heckman two-step earnings function: years of schooling, age, age^2, dummies for foreigners and part-time workers. Additional variables of the participation equation: two dummies for marital status, number of children aged between one and six years and seven and fourteen years, non wage income and number of rooms. Ordered probit earnings function: years of schooling, age, age^2, dummies for foreigners and two linguistic regions. Additional variables of the selection equation: two dummies for marital status, number of children aged 1-6, 7-14 and 15-25, non wage income and number of rooms. Log-L=-4680. N=5897.

Estimating an ordered probit equation as the first step of a Heckman selection correction (Table 15.2) gives a similar result. Returns to schooling decrease slightly for full-time workers and somewhat more for part-timers. As in the case of the simple probit model, however, the fit of the wage equation is not improved substantially. Therefore the results should not be over-interpreted and the need for this correction is minimal. The impact of the selection correction with the difference in the rates of return to education between full- and part-time working women the later seems to be far more important. This difference would deserve further investigation and underlines the need for taking into account the heterogeneity of women's labour market participation

Definition of Labour Market Experience

How we define experience is likely to have a particular impact on the returns to education for women. This is primarily because of the difference between potential experience and actual experience. Women's careers are much more likely to be discontinuous, hence a measure of potential experience is likely to be an overestimate of their actual experience. Table 15.3 shows the returns to schooling we obtain when we use potential and actual experience in the wage equation. The drop in their returns to schooling for women of 0.6 log percentage points is not statistically significant. At a first glance using *age* instead of potential experience seems to have a large impact. One has to be aware, however, that the schooling coefficient in the 'age-model' captures only part of the schooling effect. In order to get the marginal return to an additional year of schooling, one has to add the marginal return of 'becoming one year older'. The corrected rates of return to an additional year of schooling in the 'age-model' yield 0.095 for women and 0.091 for men and therefore do not deviate from the results of the reference model.

Table 15.3 Wage equations, alternative specifications for experience (1995)

	Men			Women		
	S	Adj-R²	N	S	Adj-R²	N
Potential. exp.	.090	(.0019) .360	6321	.095	(.0031) .162	5912
Actual exp.	.089	(.0019) .366	6321	.089	(.0030) .187	5912
Age	.076	(.0019) .354	6321	.086	(.0030) .161	5912

Notes: Includes experience and experience² or age and age², a part-time dummy for women (<38h per week); men: only full-time (≥ 38h); actual experience = experience without an interruption of six months or more.

Additional Control variables

The inclusion of additional control variables will, in general, lower the rate of return to education. However, as shown in Table 15.4, the returns are extremely robust to the inclusion of more control variables. For men, the return rarely moves out of the range between 8% and 9%, and for women, the range is even tighter, between 9% and 9.5%. The biggest change typically results from the inclusion of occupation-related variables such as the hierarchical position in the firm. The inclusion of such variable is, of course, very questionable. This is because these variables are typically correlated both with educational attainment and wages and are therefore not exogenous. The respective estimates are likely to be biased.

Table 15.4   Wage equations with additional control variables (1995)

	Men				Women			
	S		Adj-R^2	N	S		Adj-R^2	N
None	.091	(.0019)	.363	6282	.095	(.0031)	.164	5673
Region	.091	(.0019)	.367	6282	.095	(.0031)	.163	5673
Family	.090	(.0019)	.376	6282	.093	(.0031)	.186	5673
Foreigners	.088	(.0019)	.372	6282	.095	(.0031)	.167	5673
Firm size	.088	(.0019)	.380	6282	.092	(.0031)	.176	5673
Hierarchy	.080	(.0019)	.416	6282	.090	(.0031)	.188	5673

Notes: Including experience, experience[2], part-time dummy for women (<38h per week); men: only full-time (≥ 38h); region = dummies for two linguistic regions; family = dummy for married people and number of children in three age ranges; foreigners = dummy for foreigners; firm size = dummies for large and small firms; hierarchy = dummies for members of the board of directors and supervisors, years of tenure.

Gross versus Net Wages

Since a private investor takes into account net rather than gross returns, direct income taxes should be deducted, when calculating private rates of return. Taking into account the characteristics of the Swiss tax system lowers the rates of return to one year of schooling by 0.9 log percentage points for women and by 1.2 log percentage points for men.[2] The progression of the Swiss income tax system tends to lower private rates of return to education and therefore the individual incentives to pursue further education.

Table 15.5   Wage equations for gross and net hourly wages (1995)

	Men				Women			
	S		N	Adj.-R^2	S		N	Adj-R^2
Gross	.090	(.0019)	6334	.360	.095	(.0031)	5933	.161
Net	.078	(.0018)	6334	.348	.086	(.0030)	5933	.144

Notes: Including experience, experience[2], part time dummy for women (<38h per week); men: only full time (≥ 38h)

Non-linear Returns to Schooling

The standard Mincer equation imposes linearity between years of schooling and log wages. In Figure 15.3 these results (line) are plotted against an estimate of returns to different levels and types of education (crosses). The graphical analysis reveals that the hypothesis of linearity is fairly accurate for most educational degrees.

Figure 15.2a Testing the linearity assumption (1995, men)

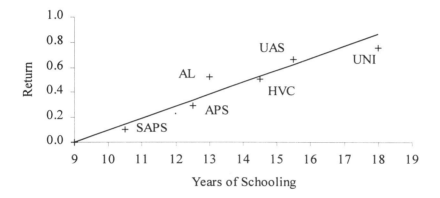

Figure 15.2b   Testing the linearity assumption (1995, women)

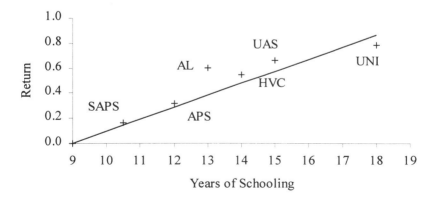

Notes: including experience, experience^2, part-time dummy for women (<38h per week); men: only full time ($\geq$ 38h). Schooling dummies: CS = compulsory schooling, SAPS= short Apprenticeship, APS = Apprenticeship, AL = school for university admission, HVC = Higher Vocational College, UAS = University of Applied Science, UNI = University.

There are some exceptions, however. For women universities of applied science (UAS) and higher vocational colleges (HVC) yield relatively higher returns. A levels (schools for university admission) display above average returns (slope between CS and A levels) whereas universities have below average returns. Conseuently, the marginal returns to university (slope between A levels and UNI) are clearly below average. If we think of educational decisions as being sequential processes, the marginal perspective is the relevant one. The results presented here illustrate that the hypothesis of linear returns would be misleading in some situations.

Sensitivity to Implicit Assumptions of the Model: Direct Educational Costs

An alternative method to estimate private rates of return to education that can be found in the literature is the so-called *Cost-Benefit Approach,* described in Psacharopoulos (1987) and Alsalam and Conley (1995). Wolter and Weber (1999a) have used the same kind of analysis to calculate private rates of return to education. Taking into account *income taxes, direct educational costs, the risk of dropping out of school and the probability of being unemployed,* they calculate rates of return as well as net-present values of lifetime earnings for men and women with different levels of education.

One of the advantages of the cost-benefit approach lies in the different simulations that can be carried out – although we can only do static simulations with this model. The case of an increase in direct educational costs for students is given here as an example.[3] The assumption is that tuition fees are to be increased to Sfr 10 000 per annum, a sum (not counting research costs) that more or less corresponds to the cost of a humanities student at university (natural science students cost roughly three times more, and medical students five times more). The simulation is carried out for university as well as for non-university tertiary level students.

Table 15.6   The effect of increasing tertiary education tuition fees (1996): relative life income (dis-) advantage compared to the next level down on the education ladder

	Men		Women	
Type of education	Normal	+Sfr 10 000	Normal	+Sfr 10 000
UAS	14%	11%	8%	4%
UNI	-5%	-9%	-2%	-7%

Notes: Database: Wage Structure Survey 1996. The calculations are based on median age-earnings profiles for people with different educational degrees. UAS = University of Applied Sciences, UNI = University. The discount rate is 5%
Source: Wolter and Weber, 1999b.

It turns out that an increase in the direct cost of education would have a considerable effect on the life income. The extra negative effect for women is explained by the generally lower wage levels of women, and to some extent also by higher dropout rates.

The cost-benefit-approach thus helps to demonstrate directly and explicitly how the way in which education is financed affects the private rates of return to education.

HETEROGENEITY OF RATES OF RETURN TO EDUCATION

A further important issue is how representative average rates of return are for the whole population. For instance it would be interesting if one could identify sub-populations (besides men and women) or segments of the labour market with different rates of return to education. In our case we are especially interested in differences between the Swiss and the immigrant population, between people living in different regions and between employed and self-employed. With the help of quantile regressions we furthermore test how rates of return vary when computed for different quantiles of the wage distribution.

Immigrants versus Natives

Table 15.7 Returns to years of schooling obtained in Switzerland versus years of schooling obtained in the country of origin (1995)

	Men		Women	
Born and schooling in Switzerland	.090	(.0024)	.101	(.0038)
Immigrants, schooling in Switzerland	.094	(.0035)	.091	(.0055)
Immigrants, schooling country of origin	.083	(.0034)	.080	(.0054)
Adjusted-R^2	.373		.167	
N	6334		5934	

Notes: Including experience, experience^2, dummy variable for immigrants, interaction term between immigrant dummy and years of potential labour market experience in Switzerland, part-time dummy for women (<38h per week); men: only full time (≥ 38h).

The question of how an immigrants' human capital is rewarded in the Swiss labour market was initially raised by De Coulon (1998). One interesting question raised by De Coulon is whether or not qualifications obtained in the country of origin are rewarded differently (to Swiss qualifications, that is) in the Swiss labour market. There is a detailed discussion of this issue in Borjas

(1999) and Friedberg (1996) has modelled the assimilation of immigrant capital in Israel.

Table 15.7 shows that immigrants' years of schooling obtained in their country of origin are significantly less rewarded on the Swiss labour market than schooling obtained in Switzerland. These results could either reflect differences in educational quality, or, what we think is more plausible, the fact that human capital is not a perfectly mobile asset. Returns to years of schooling obtained in Switzerland, however, do not significantly differ between the Swiss-born and the immigrant population.

Regional Differences

In a labour market with complete information and perfect mobility one would expect rates of return to be equal in all regions. Mobility constraints, for example linguistic or geographical barriers, might be a good reason as to why we find regional differences in rates of return. In order to test for such differences, three different estimation strategies were followed. We controlled for differences in the absolute wage levels (regional dummies), as well as testing for differences in rates of return to schooling between regions (interaction term between regional dummy and years of schooling). Table 15.8 contains the calculated coefficients for years of schooling associated with each region.

Table 15.8   Wage equations for different regions (1995)

	Linguistic regions			Urban/rural		Periphery	
	German	French	Italian	Urban	Rural	Yes	No
Men	.094	.086	.076	.089	.090	.082	.091
	(.0025)	(.0032)	(.0107)	(.0023)	(.0035)	(.0051)	(.0021)
Women	.100	.090	.084	.088	.104	.098	.094
	(.0041)	(.0046)	(.0191)	(.0036)	(.0056)	(.0080)	(.0033)
Adj-R^2	.364/.162			.363/.166		.363/.164	
N	6334/5934			6334/5934		6334/5934	

Notes: Including experience, experience[2], regional dummies to control for wage level differences, part-time dummy for women (<38h per week); men: only full-time (≥ 38h).

Although there seems to be some systematic variation in returns to education, our results hardly support the hypothesis that linguistic or geographical barriers matter in the context of rates of return to education in Switzerland. With the exception of women living in urban areas, whose returns are significantly lower compared to women living in rural areas, regional differences in the returns to years of schooling are not statistically significant (p-value = 0.05). The relatively lower returns for women in urban areas may be explained by the fact that job opportunities for women at lower educational levels are better in urban areas.

Differences Between Employees and Self-employed

Differences in rates of return to education between employees and self-employed are sometimes interpreted as the signalling value of educational credentials. This interpretation is based on the hypothesis that educational credentials are valuable for employees but not for self-employed. As Table 15.9 shows no significant differences in rates of return between employees and self-employed can be found in Switzerland.

Table 15.9   Wage equations for employees and self-employed (1995)

	Men				Women		
	S		Adj.-R^2	N	S		Adj.-R^2	N
Employees	.090	(.0019)	6334	.360	.095	(.0031)	.161	5934
Self-employed	.089	(.0098)	.108	777	.079	(.0172)	.102	289

Notes: Including experience, experience^2, part time dummy for women (<38h per week); men: only full time ($\geq$ 38h).

Quantile regression

Figure 15.4 Returns to schooling, estimated by quantile (1995)

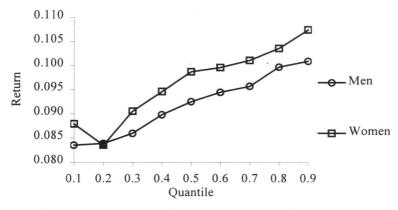

Notes: including experience, experience^2; men: only full time ($\geq$ 38h). Regression at all deciles.

The objective of quantile regression is to estimate a certain quantile of the dependent variable, conditional on the values of the independent variables. The most common form is a median regression, which like OLS describes the central tendency of the data. Since means and therefore OLS estimates are more sensitive to outliers, median regression might produce a more robust estimate. Generalized quantile regressions moreover provide estimates for percentiles other than the median. The estimates can be used to describe the distribution of rates of return.

The results are shown in Figure 15.4. They reveal that the rates of return to schooling are below average at the bottom of the wage distribution and above average at the top.This result reflects the fact, that wage dispersion is higher for people with higher educational attainment. One economic interpretation of this finding is that investment in schooling is a risky investment for the private investor (i.e. the students). Rates of return to one year of schooling according to these calculations vary between 8.4% and 10.7% for women and between 8.4% and 10.1% for men, depending on the position in the wage distribution.

When we compared the median regression results with those obtained by OLS we found the former to be slightly higher. (Median regression results: men = 0.092, women = 0.099). The differences were not statistically different from zero, however.

WAGE EXPECTATIONS

Due to the scarcity of good longitudinal data most studies of rates of return to education have to make use of cross-sectional data in order to make longitudinal statements. Such procedures may be considered reliable only insofar as cohort effects and similar can be avoided. Since in most cases this assumption cannot rightly be made, many researchers are tempted to adjust the cross-sectional data for such effects. Such corrections are of an arbitrary nature and may be difficult to justify in individual cases.

In a paper by Wolter (2000) the assumption is not so much that it is the ex post measured wage structures that are relevant in terms of educational and labour market policy but rather, and to a much greater extent, the expectations which the economic subjects have at the time they make their decisions.

Such expectations have been poorly researched to date, and moreover we do not know to what extent or in what ways these deviate from the current known cross-sectional data of an economy. Wolter (2000) attempts to take a closer look at this question with the help of a computer-assisted interactive survey in Switzerland. The methodology for the survey is mainly based on the model described by Dominitz and Manski (1996).

This research into wage expectations on the basis of an interactive, computer-assisted questionnaire has produced two main results, valid for this study compared with the US ones. First, the estimates of the wages to be earned in the future do not deviate significantly from the currently observable wage structure, as these can be measured by a cross-section. On the basis of the clearly sensible assumption that the current cross-section represents the best information on wages that can be expected in the future, the results provide evidence that the available information is being used rationally. So in this case it is fair to speak of entirely rational expectations. Secondly, the data on the distribution of expectations among individual test participants, and also the uncertainty which flaws the individual answers, indicate to some extent a high degree of heterogeneity and uncertainty, although this must be assessed in the light of the wage distribution currently to be found on the labour market. An interesting aspect of the Swiss study is that it was not possible to find a group of students that differed significantly from the other groups. The heterogeneity of expectations must thus be almost exclusively attributed to the spread between the expectations of individuals, which again supports the hypothesis of rationality for the average expectations.

These two main results from this study lead to the following two conclusions: (1) On the basis of these findings, we can conclude that even when we do not know ex ante how the relative wage profiles will develop with time, the rates of return on education that can be calculated with cross-sectional data come reasonably close to the implicit rates of return assumed by students when faced with an educational choice. It is thus to be recommended that observable cross-sectional data be made use of in empirical calculations in preference to arbitrary assumptions concerning future wage developments. (2) In view of the fact that individual expectations are rather heterogeneous and suffer from a degree of uncertainty, it would be a good idea when using cross-sectional data to occasionally include the real spread of wages in the analysis (as done here in the quantile regressions). Comparisons of medians tell too little about the real behaviours in reaching decisions and should be improved with the addition of information on wage distribution.

NOTES

1. It seems though that teaching women have higher returns to schooling as compared to women in other professions. This corresponds to a finding of Hanushek (1998) for the US that teaching is particularly rewarding for women as compared to alternative professional activities but less so for men.
2. There is no information on net earnings in the SLFS. We therefore had to build a tax model in order to estimate the individual tax burden. The model takes into account the family situation (i.e. marital status, number of children) and the household income for married couples. The tax rates were estimated with the help of a statistic of the tax burden in Switzerland.

3. One of the implicit assumptions of the Mincer model is, that direct educational costs are zero or equal to students earnings.

REFERENCES

Alsalam, Nabeel and Ronald Conley (1995), 'The Rate of Return to Education: A Proposal for an Indicator', OECD (ed.), in: *Education and Employment,* Paris: OECD, pp. 84–110.

Borjas, George J. (1999), 'The Economic Analysis of Immigration', in: *The Handbook of Labor Economics*, Ashenfelter and Card (eds.), *Elsevier Science* 1999, pp. 1697–1760.

De Coulon, Augustin (1998), 'Evidence on the Education Profile and the Assimilation of Immigrants in Switzerland', *International Journal of Manpower,* 19 (7), pp. 533–544.

Dominitz, Jeff and Charles F. Manski (1996), 'Eliciting Student Expectations of the Return to Schooling', *The Journal of Human Resources*, 31 (1), pp. 1–26.

Ermisch, John F. and Robert E. Wright (1993), 'Wage Offers and Full-time and Part-time Employment by British Women', *The Journal of Human Resources,* 28 (1), pp. 111–133.

Friedberg, Rachel M. (1996), 'You Can't Take It With You? Immigrant Assimilation and the Portability of Human Capital', *NBER Working Paper No. 5837.*

Hanushek, Eric A. (1998), 'Conclusions and Controversies about the Effectiveness of School Resources', Federal Reserve Bank of New York, *Policy Review*, 4 (1), pp. 11–27.

Heckman, James (1979), 'Sample Selection Bias as a Specification Error', *Econometrica*, 47 (1), pp. 153–162.

Heckman, James (1976), 'The Common Structure of Statistical Models of Truncation, Sample Selection Bias and a Simple Estimator for Such Models', *Annals of Economic and Social Measurement*, 5, pp. 475–492.

Mincer, Jacob (1974), *Schooling, Experience and Earnings*, National Bureau of Economic Research: New York.

Psacharopoulos, George (1987), 'The Cost-benefit Model', in: Psacharopoulos, George, *Economics of Education: Research and Studies,* Oxford, Pergamon Press pp. 342–346.

Wolter, Stefan C. (2000), 'Wage Expectations: A Comparison of Swiss and US Students', *Kyklos* 53 (1), pp. 51–69.

Wolter, Stefan C. and Bernhard A. Weber (1999a), 'On the Measurement of Private Rates of Return on Education', *Jahrbücher für Nationalökonomie und Statistik,* 218 (5 and 6), pp. 605–618.

Wolter, Stefan C. and Bernhard A. Weber (1999b), 'A New Look at Private Rates of Return to Education in Switzerland', *Education & Training*. 41 (8 and 9), pp. 366–372.

16. United Kingdom

Arnaud Chevalier and Ian Walker

INTRODUCTION

This study presents estimates of the returns to education for a variety of simple models using several of the available datasets from the UK. The UK is well endowed with datasets that allow us to address a wide variety of issues associated with the returns to education. Our aim is to illuminate the main issues in this area using the data outlined below in section two. It focuses on a number of aspects of the relationship between education and wages, estimates of which are reported in sections three and four. In particular, we investigate time stability of the returns to education using long runs of cross-section datasets; we look into the impact of education on the wages of employees compared to the self-employed to evaluate the extent to which education serves to signal innate ability; we look at returns by race and gender; and whether estimates suffer from any bias associated with a correlation between wages and unobserved determinants of participation. A further issue is the net returns to education which we investigate using a detailed simulation routine that captures all of the complications of the UK tax and welfare systems. We compare men with women and we investigate whether the returns are sensitive to sample selection.

In addition, a major issue in the literature has been the extent of bias induced by the endogeneity of schooling (see Card, 1999). Here we address the issue using educational reforms that vary across cohorts but not across individuals within cohorts (such as the minimum school-leaving age), and variables that may be associated with individual discount rates (such as smoking and gambling) as instruments. We take up this issue in detail in section five. Our conclusion is that the returns to education are relatively robust but that endogeneity is an important issue. Estimates that allow for potential endogeneity are much larger than those that do not. The returns are relatively stable over time with no evidence that the expansion of higher education in the 1960s has had any detrimental effect. We also find that returns for men are smaller than for women, for union members than non-members, and much smaller for non-whites than whites. Finally, we find evidence of only a small signalling component to the returns.

DATA

Here, we exploit the Family Expenditure Surveys (FES, also used in Harmon and Walker, 1995), the General Household Surveys (GHS, also used in Harmon and Walker, 1999), the Family Resources Survey (FRS), the National Child Development Study (NCDS, also used in Harmon and Walker, 1999, and Dearden 1998), and the British Household Panel Study (BHPS, used in Ermisch and Francesconi, 1997).[1]

The FES is a random sample of approximately 7000 households each year, and is available from the 1960s although years of education is only available in the data from 1978. In addition to education and earnings, FES contains some information relating to union status (see Lanot and Walker, 1996) and also has smoking and other expenditures (see Evans and Montgomery, 1994 for US work on this topic). Figure 16.1 shows the approximately linear relationship between full-time school-leaving age and the log real hourly wage (there are few observations above 24 and below 15 or in the 19/20 "dip") for men and women aged 21–59 in Great Britain (i.e. UK excluding Northern Ireland). Note that although men earn more than women, on average, for all levels of education, the relationship between education and wages is distinctly flatter for men than for women. The GHS, on average slightly larger than FES, is available on a consistent basis from 1984 but here we use only even years of data for reasons that will become apparent later. GHS also contains information on smoking. The availability of FES (and GHS) over a long run of years allows us to examine the stability of the returns to education which is one aspect that we concentrate on in section two. The FRS data is a random sample of approximately 25 000 households conducted every year from 1993/1994. The FRS contains information on union status and recall data on work experience but no expenditure data. The larger size and richer detail allows us to examine the stability of returns with respect to the inclusion of more extensive control variables, and allows us to examine minority groups, which we do in section three. The NCDS is a cohort study of all individuals born in a particular week in 1958 who have been interviewed on five occasions and which has detailed information about parental background, schooling and ability in early waves and about earnings in later waves. The NCDS allows us to address the relationship between earnings, ability and schooling in some detail and we explore this in section three for the 1991 earnings data at aged 33. The BHPS is a panel study of approximately 5000 households who have been interviewed in five successive years from 1991. The data contains information on current earnings and previous education as well as a wide variety of characteristics including smoking histories. The data quality in FES, BHPS and FRS is good. Only the GHS has detailed educational qualifications available as well as age left full-time education but GHS seems more prone to measurement error than other surveys. NCDS data contains some attrition and has a significant number of missing values but this is, nevertheless, not thought to be likely to produce significant biases.[2]

Figure 16.1   Education and wages – GB men and women in FES

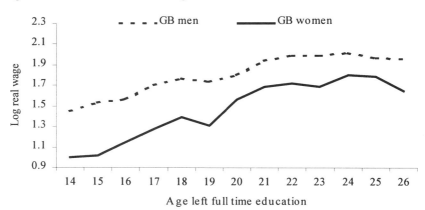

SIMPLE ESTIMATES OF THE RETURNS TO EDUCATION

A review of earlier work can be found in Dearden (1999) and international evidence can be found in Psacharopolous (1994) or in Walker and Woolley (1999) who use an internationally comparable data and find large returns for GB (and Northern Ireland).

Our principal interest in this section is to establish any trend in the return to schooling. Thus we use the FES which has the longest run of consistent data. In Table 16.1 we report estimates of the most parsimonious model where we proxy the experience effect on wages using a quadratic in age (we use age because of the potential endogeneity of experience) and capture the effect of education using simply the number of years of full-time continuous education.[3]

The data relates to employed men aged 25–59 and employed women aged 25–59 where hours of work are at least one per week and we exclude the self-employed, the disabled and those receiving sick pay or benefits. There is some tendency for returns to rise over the late 1980s and early 1990s and we find that when we interact education with a (monthly) time trend in our model estimated over pooled data that the coefficient on the interaction is 0.00051 in the male equation with a standard error of 0.00016 indicating that there is a modest but significant trend increase in the returns[4] of approximately 0.07% per annum.

Table 16.1   OLS Results using FES

	Men			Women		
Year	Educ.	Age	Age^2	Educ.	Age	Age^2
1978	0.061	0.043	-0.0005	0.096	0.004	0.00001
	(0.003)	(0.006)	(0.00007)	(0.005)	(0.007)	(0.00009)
1979	0.050	0.054	-0.0006	0.095	0.016	-0.0002
	(0.003)	(0.006)	(0.00007)	(0.005)	(0.007)	(0.00009)
1980	0.048	0.048	-0.0006	0.091	-0.003	0.00008
	(0.003)	(0.007)	(0.00008)	(0.005)	(0.007)	(0.00009)
1981	0.058	0.058	-0.0005	0.102	-0.005	0.0001
	(0.003)	(0.006)	(0.00008)	(0.005)	(0.008)	(0.0001)
1982	0.052	0.057	-0.0006	0.092	-0.003	0.00007
	(0.003)	(0.006)	(0.00008)	(0.006)	(0.008)	(0.00009)
1983	0.059	0.059	-0.0008	0.108	-0.011	0.00017
	(0.004)	(0.004)	(0.00009)	(0.006)	(0.008)	(0.000010)
1984	0.059	0.066	-0.0007	0.094	-0.011	0.00017
	(0.004)	(0.007)	(0.00009)	(0.006)	(0.008)	(0.00009)
1985	0.060	0.066	-0.0007	0.111	0.014	-0.00013
	(0.004)	(0.007)	(0.00009)	(0.005)	(0.008)	(0.00010)
1986	0.050	0.077	-0.0009	0.093	0.008	-0.00004
	(0.004)	(0.007)	(0.00009)	(0.005)	(0.008)	(0.00010)
1987	0.056	0.079	-0.0009	0.111	-0.008	0.00013
	(0.003)	(0.008)	(0.00009)	(0.005)	(0.008)	(0.00010)
1988	0.058	0.058	-0.0006	0.104	0.010	-0.00009
	(0.004)	(0.008)	(0.00010)	(0.005)	(0.008)	(0.00010)
1989	0.069	0.074	-0.0008	0.097	0.018	-0.00020
	(0.004)	(0.008)	(0.00009)	(0.005)	(0.008)	(0.00010)
1990	0.064	0.071	-0.0008	0.093	0.030	-0.00033
	(0.004)	(0.008)	(0.00010)	(0.005)	(0.008)	(0.00010)
1991	0.057	0.062	-0.0007	0.090	0.020	-0.00025
	(0.004)	(0.009)	(0.00010)	(0.005)	(0.008)	(0.00010)
1992	0.069	0.097	-0.0011	0.097	0.018	-0.00020
	(0.004)	(0.009)	(0.00010)	(0.005)	(0.009)	(0.00010)
1993	0.065	0.075	-0.0008	0.098	0.018	-0.00019
	(0.004)	(0.009)	(0.00010)	(0.004)	(0.008)	(0.00009)
1994	0.061	0.082	-0.0009	0.095	0.041	-0.00048
	(0.004)	(0.009)	(0.00011)	(0.004)	(0.009)	(0.00011)
1995	0.065	0.090	-0.0010	0.091	0.032	-0.00036
	(0.005)	(0.009)	(0.00012)	(0.005)	(0.009	(0.00010)
All	0.054	0.067	-0.0007	0.097	0.010	-0.00008
	(0.001)	(0.002)	(0.00002)	(0.002)	(0.002)	(0.00002)

Notes: Figures in parentheses are robust standard errors. The 'all' model includes trend and a trend-education interaction. Results post-1987 are for financial years.

The finding that the returns have been rising, and certainly not falling, is surprising in the light of the dramatic increases in the higher education participation rate that took place over this period. However, one issue that we uncover below is that of endogeneity and this may affect inferences about the time stability of estimated rates of return so we return to this question in section four. These results point to relatively stable, and at least not decreasing, differentials for men and women. The returns to "experience", proxied here by age, are small for women but quite large for men.

ROBUSTNESS OF THE SIMPLE ESTIMATES

In this section we demonstrate, using the pooled FRS and BHPS datasets, that the results presented above are fairly stable with respect to changes in the control variables. First, we examine how stable the results are across part-time and full-time workers. Secondly, we use alternative ways of controlling for the effects of experience on wages. Thirdly, we look at selectivity bias associated with using a sample of working individuals. Fourthly we look at how sensitive the results, particularly for education, are to the inclusion of other control variables. A related interest here is whether education has different effects on different groups (for example public versus private sector employees and by race). Finally, we look at the returns to qualifications.

We then investigate the extent to which including ability, parental background, and school quality affect the estimated returns. For example, we are concerned about the interaction between ability and education (apart from any "ability bias" that may be present which we consider later). That is, we are concerned about whether education has a different effect on the wages of high ability people versus low ability. This idea is raised in Herrnstein and Murray (1994) who argue that "... school is not a promising place to try to reduce intellectual differences ....". The school quality issue is relevant here because of concerns that quality and quantity are correlated so that the return to years of education may be picking up some quality effect.

Finally, an important issue has been the extent to which education actually increases wages through its effect on productivity as opposed to simply signalling pre-existing productivity (see Weiss, 1998). We do this by looking at the distinction between the returns to education for employees versus the returns to the self-employed. We consider these issues in turn below.

Part-time Work

In Table 16.2 we re-estimate our simple model using the pooled BHPS data and examine the returns to education for part-time, compared to full-time, workers. The estimated returns are significantly larger for part-time workers, especially for men although part-time men are a very small proportion of the sample. However, apart from non-random selection into work (which we pursue below) there is likely to be non-random selection into part-time work.[5]

Table 16.2   Hours of work effects on OLS Estimates

	Education	Age	Age^2	N
Men				
Part-time	0.113 (0.014)	0.114 (0.039)	-0.0012 (0.0005)	269
Full-time	0.062 (0.002)	0.074 (0.005)	-0.0008 (0.0001)	8015
Women				
Part time	0.111 (0.004)	0.034 (0.007)	-0.0004 (0.0001)	4285
Full time	0.087 (0.003)	0.063 (0.006)	-0.0008 (0.0001)	4702

Notes: The sample used is taken from the BHPS. Figures in parentheses are standard errors. N is the sample size. Part time is defined here as hours less than 31.

Selection Bias

In Table 16.3a we examine whether the results for women are sensitive to selectivity. We do this in the conventional way, using the method of selection correction due to Heckman (1979), and by examining informally whether *median* regression results differ from OLS where the former is thought to be robust to selection (see Buchinsky, 1994).

While the first method is conventional it does require some valid exclusion restriction to ensure identification. Here we use unearned income which we view as a determinant of labour-market participation but not of market wages. This is a satisfactory in a static model, however, in a life-cycle context it is problematic (since the fixed effect in wages is likely to be correlated with the asset position of households) and so these results should not be regarded as definitive.[6]

While there is a need for caution in this area, the Heckman results, in any case, suggest that there is no selectivity bias and the education coefficient is unchanged and this is substantiated from the median regression results where the education coefficient is only a little higher than the OLS case.

Table 16.3a   OLS, heckman selection, and median regression

	FRS women			BHPS women		
	Educ.	Age	Age^2	Educ.	Age	Age^2
OLS	0.109	0.026	-0.0003	0.103	0.040	-0.0005
	(0.002)	(0.003)	(0.00004)	(0.002)	(0.005)	(0.0001)
Heckman	0.109	0.016	-0.0001	0.102	0.060	-0.0007
	(0.002)	(0.004)	(0.0001)	(0.003)	(0.006)	(0.0001)
Median	0.122	0.024	-0.0003	0.118	0.034	-0.0003
regression	(0.002)	(0.004)	(0.00004)	(0.002)	(0.005)	(0.0001)

Notes: The sample used for this analysis is taken from the FRS and BHPS. Figures in parentheses are robust standard errors. Sample sizes are as in Tables 16.3 and 16.5. The models includes year dummies, marital status, the number of children in three age ranges, region dummies and regional unemployment rate. In each case we use household unearned income as well as the variables from the wage equation in the participation equation.

In Table 16.3b we show the effect on the education coefficient of correcting for selection bias for part-time status as well as non-participation. The returns are stable at around 8% for men and 11% for women.

Table 16.3b   Part-time and full-time wages: OLS and Heckman selection

	Men		Women	
OLS	0.0786	(0.0014)	0.1082	(0.0015)
Heckman	0.0798	(0.0014)	0.1050	(0.0015)

Notes: The sample used for this analysis is taken from the FRS. Figures in parentheses are robust standard errors. Sample sizes are 39 029 women and 36 536 men. The models include year dummies, and region dummies. In each case we use household unearned income as well as the variables from the wage equation in the full-time/part-time/non-participation ordered probit equation.

Race Effects

In Table 16.4 we investigate race. Non-whites represent less than 5% of the sample, but FRS is large so we do have sufficiently large groups to support separate estimation of black (mainly Afro-Caribbean) and Asian (mainly Pakistan, Bangladesh and India). The results (which are not reported here) suggest strong discrimination in the levels of wages. However, as well as intercepts effects we interact education with the race dummies and find significantly lower returns to education for non-white men and women relative to whites suggesting that education has a smaller impact on productivity for non-whites perhaps because the *quality* of the education treatment is different for the two groups.[7]

Table 16.4   Race and the Returns to Education

	Men	Women
White	0.0824 (0.0013)	0.1138 (0.0015)
Black minus white	-0.0563 (0.0111)	-0.0867 (0.0098)
Asian minus white	-0.0313 (0.0061)	-0.0559 (0.0078)

Notes: FRS sample. Figures in parentheses are robust standard errors. The models includes year dummies, marital status, the number of children in three age ranges, region dummies and regional unemployment rates.

Experience Definition

Here, we contrast the effects of using a quadratic in *potential* experience (age minus age left full-time education) and in *actual* experience (measured in the data by recall and giving a weight of 0.5 to years of part-time experience). The results, in Table 16.5a and Table 16.5b, differ significantly because they are very precise but the differences are not dramatic.

The most pronounced difference is between potential and actual experience for women since it is for this group that these measures differ most. However, the education coefficient differs little across specifications. Note that the age definition of experience gives the most conservative returns to education and we use this definition in subsequent analysis below. [8]

Returns to Qualifications

In Table 16.6 we estimate the returns to educational qualifications. The motivation for this is partly "credentialism", which views the returns to education as being signalled by the credentials obtained, and partly to detect nonlinearities in returns. Since credentials are acquired through a combination of years of education and effort/ability the coefficients on the credentials are generally thought to overestimate the returns to education *per se*.

However, in Tables 16.6, we attempt to control for the education component of credentials by including years of schooling as well as the highest credential obtained with the BHPS data: the precise interpretation of the acronyms is unimportant – CSE is a now defunct qualification once taken by non-academic children at the end of compulsory secondary schooling; GCSE are qualifications now sat by all children at the end of compulsory education; while A levels are academic exams requiring two years' post-GCSE; a degree which requires a further three years' full-time study (more in some vocational subjects); and a higher degree which requires one or more full-time years of postgraduate study.

Table 16.5a   Sensitivity of OLS results to the experience measure, men

Definition of experience	Education	Experience	Experience^2
FRS			
Age	0.079	0.089	-0.0010
	(0.001)	(0.003)	(0.00004)
Potential experience	0.094	0.051	-0.0009
	(0.001)	(0.001)	(0.00003)
Actual experience	0.096	0.051	-0.0009
	(0.001)	(0.001)	(0.00003)
BHPS			
Age	0.064	0.076	-0.0008
	(0.002)	(0.005)	(0.00006)
Potential experience	0.076	0.043	-0.0008
	(0.002)	(0.002)	(0.00005)
Actual experience	0.078	0.043	-0.0008
	(0.002)	(0.002)	(0.00004)

Notes: Figures in parentheses are robust standard errors. Sample sizes are as in Tables 16.3 and 16.5. The models include year dummies.

Table 16.5b   Sensitivity of OLS results to the experience measure, women

Definition of experience	Education	Experience	Experience^2
FRS			
Age	0.108	0.023	-0.0003
	(0.002)	(0.003)	(0.00004)
Potential experience	0.115	0.021	-0.0004
	(0.002)	(0.001)	(0.00003)
Actual experience	0.122	0.042	-0.0007
	(0.001)	(0.001)	(0.00004)
BHPS			
Age	0.103	0.040	-0.0005
	(0.002)	(0.005)	(0.00006)
Potential experience	0.106	0.017	-0.0003
	(0.003)	(0.002)	(0.00004)
Actual experience	0.116	0.031	-0.0006
	(0.002)	(0.002)	(0.00005)

Notes: Figures in parentheses are robust standard errors. Sample sizes are as in Tables 16.4 and 16.3. The models include year dummies.

The vocational qualifications are more disparate. "Commercial" is often ONC, obtained through part-time courses over two years. "Other" is often HNC typically requiring a further two years' post-ONC. Nursing qualifications can be either obtained on-the-job through experience and part-time study over two years or, for a more advanced qualification, through close to full-time study with some experience over three years.

Table 16.6   The returns to education qualifications, BHPS

	Men		Women	
Years of education		0.026		0.036
		(0.003)		(0.003)
Age	0.067	0.069	0.027	0.031
	(0.005)	(0.005)	(0.004)	(0.004)
Age^2	-0.0007	-0.0007	-0.0003	-0.0004
	(0.0001)	(0.0001)	(0.0001)	(0.0001)
Nonvocational				
Higher Degree	0.773	0.632	0.929	0.747
	(0.032)	(0.036)	(0.039)	(0.042)
Degree	0.660	0.525	0.824	0.636
	(0.018)	(0.024)	(0.018)	(0.023)
A Level	0.379	0.348	0.345	0.276
	(0.017)	(0.017)	(0.021)	(0.021)
GCSE	0.265	0.246	0.233	0.195
	(0.016)	(0.016)	(0.012)	(0.013)
CSE	0.252	0.246	0.011	-0.008
	(0.023)	(0.023)	(0.024)	(0.024)
Other	-0.081	-0.107	0.294	0.243
	(0.041)	(0.040)	(0.050)	(0.053)
Vocational				
Teaching	0.450	0.383	0.847	0.689
	(0.031)	(0.031)	(0.023)	(0.026)
Other higher	0.418	0.384	0.412	0.338
	(0.015)	(0.015)	(0.017)	(0.019)
Nursing	0.303	0.278	0.493	0.446
	(0.067)	(0.066)	(0.023)	(0.023)
Commercial	0.375	0.357	0.153	0.140
	(0.104)	(0.105)	(0.017)	(0.017)
Apprenticeship	0.174	0.166	0.027	0.037
	(0.024)	(0.024)	(0.058)	(0.058)

Notes: Figures in parentheses are robust standard errors. The models include year dummies, marital status, the number of children in three age ranges, region dummies and regional unemployment rates. Omitted category is no qualifications.

The estimates, of degree relative to A level of around 30% for men and 50% for women, are the same order of magnitude as in Blundell *et al* (1997) using NCDS, and Harkness and Machin (1999) using GHS. Note that the interpretation of the year of education is less clear-cut since we are already controlling for the level of qualification. The most appropriate way of interpreting these effects is as the return to years of education that do not directly contribute to a qualification. For example, an individual might spend two years studying for A levels but not actually pass and the return on those two years would, not surprisingly, be lower than earlier results would lead us to expect. Since these results are broadly consistent with our earlier ones we do not subject them to further testing for stability.

The average years of full-time continuous education corresponding to each qualification is a reasonable guide to how long it typically takes to achieve a particular standard except in those cases where the vocational training is on-the-job. Thus, in Figure 16.2 we graph the estimated returns for males against the average years and the slope of these relationships seems broadly consistent with the earlier results. Moreover the results suggest that the education/log wage relationship is close to being a linear one. While the results on the returns to qualification suggest that the common assumption that log wages are linear in schooling is a reasonable approximation there are still possible "sheepskin" effects associated with particular levels of schooling.

Figure 16 2   Estimated returns to qualifications, men in BHPS

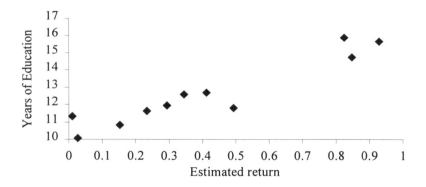

In Figure 16.3 we see that there are marked nonlinearities in the relationships especially between 18 and 21 and after 22 (F-tests of linearity are strongly rejected for both men and women). One should be cautious about assuming that this is support for "credentialism" since those individuals who do leave at untypical ages may be untypical in other, unobservable, ways. For example, typically individuals leave school at the end of study programmes marked by GCSE-level qualifications at age 16, A level at 18 and a degree at 21 so that those that leave at other ages may be low-motivation drop outs or low-ability failures.

Figure 16.3   Years of schooling sheepskin effects in FRS

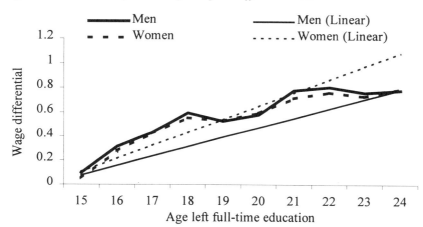

Returns to type of degree

The GHS dataset allows us to disaggregate degrees by broad subject of study. In Table 16.7 we present results for individuals who have at least A levels (the minimum qualification to gain entry to a degree course).

We pool successive pairs of years to obtain sufficiently large samples and the results show rising returns for women in arts/humanities and in science (including medicine)/engineering and decreasing returns in the other category (largely joint degrees and law), and returns for men rise until the late 1980s and then fall for all subjects except arts/humanities where the returns are never significantly different from zero. Similar results can be seen in Harkness and Machin (1999) over a longer period of time.

Signalling

It has been suggested that the returns to education are not entirely due to its impact on productivity but because it conveys a signal about pre-existing productivity (see Weiss, 1998). Testing for this is difficult but it has been suggested that the distinction between public and private sector can illuminate the signalling role of education.

Table 16. 7   Returns to Degrees (Relative to A Levels): GHS

	1980/1982	1984/1986	1989/1991	1993/1995
Men				
Arts/humanities	0.021	0.043	0.019	0.049
	(0.032)	(0.035)	(0.036)	(0.045)
Science/engineering	0.120	0.176	0.243	0.177
	(0.023)	(0.024)	(0.023)	(0.027)
Social	0.166	0.197	0.248	0.221
Sciences/business	(0.026)	(0.026)	(0.026)	(0.031)
Other	0.223	0.252	0.263	0.165
	(0.031)	(0.031)	(0.035)	(0.040)
Women				
Arts/humanities	0.109	0.192	0.193	0.267
	(0.037)	(0.036)	(0.034)	(0.049)
Science/engineering	0.243	0.314	0.319	0.366
	(0.048)	(0.043)	(0.034)	(0.042)
Social	0.223	0.220	0.263	0.203
Sciences/business	(0.041)	(0.037)	(0.030)	(0.039)
Other	0.278	0.343	0.234	0.202
	(0.041)	(0.037)	(0.036)	(0.044)

Notes: Standard errors in parentheses. Samples contain only individuals with at least A levels as highest qualification.

The difficulty here is that, unlike race, sector of work is unlikely to be randomly assigned. In particular, there may be a correlation between the fixed effect in wages and sector of work. For example, risk-averse individuals may be more likely to choose the public sector and are also likely to have lower wages. This is particularly acute when it is borne in mind that certain occupations are associated with certain sectors almost exclusively: medics and teachers are almost invariably public sector workers. Thus, even ignoring the endogeneity of sector, it is difficult to disentangle sector effects from occupational ones.

Simply entering sector into a least squares model is rather uninformative but we do so here for comparability with other studies and report the results in Table 16.8 where we find: a 9% public sector differential for men and a 21% one for women; [9] no difference in returns to education for women and just 1% lower for men in the public sector.

A further test of the role of signalling could be based on self-employment: the self-employed know their own productivity so that education has no value as a signal to them. Here we exploit the information we have about the income of the self-employed in BHPS. [10]

Table 16.8   *Returns to education in the public and private sectors*

	Men		Women	
Public/private differential	0.090	(0.003)	0.209	(0.010)
Public sector return	0.065	(0.003)	0.093	(0.003)
Private – public return	-0.011	(0.004)	-0.0008	(0.004)
Sample sizes	8284		8987	

Notes: The sample is from the BHPS. Figures in parentheses are robust standard errors. The models include year dummies, marital status, the number of children in three age ranges, region dummies, and regional unemployment rates.

Table 16. 9   *The signalling value of education*

	Employees		Self-employed		Signalling value
	Return	N	Return	N	Return
BHPS-OLS					
Men	0.064	10001	0.051	1717	0.013
	(0.002)		(0.008)		(0.012)
Women	0.103	9550	0.076	563	0.026
	(0.002)		(0.015)		(0.019)
BHPS-Heckman					
Men	0.069	10001	0.055	1717	0.014
	(0.003)		(0.022)		(0.025)
Women	0.103	9550	0.078	563	0.025
	(0.002)		(0.066)		(0.070)

Notes: The sample is from the BHPS. Figures in parentheses are robust standard errors. The models include year dummies, marital status, the number of children in three age ranges, region dummies, and regional unemployment rates. The Heckman selectivity estimates use father self-employed, mother self-employed and housing equity as instruments.

The idea here is that education has a value from its effect on productivity and a value from signalling innate productivity and, for the self employed, the latter will be zero. Thus, the difference between the rate of return to education for employees and for the self-employed provides a measure of its value as a signal of innate productivity.   Self-employment is also unlikely to be randomly assigned and we control for the endogeneity of self-employment using information on whether one's parents were self-employed and on housing equity, [11] where the rationale for the latter is that one can use housing equity as collateral to finance a business overdraft. The results are presented in Table 16.9 and indicate[12] that the value of education as a signal is rather low and, once the endogeneity is controlled for, the estimated values are not statistically significant for either men or women.

Additional Control Variables

In Table 16.10 we investigate the extent to which the returns to education are sensitive to the inclusion of other variables. We augment the basic specification with: children and marital status variables, part-time working dummy, union status and plant size. While many of these characteristics are not randomly assigned across individuals, the table suggests that the least squares estimated returns to education are relatively stable to such changes in specification.

Consistent with many earlier studies we find: large plant size effects on wages for both men and women; an 8% union differential for men and a substantially larger one for women; a large marriage penalty for women relative to being single never-married and a large marriage premium for men; and, as before, a large negative effect of part-time work for women but not for men. However, whatever controls are included the estimated return to education remains unchanged.

Gross and net returns

A final issue that is almost entirely unresearched is the *net* return to education[13] – that is, net of the impact of income related taxes and transfers. One approach to this issue would be to redefine the dependent variable to be wages net of income tax and social security liabilities (and, perhaps, including income-related welfare entitlements).

We report on this in Table 16.11 where we use the net earnings data that is available in BHPS and GHS datasets.[14] The net returns are approximately 20% lower than the corresponding gross returns given in earlier tables. As before, we find that using potential experience (age minus education) yields a higher education return than using age.

However, the presumption here is that the average tax rate is exogenous and this will not be true except if the tax system is proportional. Thus we also estimate the gross return and then simulate what impact raising education would have on net incomes by simulating the impact of adding an additional year of education to individuals in a large sample where we can accurately compute tax liabilities and welfare entitlements. This allows us to estimate the net marginal return. Indeed, we can also compute the consequences of educational expansion for government net revenue. Since education affects labour force participation and hours of work we estimate a Heckman selection model and, since hours of work affect welfare entitlements and the income tax rate faced we estimate reduced form Tobit hours equations.

Table 16.10   BHPS: Changes in control variables

	None	Plant size and union	Children and marriage	Part-time	All controls
Men					
Education	0.064	0.062	0.065	0.064	0.063
Age	0.076	0.070	0.063	0.076	0.057
Age^2	-0.0008	-0.0008	-0.0007	-0.0008	-0.0006
Medium Plant		0.157			0.153
Large Plant		0.241			0.243
Union member		0.079			0.080
No. of children			0.017		0.019
Married			0.144		0.144
Cohabit			0.095		0.107
Divorced			0.050		0.058
Part time				-0.020	0.036
Women					
Education	0.103	0.095	0.101	0.097	0.092
Age	0.040	0.041	0.060	0.049	0.053
Age^2	-0.0005	-0.0005	-0.0007	-0.0006	-0.0006
Medium Plant		0.158			0.130
Large Plant		0.258			0.216
Union member		0.214			0.195
No. of children			-0.077		-0.032
Married			0.001		0.025
Cohabit			0.021		0.025
Divorced			-0.009		0.003
Part time				-0.220	-0.156

Notes: Figures in parentheses are robust standard errors. Sample sizes are as in Table 16.4. The models include year dummies, region dummies, and regional unemployment rates.

Thus, we simulate the wage, participation and hours effects of education changes by predicting pre- and post-ducational reform positions. Here we simply add one additional year of education to all individuals in the data. The system used is estimated over the pooled FRS data and reflated to current prices using the RPI. The estimates are reported in Table 16.12 and show that education has a gross return of 7.5% for men and 11% for women, consistent with our earlier results. Moreover, education positively affects the participation probability and hours of work especially for women. Furthermore, we find that education raises wages, participation probability and hours for both men and women. Unearned income has a significant effect

Education and Earnings in Europe

only for female participation. Being married raises hours and participation and having an employed partner raises hours and participation. Husband's predicted wage has a negative effect on hours and on the participation of wives.

Table 16.11   Net returns

	GHS		BHPS	
	Men	Women	Men	Women
Education	0.051	0.069	0.052	0.076
	(0.001)	(0.002)	(0.002)	(0.002)
Age	0.057	0.018	0.069	0.036
	(0.003)	(0.003)	(0.004)	(0.003)
Age^2	-0.0006	-0.0002	-0.0008	-0.0004
	(0.00003)	(0.00003)	(0.00004)	(0.0004)
Marginal return at 10 years	0.045	0.014	0.067	0.028
Education	0.061	0.075	0.073	0.098
	(0.001)	(0.002)	(0.002)	(0.002)
Potential experience	0.034	0.013	0.046	0.019
	(0.001)	(0.001)	(0.002)	(0.002)
Potential experience^2	-0.0006	-0.0002	-0.0008	-0.0004
	(0.00003)	(0.00003)	(0.0004)	(0.00004)
Marginal return at 10 years	0.022	0.008	0.030	0.012

Notes: Robust standard errors in parentheses. Specifications also include year and region dummies.

These results are used to simulate the impact of adding an additional year of schooling to all observations (not retired, self-employed, disabled or sick) in the three years of pooled FRS data, reflated to January 1999 prices. We account for the effect on the participation probability, via the reduced form participation probit equation, and thence on wages conditional on the participation probability (i.e. adjusted for the selection term) and, since tax and transfers depend on hours of work, we also allow for the effects on hours of work via our reduced form Tobit hours equation. [15]

Table 16.12   Results for simulating net returns, FRS

	Participation Probit	Wages	Hours Tobit
Men			
Education	0.087	0.075	0.220

	(0.005)	(0.002)	(0.047)
Unearned income	-0.0025		-0.0021
	(0.012)		(0.14)
Married	0.930		11.828
	(0.026)		(0.315)
λ		-0.245	
		(0.041)	
Women			
Education	0.091	0.107	1.716
	(0.005)	(0.002)	(0.060)
Employed husband	1.085		17.245
	(0.032)		(0.526)
Husband's predicted wage	-0.072		-1.209
	(0.005)		(0.069)
Unearned income × 100	-0.047		-0.010
	(0.015)		(0.002)
Married	0.139		-0.0075
	(0.049)		(0.749)
λ		-0.148	
		(0.025)	

Notes: Figures in parentheses are robust standard errors. The estimations also include as independent variables age and its quadratic, region dummies, regional unemployment, and the number of children in each of three age ranges.

Although the UK income tax system is based on individual incomes, a difficulty in computing net returns is that transfer incomes are usually related to benefit unit (defined as an individual or a couple with any dependent children) incomes. Thus we equivalise the transfer incomes received by the benefit unit using the equivalence scales implict in the DSS income support rules and allocate equivalized means-tested transfer payments to each individual in the benefit unit. [16]

In Figure 16.4 we plot these net returns at each level of education. The first thing to note is that the net returns here are comparable with the gross returns estimated previously since they both correspond to the proportionate change in wages from a one-year change in education. However, in Figure 16.4 we also allow for education to affect participation and hours of work so that the net returns are higher because of this but lower because of net tax liabilities. Thus at low levels of education the returns are lowered by the poverty trap implicit in the welfare system but raised by the effect of education on the probability of being in work[17]. Corresponding to the net return to the individual being lowered by the operation of the tax and transfer system there is a benefit to the government in the form of additional revenue and reduced expenditure on transfer payments. Moreover, the effect on the probability of being in work reduces government expenditure and raises tax revenue as well as generating a gain in net income for individuals. Thus, we can compute the implications for overall government net revenue and we find that the additional net revenue from the additional education is in the order of £440 per annum per individual. At any reasonable discount rate this would represent a present value that far outstrips the additional tuition expenditure which, at the margin, would be approximately £3400 per annum per individual.[18]

Figure 16.4   Net returns to education, FRS

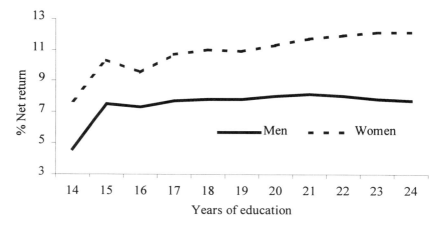

These results have important consequences for policy design. Raising the school-leaving age for those with low schooling levels is likely to be relatively inexpensive for the government since it can recoup much of the tuition costs from lower transfer expenditures. However, the corollary of this is that individuals with low levels of schooling have the lowest net return to education and so have little incentive to participate beyond the minimum (and have little incentive to comply with any increase in the minimum). This effect of low net returns might be strengthened by the high discount rates that are associated with individuals with poorer family backgrounds. Thus, raising school participation may require in-school transfers (such as those recently proposed for the UK). There are a number of deficiencies with this analysis. A substantial methodological object is that the modelling assumes that such widespread increases in the supply of skilled labour (and decreases in unskilled) will not affect the distribution of wages. These results are, of course, sensitive to the estimated gross rate of return. We have already pointed out that the returns may be particularly low for non-whites and this would be exacerbated by the effect of the poverty trap on education incentives. However, the next section suggests that, overall, the estimates used above may be too conservative.

Table 16.13   Differences in returns across standard regions, BHPS

	Men		Women	
Education	0.053	(0.004)	0.087	(0.005)
Education × North region	0.001	(0.007)	0.013	(0.008)
Education × Yorkshire region	0.022	(0.007)	0.005	(0.008)
Education × North West	0.005	(0.006)	0.019	(0.008)
Educucation × East Mids	-0.006	(0.007)	0.009	(0.009)
Education × Greater London	-0.001	(0.006)	-0.010	(0.007)
Education × South East	0.011	(0.005)	0.019	(0.007)
Educucation × South West	-0.001	(0.008)	-0.017	(0.010)
Education × Wales	0.028	(0.009)	0.018	(0.012)
F-test of equal returns	3.21		4.47	

Notes: Robust standard errors in parentheses. Omitted category is West Midlands. Regional controls are included as intercept shifts.

Table 16.14   Differences in returns by father's occupation, BHPS

	Men	Women
Education	0.075 (0.004)	0.047 (0.004)
Education × Professional	-0.020 (0.008)	0.008 (0.007)
Education × Technical	0.026 (0.009)	-0.010 (0.009)
Education × Clerical	0.009 (0.012)	0.027 (0.007)
Education × Manual	0.019 (0.006)	0.010 (0.005)
Education × Services	0.024 (0.012)	0.001 (0.009)
Education × Sales	0.057 (0.016)	0.017 (0.008)
Education × Plant operative	0.025 (0.007)	0.013 (0.006)
Education × Other occupation	0.034 (0.010)	0.031 (0.008)
F test of equal returns	7.36	4.09

Notes: Robust standard errors in parentheses. Occupational controls are included as intercept shifts. The omitted category is Father and manager.

Returns across Regions

Perfect markets ought to equalise returns and we test this here by comparing the returns to education across regions in GB. We do this by interacting education with regional dummies and report the results in Table 16.13. There are substantially higher returns in Yorkshire and Wales for men and in the North West for women. F-tests of equal returns in all regions is rejected for both men and women.

Returns across Family Backgrounds

It is common to use parental background variables as instruments for education by excluding them from wage equations. Here we interact father's occupation with individual education to see if parental occupation affects the returns to education (as well as through an intercept shift). In Table 16.14 we find that the interaction terms are jointly significant and we can reject the exclusion restriction.

Figure 16.5   Estimated returns to education, UK GHS 1984–1996

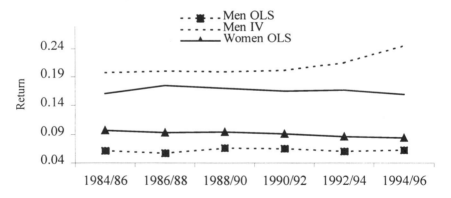

Notes: Each estimate is obtained from pooling consecutive pairs of even years. Estimates control for quadratic in age, region and year dummies. Instrument is smoking dummy. Total sample is 16780 women and 25200 men.

In Figure 16.5 we summarize our estimates of the rate of return obtained by pooling successive pairs of even GHS years using OLS and IV where we instrument education by a smoking dummy (see Evans and Montgomery, 1994). We adopt a parsimonious specification since our earlier results suggested that more general models make no substantial difference to the return to education. The estimates are significant and the differences between men and women and between IV and OLS are also generally statistically significant. Tests of the stability of the estimates over time in OLS specifications that pool the datasets across time and include a trend/education interaction show stable returns for men and women. However, for the IV results the data shows a significant rise for men but no significant trend effects in the returns for women.[19]

The results are dramatic: IV returns of the order of 20% for men and 15% for women compared with OLS estimates of around 6% for men and 10% for women. Nevertheless large increases in IV results are typical of those reviewed in Card (1999) and, for the UK, Harmon and Walker (1995) find results of a similar order of magnitude based on a cohort discontinuity associated with the raising of the minimum school-leaving age. However, one potential weakness of the analysis behind Figure 16.5 is that we only use current smoking behaviour and this may be correlated with current wages rates, perhaps because smoking is a normal good. Thus, we check the pooled GHS results in specifications reported in Table 16.15 with a variety of datasets and definitions of the instrument.

Firstly we use dummy variables for individuals who were smoking at 14, 16 and 18 in the GHS data to compare with the results using current smoking and find that the male/female returns fall from 0.205/0.163 to 0.095/0.126, compared to OLS returns of 0.064/0.092. The advantage oto using smoking in the past as an instrument is that it is unlikely to be correlated with current wages through an income effect and it allows for the possibility that those who quit smoking post-18 are more like those never smoked than are smokers.

NCDS data records parental smoking and own smoking at age 16 so we report results that use these variables as instruments and we do this with and without controls for other family background characteristics. The NCDS results are similar to GHS: for example with controls for family background we find that current smoking yields male/female returns of 0.191/0.215 compared to smoking at 16 which yields 0.080/0.207, compared to OLS returns of 0.061/0.107.

These results based on smoking suggest that there are some grounds for believing that the earlier results of IV returns of approximately double the OLS returns are probably too high – perhaps because the instruments picked up cohort effects. Nevertheless, the results here suggest that previous smoking behaviour yields estimates which are still significantly higher than OLS. Eventhough the rate of return is higher once endogeneity is corrected for, some care needs to be attached to the interpretation of the IV results.

Since the rationale for using smoking as an instrument is that it picks up discount rate differences, it is reasonable to compare the resulting estimates with OLS. However, the analysis based on raising the school-leaving age is probably best interpreted as a local effect – the effect of an additional year of education for those who would have left school at the minimum. We would expect that, because of diminishing returns, the marginal return would be high for such individuals. On the other hand, it is probably important not to overstate this legitimate concern – Harmon and Walker (1999) use a variety of educational interventions and find that the estimated return is high regardless of whether it is interventions that affect the top of the education distribution or the bottom.

Table 16.15   Further IV Results

	Men		Women	
GHS: OLS	0.064	14424	0.092	11759
	(0.002)		(0.002)	
GHS: Current smoking	0.205	14424	0.163	11759
	(0.012)		(0.011)	
GHS: Smoking at 14/16/18	0.095	17907	0.126	17047
	(0.007)		(0.008)	
GHS: Current smoking and at 14/16/18	0.137	14424	0.139	11759
	(0.007)		(0.007)	
BHPS: OLS	0.064	8284	0.103	8987
	(0.002)		(0.002)	
BHPS: Raising of school-leaving age	0.205	8284	0.175	8987
	(0.062)		(0.047)	
BHPS: Smoking	0.209	8284	0.168	8987
	(0.014)		(0.011)	
NCDS: OLS [a]	0.061	3169	0.107	1981
	(0.006)		(0.007)	
NCDS: current smoking [a]	0.191	2311	0.215	1978
	(0.031)		(0.043)	
NCDS: ever smokes [a]	0.135	2319	0.205	1981
	(0.034)		(0.043)	
NCDS: smoked at 16 [a]	0.080	1972	0.207	1692
	(0.033)		(0.032)	
NCDS: OLS [b]	0.075	3169	0.120	2739
	(0.005)		(0.006)	
NCDS: current smoking [b]	0.203	3169	0.241	2739
	(0.029)		(0.030)	
NCDS: ever smoked [b]	0.142	3169	0.206	2739
	(0.032)		(0.030)	
NCDS: smoked at 16 [b]	0.084	2486	0.219	2150
	(0.030)		(0.025)	
NCDS: parent smoked when 16 [b]	0.133	2236	0.169	1895
	(0.027)		(0.024)	

Notes: Figures in parentheses are robust standard errors. The models include year dummies, marital status, the number of children in three age ranges, region dummies, and regional unemployment rates. Numbers of observations differ because of missing values for some variables. a. Specification includes family controls. b. Specification does not include family controls.

Finally, in recent work, Card (1999) has pointed out that heterogeneity in the returns to schooling (the return is a random parameter) undermines the properties of IV. Card notes that the control function approach used in Garen (1984), whereby the estimated residuals from the schooling equation are included in the second stage regression, interacted with both the intercept term and with schooling, allows one to interpret the coefficient on schooling as the mean return.

In Table 16.16 we implement this procedure and compare the results with regular IV. The results suggest that the heterogeneity issue is relatively unimportant. The methods used above yield quite similar results and both are substantially higher than GLS estimates of the standard model with exogenous education, where here the model is a random coefficients one which induces heteroskedasticity in such a way that the variance is proportional to education.

Table 16.16   BHPS: Heterogeneous Returns to Education

	Men	Women
Random coefficient, education exogenous	0.045 (0.002)	0.103 (0.002)
Homogeneous returns model, education endogenous	0.209 (0.014)	0.162 (0.011)
Heterogeneous returns model, education endogenous	0.230 (0.012)	0.172 (0.011)

Notes: Figures in parentheses are robust standard errors. The models include year dummies, marital status, the number of children in three age ranges, region dummies, and regional unemployment rates. Instruments are smoking and minimum school leaving age.

CONCLUSION

The results suggest that the rate of return is reasonably stable (at approximately 6-9% for men and 8-12% for women) in the face of a variety of specification changes. Our data also points towards much lower returns to education for non-whites and for union members relative to non-members. There is some suggestion that the returns have risen over timebut the evidence is not strong. The signalling value of education is a rather small proportion of the total. The returns to education net of tax and welfare transfers are low for low education individuals, because of the poverty trap, implying that the incentives to invest in education is low for precisely the group who seem likely to have high discount rates. This suggests that there needs to be a subsidy for post-compulsory education especially for children from poorer backgrounds. Thus, our results support the idea that subsidies ought to be means tested against parental incomes.

Consistent with earlier UK results, we find that education is endogenous so that estimates which instrument education yield substantially higher returns (approximately 10-15% for men and 12-20% for women) than least squares – although some caution needs to be given to the interpretation of IV results.

We presented some rather simple results on: signalling and self-employment; the random parameter framework; "sheepskin" effects; smoking and IV estimation; and the net *vs* gross returns, and more detailed work is reserved for the future.

In addition there are several topics that we have neglected altogether which we regard as potentially important. For example, we are interested in the returns to a degree for those degree holders not in "graduate" jobs relative to those that are since an excess supply of graduates may manifest itself by graduates taking the jobs normally done by non-graduates.

Secondly, we are interested in "composition bias" associated with selection into employment which arises if education affects the probability of being in work. Thirdly, we have said nothing about the potential *general equilibrium* effects of reform. Finally, we are interested in the extent to which there is a consumption benefit associated with education which may manifest itself as educated individuals, *ceteris paribus*, having higher levels of satisfaction with their lives[20]. Thus, there is much still to be learned.

NOTES

1. There are several other surveys that are particularly useful for international comparisons: the British Social Attitudes Surveys (used in Blanchflower and Oswald, 1995) some of which is abstracted into the International Social Surveys Programme (see Trostel and Walker, 1999) and Walker and Woolley (1999); the International Adult Literacy Survey (see Denny and Harmon, 1999); and several surveys that contain retrospective data (the Working Family Lives Survey, for example). Finally the Labour Force Survey is a large annual survey of individuals that contains detailed education and hours of work information but the earnings data is only available from 1992 and is regarded as being of a poor quality with a large number of missing values (see Blackaby, *et al*, 1999).
2. See Chowdury and Nickell (1985).
3. It is conventional to make the log wage relationship linear in schooling and there seems a reasonable degree of agreement in this in the literature. However, we find, using BHPS, that the relationship is significantly concave. We intend to pursue this nonlinearity in further work.
4. There is a small and insignificant coefficient on the interaction for women of 0.0001 (standard error, 0.0002).
5. See Ermisch and Wright (1993).
6. See Imbens *et al* (1999) for a labour supply model where the income effects are estimated from the random assignment of lottery winnings.
7. See Blackaby *et al* (1999) for more detailed evidence from LFS which also suggests lower returns to education for minority men. Bell (1997) uses GHS data and shows that years of

education for immigrants have a substantially lower return. These results contrast with the US where returns do not appear to differ by race. See Ashenfelter and Rouse (1999).

8. Note that the returns to potential and actual experience are the same for men but smaller for women because of the large discrepancy between them for women. See Ermisch and Wright (1994) for further evidence on the definition of experience on measures of discrimination.

9. However, BHPS offers the opportunity to attempt to assess the effects of sector by exploiting the "contracting out" of many activities that had traditionally been the preserve of the public sector but which, during the 1990's were progressively privatised. Disney *et al* (1999) identify such changes from individuals whose occupations remain the same but who record a move from the public to private sectors. This was largely associated with manual work in the public sector in the health sector and in local authority services. Despite our concerns, their results are consistent with the simple ones presented here.

10. The FRS data reports gross income from self-employment, while the BHPS reports monthly self-employment profit.

11. Housing equity is the difference between the subjective value of the home and the mortgage balance.

12. See also Brown and Sessions (1998) who use BSAS data and control for self-employment in an essentially arbitrary (and rather unsuccessful) way.

14. This section is drawn from Walker and Zhu (1999).

15. This is net of all deductions including pension contributions.

16. We use a Tobit for hours since we have no convincing way of identifying participation separately from hours conditional on participation.

17. We compute income tax and employers social security (National Insurance), and entitlements to Family Credit, and Housing Benefit. Equivalence scales are those used in the annual official poverty analysis (DSS, 1998). We assume that all the factors that affect transfer entitlements such as marital status, housing tenure, rent, and the number and spacing of children are unaffected by the additional education. We also compute entitlements to Income Support (for lone parents) and Job Seekers Allowance (for everyone else) since we compute weight the predicted incomes in and out of work by the predicted probability of being in work. Our analysis is based only on households containing single benefit units. For any predicted wage below the minimum wage we replace with the minimum wage but make no allowance for a possible effect of the minimum on unemployment.

18. Higher rate taxpayers are few in number so there is no discernible maximum to the figure.

19. This is the average expenditure by Local Education Authorities for "sixth form" students.

20. The OLS coefficients (standard errors) on the interactions are 0.0001 (0.0004) and -0.001 (0.0004) for men and women respectively. The IV coefficients (standard errors) on the interactions are -0.011 (0.002) and -0.003 (0.002) for men and women respectively.

21. See Park (1999), Heckman (1998), Dearden (1999) and Oswald (1996) for existing work in these areas.

BIBILOGRAPHY

Ashenfelter, O., C. Harmon and H. Oosterbeek, H. (1999), "Empirical Estimation of the SchoOling/earnings Relationship – A Review", *Labour Economics,* 6 (4), pp. 453-70

Ashenfelter, O. and C.Rouse (1990), "Schooling, Intelligence and Income in America: Cracks in the Bell Curve", NBER Working Paper 6902.

Bell, D. (1997), "The Performance of Immigrants in the UK: Evidence from the GHS", *Economic Journal* 107 (441), pp 333-344.

Blackaby, D., P.D. Murphy, N.O'Leary, and D.G. Leslie (1999), "The Wage Effect and Occupational Segregation of Non-white Male Employees in Great Britain", mimeo, Swansea.

Blackburn, M.L. and D. Neumark (1995), "Are OLS Estimates of the Return to Schooling Biased Downward? Another Look", *Review of Economics and Statistics*, 77 (2), pp. 217-30

Blanchflower, D. and A. Oswald (1997), The Wage Curve, MIT Press, Cambrifdge, MA.

Blundell, R.W., L. Dearden, A. Goodman, and H. Reed (1997), Higher Education, Employment and Earnings in Britain, Institute for Fiscal Studies, London.

Brown, S. and G. Sessions (1998), "Education, Employment Status and Earnings: A Comparative Test of the Strong Screening Hypothesis", Scottish Journal of Political Economy, 45 (5), pp. 586-91

Buchinsky, M. (1994), "Changes in the U.S. Wage Structure 1963–1987: An Application of Quantile Regression", Econometrica, 62 (2), pp. 405-58

Card, D. (1999), "The Causal Effect of Education on Earnings" in O. Ashenfelter and D. Card (eds.) *Handbook of Labor Economics*, Amsterdam: Elsevier, pp. ????-????

Chowdhury, G. and S.J. Nickell (1985), "Hourly Earnings in the United States: Another Look at Unionization, Schooling, Sickness, and Unemployment Using PSID Data", *Journal of Labor Economics*, 3 (1), pp. 38-69

Dearden, L. (1998), "Ability, Families, Education and Earnings in Britain", Institute for Fiscal Studies Working Paper 98/14.

Dearden, L. (1999), "Qualifications and Earnings in Britain: How Reliable are Typical OLS Estimates of the Returns to Education?" IFS Working Paper W99/07.

Denny, K, C. Harmon and S. Redmond (1999), "Cognitive Skills and the Return to Schooling – Evidence from the International Adult Literacy Survey", mimeo, University College Dublin.

Disney, R., A. Goodman, A.Gosling, and C. Trinder (1998), "Public Pay in Britain in the 1990s", IFS Commentary.

Dolton, P.J. and A. Vignoles (1999), "The Labour Market Returns to Different Types of Secondary School Curricula", mimeo, Newcastle University.

Ermisch, J. and M. Francesconi (1997), "Educational Choice, Families and Young People's Earnings", ESRC Research Centre on Micro-social Change Working Paper 97–6, University of Essex.

Ermisch, J. and R. Wright (1991), "Gender Discrimination in the British Labour Market: A Reassessment", *Economic Journal,* 101 (406), pp 508–22.

Ermisch, J. and R. Wright (1993), "Wage Offers and Full-Time and Part-time Employment by British Women", *Journal of Human Resources*, 28, 111–33.

Evans, W.N., and E. Montgomery (1994) "Education and Health: Where There's Smoke There's an Instrument", NBER Working Paper 4949.

Feldstein, L and J. Symons (1999), "Attainment in secondary school", *Oxford Economics Papers*, 51 (2), pp. 300-21

Garen, J. (1984): "The return to schooling: a selectivity bias approach with a continuous choice variable," *Econometrica*, 52 (5), pp. 1199–1218.

Harkness, S. and S. Machin (1999), "Graduate Earnings in Britain, 1974–1995", DfEE Research Report 95.

Harmon, C. and I. Walker (1995), "Estimates of the Economic Return to Schooling for the UK", *American Economic Review*, 85 (5), pp. 1278-86.

Harmon, C. and I. Walker (1999), "The Marginal and Average returns to Schooling", *European Economic Review*, 43 (4-6), pp. 879-87.

Harmon, C. and I. Walker (2000), "Selective Schooling, School, Quality and the Labour Market Returns", *Economica*, 67 (265), pp. 19-35.

Heckman, J. (1979), "Sample Selection Bias as a Specification Error", *Econometrica*, 47 (1), pp. 153-61.

Heckman, J. (1998), "What Should Be Our Human Capital Policy", *Fiscal Studies*, 19 (2), pp. 103-119.

Herrnstein, R.J. and C. Murray (1994), *"The Bell Curve: Intelligence and Class Structure in American Life"*, New York; London and Toronto: Simon and Schuster, Free Press.

Imbens, G., D.B. Rubin and B. Sacerdote (1999), "Estimating the Effect of Unearned Income on Labour Supply, Earnings, Savings, and Consumption: Evidence from a Survey of lottery Players", NBER Working Paper 7001.

Lanot, G. and I. Walker (1998), "The Union/Non-Union Wage Differential: An Application of Semi-parametric Methods", *Journal of Econometrics*, 84 (2), pp. 327-49.

Oswald, O. and A.E. Clark (1996), "Satisfaction and Comparison Income" *Journal of Public Economics*, 61 (3), 359-81.

Park, J.H. (1999), "Estimation of sheepskin effects using the old and new measures of educational attainment in the CPS", *Economic Letters*, 62 (2), pp. 237-40.

Psacharopoulos, G. (1994), "Returns to Investment in Education: a Global Update", *World Development*, 22 (9), pp 1325-43.

Trostel, P. and I. Walker (1999), "Education and Work", mimeo, University of Warwick.

Walker, I. (1998), "The Economics of Lotteries", *Economic Policy*, 0 (27), pp. 357-392.

Walker, I. and P. Woolley, P. (2000), "The Returns to Education across 28 Countries", *Labour Economics* 5 (3), pp 245-260.

Walker, I. and Y. Zhu (1999), "Education Incentives and the Poverty Trap", mimeo, Keele University.

Weiss, A. (1998), "Human Capital *vs* Screening Explanations of Wages", *Journal of Economic Perspectives*.

Index